AF252107

a Bel,
cruzando fronteras,
un abrazote
Marc Zimmerman
24/9/07

South to North:
Framing Latin and Central American, Caribbean and Latino Literatures

Marc Zimmerman

2006

Published in Santiago, Chile
Prepared by Global and Latin American and Latino/a CASA
(Cultural Activities and Studies Arena) Publications,
with the support of the GEAR Program of the University of Houston.
Co-published with Bravo y Allende Editores

U.S. Library of Congress Cataloguing-in-Publication Data

1. Literary Theory
2. Latin American Literature
3. Caribbean Literature
4. U.S. Latino Literature
5. Comparative Literature

Primera Edición 2006
ISBN 0-9767019-3-6

Diseño y diagramación:
J. S. V. B.

Se terminó de imprimir en
el mes de enero de 2006.

Impreso en Chile / Printed in Chile

Table of Contents

To my son,
Carlos Eduarte
and his family
for support and light from pre-post times to now.

Preface

1. Frames, Entry Points, Postscripts

Frames, entry points and post-scripts-that's what it's all about.

Frames are always important, and so are points of entry. And there is always the temptation to add postscripts or even framing introductions, which are pre- and post-scripts at once, in the ever futile effort, pre-text or post-text, to update a text, which is always on the verge of being outmoded from the day of supposed completion or the day of publication. Frames provide context; they enhance pictures; they may even transform them. But frames always falsify, as in "I've been framed!" And changing frames at least seem to change pictures, just as different pictures can make frames seem different, and sometimes or almost always quite inadequate.

Framing any topic is like framing the wind. Artistic and literary movements, currents and works always transcend or deviate from their framing contexts or their most complete conceptual description. And yet we always need frames, we always need entry points, even if they mislead, leave out and ultimately raise more questions than answers, about the subjects they presumably seek to make more intelligible. And we always need postscripts as we ever seek to further frame our frames and make our entry points correspond to what, in the course of framing, has now required new roads and maps to find them.

Somehow it fell to me over the years to be one of those who had to do that overview text for one book or another. Somehow I became the framer of several collective projects. So I came to write the essays that make up this collection-framing efforts to be judged now in the light of better, often richer and more precise overviews, to be corrected by many individual studies, but still of value, I would hope, in both introducing given areas of literature and setting forth limited models which readers can modify through their own reading and discernment.

In spite of all the trouble with frames of references, points of entry and ever-outdated prescripts and postscripts, I decided it was time to bring together my most significant efforts to frame Latin American, Central American, Caribbean and U.S. Latino Literatures in one, relatively succinct volume that I hope will help those interested to understand and inter-relate complex dimensions of a very complex field.

The first caveat I must offer in this regard is that these texts have very different dates and contexts of origin, and are inconsistently outdated in their framing and entering viability. To be sure, I have edited each essay with an eye to updating, but such a process is doomed to failure. To be sure, also, I have frequently added postscripts and yes the back cover, this preface and the introductory materials which follow, in an attempt to out-maneuver time itself.

In choosing how to present this material, I was faced with two major options: offer them in the chronological order of their genesis, or order them according to a logic extending from the most general to the most particular. I have chosen the second principle, since the subject of this book is an effort to understand given literary phenomena and not understand Marc Zimmerman's diachronic processes. However, I would urge the reader to pay attention to the dates of publication of these articles and to try to go beyond the indications I give of the particular contexts in which these articles were written.

In this regard it is important to note that the earliest drafted essays, Chapters III and V, were first written in the early 1980s and thus reflect views about Marxism, socialism, and "class struggle" that would become very modified by historical events and my relation to them especially in the 1990s. A second useful point to keep in mind is that Chapters I and II, while drafted in 1992 and 1987 respectively, had never been final-edited for publication, and thus bear, unconsciously or not, the fullest brunt of my postscripting proclivity and indeed inevitably reflect a larger knowledge base, about the literatures and contexts in question than do the subsequent chapters, which perhaps might best be considered in their light.

This said, and the inevitable problems my procedures might bring placed in relief, I believe I have framed, provided points of entry and indeed postscripted the essays which follow to now offer them to interested readers as the product of considerable work and thought over the years that hopefully will frame many issues, open many doors, and lead to your own updating and revising postscripts in our constant pursuit of an understanding of Latin American, Central American, Caribbean, Latino and indeed world literary and broader processes.

2. Acknowledgements

While the introduction to this volume as well as Chapters I and II appear here in print for the first time, still parts or other versions of some of their materials have appeared elsewhere, and the Chapters III-VI, in modified form, have also appeared. In each case, I note the last previous public appearance of the essays or significant parts thereof following the order of the chapters in the book:

Introduction. Some materials from "Latin America, Latinos and Postmodernity: Frames of Reference and Points of Entry." In Michael Piazza and Marc Zimmerman, ed. *New World [Dis]Orders and Peripheral Strains: Specifying Cultural Dimensions in Latino and Latin American Studies.* Chicago. MARCH/Abrazo Press, 1998: 38-67. Some materials also from an unpublished paper on World Systems Theory and Literature, presented at a session of the Marxist Literary Group, held at the MLA Convention in Los Angeles, 1982.

Chapter I. Some materials from "La novelística postmoderna, el testimonio y la literatura latina en el sistema literario latinoamericano." Chicago. *Arena Cultural* núm. 3. *La Raza*. Junio 1999: 4-6.

Chapter II. Some materials drafted for, and then modified for use in, John Beverley and Marc Zimmerman, *Literature and Politics in the Central American Revolutions.* Austin: University of Texas Press, 1990; also some materials from my book, *Literature and Resistance in Guatemala: Textual Modes and Cultural Politics from El Señor Presidente to Rigoberta Menchú.* Athens, Ohio: Ohio University Press, 1995.

Chapter III. "The Unity of Caribbean Literature." in Ileana Rodríguez and Marc Zimmerman, eds. *Process of Unity in Caribbean Societies: Ideologies and Literatures.* Minneapolis: Institute for the Study of Ideologies and Literature, 1983: 28-56.

Chapter IV. "La teorización de las literaturas caribeñas: Perspectivas latinoamericanistas." *La Torre: Revista de la Universidad de Puerto Rico* III, 11 (Julio-septiembre 1989): 531-560 (the English language original was never previously published). Also some materials from "Postmodernidad y globalizacion: Transformaciones de los paradigmas teóricos en América Latina," in Luis Felipe Díaz y Zimmerman, ed. *Globalización, nación, postmodernidad. Estudios culturales puertorriqueños.* San Juan, Puerto Rico. Editorial LACASA Puerto Rico, 2001: pp. 19-56.

Chapter V. «Latin American Literary Criticism and Immigration.» *Ideologies and Literature* VI, 2nd Cycle, 16 (May-June 1983): 172-196.

Chapter VI. Introduction to *U.S. Latino Literature: An Essay and Annotated Bibliography.* Chicago: MARCH/Abrazo Press, 1992.

Just a glance at the public venues cited evokes my gratitude especially to my publishers, Hernán Vidal and Tony Zahareas of the Institute for the Study of Ideologies and Literature, as well as to Carlos Cumpián of MARCH/Abrazo Press, Susan Homar of the University of Puerto Rico-Río Piedras Comparative Literature Program, and my co-editors and co-writers, John Beverley, Ileana Rodríguez, Michael Piazza and Luis Felipe Díaz. I would also like to acknowledge the help and support I received in the Department of Modern and Classical Languages (MCL) at the University of Houston: Yenny Labrador and Flor Velásquez for their help in preparing this text, to Norma Quiñónez for helping to facilitate our work; also to graduate students in my seminar on literary theory who had to bear with some of these texts while trying to develop their own work; finally to Gabriela Ventura Baeza and Stella Cruz, who helped with final details.

I wish to acknowledge the College of Liberal Arts and Social Sciences, which provided funds for projects developing under the aegis of Comparative Critical and Cultural Studies, and the GEAR Grants to Enhance and Advance Research Committee of the University of Houston which funded the publications proposal which made possible the infrastructure to develop this project and the other ones which appear under the aegis of LACASA Publications of the World Cultures and Literatures (WCL) program of the Modern and Classical Languages Department. Finally I wish to thank Tom Gutting and Nicolás Kanellos, whose advice helped me to shape the final draft of my proposal.

This publication of LACASA's series on literary theory is meant to showcase UH's new Latin American Studies program, as well as MCL's WCL and Spanish Graduate Programs it is meant to spur on further publishing projects. Casa stands for Cultural Activities and Studies Arena, but that arena is also our home. Let LACASA be your home as well in this globalized world.

3. A Final Framing Note

As I completed the penultimate draft of this preface and book, I received word from my good friend, Ángel Quintero Rivera about the death on January 6, 2005 of Antonio Benítez Rojo whose fine book on Caribbean culture and literature, *The Repeating Island*, receives some small criticism in Chapter IV below. In justice to this crucial thinker, a major player in a field of major players, I wish to cite only a small fraction of Quintero-Rivera's first draft words of homage written the day after Benítez Rojo's death, as a final frame, entry point or postscript for this preface and as pre-script for some final comments on the Caribbean that will appear in the postscript for Chapter IV. Quintero notes that

> *Antonio died on Three Kings Day, so important in our Caribbean* creolité, *which he had helped us so much to understand. With his death, the Caribbean loses one of its must incisive analysts and thinkers. Although he considered himself mainly a narrator, his interpretative analyses and essays are for many of us as important as his literary writings. [But]... the fact is that for Benítez Rojo, the distinct forms of writing were diverse vehicles to approximate, describe and attempt to understand this "Caribbean which repeats itself." That is, to understand a living reality that is one, but is at the same time multiple, and that therefore requires diverse approximations that distict "genres" of writing bring.*

It is of course the case that Benítez Rojo's work can be said to frame not just the Caribbean but the Latin American/Caribbean world which my own book evokes, for to define the Caribbean as a "discontinuous order in the chaos" is to help define a major dimension of the overall world we explore here, even though, inevitably, the Caribbean version remains a distinct variant worthy of distinct framing and study. Defining, framing-these are tasks Benítez Rojo helped so many of us to undertake, always aware that the role we play is necessary but impossible: impossible to frame chaos, to bottle or frame the wind.

Marc Zimmerman,
Houston. August, 2005.

Introduction

Prescripts/Postscripts for Latin and Central American, Caribbean and Latino Literatures

1. New World Literatures in the World Systems Process

At the end of the twentieth century, as the world economic order disrupted national developmental processes, many contradictory forces manifested themselves on the social level and registered also on literary modes of production and their study.

Throughout the world, and most dramatically in what some have called the "Third World" and some are re-articulating as the "global south," national projects have been disrupted, destroyed or altered by global processes. In the Latin American/Caribbean context, efforts at national development, whether in Brazil, Argentina, the Dominican Republic or Mexico, suffered serious long-term setbacks. Whole ideologies whether of ameliorist, developmentalist or revolutionary origins suffered as well. Revolutionary movements of the 1980s collapsed; and new social movements of NGOs, etc. which responded to neo-liberal reform measures in the 1990s continue to operate in relation to the developing scenario of globalization. Now as never so obviously before, the weight of global factors and the force of contradictions external to regional and national entities have fallen on the area and emphasize its structural weaknesses, vulnerability and, to evoke a discredited word from the 1960s... dependency.

To be sure, in Latin America as in other parts of the underdeveloped world, initial structural weaknesses played their part in the current circumstances. Whatever internal weaknesses there were, external capitalist domination led to the exacerbation and institutionalization of the weaknesses in ways that are still registering their full impact.

Many changes have occurred in the world economic and political order, as well as in the place of the U.S. and other capitalist powers in the midst of these changes. From the early 1970's on, key capitalist countries suffered stagflation, internal crisis and a series of realignments within their internal and external relations; meanwhile, underdeveloped countries have undergone nationalist, religious and cultural turmoil, so that the configuration of global power relations and possibilities has changed considerably, in the wake of the cold war's termination and, more recently, in the aftermath of 9/11/01 Many advanced countries have been crippled; underdeveloped countries, oil-rich or not, capitalist or not, have been unable to underwrite or attract the ever-escalating sums required for modernization. Countries marked to begin with by the most unequal distribution of income and goods, are suffering more than ever before. Indeed each injection of foreign productive plants taking advantage of lower wages in these areas has only further exacerbated the total negative tendency, and as concomitant of this and the larger picture, an exponential migration of people from the countryside to the cities or from immiserated to relatively more prosperous countries has unleashed additional processes which jostle the existent field of relations and create new complications and contradictions in our very conception of Latin America, the Caribbean, the U.S. and the world.

How can we conceptually maintain a geographically bound image of Latin America, the Caribbean or the U. S. when such large numbers from the first two areas are inserted in the third? How can we maintain our sense of the U. S. role and status when within that nation, we find such massive instances of peripheral life, culture and even economy, when massive third world style unemployment becomes rampant and we even talk of "industrial free zones" that will compete, in effect, with the runaway shops of Mexico, El Salvador and so many other points of the Latin American and Caribbean global south?

The conflict between advancing and declining capitalist states, between these states and multinational corporations, between the powers that be and those representing marginalized or subaltern groups-all these have had a far reaching impact on economic and political policies and strategies, on ideological and cultural structures and on the expressive artistic systems in which literary systems and specific literary expressions are born and operate; they also have had impact on the institutions and entities in which the study of literature takes place, and, of course, on literary study itself. Indeed, as the world forces inundate and transform Latin America and the Caribbean, and as these forces make Latin America (not to speak of other areas of heavy immigration to the U.S.) a matter internal to the U.S. itself, indeed, so the very field of Latin American literary studies and the effect and value of work in this terrain have become problematic, and has required rethinking and exploring with a look to summing up past achievements and projecting new directions.

The situation in our discipline-the sense of critical work as ultimately just sub-functional in a basically capitalist system-significantly parallels the macro-theoretical perspective which had its advent in the early 1970's and which brought together strands from Marxism, structural historicism and Gunder Frankian dependency orientations to produce a kind of mini-revolution in socio-historical epistemes under the rubric of world systems theory.

What could be more in keeping with this theory than the notion a systemic subunit empirically found to be constituted for the sole purpose of opposing a given system and promoting another one would in fact only really serve that prior system? And what could be more logical than the production of this theory at a time of great disillusionment with respect to revolutionary movements that only some years before had, often through the prism of dependency theory, seemed to be particularly imminent?

In the face of a disrupted world order and the conservative tendencies within most versions of system theory, the question has become to what degree world systems theory as a general orientation and irrespective of our agreement or not with any of its particularities, may help us to understand and ultimately deal with the processes affecting, conditioning, and often overwhelming particular national, local and institutional developments which have had the effect of limiting progressive Latin American, Caribbean and Latino literary studies even as they develop. A further question might be how the investigation of this question might serve the problems facing Latin American and Caribbean literary studies related to other literatures and problematics within a global frame.

2. The Logic, Goals and Procedures of this Book

This introduction seeks to deal with some basic questions of world systems theory as it relates to Latin American, Caribbean and U.S. Latino literature and their criticism, as well as the relations between these literatures at this historical moment. I start with an empirical given: the apparently changed historical situation in which literature production (also changed in its nature and the way its relational field is seen) takes place. The goal is not really to explore world systems theory in every area of its development, but to invoke and trace the broad conceptual field which, validly or not, theories of imperialism, dependency theory and then their extension in world systems theory pressured into place for all socio-historical studies of Latin American literature. In this light it would be well to note that, however partially, world systems theory should be seen as playing a sobering or qualifying and ultimately pessimistic role vis-avis the analysis of revolutionary change in the modern world. If we can say that dependency theory posed a conceptualization by which Latin American national liberation struggles were not merely repetitions of the French revolution, but were themselves revolutions against states and systems that were in fact already capitalist, then world systems theory took the more negative dimensions of this attack on Marxist orthodoxy (that is, the notion that prior to the industrial revolution, Europe was feudal, and that Latin American social formations are fundamentally based on feudal modes of production within a capitalist system) to suggest that such national liberation struggles in small and/or weak countries cannot in fact be revolutionary, no matter what their ideologies and overt intentions are, because there are few ways such countries can maintain their autonomy vis-à-vis the larger capitalist world economy of which they are a part.

It would be easy to see this theory as completely regressive or negative; however, we might best describe it as constituting a field of negative possibilities that provides a healthy corrective to over-zealous and romantic optimism, suggesting the realistic difficulties which posited forces of change must face. But the specific question which this introduction and this book will address is ultimately the functioning of Latin American, Caribbean and U.S. Latino literatures and literary criticism in relation to these possibly changing overall social forces, movements and systems.

In this context, we may point to the role of discursive formations in relation to cultural and psychological transformations connected with the transformations of overall social systems at national, regional and global levels. The constitution of what are considered specifically literary discourses with their own internal and external relations is also crucial here. Literary discourses and literature as a whole has played its role in the construction and maintenance of socio-economic and political power. Some argue that literary movements, currents and specific works are can contest, question or at least problematized larger structures of power, and might even have some force in the construction of counter-hegemonic forces; others argue that no matter individual or broader intentions, literary processes and works are so caught up in the configuration of power that they can never be truly oppositional. Such arguments have raged around the Latin American, Caribbean and Latino literary fields, with Ramón Saldívar (1990) a Latino example of the first position and John Beverley (1993) a Latin Americanist version of the second.

This book will seek to deal with questions of literature in relation to broader socio-historical processes. To accomplish the overall task at hand, and to give some unity and systemicity to a text which speaks both to broad unity and fragmentation, broad forces and particular themes, I will give a brief overview of dependency theory and more fully, world systems theory, and describe the theory's trajectory before and throughout the postmodern period, and on into the era of globalization. This will provide some contextualization for the Latin and Central American, Caribbean and Latino literary questions which, while introduced in this essay, will be discussed more fully in the essays which follow.

3. Backgrounds in Marxism, Structural Historicism and Dependency Theory

We might best approach world systems theory in its relation to literature by considering its relations with other theoretical constructs which precede it and which it attempts to totalize: Marxism, structural historicism, and dependency theory. In the broadest sense, the first two terms are most fully discussed in my recent volume, *Pre-Post Positions* (2005), while dependency theory and its role in developing Latin American socio-historical critique is most fully articulated in one of my forthcoming volumes, *América Latina en el nuevo [des]orden* (2006).

For the many readers who will find the analysis which follows a repetition of what they already know, I suggest that they move on to last sections of this introduction; for the many readers not deeply familiar with these themes, I urge a careful reading of this analysis, since it provides a minimal framework and entry point for matters that are often implicit in and assumed as macro-frames in my discussions of particular literatures or literary dimensions.

Drawing on Chapter VII of *Pre-Post Positions*, I may start by simply noting that with capitalist development, Marx saw the emergence of a "world literature" which required a complex mode of analysis. With the coming to dominance of the commodity form, he saw apparent tendencies toward the commodification of artistic and literary forms. Marx realized that in attenuated ways literature embodied the values and beliefs of social groups, and this made literature a matter of importance. But he also saw literature as a vehicle for values that transcended their particular historical moment of genesis-for values expressive of periods in which lesser degrees of social alienation reigned than under full capitalism, for values embodying aspirations which, however distorted, spoke to a time beyond the period of capitalist domination.

In brief, literature for Marx confirmed the historicity of all social phenomena-their place in given social formations, expressions and institutions. But literature also confirmed for him the complexity of social life, the possibility for certain phenomena to lag behind, and resist , and yet also to leap beyond the dominating elements of the historically given moment, to affect that moment as that moment affects them, and in fact, to express simultaneously elements of a past and future which are contrary to the given moment and which contribute, in difficult to determine but ultimately determinate ways, to the making of a future beyond the present.

Unfortunately, the subsequent development of Marxism throughout much of the period of the Second International involved a narrowing of Marxism's holistic theoretical promise to a matter of economic determinism. Literary studies tended to relate the contents particular works and genres to specific serial tendencies. The implications of Marx's total dialectic were drowned in a wave of positivism which reduced historical phenomena to fairly simple economic effects along a linear continuum. The rich array of historical possibilities and interactions were reduced to a series of fixed universal stages based on the organization of labor through which all societies must pass. Pseudo-problems such as the possible leaping of stages, the failure of revolutionary consciousness in the midst of their objective facilitating object context-that is, band-aid theorizations trying to explain what the theory by the narrowness and dogmatism of its applications could no longer really explain.

And while there were Marxists who sought to remedy the problem by drawing on Hegel and other sources, really many of the solutions were being sought, at least in terms of social and historical theory, in spheres that were hardly Marxist in their central orientation. One of these spheres was structuralist theory whose subsequent development even involved crucial Marxist transformations such as those by Althusser and company. More directly central to our subject, however, were the attempted Marxist transformations by those theorists drawn to the post-structuralist historicist formulations of Ferdinand Braudel and the "*Annales* group" of structural historicism.

Annales historians applied the model-building techniques developing in economic history to elaborate an integrative historical method aimed at grasping the interrelation of socio-economic processes in a way that balanced out and conceptualized historical elements, de-emphasized events and individuals, and accounted for historical constraints and continuities, as well as dynamic relations and transformations. At the center of structural historicism's theoretical apparatus is the notion of the varying historical elements achieving relatively stable and hierarchical relations to constitute a virtual structure, or pattern of relations which encapsulates forces of change and tends to endure overtime. This structuration process leads to a historical verticality of "structural-levels" whose interrelatedness, relative autonomy and possibilities for change and for effect on other levels can only be grasped through the construction of models. Until Braudel, even *Annales* writers had centered their work on the relation between relatively long-range processes and short term conjunctures. Braudel sought to conceptualize history in terms of the intersection of various temporalities and rhythms, including those deep, seemingly unchanging forces that he related to the "long duration." The question of historical analysis becomes one of determining the basic structural field of analysis and plotting the possible shifting relations and transformations on basic structures-transformations which are generated by inter-structural relations and which cannot be grasped by focusing on any "aspect" of history, but only in terms of the structures themselves. In the structural historicism framework, literature has its own relatively autonomous developmental rhythm and its own mode of historical relatedness. But Braudel's theorization assures that literature is related to other historical phenomena-that it is important in history and that history is important to it and its understanding.

Thus structural historicism emerged as an alternate holistic theory, one able to mediate and integrate structuralist and Marxist elements. Unlike structuralism, it makes no necessary ontological-epistemological assertion about any basic underlying trans-historical structures (long durations are not necessarily eternal; structural historicist models are provisional). Unlike most versions of Marxism, it makes no theoretical assertion about the underlying determinations of historical structures by any supposed economic base-though concrete historical research could determine when and how modes of economic production are determinate in given social formations in given periods. Clearly such an intermediate theorization could be decentered in any number of directions; Levi-Strauss could draw on Braudel to elaborate a theory of "hot" and "cold" societies; Althusserians drew on Braudel to constitute a new reading of Marx. But what most concerns us here is how structural historicism could link up with another developing mode, dependency theory, which it had itself influenced, to constitute the basis for a synthesis in world systems theory.

Like structural historicism, dependency theory challenged the fixed categories, economic causality and stage theories of 2nd International Marxism. While Latin American social formations might have certain of the characteristics of supposedly feudal European societies, they were in fact dependent parts of an overall capitalist system and in fact products and representatives of that system. This stance, clearly differing from orthodox Marxist and liberal stance which both posited a bourgeois revolution, implied new analyses of regions and polities in the question of labor distribution, accumulation of capital, modes of production and state formation, classes and truly oppositional and revolutionary alliances and movements. The stance meant essentially that national liberation struggles should not be seen as in standard dominant models as constituting bourgeois revolutions, and that alliances with a supposed national bourgeoisie were not the road to revolution.

Despite attacks on the initial theorization and subsequent elaborations of the dependency model, it functions as a significant theoretical vessel for the reconceptualization of Latin American and Caribbean culture, ideology and literature, especially when dovetailed with Althusserian perspectives on the ideological apparatuses of the state.

World systems' theory resulted from a comparative analysis of African development vis-à-vis the work of dependency theorists on Latin American and structural historicist-influenced work on Europe. And this synthesis had the virtue of raising dependency perspectives out to the global reaches initially evoked in Marx's totalistic theory. It attempted then to pose the relation of the world's diverse social formations to an overall perspective which then looked back at the specific entities as local variations and components in a total system. The theory attacked bourgeois and Marxist stage approaches to historical development, and it sought to cure the apparent market bias of its theoretical antecedents by demonstrating that supposedly pre-capitalist agricultural production in sixteenth Century Europe and twentieth Century Latin America were in fact capitalist, and that by virtue of the total orientation of Marxist theory, we could judge as incorrect his implicit identification of capitalism with the industrial revolution.

If dependency theory suggested possibilities for revolutionary action on the part of Latin American workers, peasants who were now to be seen as workers, no matter what their specific status as landed or dispossessed, etc., then world systems theory seemed to stress the idea that supposed national liberation or socialist revolution in backward conditions could only constitute a precarious struggle for modernization in relation to a total system in which even existing socialist states could only be in essence subsets of capitalism, and therefore capitalist.

What are the main tenants of world systems theory? What are its obvious strengths and weaknesses as theory? How does it change our way of dealing with literary phenomena, including criticism? What directions are suggested in developing a literary method from this theory and its criticisms?

4. Some Basic Dimensions of World System Theory

The theory has its first full formulation with the publication of Immanuel Wallerstein's book, *The Modern World System*, in 1974. In this book Wallerstein aimed to achieve a coherent grasp of the modern world and the development of modern capitalism within it. To do this he attempted to fasten on units and categories of analysis that were adequate to understanding the origins of his subject and its subsequent development. In fact, Wallerstein's overall historical project, still in progress, was to be the subject of four volumes of history.

Leading up is consolidation of the capitalist world economy and particular revolutionary tensions this consolidation has involved from 1917 to the present. But what is crucial in this plan was there counting of this history through a synthesis of the best of recent global historiography by means of a compressed, yet totalistic framework which could be a scientific view of the past in function of possibilities for transformative action in the present.

Wallerstein's initial assumption is that history must be conceptualized in terms of existing and developing socio-economic systems with respect to such matters as national states, area-wide, national, and local social, political ideological and cultural formations are to be seen as functions. That is, we cannot grasp what is systematically taking place in an area or state on the basis of what we see happening there, but in terms of a broader structured system which in fact governs and lends significance to those occurrences.

Thus central to Wallerstein's conception is the notion of a world system as a social system that has boundaries, structures, member groups, rules of legitimation and coherence. Its life is made up of the conflicting forces which hold it together and tear it apart as each group seeks to mold it to its advantage. It has a life span over which its straits change in some respects and remain stable in others and over which its structures are strong or weak in terms of the internal logic of its functioning and its capacity to hold the tensions it encapsulates in check.

A social system is characterized by the fact that the life within it is largely self-contained and the dynamics of its development are mainly internal. Social units which do not meet these criteria of internal self-sufficiency are not systems and hence cannot be valid objects of scientific study.

Most entities described as social systems are not total systems. The only real social systems are those relatively small, highly autonomous subsistence economies not part of a larger subsistence-demand system and world systems. These are few and large and they constitute "worlds" whose self-containment as an economic-material entity is based on their extensive division of labor and their containment of a multitude of cultures.

Only two varieties of world systems have existed: (1) world empires with a single political system over most of the area; and (2) world-economies in which a single political system does not exist. Prior to the modern era, world systems were rarely economies, which tended to be unstable, converting into empires or disintegrating. The strength of the modern world system is that it is a world economy that has survived for 500 years and has not yet been transposed into a world empire. This is the corollary of the fact that the world-economy's capitalist character has flourished because it has had within it a multitude of political systems.

What are the main points Wallerstein makes about the development of the modern world economy that underpin his concrete studies? He argues that Northwest Europe, formerly a marginal part of the world, emerged in the sixteenth Century as the social and geographic area destined to overtake all others and eventually change the entire structure of the world. Only Europe established modern capitalism; and this development, in concert with modern technologies (including transportations and communications) created a world economy and a world system.

The fact that the European world-economy was never transformed into an empire points to one of its systemic character as representing an economic but not a political unit. Nascent world capitalism could only flourish in a world economy, not in a unitary political world empire. Modern nation states emerged in the European system and took political forms appropriate to their functions within that system, both in Europe and in relation to the later overseas empires of which they formed the nuclei. Overseas expansion was a key development in the creation of a capitalist world-economy. Together with a new organization of production, a new form of surplus appropriating, the organization of new administrative machinery and rise of new social classes, the world-economy ushered in the changes that led to the modern world.

The world system is the general frame of analysis in which sovereign national states and regional or national social formations are to be seen. Capitalism and statism form dialectically related nuclei in the whole system. Capitalism is based on the fact that economic factors operate in an arena larger than that which any political entity can totally control. Hence there is a structurally based freedom of maneuver for the capitalists which has made possible the system's economic expansion and flexibility despite a skewed distribution of rewards.

Indeed, the only alternative world system that could maintain high productivity and change the distribution system would involve reintegrating the levels of economic and political decision making. This would be a third world system- such as we have not seen as yet: a socialist world government. The size of a world economy is a function of the state of technology, and especially transportation and communications. The extensive division of labor is not only functional or occupational, but also geographical. The range of economic tasks is not equally distributed throughout the system, and is a function of ecology but also of the social organization of work which magnifies and legitimizes the ability of some groups to exploit the labor of others and receive a larger share of the system's surplus.

Further, an empire's political structure links culture with occupation; but in a world economy, political structure tends to link culture with spatial location. So it is that the first point of political pressure available to groups is the local state structure and its nationalistic ideologies. Cultural homogenization serves the interests of key groups, and pressures build up to fend against uncontrollable divisions by creating national cultural identities.

For capitalism, it was essential that the world-economy developed on the basis of a global division of labor into three different but closely related zones:

the core, the semi-periphery and the periphery. These zones are distinguished by the different economic functions, class structures, political organizations and modes of labor control. By 1650, the core states had free labor, the semi-periphery, sharecropping and the periphery (Hispamerica and Eastern Europe) coerced labor. The essence of capitalism was this combination of labor in core and peripheral zones.

The division of social relations of production went hand in hand with the developing world economy. This economy's social, economic and political structuring facilitated the essential processes of capitalism: the flow of surplus from lower to higher states, from periphery to core, from majority to minority. The structuring had deepened in the modern world, so that the gap has widened between developed and underdeveloped countries, even as certain countries have changed their relative position in the whole. In core states, the creation of a strong state machinery coupled with national culture (the process known as integration) protects disparities that arise from the world system while ideologically masking and justifying them.

We may in fact see world economies as divided into cores states and peripheral areas. A trait of peripheral areas is the weakness of their states, non-existent under colonialism and with little autonomy under neo-colonialism. Semi-peripheral areas are half way in terms of their complexity of economic activity, the strength of their state machineries, their cultural integrity, etc. The areas may shift historically in their status and identity, but the existence of areas in such positions is essential. Such entities serve the role of middle trading groups under capitalism; they deflect oppositional political pressures coming from the periphery toward the core and the groups operating within and through the state machinery. Interests in the semi-periphery may absorb peripheral concerns but in ways that can hardly penetrate or disturb the core with ease.

In fact three mechanisms enable world systems to retain relative political stability as systems: 1) concentrated military strength in the hands of dominant forces, 2) pervasive ideological commitment to the system as a whole and 3) the division of the majority into a larger lower and smaller middle stratum. The last recourse of the system is the buffer semi-periphery and the middle strata. The semi-periphery, then provides political stability to the system. Indeed, all oppositional energies proliferated in the system, including those which emerge in such institutionalized cultural forms as literature are so structured as to maintain and not overthrow the system.

The world economy's tripartite division involves a hierarchy of occupational tasks. Those requiring a higher skill level and greater capitalization are reserved for higher-ranking areas. The system regards accumulated material and human capital at a higher rate than raw labor power. Thus the geographical mal-distribution of skills involves a strong trend of self-maintenance. The marketplace enforces rather undermines this pattern. And the absence of a central political mechanism for the world economy makes it difficult to counteract the mal-distribution of rewards which is determined at the global level. Thus the world economy expands economic and social gaps as it develops. Technological advances making the extension of the world economy possible may reward particular regions even changing their structural role. But the disparity of rewards between different sectors in the world economy are widening. Regions external even to the periphery may become periphery. Core areas may become semi-peripheral, etc. But the system remains. Core state advantages have grown, but different states have served as core. Thus the system is characterized and not necessarily threatened by the rise and fall of particular core states.

These are only a few of the key ideas of Wallerstein's initial formulation important for understanding matters relating to Latin America. True, even in his initial formulations, Wallerstein goes much further in elaborating his theoretical framework for charactering the development and structural stability of the system. Wallerstein develops his views on the role of ideology and the definition and role of social classes, and those special social groupings which he calls migrating ethno-nations and which have different functions in their homebase than they do in the locales in which they settle.

These early formulations of world systems theory and its subsequent development were criticized by Marxists and non-Marxists alike. On the theoretical level, the main complaint was his functionalist subordination of religions, cultural and scientific dimensions of historical development by the operations of the socio-economic system. Furthermore he has been criticized along the lines of Gunder Frank for overplaying the whole and thus under-playing the dynamic role of indigenous developments, including the effect of like epiphenomena on consciousness and culture in the third world, on confusing the capitalist mode of production with participation in a world capitalist economic system.

The result of the global approach of Wallerstein is a reduction of the efficacy and integrity of local and national developments, even as his theory attempts to contextualize and thus establish the bases for the only real social systems today and the role of classes, and even the phenomenal forms of a nation's economic life are subordinate to their role in the total system.

Even though he claims his goal of providing an understanding which leads to revolutionary practice, the functionalist and virtually mechanistic implications of his model leave, as we have suggested, a sense of pessimism about genuinely revolutionary possibilities in small, peripheral and even semi-peripheral states. He pathetically uses China as a model for a possible socialist road in the midst of the forces of capitalist engulfment. How could such a construct, we might ask, anticipate the revolutionary energies released in South and Central America during and after the 1960s and 70s? What value could they have for plotting the future possibilities of Nicaragua, for example, except of course to point to grave difficulties these nations would face in actually moving toward relative independence and progress.

It is true that since his early formulations, Wallerstein and his followers have extended his theory and applied it on an ever broader number of themes, especially through his journal *Review*, and a series of collective volumes. Let us turn to some of these later views, first placing them in historical and theoretical context, as we move from the Cold War era to a new one marked first by theories of postmodernity and then globalization.

5. Recent Developments in World Systems theory in the era of postmodernity and globalization

According to Best and Kellner (1991), events and transformations in the 1990s, including many taking place in the global south) made this period "the most tumultuous in the postwar era" (Best and Kellner 296) -at least until 9/11. In this context, they argue, that with the collapse of the Soviet World, and the extension of inter-capitalist and local struggles, the need for critical theory with respect to modernity and development and underdevelopment seemed more crucial than ever.

> *Since capitalism continues to be a major constitutive force in many contemporary societies, the Marxian theory and critique of capitalism continues to be a crucial element of a critical theory of society... Yet since Marx failed to provide an adequate theory of the state, bureaucracy, nationalism, the public sphere, society, the psyche, gender, race and culture, a reconstructed critical social theory must draw on other traditions as well. Likewise, since the Marxian theories of revolution have so far failed to produce an adequate version of democratic socialism, the theory of political transformation also needs to be revised and updated. Critical theory is by nature historical and must revise its theories and practices in light of historical transformations. It is also methodologically self-reflexive, normative, and willing to explicate and defend its theoretical and political commitments (296).*

Clearly poststructuralist and postmodernist theories help in reconceptualizing things even as advancing critical theory critiques them and finds them wanting. The underlying theoretical drift in this essay and this book as a whole points toward an unstable, evolving synthesis which is ultimately incoherent but seeks to keep things open and yet guided enough to point toward better future theorizations based on the partial kinds of knowledge which the unstable synthesis shows itself more or less able to deliver. With regard to global and Latin American theorizations, I maintain here a greatly revised *dependentista* perspective represented by writers grouped around the journal *Latin American Perspectives* and projected out toward the dimensions of a Wallersteinian orientation which has in my hands only recovered its weaknesses of cultural analyses involving cultural causalities and not mere effects by drawing on Jameson and his relevance for our own cultural turf.

In this regard, it is interesting to read Jameson's pronouncement in 1992 on the question of what he sees as the priorities in the new historical millennium. With the entrance into postmodernity, Jameson writes,

> *Doctrines such as reification and commodification which played a secondary role in the traditional or classical Marxian heritage are now likely to come into their own and become dominant instruments of analysis and struggle. In other words cultural politics, a politics of everyday life, which emerged in earlier decades but as something of an adjunct and a poor relative, a supplement to 'politics' itself, must now-at least in the First World-be the primary place of struggle (Jameson 1992: 212).*

But the fact is, cultural politics and the politics of the everyday are crucial for the Third World as well-or at least the Latin American and Latino sector of what was called Third and now is often called the Global South, even though that South is migrating north just as the North has migrated south. In this context, I would wish to invoke Wallerstein's evolving views on the socio-economic but also cultural and ideological dimensions of recent conjunctures as globalization theory has moved to the forefront, to see how those establish a perspective on the global future in which Latin American socio-economic, political and, yes, cultural and literary developments may receive some final, predictive consideration.

In an early article, Wallerstein attempted a richer critique of culture and class in function of the concept of "ethno-nations" and tried to show the relation of his theory to the Marxist tradition on such issues as historical periodization and transition. In one generally theoretical volume which he co-edited with Terrence Hopkins (1980), Wallerstein seeks to distance himself from mechanistic reductionism posing the concept of process in opposition to that of structure (Jameson 1992: 212). Another volume, with Samir Amin, Giovanni Arrighi and Andre Gunder Frank (1982), addresses many questions of economic and state development in Latin America, and even contains an important article attempting to integrate the question of women's work and oppression into world system theory. in still another volume, his associates (Kritz, Keely & Tomasi, ed. 1981) attempt to sum up work relating to the crucial question of immigration to that of core transformations in the world system. In the light of these and countless other texts, and especially his co-edited volumes dealing with anti-systemic social movements (1989 and 1990) as well as questions of race and ethnicity (1991), we may focus on one of Wallerstein's major post-Cold War texts, *Geopolitics and Geoculture* (1993), where Wallerstein attempts to rethink his world systems views giving more weight to contemporary or postmodern intersections of culture and ethnic identifications.

First, a central driving thesis of Wallerstein's work throughout the 1990s was how Soviet bloc collapse and subsequent developments in Western Europe could only be understood in terms of the cyclic rhythms and overall hegemony of the capitalist world economic system in which diminished U.S. hegemony played a crucial, systemic role. U.S. economic decline (which was in part the counterweight to its military and world system-policing functions) points to other shifts that make the possible construction of new radical, and even specifically socialist social modes more possible within the evolving world system.

Wallerstein points out that since the 1960s there has been a rejection of universalist liberalism through an intellectual focus on "cultures" as opposed to economics and politics, and that this has involved a development of challenges to the dominant "geo-culture" or cultural framework through which the world system has operated. Logically, the role of the dominant geo-culture (capitalist construction, modernization, leveling of differences, but within limits requiring the survival and further articulation of racist and sexist dimensions as useful in given developmental phases) and the predominant challenges thereto, actually bred and encouraged by the further development of the system but potentially oppositional thereto (e.g., anti-sexist and anti-racist, but also pro-ethnic and culturally affirming ideologies) in Latin American contexts, will be the ultimate concern of our interest in Wallerstein here.

Early in his book, Wallerstein argues that it is false to conclude that the collapse of Leninism leads to a decisive weakness in Third World countries, when the fact is that Soviet existence and rhetoric had only marginal value to these countries, whose weaknesses derive primarily from the continuing functioning of the capitalist world-economy, secondarily from the inefficacy of their strategies of national development, and only tertiarily from their lack of Soviet support (Wallerstein 1993: 2).

Indeed, for Wallerstein, the very nature of the capitalist system implies that only some of the peripheral countries and peoples will move to semi-peripheral status and those that do will probably contribute to the fall-back or decline of some others-or, because of existing patterns of wealth and resource distribution, will become all the more unevenly developed and structurally weak (as well as volatile) in the process. Then, with respect to most of the "peripheral" countries and peoples which will not "develop," it is probable that they will still harbor predominantly pre-modern socioeconomic subsystems, ideologies and cultural patterns that will stand against their integration as equals in the system, but which might be converted into elements which, while, and indeed *because,* they are *in* the system, can seek to rupture it.

In the vision of world capitalism in the post-Communist era, the need for third world or peripheral social formations and peoples as sources of production and as markets will increase, as will the overuse of resources and the limited post-Fordist exploitation of labor. The inroads that will be made on ethnic, gender and other patterns that are not consonant with systemic functioning, the pressure on resources which peoples see as tied to their identity, and the very breaks with previously constituted identity through migration, mass media impact and other factors that lead to deterritorialization, decontextualization and other processes theorized in Deleuze and Guattari (1987) will inevitably lead to a new wave of conflicts that will emerge in the years to come -a wave perhaps more intense than what we've seen in this century (132-33)- and one with a larger repertory of oppositional possibilities, given the expanded, if uneven, distribution of materials, "know-how" and motives.

In these instances, national liberation movements and other coalition anti-systemic resistance struggles will play their part and may lead toward an unmaking of the subsystems (and the total system?) from within-though not, perhaps, through the kinds of apocalyptic working-class or guerrilla revolutionism which was part of our sense of things in this century. Furthermore Wallerstein notes, for example, that "third world" struggles in the past few decades have led to a better political positioning for many subaltern groups, even while their economic or material conditions have not much improved. If political positioning is better, will that help groups economically, and if so, will improvement of material conditions improve or undermine radical resistance? It is true that the end of the Cold War may mean some lost illusion of support to offset hegemonic capitalist power, but that resistance will not readily be ascribed or fold into macro-geo politics, so that the subaltern may be freer to speak and fight than ever before.

In this vision, of course, Wallerstein takes us to the heart of questions for Latin America's future-its capacities for internal development and resistance, its relation to the U.S. and other power points within the world economy, the effect of the postmodernist culture dominant on other cultural (including ethnic) forms. Ironically, Wallerstein, who draws so much of his theoretical frames from those developed in Latin America, has little enough to say directly about this part of the world. Indeed, the implications for the peripheral or "southern" social formations which make up the Latin American variant of the third world or Global South are not fully or systematically explicated in his work. But at least some further extrapolations may be explored.

First, if U.S. hegemony continues to decline globally, still, it will attempt even more so to dominate its weak, hemispheric neighbors. Second, it will attempt to maintain control of growing ethnic and other modes of resistance through hegemonic, cultural ways which are already in march through religious, mass media and other forces. To a certain extent this effort to cripple will propel counter-hegemonic efforts and alliances. But it is probable that internal developments will more directly respond to internal dynamics that are strongly conditioned but not clearly determined by the larger systemic whole. To the degree that external and internal forces conspire to throw off ethnic, regional and other modes of Latin American "otherness," those forces will run into renewed and intensified resistances that could result in some renegotiated power structure that favors or weakens the U.S.

Finally, maintaining a larger, systemic eye, there may well be challenges to U.S. hemispheric hegemony as technology lessens the significance of geographical, geocultural or geopolitical proximity. Whether Latin American parties and their leaders, either the worst demagogues or the most saintly servants of humanity will exploit such rivalries or succumb to them, whether genuine local resistances are manipulated or achieve a genuine and viable articulation- these are matters that are difficult enough to predict, but past indications are hardly very reassuring.

Since the shift to formal democracy in much of Latin America, the U.S. has indeed continued to play a major role in reorganizing internal dynamics of different countries (vis-à-vis narco-traffic and policies related thereto, regional trade agreements and IMF restrictions, and, at select times, human rights questions), so that they have yet to break out of an overriding hegemonic structure. If repressive violence was crucial in the years of South American crisis in the 1970s and the Central American crisis in the 1980s, ideological hegemony, including the advance of neo-liberalism and U.S.-based evangelical movements, were of growing importance in the 1990s and persist into the new century. But the growth of conformity-inducing ideological and cultural projects, including all that may be seen as negative in the growth of mass media, the impact of telenovelas, and the overall erosion of non-commodity dimensions of Latin American culture occurring from reverse migration, but above all from the "miamization" of Latin America taking place through media control and the use of right wing Cubans as U.S. "middle men" and sometimes women throughout Latin America, may be partially offset by progressive media uses, and the incursion of ecological, feminist and other currents developing more readily in the humous of developed social formations and now turning toward concerns with globalization.

In spite of the trend toward hegemonic as opposed to direct power, the resort to violence, however officially condemned by the U.S., is constantly in use in relation to narco-capitalism and other concerns; and the resort can become systemic to the degree that the situation of crisis might override concerns for international image and at least the appearance of relative, if constantly disrupted, social peace, to serve counter-insurgent goals which the U.S. ultimately has supported.

Nor is it reassuring to conjure up the growth of Japanese and Chinese economies, the continuing effects of Middle East oil and enmity. In this context, Latin America will have great difficulties in competing; and the resultant processes of migration, transnational or otherwise, will lead to internal problems in the U.S. and other Western countries, so that their capacity to defend their internal and global interests will be severely eroded. In the case of the U.S., it is questionable whether relations with Latin America, fostered by free trade or whatever, will create an areawide capacity to resist more global patterns and maintain, let alone, improve the U.S. and area situation in the global economy. In the meantime, continued upheaval and migration in the New World, joined with migrations from Europe and Asia, may create even more internal problems than opportunities. Indeed, the specific Latinization of the U.S. may have positive or indeed negative results, both in material and human terms. Efforts to reform the U.S. infrastructure now (including the economy, welfare, education, etc.), may well, even in the midst of capitalist functions and privileges, have some effect on capacities for the future, to elude the kind of heavily deterministic logic which a Wallersteinian vision seems to enjoin.

Turning inward toward Latin American cultural production itself, several futuristic visions compete in our mind's eye. How many scenarios of deculturation, of enormous cities and eroded countrysides, of smog, drugs, prostitution, tin hovels, favelas and universal AIDS. Films like those of Gaviria speak to an unspeakable world of destruction and loss. In such a world, perhaps subaltern silence is often the loudest articulation.

Indeed we may come to the conclusion that unless Latin America can resolve its deep problems, its chances for positive change, for fully participatory democracy, for resistance that doesn't feed but actually transforms the systems in which it is encased are unlikely enough. As Skidmore and Smith argued as early as 1992 in their standard overview, *Latin America* the basic socio-economic and political structures of given Latin American countries projected to many variants in the years to come without offering necessarily positive resolution.

Among their charming conclusions are (1) "*a large share of influence on Latin America's future development will continue to come from outside the region*"; (2) the action of any particular social group or class will depend not only on its own growth and strength [but]... *on what is happening among other social groups*"; and (3) -if we may extrapolate here-, the structure of international and internal class/group interactions make democratic or violent transformation of the underlying structures of Latin America matters of great difficulty (Smith and Skidmore 392).

Clearly demographic and economic data in general point to severe problems, shortages, employment and productive crises (Skidmore and Smith, 394-396); the growth of informal economies, the loss of ethnic identities through rural penetration, migration and modernization efforts, leading to the re-articulation of older patterns, new syncretic religions, musical revolutions-new transculturations which will probably not, after all, lead us readily to any new state of grace.

Indeed, in spite of the growing Mayan population, in spite of other indigenous group growth, they will still be subject to transformations that will tend to their being less Indian, at least less what they were even if more something else. They may still fight for sacred space, even if it is no longer the space of their ancestors, or even their older brothers or sisters. Or the affirmation of sacred space may transfer to the slums, only to be diluted or become rechanelled as a basis for modern urban turf wars. To the degree ethnic identities do hold it will be in part due to government collusion with ethnic entrepreneurs, the new ethnic bourgeoisie, who will seek to commodify ethnic otherness as a source of tourist dollars in an overall modernization drive that may well end up obliterating the bases for that otherness without bringing the economic prosperity for which all would be traded (Skidmore and Smith: 403-404). And to the degree ethnic identities hold, they will be at war with new gender transformations, and even new points of unity with other groups in a modernization struggle that transcends old blood, clan, *compadrazgo* and territorial lines.

It is possible, of course, that the commodification of native cultures will enable them to survive, even if modified, and that the ethnic bourgeoisie will be the origins of new dissenting leaders able to vanguard indigenist causes. It is possible that protestantized Indian groups will then transform evangelical values in function of older indigenous ones so that the net result will be the preservation of Indian resistance in a still more dynamic mode.

Ethnicity may continue to serve as a brake on broader unities which must be achieved if destructive patterns of corporatism, right wing populism and other hierarchically or patriarchically bound social and political forms do not erode any possible gains to be achieved by espousing or supporting them.

The deep structures do not necessarily bode well; and as our normative Latin Americanists tell us, "Revolutionaries have few grounds for optimism" (Skidmore and Smith 403). Where do they exist? In base communities? In new, non-hierarchical religious forms? In old or new testimonial books? In the telenovelas? In mass ecological, feminist and ultimately, new, revised workers' movements, including the new technical and assembly workers of a more advanced Latin American labor force some would say. And virtually no one opts for bearded revolutionaries setting up their mountain bases. But, then, how do we get from micro-politics to the kinds of movements able to have major effects? Surely we have not answered that question.

Over the years, we come to understand how important it is for popular memory to be kept alive. But how can older dimensions be forged in terms of a positive social future? Where can we go? Where can we even begin? And what are the implications of all this for literary theory and work?

6. World Systems Theory and Literature

What indeed are some of the issues and problems involved in applying world systems theory to Latin America, the Caribbean and U.S. Latinos?

World systems theory has served to build on dependency theory in completing a totalization process in which particular literary movements, currents, genres and works are to be seen. Whatever the final world might be on dependency theory itself, (and its inter-relation with Althusserian perspectives), world systems theory establishes a general orientation that pressures an extension of existing orientations toward an examination of Latin American, Caribbean and Latino literary phenomena in a way that can be more adequately particular because it can be, potentially, more adequately seen in a general comparatist frame. Indeed, Walter Mignolo and those working with him have attempted to incorporate world system frameworks, beyond Wallerstein's stated views on ethno-nations, to areas and modes of research anticipated but never fully taken up in directly Wallersteinian efforts (cf. Mignolo 2000).

As noted earlier, considerable work has gone into establishing the framework for a study of Latin American literatures in themselves and in relation to broader literary, cultural and social forces and in their internalization of such forces at the level of individual works. Efforts have been made to define Latin American literature as a totality in relation to more comprehensive frames, in relation to semiological mass media, oral tradition, the mythemes and ideologemes of different groups ad blocs operative in varying settings-in relation to whole semiological systems. Researchers have tried to see literary movements as responses to international forces as they affect local areas and they have tried to plot Latin American literary production in relation to macro-ideologies developed by class sectors in response to different phases of dependent development. And the effort has sometimes been to dovetail these concerns with an Althusserian dimension which places literature in relation to state apparatuses viewed within a dependency theory perspective on the socio-economic field in which legitimizing oppressive state institutions function. In these model efforts, the question has been of the relative efficacy and ultimate relation of particular literary modes to other ideological, cultural, political and socio-economic modes in a model that ultimately transcends national determinations.

As just some suggestion as to where world systems theory may lead us, we may get a more precise understanding of works in relation to literary apparatuses of the kinds of state formations facilitated by the world system in Latin American politics. We may find bases for determining the relative objectivity of works in their progressive contours as related to the status of Wallerstein's "ethno-groups" or classes in particular social formations in particular relation to larger processes. We may be able to understand the objective function of international and "indigenous" dimensions involved in the works of given authors and whole movements or trends in Latin American literature.

Indeed, we may approach the question of the relative international, Latin American and national weight in works or genres in a given era or area. One question of great interest may be that of literary systemicity in relation to clear and continuing signs of relatively autonomous national literary systems coexisting with other writings that more directly partake of international dimensions. For instance, to what degree are figures like Vargas Llosa, Cortázar or Jorge Amado and García Márquez tied to national as opposed to Latin American or even broader international literary processes. What is the "mode of production" to which their literary modes should be related? So too, we may wish to ask to what degree Black writers in Latin America are related to their native polities or even the whole of Latin America as opposed to a more general Pan-African trend. And could not the same question be asked with respect to women's literature in Latin America?

And yet we know of other writers who are absolutely crucial to their national literary life who have simultaneously little direct international significance or impact. Much will be said about these and like developments in the chapters which follow, but here I wish to point toward just two dimensions affecting literary phenomena about which I will then seek to make a few limited remarks.

Both dimensions arise from the current conjuncture and may be seen in function of the conjuncture's phenomenal expression in the migration of capital and labor as the impact on literature and literary related matters in home base and host areas-leading to transformations in the total literary, ideological and cultural fields in which literature functions.

Even as the global forces came to most overtly determine the hegemonic contours of each area and polity, and as the role of those forces became more devastating to national bourgeois and revolutionary projects and ideologies, the end result on the level of ideological, cultural and literary production has been a recent tendency toward what Jean Franco has termed a new nationalism or, in effect, a turning of backs to the world system.

For many contemporary Latin American writers, recent circumstances, including the collapse and decline of revolutionary movements, as well as national modernization projects (that is, the inundation by the world system) could only spell out an effort to "shore up ruined fragments" of prior local concerns, to focus on the local and particular in an effort at a kind of psycho-cultural defense in the face of enormous penetration and disintegration. Indeed, instead of viewing local details in function of broader material (or, subliminally, spiritual or metaphysical) forces, a tendency which crystallizes in Dario and becomes a basic orientation of the boom, we see a kind of reversion to the opposed option-that of taking in the global and general and using it in function of the particular and local-that is, the approach of Marx, the social novelists, and as apolitical a writer as Rulfo, just to cite one example.

The effort would seem to be to only grasp the global to the degree that it nurtures a hoped-for local project and to look constantly within the received existent patterns of everyday life, language and customs, for the creative possibilities in generating an enriched national or subnational community. As if to say, as impoverished as we are in the massive, totalizing scheme, let us find what we have within to make what we can. Many of the overt products of this process are not political, but the process would seem to crystallize most in conjunctures such as Nicaragua's in the 1980s and is in fact anticipated there by the development of a radical, Sandinista nationalist valence within the politically conservative modes of vanguardist cultural orientations and poetic practices resulting in Cardenal's exteriorismo and its transformations as insurrectional and then post-insurrectional workshop poetry (cf. Beverley and Zimmerman 1990).

This process, which may be referred to as centripetal, is countered by another one most commonly dominant in Latin American immigration literature and which is centrifugal in relation to the home base. Here, in the literature representing those who have been impelled out of their native lands by the forces of the world capitalist system, we find expressions that evoke, perspectivize and sometimes disassociate themselves from home base values and whose core problematics are tied increasingly (but with key differences based on given class orientations) to the dominant modes of the host, most often core country.

The result is a literature of exile or immigration, but a literature which is also one of U. S. marginality in relation to its own norms and relations with other literatures and broader fields; frequently it is a literature more radically valenced toward oppositional currents than is literature from the home base itself. And in this epoch of penetration and threat, it is, like other Latin American national literatures and works, in the process of shoring up remnants of a ruined past, gathering up things that have been falling apart, seeking new directions in the wake of collapsed projects. Here we note that the very mention of these literatures and their developments suggest how the very object of study in Latin American socio-literary theory has escaped definition, in part through colonial prisms, but in part too through global transformations on our specific objects and their real and conceptual fields.

It is to the objects of Latin socio-literary theory-that is, Latin and Central American, Caribbean and U.S. Latino literatures, with some special consideration of the literatures of immigration generated by local and international economic and cultural processes-that we will examine in this book. In this regard, let me make a few final comments relevant to the chapters which follow.

7. Latin American Culture and Literature in Postmodern and Globalization Contexts

Many current discussions of Latin American literature seem to negotiate two sets of important problems. One is national or regional as opposed or in relation to more general Latin American and global literary structures. Another is that of a theoretical perspective adequate to conceptualizing intra-literary and socio-literary relations from the perspective of contemporary norms and frames-and here the question is the relation of general, subaltern or third world, or Latin American or even area or nation-specific perspectives with respect to a literature or literatures whose nature, relations and functionality remain variable or unresolved.

In one sense of course, to speak of Latin American, Caribbean or Latino literatures is to speak of beasts that are at once many headed and non-existent. As if in anticipation of encroaching cultural imperialism, some critics write as if there are no such systemic reality as Latin American, Caribbean or Latino literatures, but rather a series of national or regional literatures related in some ways yet different in others, in Latin America. However in addition to national, regional, subregional or group forces at work on the various literary currents or trends existing often within the same contiguous geographical, politically discrete or group spaces, there are also forces of homogenization and diversification at work.

In the case of Latin American literature, those forces stem from the two major systems affecting the area-very loosely: 1.) the western (Madrid, but preferably Paris, sometimes New York or even London, and now perhaps L.A. or Miami) culture of the cosmopolitan, urban or urbanized Latin American elites; and 2.) the various local popular cultures, transformed by the impact of modernization from the conquest on, but still existing, especially in those less cosmopolitan and less "whitened" areas of Latin America.

To the degree that they survive, these latter cultural strains impact the literature of the elites, even if it is only by conditioning, if not determining, the cosmopolitan-affirming denials of Darío and scores of writers who pre-figured and followed him. For many these popular strains are much the continuing source of Latin America's residual "otherness," what remains of the non-Western tradition in America-what Unamuno called the "feather" in Darío's hat: the source of non-instrumental, magical and mystical energies some look to in the area-forces that are threatened, and even dying, perhaps, and transforming certainly, but which have somehow at least partially eluded "Latin America's dependent, peripheral capitalism" and which continue to incite concern, and sometimes, even provide bases for hope and change (even when and if they themselves begin to take on monstrous hybrid, cosmopolitan-influenced forms) in a world whose horizon of possibility seems more reduced today than even under the old dictatorships and older forms of domination.

In effect, as advanced capitalist cosmopolitan forces impact Latin American literary work, they are met by pre-capitalist cultural residues which largely limit and characterize their disposition and "season," "tropicalize" or in the last analysis profoundly transform the very patterns which seek to encapsulate them. Ironically, it is this very situation of hybridization or transculturation which constitutes Latin American literature's oblique relation to modernizing, Eurocentric traditions, and which positions at least some Latin American work as "postmodern" even in the context of social formations which are primarily "pre-modern" in virtually every other way.

There is no doubt but that the peculiar synthesis which characterizes Latin American literature and its own problematic relation to literary modernism-in sum, the equation of at least some key works of the so-called Latin American literary boom and post-boom with postmodernism-is the source of the continued intense interest in the literature. There is also little doubt that this is where an effort to understand the social basis of Latin America's literary development might find its clearest contemporary path to explication.

For all its cosmopolitan overlays and transculturations, Latin American literature, as an expression of Latin American history and overall culture, is clearly the dominant question in this book, affecting our look at Caribbean and U.S. Latino literatures as well. In relation to this question, I will explore first of all how the so called "boom" literature affected thinking about Latin American literary history, and then how the critique of that thinking led to the revisionist historicism explored in my own essay-a historicism which stresses previously submerged, unnoticed or uncommented continuities and discontinuities. In the context of a brief review of the revised history itself, I will turn to a discussion of the social meaning and significance of the boom; and then finally I will move beyond a discussion of the much heralded boom novel period to consider other emergent forms which have received considerable attention in recent years with the effort to broaden our understanding of the realities of Latin America through a study of the overall patterns of popular culture in the area. The first is political poetry, an area where much of my own work has been concentrated (but about which I will make only a few comments in this essay), and then, perhaps more important of all for our focus here, Latin American testimonial discourse.

In the course of developing a schematic view of Latin American socio-economic, cultural and literary history, centered on the boom and subsequent developments, I shall be drawing on several theoretical constructs which have emerged and have been somewhat discussed or at least mentioned in other books of mine. Clearly the primary theoretical thread of concern for recent socio-historical students of the literature is that of dependency theory as it developed virtually in tandem with Boom narrative creation; a second thread is how dependency theory itself became modified as a construct in the light of Althusserian and then poststructuralist/postmarxist formulations, involving the theoretical transformations leading to world systems theory as described in earlier in this introduction.

In Chapter I, these transformations are for the most part assumed and we look more specifically at the way in which the revised theoretical field enables us to negotiate between dependency and other, more recent perspectives. Nevertheless, we should note the persistence of some aspects of dependency theory in contemporary conceptualizations. Indeed, throughout much of the book, several of the critics we will be drawing on in one way or another formulated their views on Latin American, Central American and Caribbean literary history under the sway of dependency and world systems theory. And that theory even has effects on Latino literary studies. Even as we diverge from the theory in function of contemporary critique as specified above, nevertheless dimensions of the theory inevitably inflect and at times even underpin aspects of our analysis and may at times elude our contemporary corrections.

8. The Question of Latin American Poetry

Not much particular attention to Latin American poetry is paid in Chapter I. So we take the opportunity to fill that relative blank here, beginning with certain questions we must now confront and understand. First, poetry is a dominant mode of cultural production throughout Latin America as it is in every underdeveloped part of the world. Second, the importance of poetry has not remained in the cultural sphere alone, but has extended its "cultural space" to register a considerable impact on the total social formation and on the political realm in particular. Third, the poetry of each Latin American country, in spite of its own particularities and relations to specifically national cultural social and political patterns, shows many characteristics which makes it part of a larger regional literary system. To a certain degree, this applies to Caribbean and U.S. Latino as well as Latin American poetry perse; it would seem especially true for Central American poetry. On the question of Latin American poetry as a whole, John Beverley had noted in the 1980s:

> *The political centrality of literature, and of poetry in particular, is due among other things to the paradoxical effects of capitalist combined and uneven development in Latin America, which, together with the introduction of a bourgeois commercial mass culture, leaves intact elements of earlier strata of cultural expression: for example, the rural tradition oral songs and storytelling with roots at once in the survivals of the pre-Colombian Indian civilizations and popular Catholicism; or the role of the writer consecrated by Liberal Romanticism in the epoch of the Wars of Independence as a sort of Moses, "informing" through his rhetoric the processes of national liberation and identity-formation.... Where illiteracy, or marginal literacy, were still widespread, poetry and political rhetoric had the virtue of being susceptible to memorization and oral recitation. In small rural towns, where TV had not yet penetrated, young people gathered in the evenings to sing songs together and gossip. The spoken word conjured together the presence of the sacred (as produced by the people rather than for it), the communal and the erotic. The task of elaborating that plain-speaking Democratic Vistas voice which was supposed to be the responsibility of the "great tradition" in U.S. poetry now passed on to those countries which are the main antagonists of U.S. imperialism. (Beverley 1983: 127).*

Latin American poetry has been the space of state power and of subjective differentiation among the elites; it has had its share of those seeking to keep it a sacred practice removed from the mundane, unsoiled by the everyday, the political, the commercial. But even among those who have most mastered its formal complexities, its powers for evocation for identity exploration, for conjuring, equating and differentiating, poetry has often served as means of connexus with the concerns of people, with their struggle to survive in a hostile and alien space, with their everyday concerns, even with their vulgar hopes, dreams and language.

The question important for our understanding of Latin American and U.S. Latino poetry is that of the forces which led to the cultural and ultimately political importance and systemic nature of the poetic sphere. For Latin America, the answer may be found in the force of the state apparatus placed in domination by the area's agro-export models, and, in response, the configuration of pre-existing and developing cultural norms and forms in increasingly direct stances of opposition and resistance. To put this matter in another way, the fact is that in the face of military dictatorships throughout much of the twentieth century, Latin America has proliferated a group of poets who have forged a region-wide mode of literary and cultural production which, according to the variants generated by the concrete differences in each national poetry, has represented an active opposition to economic and cultural dispossession or domination. The emergence of this system has anticipatory moments even in the cosmopolitan *modernismo* of Darío, Julián Casal, and others; but it has its virtual "takeoff" in the vital, nationalistic, radical (and sometimes even reactionary) poets who emerge in the 1920s and 30s in Chile (the poetry of Huidobro, Neruda), Perú (Vallejo), the Caribbean (the Negritud movement in Cuba, Puerto Rico and the "Dominican Republic) and Central America (above all the vanguardists of Nicaragua) at a time of intervention, reasserted dictatorial power, and emerging popular resistance.

If current Latin American poetry frequently involves an appropriation and development of avant garde techniques in a mix with indigenous traditions as a means of entering into cultural and literary modernity, then what are we to make of this endeavor when the advanced capitalist world has moved on to its encounter with postmodernity and globalization?

It is certainly true that to understand the history and future of Latin American poetry and literature, we require more complex, contemporary models, ones that correspond to a modified sense of the nature of our situation in postmodernity in its Latin American and more global dimensions. Feminist perspectives, poststructuralist ones, comparative studies involving North American majority and minority literatures, other third world literatures, (e.g., Asian subaltern, post-colonial studies, etc.)-all these and other dimensions will come into play, as will the relation of these dimensions with broader cultural ones.

Here we return to the view that literary transformations indeed anticipate rather than reflect changes at other social levels. In the continuing expressions and silences of Latin American literary and cultural discourse, in all its new and emergent forms and processes, we may find symbolic patterns which not only anticipate but also help forge a Latin American future in which some of the most important, best and nearly forgotten dimensions of Latin America's past live and find fruition.

In this regard too, we should note how successive immigration waves into New York, Chicago and elsewhere have produced new Mexican, Puerto Rican, Cuban and now other Latin American voices, each with their own intonations, but all together generating an overall Latino discourse which has long begun to etch out new modes of Latino identification which in turn impact this nation and even have their effects on the Latin American and Caribbean worlds from which the writers or their families initially came. The transnational migration of peoples and poetry is central to the future of the Americas.

9. Central American, Caribbean and U.S. Latino Literatures

All we say about Latin American narrative and poetry here and in Chapter I will be even more important in Chapter II, in regard to Central America. Historical circumstances and the difficulties of Central development have perhaps given Central American poetry a special displaced significance and weight. However this weight clearly varies from country to country, place to place. In Chapter II, we attempt to mark points of similarity but also ones of divergence and disparity in literary qualities and achievements, country to country on the basis of a differential and ultimately *dependentista* model, though evidence of world systems traces appear also. In this context, I extend my initial remarks about testimonio in Chapter I to a more specific treatment of Central American testimonio. But what distinguishes this chapter above all is my major attempt to do an overview analysis on the basis of theories and perspectives derived from dependency theory views of political economy, extending to questions of indigenous and ladino identities and the complexities of literary production. I suppose my extended years of work on Central American literature and politics gave me a certain license to give an extended analysis in this essay, which is marked by the reading and writing of different texts on Central American politics and literature for over twenty-five years.

Perhaps less informed but more theoretically rich are my two essays on Caribbean literature. The first essay is marked by my abiding concern with world literature in the context of a world systems analysis. However, as an essay drafted in 1976 and only re-written for publication six years later, this chapter, while still valuable, I believe, in its Gramscian move to develop a cultural process model as an essential mediation between political economy and literary analyses, requires a second level commentary and updating which Chapter IV provides. Chapter IV indeed serves as a kind of extended "postscript" to Chapter III, in its admittedly partial and selective treatment of developments of literary study in the years extending from the late 1980s through 2004. And this postscript chapter indeed concludes with further extended version beyond the essay's initial appearance in the late 1980s-a postscript involving a critique of Antonio Benítez Rojo and other recent theorists of Caribbean literature, and projecting us toward future developments.

Very much related to my Caribbean work, but also to the immigration dimensions of my discussion of Latin American literature, is my initial meditation dating from the early 1980s, on Latin American Literature and immigration, perhaps the article that first gave me some standing as a Latin Americanist by combining my work in literary theory with my observations as a social worker of Mexican and Puerto Rican migrants in Minnesota during the 1970s. This short chapter draws on the question, also of political exile, and stresses the distance between Latin American economic migrants and Latin American academics who can only gradually come to an understanding of the lives and cultural production of their poorer cousins, many of whom are treated and come to see themselves as an ethnic minority. This is clearly an essay and not an article, without a single footnote and making suggestion after suggestion on the basis of lived experience as opposed to academic research. Nevertheless, the essay contains an extended theorization of immigrant processes and immigrant literature (from Latin America, the Caribbean, etc.); and in general I believe the essay shows some prescriptive and predictive power, even as it sets forth a program of work that is still viable to this day.

One of the major themes of contemporary Latin American studies begins its story in what are the border areas, and that theme may in fact have things to tell us about what is going on both sides-how north hits south, how a now transformed south responds and in turn transforms itself; how outward and return, limited and extended, transnational migrations, as well as the deterritorializations and identity shifts involved, may speak to and anticipate new constellations, new relations both in our hemisphere and elsewhere throughout the world, as the planet heats up and as ethnic identifications and enmities grow in the interstices of the postmodern, globalized world.

But we should be clear that, while the story may begin and much of it take place at the border, and while border as metaphor has been a distinctive feature of contemporary discourse, nevertheless, if our subject is Latino people, culture and literature, the metaphor dangerously becomes overly fixed, so that southwestern patterns, certainly a predominant U.S. Latino experience, come to "colonize" other ones, so that non-Mexicans and Mexicans in the Midwest (many of whom arrived from their homebase without touching the Río Grande or the Tijuana fence), are virtually subsumed in the metaphorical operation.

So, even New York-based theorists like Juan Flores and George Yúdice (1989) pick up on the metaphor and apply it to the overall Latino experience; so *Latino* itself becomes a dangerous generalization, concealing regional, class and ideological differences, causing us to forget how different urban experiences may make very different people and groups even of people from the same town or region of origin, to the point that a terminology designed to both designate diverse peoples as having points of unity comes to obviate, cancel and yet simultaneously structure experience. So a Latino event is really a Mexican or Cuban one; a Cuban one a "Caribbean" or "Latin American" one, etc.

And yet we know that such terms, "Latino" or even that term so despised by the "politically correct," including myself-Hispanic-and the term, "borders," are very useful, even as we know we must resist their totalizing and colonizing tendencies. So too, the recent, if still-to-be-detailed, effort to explore postmodern dimensions of U.S. Latinization (cf. Olalquiaga 1992) or the largely still-to-be-written story of the "Miamization" of Latin America in past several years are important to the overall question of emergent Latino identities in relation to postmodernity and its impact in Latin America.

So Latino culture and literature must be studied as part of Latin American postmodernity and part of the new postmodern world in the globalized Americas, as we seek to do so in Chapter VI. And so too, this discussion will not only mean applying Latin American and Chicano, Puerto Rican and other perspectives to the question of Latino identities, but will mean too a consideration of how the Latino totality affects the overall Latin American and broader world in the Americas. Here, we may evoke a sense of the transformations involved in the larger "Latino question.

This is a time when a Chicano intelligentsia has been firmly established, but also when Mexican and broader Latin American immigration have taken us from discussions of Oscar Lewis's "culture of poverty" and patterns of assimilation to ones more specifically centered on questions of the "underclass," transnational migration and "effective citizenship." This is a time when Chicanos are not the only oppressed Latinos in many areas and when in fact there is a struggle to maintain or decenter things Chicano in function of a larger (perhaps more diluted and unconcretizable) Latino whole. And of course, this is a time of ever-more sophisticated feminism, when in fact the older struggle against the external other (the Anglo, the *gabacho*, *bolillo* or *quién sea*) has been turned inward, when the very issue of cultural affirmation and change has been complicated by the critique of gender construction and oppression as part of culture. Chicano and Latino culture are being deconstructed and reconstructed, de-centered and re-centered, as we seek to plot what to hold onto, what to lose, how can we retain *X* as a value when it is tainted by class privilege, or sexist oppression.

Identities and identifications have been transforming in relation to the global economy and global perspectives. Immigration surveillance and English-only movements, Proposition 187, Welfare reform, attacks on Affirmative Action, bilingual education -these and other issues- spell the re-intensification of anti-Mexican and anti-Latino feelings, as well as splits in Latino communities. But ongoing economic crisis continues to send thousands north; and the explosion of mass media (and especially Spanish-language television) now gives Spanish a stronger foothold north of the border with Mexico.

The possibility of a Latinized U.S., of a reconquest by the older peoples of America (transformed, of course in varying degrees by U.S. modernist and now postmodern cultural hegemony) looms before us as a millennial prospect that could make all previous Chicano history and all previous critiques and theories of Chicano identity and culture into mere phases and aspects of the pre-history of a remade cultural hemisphere.

But in all this picture, of course, the question of the world of gangs and drugs, of informal economy and drug-running enclaves, of continuing and extending anomie, of dropouts and welfare dependency, of growing parental absenteeism, growing and deepening racial conflicts, and intensifying gender conflicts, class differentiation and the like have prevented Chicanos, Chicanos and Latinos, Latinos and Blacks, Latinos, Blacks and others, from forming a bloc, from struggling in the most meaningful ways. Now, bereft of older revolutionary illusions and horizons, and without a sure sense of new ones, the whole world and all of Latin America in or out of what is legally Latin America dance to the rhythm of postmodern commodity logic; and those who can't go with the flow and who can't get with the diffused, de-centered, post-industrial universe are doomed to live in its back alleys, unable to adjust or react creatively to new cultural transformations, and only able to hold on to the most questionable aspects of the "older cultural bases-precisely those which may best conform to and then lend themselves to becoming transformed by the logic of the informal economy and underclass patterns, the bartered communalism of gang and druggie loyalties, the nostalgic feudalism that feeds on as it fends off of advanced capitalist marginalization, a misplaced, communally destructive *compadrazgo*-even as a new Latino middle class intelligentsia takes shape and as young professors find themselves lucky to have their problems to deal with even as they scurry to their conferences in Santa Barbara or San Juan, publish their articles and go about their lives.

Here, as in the case of cultural studies in general, world changes inevitably affect our views with respect to things Chicano and Latino, just as thoughts about Chicano and Latino culture as the life form of a significant subaltern population may potentially affect the overall theoretical field. Recent anthropological, historical and literary studies (cf. the work of Renato Rosaldo, Mario García, Rosaura Sánchez, Norma Alarcón, Ramón, José David and Sonia Saldívar, etc.) point to dimensions crucial to any overall synthetic perspective on U.S. Latino culture, and especially the matter of counter-hegemonic modes which directly or indirectly express human groups attempting to cope with the various forms of oppression that exist throughout the Americas and affect the very psychology and being of those coming to, or living in, U.S. enclaves. The questions for U.S. Latino, as well as Latin American, culture posed by this perspective have mainly to do with the overlays of postmodern cultural forms and norms. The current task is to draw on contemporary work as a means of articulating an approach to the particularities of U.S. Latino social life in ways, however critical and however respectful they are of the irreducibility of Latino experience, also point to global contexts and link up with broader theorizations in expressing present realities and future potentialities.

The goal in contemporary and future work in Latino studies, then, will be to consider some dimensions of the theoretical revolution to see how they make us rethink Latino cultural questions since the 1960s. This consideration will inevitably take place in the shadow of our deliberations over post-Marxian and Gramscian currents which point to a cultural emphasis as implicitly given space by the work of Jameson, Laclau/Mouffe, Wallerstein, etc. Clearly, we should add here that this cultural focus is especially valuable for Chicanos and more broadly, Latinos, among whom the question of culture or "cultural dimensions" in the midst of and even at times opposed to civilization, is more central than it is for the more modernized peoples sharing the American landscape.

In dealing with such theoretical concerns, I would like finally to suggest that Chicano and more broadly Latino resistances and accommodations will be important to the future of U.S., Latin American, and even more broadly international configurations in which humanity makes or does not make its future. In this frame, it is of course important to examine the effects of contemporary patterns of post-Wallersteinian concerns with transnational processes of immigration (cf. Schiller, Basch and Banc Szanton 1992 and Báez, Bencomo and Zimmerman, ed.). As Flores and Yúdice (1992) have been pointing out, Latino identity with all its previous characteristics and contours, crosses over in postmodern culture as posing some combination of the most retrograde and progressive possibilities for future patterns of resistance and creativity, posing some of the most dynamic points of convergence and alliance with other, non-

Latino groups in a broader field of new oppositions internal to and at least possibly transformative of the entire social system.

In this context, the final chapter, drafted in 1989 and rewritten in 1992 and other times over the years, is in some sense a postscript to Chapter V, developing questions related to U.S. Latino populations and developing discussions over Chicano and Rican literature as parts of a posited "U.S. Latino literature." In the preface to the bibliography which my essay introduces, I noted in 1992 how the "text attempts to address... questions... relating to Latino cultural identity as the context for... literary works; it also touches on the way in which the recent theoretical and creative works change our way of conceiving the literary corpus, and how that corpus has been extended by new feminist, new non-Chicano/ Puerto Rican/Cuban works."

This essay has proven seminal to many, but the work of Nick Kanellos's Recovering the Hispanic Literary Heritage project has indicated an enormous pre-history of Spanish language writing in what is today U. S. territory from the sixteenth century on. And of course considerable literary, critical and theoretical production, especially with regard to feminist and overall gender questions, in the years after this chapter was first drafted, are only partially subsumed in subsequent rewriting efforts. So the text, even as rewritten, immediately requires updating and yes, postscripting as we make our way in the new millennium.

Postscript

Such is the overall perspective stemming from the final essay and providing a final postscript to the essay and the book as a whole. A still more final postscript to the essay itself attempts to overcome some of its limitations; but postscripts can never outrun time and change. The same may be said for the brief postscript which closes this book, and so too for this introduction, which may of course be seen as the penultimate reference frame, entry point and postscript for the entire effort contained within the covers which are the framing entry points and postscripts of all.

Works Cited

Baez-Hernández, Sonia, Anadeli Bencomo, & Marc Zimmerman, ed. forthcoming. *Ir/Venir: Migración transnacional y procesos cultures entre América Latina y el norte.*

Basch, L., Schiller, N.G., & Blanc-Szanton, C., ed. 1997. *Nations Unbound.* Amsterdam.

Best, Steven & Douglas Kellner 1991. *Postmodern Theory: Critical Interrogations.* New York. The Guilford Press.

Beverley, John. 1983. "Sandinista Poetics". *The Minnesota Review.* Ns 20 (Spring): 127-134.

Beverley, John. 1993. *Against Literature.* Minneapolis. University of Minnesota Press.

Beverley, John & Marc Zimmerman. 1990. *Literature & Politics in the Central American Revolutions.* Austin, TX: University of Texas Press.

Deleuze, Gilles, & Felix Guattari. 1987. *A Thous & Plateaux: Capitalism & Schizophrenia.* Minneapolis. University of Minnesota Press.

Flores, Juan & George Yúdice. 1990. "Living Borders/Buscándo América: Languages of Latino Self-Formation." *Social Text* 24 (Fall): 58-84.

Hopkins, Terence K. & Immanuel Wallerstein, ed. 1980. *Processes of the World-System.* Beverly Hills. Sage Publications.

Jameson, Fredric. 1992. *Postmodernism, or, the Cultural Logic of Late Capitalism* Durham, NC. Duke University Press.

Kritz. M.M., Keely, C.B. & Tomasi, S.M., ed. 1981. *Global Trends in Migration: Theory & Research in International Population Movements.* New York. Center for Migration Studies.

Laclau, Ernesto & Chantal Mouffe. 1985. *Hegemony y Socialist Strategy: Towards a Radical Democratic Politics.* London. Verso.

Mignolo, Walter. 2000. *Local Histories/Global Designs: Coloniality, Subaltern Knowledges, & Border Thinking.* Princeton, NJ. Princeton University Press.

Saldívar, Ramón. 1990. *Chicano Narrative: The Dialectics of Difference.* Madison. University of Wisconsin Press.

Skidmore, Thomas & Peter Smith. 1992. *Modern Latin America.* Oxford University Press.

Wallerstein, Immanuel. 1974. *The Modern World-System, I: Capitalist Agriculture & the Origins of the European World-Economy in the Sixteenth Century*. New York & London. Academic Press.

Wallerstein, Immanuel. 1993. *Geopolitics & Geoculture: Essays on the Changing World-System*. Cambridge: Cambridge University Press.

Wallerstein, Immanuel, Samir Amin, Giovanni Arrighi, & Andre Gunder Frank. 1982. *Dynamics of Global Crisis*. New York. Monthly Review Press.

Wallerstein, Immanuel, Giovanni Arrighi & Terence K. Hopkins. 1989. *Antisystemic Movements*. London. Verso.

Wallerstein, Immanuel, Samir Amin, Giovanni Arrighi, & Andre Gunder Frank. 1990. Transforming the Revolution: Social Movements & the World-System. New York. Monthly Review Press.

Wallerstein, Immanuel & Etienne Balibar. 1991. Race, Nation, Class: Ambiguous Identities. London. Verso.

Zimmerman, Marc. 2005. Pre-Post Positions: Essays on Structures & History, Literature & Aesthetics. Santiago, Chile. Bravo y Allende; Houston, TX LACASA.

______. 2006. América Latina en el nuevo [des]orden. TBA.

Chapter I

LATIN AMERICAN LITERATURE AND THE CONTEXT OF THE POPULAR

1. Introduction: The Effect of the Boom on Literary History

During the late 1970s, as Latin American literature moved toward what some have characterized as the post-boom, several critics complained how the reification of Latin American literary production into the commercial or publicity category, "the Boom," had denied the validity and obscured the study of previous Latin American literary works, and indeed led to a generation of Latin American literary students only interested in avant garde narrative, its antecedents, its main texts and then its recent successors. In some paradoxical ways, the very literary development which most spurred interest in Latin America and Latin American literature simultaneously blinded people to the full range of that literature and its history. The fascination with "boom literature" led to a situation by which all of Latin American literary history was seen as a series of stages leading to and subsequent to the boom. There was no doubt that contemporary Latin American fictive practice was producing the greatest number of major texts, the greatest density of literary creation, in Latin American literary history. But the so-called boom, critics and teachers began to shout, was not all there was to Latin American literature. Furthermore it was not the only thing that was good or valid in Latin American literary or cultural production. Indeed, they argued that without seeing that production in fuller, more systematic ways, critics were losing the very significance of the "boom literature" they were so intent on heralding.

At least some of the critics, formed in the 1960s and 70s, and now middle-aged power-brokers in the academy, are post-boomers seeking an alternative but fully loaded canon. And now we must see the debate over the centrality of "boom fiction" in function of the fact that, combined with the larger social circumstances which accompanied it, the literary production labeled as Boom in fact generated the need which it initially seemed to repress: the reconstitution of

Latin American literary history. This was the point of Nelson Osorio's important article of 1977-that the new Latin American narrative designated a change inside the Latin American literary system and also in that system's theoretical conceptualization. For Osorio, the "new novel" should cause critics to rethink Latin American history and literature; it should cause us to think of repressed aspects of Latin America's social and literary past. It undoes previous canons, the selective schemas of "significant movements and works"; it also generates the need to rethink critical tools of analysis. Indeed the emergence of the new novel forces critics and teachers to determine the "real physiogamy of previous literature as an ensemble, in order to know how and with what elements we can establish the relation of literature's internal historical continuity with socio-economic and political developments."

Osorio notes two dominant tendencies (the formal and sociological) in most approaches to Latin American literary history which had been practiced separately and without unity and which the new Latin American criticism (Marxist and otherwise) was bringing together. Both tendencies were partial and ideologically limited. Immanent literary studies, in their effort to achieve "objectivity" restrained the limits of the field of inquiry to the determination and analysis of formal linguistic elements. The second properly insisted that we cannot understand literary phenomena with grasping social context, but it tended toward a positivist procedure of reducing literary phenomena to their thematic contexts and then confronts them with social life.

In the study of Latin American literary history, the dominant tendency has been justifying projects of the present which obscure the past. Whether in "immanent formalist" or "vulgar sociological" studies, Latin American literary history had been guided by the same ideological perspective. For example, immanent histories dealing with the wealth of Latin American narrative genres have focussed only on those forms privileged by the metropolis, and have thus distorted our view of the total Latin American narrative system and literary tradition. Retrospective studies were realized on the basis of a catalogue of authors and works elaborated by a metropolitan-dominated critical tradition-with little effort to account for or even identify tendencies which emerged to oppose the dominant tradition or to account for changes in terms other than internal ruptures in a virtually hermetic literary system. Finally, literary study, evaluation and classification were mainly based on implicit content, reducing our view to a one dimensional perspective that impoverished criticism and made appreciation of concrete functions of literary phenomena and their evolution impossible. The result was an ideologically distorted apprehension of literary history which failed to establish believable continuities of literary development in relation to social history. We had a relatively fixed catalogue and hierarchy of works uncritically based on socially dominant tastes -a veritable system of inclusions and exclusions which failed to account for the very literary history it claimed to present. We had the canonized literature of the critical elites, which during the 1960s caused us to see all in function of "the boom," and to leave out much that previous literary historians had seen as anomalous during a period of lineal social realist literature; and then we have a more popularly inflected series of texts which some would even reject calling "literature."

And yet as Roberto Fernández Retamar argued in a seminal essay (1975), it is a fundamental characteristic of Latin American literature that genres, modes and currents which are secondary or minor in European literatures are more primary and crucial in the overall Latin American system. The essay, for example, had played a crucial role; so did chronicle and travel books in earlier historical phases; so does testimonial literature in the 1970s and 80s. So while we may start with the mainstream tradition of elite literature, we would want to keep other traditions and currents in mind

The texts by Osorio and Fernández Retamar to which I have been referring are products of an era now already very different from the new period beginning in 1989. In the present moment, we may see that they were struggling against the imposition of a new cultural hegemony which many of us came to call postmodern and now we have come to characterize under the rubric of globalization. Indeed, in a perceptive article written some fifteen years ago, Jorge Ruffinelli (1990) corroborated the view held by Gerald Martin (1989) and others that postmodernity first began to consolidate itself in Latin America in Borges and a few other writers; it did so to such a degree, it has been argued by George Yúdice and others (see below), that the effort to promote other discourse modes and alternative literary histories in Latin America became a struggle against boom hegemony taking place nevertheless in the frame of that very hegemony. Whether we see one or another example of Boom modernity as simultaneously or at least "at times" postmodern, or as a specifically "pre-postmodern" occurrence, we would most likely agree that the struggle to emphasize other narrative and literary discourses and to decenter Latin American literary history from a focus on what leads to "the boom" as opposed to these discourses, occurs and is given its configurative character by Latin American high narrative itself and of course the broader socio-historical context which the boom and recent post-modern and now post-9/11 Latin American history have been a part.

Throughout the entire period designated as the boom, leftist Latin Americanist critics were indeed responding to boom hegemony and attempting to constitute an alternative literary history. They emphasized the "ancillary literary modes" Fernández Retamar had championed -or uncanonized works within already recognized literary modes. Following Angel Rama's re-inscription of Ortíz's transculturation as the predominant basis of Latin American cultural processing (Rama 1982 and Ortíz 1978), they sought to find the discourses blocked out, hidden or otherwise marginalized by the dominant ones. Drawing on developing poststructuralist methodologies to recover patterns that were displaced, decentered and structured out, they pointed to lost works, lost movements and currents, and went so far as to find other discourses submerged in the patterns of presumed dominance.

Such efforts have only deepened with the full advent of poststructuralist, feminist and now postmodernist perspectives. With relation to the literary past, we may note the effort by John Beverley (1993) to see Latin American literature as another structure of first colonial and then Creole capitalist domination even as a problematic colonial and then bourgeois sector began to turn literature into a mode of apparent oppositional discourse increasingly open to popular currents if only to encapsulate them; and we may also note Martin Lienhard's seminal volume (1990) in which we begin to recover the forgotten history of oppositional writing beginning with indigenous works and projecting as alternative repressed texts or submerged dimensions actually alive in apparently elite discourse structures.

With reference to the colonial period, Rolena Adorno (1982, 1994. 2000), Walter Mignolo, Beatriz Pastor (1983), Ileana Rodríguez (1984) and Hernán Vidal (1985) produce major re-interpretations recovering lost traditions and projecting previously unnoticed or undeveloped continuities. With respect to the nineteenth Century, we might well turn again to Vidal (1976), and to such writers as David Viñas (1971), Beatriz González-Stephan (2002) and Doris Sommer (1991a). As far as the transition between the nineteenth and twentieth centuries, we have the work of Rama (1970), but also Françoise Perus (1976), Hugo Achugar (1985), Julio Ramos (1989) and countless others. And the list is of course even greater when we look at the century as a whole or other given periods or genres therein. With reference to the literary present, the critics have emphasized popular poetry, lyrics, graffiti and testimonio, seeking to constitute these forms as ones oppositional to postmodern ones (cf. Yúdice 1991) or as constituting a left postmodernism in relation thereto (cf. Larsen 1995).

Recent studies of Latin American popular culture, synthesized best perhaps in Rowe and Schelling (1991) create a more general context of cultural history in and against which elite and subaltern discourses act, interact and intertwine. Thus the written word has tended to play an oppressive role in Latin America history (cf. Beverley 1993), but it is also true that many writers and critics have tried to reverse the view from one that legitimizes Latin American literature by reference to Europe and have, intentionally or not, evoked or represented popular sectors at least partially in countering the hierarchical ordering patterns and traditions inscribed in the writing process.

In sum, what was called the "novelistic boom" was seen as the final achievement of 'maturity', among Latin American as well as European critics. But a European focus can't explain the actual production and reception of the literature in situ. Since Angel Rama and then Antonio Cornejo Polar, the emphasis on intertextuality has gone from exploring a work's relations not only with broad, usually European traditions, but also specifically Latin American ones.

Today, Latin American socio-historical literary criticism continues reversing the trend of imposing Eurocentric paradigms and thereby obscuring differences. Indeed, the recent post-Gramscian constructs derived from Laclau and Mouffe, Michel de Certeau, Néstor García Canclini and other thinkers have transformed the conceptual field of analysis; and we are clearly in a post-dependency and now, for many, a post-Marxist phase of Latin American historical analysis.

Inevitably, this situation corresponds to the new postmodern phase marked by Neo-Liberalism, New Democracies and Debt Crisis -and this in turn implies a new cultural and literary terrain now characterized by the globalizing processes of recent years. But even evoking a new theoretical stage beyond dependency shows how that theory still casts its shadow over socio-historical conceptualizations of Latin American realities. In this sense, the theory's orientational frame still helps us to map out certain socio-economic, political and literary correlations which enable to begin to enrich our understanding of the history and the literature itself.

In the present chapter, inevitably written within the paradigms available during the historical conjuncture of its genesis, I wish to review certain of the key stages in the development of Latin American literature in function of its dialectical relation with "the nation", popular culture and the subaltern, etc. I wish to outline certain of the major characteristics, movements, trends and currents of different periods of Latin American literature before, during and after the literary explosion we know as "the boom"; but I want to place the development of that explosion in relation to the socio-economic and political history of recent years, as well as the system of cultural and literary production which is impacted by that overall system and of which the cultural/literary system is itself a part. Inevitably I wish to emphasize the contradictory patterns, and the forgotten currents, the forgotten people and dimensions of "people's culture" which recent, postmodern contexts are in fact helping us to recover.

What follows, then, is a brief account of the different phases of Latin American socio-economic and literary development, with an emphasis on ways which, at given stages, certain kinds of literature affirm or undermine givens within the literary and overall cultural, political and socio-economic system in which various parts of Latin America are embedded. The reader should in no way view this chapter as definitive, but as a summing up of certain directions and perspectives which underline current problems and point, however uncertainly, toward the future. In all of this, literary and non-literary cultural phenomena should be seen as not merely reflecting but actually anticipating new directions and possibilities for Latin America.

2. Latin American Culture and Literature in Historical Phases

A. The Colonial Phase

For this exercise, I quite purposely leave aside the vast array of pre-Conquest oral and written literature; even while acknowledging that the transculturation of colonial and post-colonial literary characteristics have their roots in this older corpus of practices and processes that represent the indigenous cultures of the Americas. .During the Colonial period, whose cultural effects endured deep into post-colonial social formations, the metropolitan countries monopolized production and commerce, concentrating on the hacienda, the mine and the city. Beyond the trading enclaves lay vast spaces outside of systematic control. The urban elites posed the problems they faced in function of the oppositions between "civilization and barbary," enclave and rural cultures, the Republic of Spaniards and the Republic of Indians, which supplied the labor force for the mines and haciendas. The enclave was controlled through censorship, Inquisition, and monopoly of the printing press. Clearly modes of literary expression developed in function of print culture in these circumstances and according to given conditions. The Indian world had some printed expressive modes, to record their own history and traditions; and Lienhard, building on the work of León Portillo and others, has shown how Indian written expression persisted throughout the colonial period and even up to the present, and how Indian perspectives seeped into or unconsciously structured aspects of creole discourse. Nevertheless, we may still safely assert that the primary "weapons of the weak" (Indians Africans, women, others) throughout the colonial period and beyond were to be found in popular cultural oral and extra-verbal traditions (music, dance, religious ritual, etc.). So, the colonial period was marked by an oral culture dependent on a community and a written culture associated mainly with domination.

Part of the problem of understanding the colonial world rests on the fact that oppositional discourse was relegated to oral traditions difficult to reproduce and study. And this problem affects us to this day, since in addition to an extensive narrative system, we have persisting elements and forms from earlier stages of development, which are coming to the fore through testimonial and other modes down to our own times.

The importance of the oral cultures of Latin America has been lost in the shuffle with talk of García Márquez, Vargas Llosa and company's internalization of the popular as "marvelous" and "magical" dimensions in their literary structures. To be sure, much of the oral tradition is one of negotiations and accommodations within the system of colonial dominations and contradictions. While we have too little in the way of popular records of these processes, and while many popular movements rose only to fall and are only sporadically expressed in colonial literature, nevertheless, these processes and movements are crucial to understanding that literature as a series of repressions and "structurings out" that are significant in relation to future transformative possibilities in Latin America. And yet, even when elite writers have appropriated popular elements or whole traditions related to patterns of rebellion, resistance and opposition, they have tended to subvert them in function of aestheticist or, if more directly political, as conservative or self-serving populist projects.

In the colony, we have, in effect, two primary modes of reproducing culture belonging to two different methods of organizing experience. The colonizer controlled the press and written word production. Because of the Inquisition and government power, subversive, counter-hegemonic discourse for the *letrados* was forced into an elaborately symbolic, Gongoran mode (cf. Beverley 1988 and 1993). But for the most part, print culture was a direct apparatus of the state, and those who wrote were frequently members or at least organic intellectuals of those who constituted state power. Of the elite modes, the main one to escape colonial domination and instrumentality was poetry, precisely the arena most accessible to otherwise silenced colonial women-the most celebrated case being that of Sor Juana Inés de la Cruz. Indeed, the triumph of the Baroque and, at the extreme, of gongorismo (or a seeming superabundance of decorative elements, exaggerated metaphor, etc.), suggest, as Jean Franco has noted, "an emptiness, a multiplication of the signifier as a sign of the poverty of the signified among colonial elite writers and pointed to their search for a means to preserve individual perspective in a literary system expressing hierarchical control" (Franco 1973: 70).

If Beverley is correct, the triumph of Góngora in Latin America from colonial times through Darío and García Márquez, meant the triumph of a kind of sublimating utopian discourse, primarily conforming to colonial models, but capable of some veering toward subversive or at least iconoclastic Aesopian discourse. However, the literary radicalism it promotes May well be as a substitute for genuinely political radicalism and may in fact imply an overall conformism that maintains the sphere of symbolic transformation to a chosen elite of the lettered (1988: 96).

To be sure, dissidence among the colonial lettered parallels the political, cultural and ideological struggles involved. So, alongside the chronicles of Iberian glory, we have writings like those of Las Casas who saw the Conquest as invasion. Meanwhile the native accounts point to colonial destruction, but also the creative reappropriation of European influences by cultures which refused to die. Mutual transformations did occur, even where native populations disappeared (cf. Lienhard 1990).

The colonization of native consciousness met only varying degrees of success. The combining of traditions was limited due to the decimation of the population. By the end of the sixteenth Century, the material basis of native memory had suffered drastically. But many sites of resistance escaped suppression. To a degree, landscape and its magical/religious significance remained. The development of the Christian belief systems in syncretic relation to native ones is the key model of accommodation and resistance processes studied today. The question always is whether the process is primarily one of colonial imposition or native appropriation. The tug of war is the constant Latin American reality, with the Virgin de Guadalupe serving as a prime instance (Rowe and Schelling 23).

Christian ideas often masked native thinking in the colony. Foreign elements came to stand for native ones and refigured native beliefs. Counter-documents, counter-belief systems emerged. Idolatry, "fluidity of time and space, a permeability of beings and things, a multi-dimensionality, undermined the stable categories of western thinking" (ibid.).

The Jesuits reduced native multi-dimensionality to their own more instrumentalist categories. But how far did the Christian grid distort native thought and how far did native thought penetrate Christian? Christian concepts were changed and reappropriated into native or non-orthodox codes. Also native culture declined in the public sphere only to be displaced to and survive in the domestic, and then retransmitted back to the public.

Women became the prime transmitters of indigenous culture, in a process of counter-acculturation. Native practices continued in relation to misfortune, illness, death; and women played the major acculturation role in efforts to conjure up lost animals, lost objects and lost loves. Native practices drifted from their original meanings and contexts, but idolatry survived as a repertory of actions, conducts and ruses giving some coherence to emotional states, but no longer surely relating cosmos and organized memory, generally becoming isolated, esoteric formulae. However this decontextualization process of actually helped customs to survive in *curanderismo* and other forms. Even as the practices became disconnected from their original group meanings, they were able to extend to other groups, even Spaniards. The more they lost, they more they extended and in effect gained. Thus, Rowe and Schelling see decontextualization as reducing a native culture's main strength-its ability to store old and process new information. However reduction did not mean disappearance (ibid.: 22).

"Colonial magic"-a synthesis of European and non-European practices-come to characterize subaltern groups finding ways of getting around colonial hierarchy. Erotic magic could overcome barriers of caste to gain socially forbidden sexual attentions. Such everyday practices lived within the interstices of the rigid hierarchies of colonial society and formed a substratum of popular culture. What became the basis of "magic realism" was mainly transmitted by women as they negotiated between tactical obedience and pragmatic evasion. Magic responded to a lack of mechanisms for mediating relationships in colonial society. Women transmitted popular attitudes in those spheres of life most eluding colonial institutional controls. With variations, this process would continue, in part fostered by the limited role usually assigned to women in civil society (cf. Franco 1989, cited in ibid.: 22-23).

B. Independence and Liberalism in Latin America

The Independence and subsequent nineteenth Century processes involve significant efforts at modernization and an attack on the accommodational syntheses achieved throughout the colonial period. The elimination of the native, *blanquiamiento*, etc. are just the most famous and extreme modes of nineteenth Century modernization schemes. If the wars of independence meant a breakdown of order and authority, the creoles in power did everything they could to reestablish order, but they waged war in terms of competing Liberal or Conservative projects. Creole-led armies recruited rural Indians and Blacks, *mestizos* and mulattos, whose own projects and aspirations were generally swept into the dominant programs and oppositions; these same social sectors were brutally repressed when they asserted themselves outside of the dominant frames. Indian and slave uprisings were not infrequent processes and were often encouraged to the degree that they fed creole interests. Ultimately Indian lands were encroached upon even as the slaves were freed in function of overall projects which hardly respected Indian or Black interests.

If with few exceptions, colonial writers catered to colonial elites, most post-Independence writers, addressing a narrow, ambiguous public, transcribed the European equation of romanticism and liberalism. Liberalism meant free trade, a shift from Spanish to English hegemony and from a nationalist ideology which championed independence but underplayed class antagonism. Limited industrialization and entrenched agrarianism increasingly drawn into the international market (hence the victory of Liberals over Conservatives) would prevent the full emergence of a modern proletariat. Literary forms entered a narrow internal print-culture market of small elites headed by a caste of nascent commercial oligarchs that would only internationalize the market (and book production therein) after the "caudillo wars" and their coming to hegemony during the last third of the century.

According to Vidal (1976), revolutionary liberalism became the dominant ideological expression of Latin America's emergent bourgeoisie projecting a new vision of a Latin American space to be mastered and transformed. Principles basic to the project were *free trade*, involving self-regulating mutual interchanges leading to progress for those involved; *difusionismo*, or the provision of bases for penetrating and civilizing unsettled areas; and *Republicanism*, defined as the appropriation of the state apparatus for the sake of propelling modernization.

Corresponding to these three tendencies was a series of myths inscribed in the literary system with the object of creating a mentality appropriate to the consolidation of new and sovereign nations. These myths seek to incorporate the American subject within the liberal project with the end of capturing and stabilizing the national states and promoting the conquest of the interior. The writer is a spiritual conductor of a child people still submerged in barbarism, lacking self-consciousness, discipline and emancipated will. The social utopia involved a pilgrimage from primitivism to the Promised Land. Of course there would be a need or a directive will, which corresponded to the political needs of the Liberal free trade project. The epic of the era presented the conquest of the interior -as the project of a class as a national question to overcome barbarism and establish democratic order against regional anarchy and *caudillismo*- a project claiming to involve all national classes. But the epic's hero is a classist figure, a superior being whose presence implies the passivity of the masses, who are moved to incorporate themselves in a new European-style order which only the hero can constitute by overcoming their debilities.

The classic novel expressing the processes in question is Sarmiento's *Facundo*, a work presenting the formation of Argentina as a modern nation, with Buenos Aires as the central civilizing force opposing federalism, fragmentation and chaos. Sarmiento proudly flaunts his European bias in function of his view of Civilizaton over Barbarism; but, Viñas shows, he also incorporates popular Latin America dimensions which undermine or challenge his dominant focus and anticipate future problems. The pampa "resists mapping according to the grids of European civilization." Frontier freedom challenged European capitalist centrality; and "the civilizing project of the Argentinean bourgeoisie failed to supply the affective connections necessary for the construction of a national identity" (Rowe and Schelling 200).

As Sommer (1990a) has now well shown, the bourgeois dream was to make novels an instrument of nation-building in the nineteenth century. But the reality was something else, in that the major works show the fundamental divisions of culture and territory that made the formation of modern states in the European image no easy matter. And Sommer's appropriation of Benedict Anderson's view (1983) of the novel as the space for nation-building is problematic with respect to Latin America. Indigenous rejection of national borders remains in Latin American consciousness (Rowe and Schelling 204) -a matter which emerges in Sommer's own treatment of "counter-narratives," such as testimonio, both in the final pages of her book and her article of 1990 (Sommer 1990b).

The contradictions between individual and collective projects, the confusions of national and class interests, dependency and independence, characterize nineteenth century romantic writing. There is a costumbristic interest in the folk, but an emphasis on submerging or even destroying-or at least ordering- it in relation to metropolitan models: the image of Ariel. So the utopian impulse can lead to genocide, whitening, bettering a primitive "colored" race; it can lead to the takeover of common lands in the name of progress; and thus, as it occurs, the further impoverishment and displacement of rural populations. As the liberal modernizing project wins over, the bourgeoisie becomes willing to sacrifice the democratic pretensions of their ideological project to struggle against the stirrings of a landless proletariat it has been instrumental in creating. The illusion of national progress fades, and the necessity of military control or dictatorship as the basis of national progress against satanic forces comes to the fore. We move from the liberalism of Benito Juárez in México and Rufino Barrios in Guatemala, to the *porfiriato* and *El señor presidente*.

In sum, the peculiar nature of Latin American liberalism becomes the inscribed mode of dominant Latin American literature in the nineteenth century. The liberal project is never fully eroded and, according to Vidal (1976), it is still the driving force in a transformed sense, into the 20th even in the ideology of the so-called Boom. However, prior to the Boom are the successive phases of modernism, social realism and vanguardism.

C. The Victory of Liberalism, Imperialism and Modernism

The market expands between 1875 and the first years of the new century, the famous, ubiquitous first phase of modern imperialism, in which several countries are incorporated in the international division of labor. Latin America's role was to export raw materials and agricultural goods and to import finished products. This meant riches for the oligarchs, who equated their prosperity with the wealth of the nation. The financial-industrial phase of dependent development brought into being national entrepreneurs whose wealth was directly dependent on the demands of the commodity market. Their many European-style monumental buildings reveal the nature of their project, as well as their wealth. Here Rowe and Schelling (28-42) provide a useful summary.

The victory of free trade and authoritarian liberalism toward the end of the last century meant political, technological and cultural modernization, always carried out within but often coming up against, the limits of established order. Telegraph, the railroads and rifles "immobilized cultural flows and meant that movements of population would be those of immigration to the capital from rural areas and from other countries. Nineteenth century ideologues continue to use conquest ideology to justify eliminating all elements threatening the state. The Indians are the object, the military the "hidden god" (cf. Viñas 1982, cited in ibid.: 30). By the 1880s technological modernization was accelerating, and popular continuities with the colonial period began to break down. Mass social forms emerged offering a mode of enforced peasant and urban poor integration and a means of asserting their access to goods, services and cultural pleasures which the elites had previously monopolized. Political independence is less significant in this sense than modernization. But, the key point of Latin American development is its unevenness and contradictoriness.

Modernization is not narrowly technological. Just because some social sectors get updated doesn't mean that the overall situation advances or improves. The progress of some may well reinforce the partial marginalization and super-exploitation of pre-capitalist peasant and other sectors. Economic modernization may in fact sponsor or maintain feudal and paternalistic features. Latin American modernization was uneven, partial and "distorted," occurring mainly in coastal regions, mainly benefiting landed elites and their client population pools, mainly involving a continually inadequate infrastructure and a continuation of monocultural production. Authoritarian liberalism combining economic liberalism with social authoritarianism became modernity's main political mode of implementation.

In the major cities, a new urban culture emerges with its own cultural norms and forms. It is the period of newspapers, folletins, circuses, popular theater, photography, printmaking, the beginning of filmmaking, new musical forms: the tango, the bolero (ibid.: 33). The new urban popular culture means the intensification and transformation of high culture and the decline of rural traditions in the cities and in the *campo*, even as the new urbanized cultural modes preserve some potential oppositional thrust.

In the transformations taking place at the end of the nineteenth century, involving rural and urban populations, older and newer bourgeois sectors, native and newly arrived immigrant populations, we find the basis for Latin America as we know it today. Modernizing ideology and traditional practices join in contradictory patterns and problems, which intensify in the more urban areas and became the basis for a "peripheral modernity" (Sarlo 1988), in which a stubborn pattern of patrimonial social relations are overlaid by European cosmopolitanism and liberalism (belief in progress, etc.) and involve a varied discrepancies between cosmopolitan representational forms and the national realities to which the forms supposedly relate. Art and architecture oppose the habits and customs tied to traditional society. Popular culture, seen as disturbing the civilized Paris-centered image promoted by the elites, is negated-just as vagrancy and other laws exclude popular sectors from city plazas. The rural population, popular religion and festivals, hold the nation back. Sarmiento's old civilization versus barbarism-or modernity versus tradition-takes on its more modern forms.

Ideas and attitudes, state policies and actions, seek to uproot native and African "barbarism" and to impose modernization from above. Positivist science and authoritarian social engineering, order and progress, are often backed by police and military, who control popular sectors, and seek to "construct them in function of the new disciplines" (*Ibid*.: 41).

According to Perus (1976) and Cueva (1977), what is imposed are Latin American variants of Lenin's "Junker model" of development, in which old class relations and authoritarian forms selectively draw on modernizing economic practices and ideologies to reinforce, deepen and extend traditional power-even though the modernization processes inevitably stir often explosive oppositions to the drive for a mode of economic development which preserves and intensifies class privileges. In this sense, Mexican, Argentine and other Latin American positivisms had little enough in common with the uneven application and transculturations of transplanted French models. In literature also, modernizing, cosmopolitan aesthetic and discursive elements, especially those which congeal in *modernismo*, follow the same pattern as do ideological ones, in their essential correlation to Junker model established hierarchies, and even in their sometimes appropriation of anti-referential, aestheticist, irrationalist and symbolist dimensions which mark out their anti-positivist space in the cosmopolitan cultural mix.

According to *dependentista* reductionism portrayed in Franco (1973) and Blanco (1976), literature at this time could be characterized as involving less restriction and more free trade, with the assumption that a good product would make its own way on the market, whereas a poor product would fail. The only problem was that there was no market and little in the way of an infrastructure of publishing and criticism. Thus the differences between metropolitan and dependent economies were reproduced in terms of the differing conditions in which literary production took place. For a Latin American writer to enter the pantheon of Eurocentric letters meant shedding local eccentricity. Cosmopolitanism was *modernismo*'s clarion call, but the movement also reflected "the schism of the bourgeois artist from bourgeois society itself," at least in terms of questions of taste in Bourdieu's sense (1984). Ruben Darío cannot counter positivism and materialism by referring to nature since this would bring him too close to Calibanesque Latin American realities; but he cannot accept bourgeois culture which is based on utilitarian instrumentalism. Sensuality tempered by taste is the solution, with cultural allusions mediating between the poet and productive relations.

So in the key essay of the period, Rodó's *Ariel* (1967), taste allows the aristocracy of the best to be distinguished from the Calibáns of the democratic horde. Modernista authors define their superiority over the masses while rejecting their society's overt ideology. Their aestheticism and hermeticism express a sensuous enjoyment contrary to puritan sublimation or apology of modernization. Their vitality broke through utilitarianism and instrumentality, promoting values contrary to productive and a devotion to sensuous pleasure constrained by a Catholic sense of sin, rather than a capitalist/protestant labor imperative. Print culture exaggerated the schism between writer and masses, especially in countries with high illiteracy rates. The very possession of books was as mark of cultural superiority and divided the writer from the illiterate. Authorship was the guarantee of nobility and disinterestedness. Literacy was redemption.

To be sure, the class contradictions in *fin de siglo* European literary production were not so developed in Latin America, so that José Martí, the "first great anti-imperialist American, the most passionate defender of social equality in his times, believed in the united struggle of all classes against imperialism and or an economic development which he cannot recognize as necessarily dependent. The most advanced writer of the day could not see that the literature of the nation was the literature of class domination (cf. Blanco 1976).

In Carlos Blanco's view, Martí's modernist contemporaries were much less clear-eyed-at least the main ones. Critics speak of their alienation from Latin American reality, since they pose an anti-market, anti-bourgeois struggle against the growing commodification of art impelled by the new economic order. But these poets are seeking to preserve a declining patronage system by taking on, praising and defending the cosmopolitan, consumptionist values of the dominant groups. They may oppose the most vulgar, utilitarian traits of the bourgeoisie; they may even come to attack U.S. intervention as an arm of economic and cultural imperialism. But they depend directly on an oligarchic reading public which they must seek to please; they accept the international division of labor which they recognize as essential to the wealth which sponsors their work. Thus their voluptuous poetic images and forms affirm a world of luxury consumption. Thus, in spite of all their fascinating contradictions, the more famous *modernistas* furnish one of the needed languages to absorb the criticism of bourgeois values and thus celebrate all the better the bogus bourgeois kings of a world they overtly satirize but upon which they are inevitably dependent. Nevertheless, by cultivating a relative autonomy from history, the modernists established a space or a development of literary modes that could then do other than merely express bourgeois domination.

D. From the early 1900s to the 1930s

If an exotic, modernist poetry develops in polar relation to a positivist-rooted journalism, both frequently practiced by the same writers, then too the development of the novel, and to a lesser extent theater and other literary and artistic modes, may also be seen in relation to more popular or everyday modes of urban culture. In this regard, novelistic production can be related to the production of newspapers, pamphlets and other forms popular publications, etc. In the 20th century, there is a shift from transitional to hybrid art forms. Hybridization means a break with tradition as accumulation over time and an emergence of new simultaneities whereby elements form previously separated territories and histories combine. This is a phenomenon traceable to the early 20th century avant garde movements, but it was to accelerate greatly with the spread of mass media in the course of the twentieth century.

If until the 1960s, *modernista* poetry remained Latin America's prime defining contribution to world literature (and of course it has remained important), still, Latin American writers attempted to develop the novel as a full expression of the area's coming of age. As Sommer has shown (1990a), the novel's popularity, its status as a sign of modernity, as the modern epic of any nation worthy of the name all contributed to making that genre a powerful source for the expression of dissidence. The very choice of a genre that could claim to plot the social reality of otherwise voiceless masses showed the fundamental Latin American contradiction between the writers and the illiterate multitude. In general, the novelists used their modernized literary mode as a platform for modernization projects. The masses must be modified by modernizing civilization. In 19th century narratives, the people were dealt with in function of *costumbrismo*, or the description of quaint local manners, with a heavy influence of European romanticism, only later joined by more realistic and naturalistic strains, but also opposed fantastic ones, as the century came to an end. In the new century, the Mexican revolution and other social movements, proletarianizing field and urban workers throughout Latin America, implode on the world of the enclave which would absorb them, and they find more dynamic, contradictory representation in the development of a literature in which fiction turns primarily toward the realistic, referential conventions of the social novel, but in which, also, even poetry, conspires to produce the *vanguardista* mutation of literary hegemony, culminating in Neruda and Vallejo.

What is the situation of Latin America as this new period begins and how do subsequent developments affect or relate to cultural and literary ones? First, in order to rise above the limited and stagnant state of achieved development, the more entrepreneurial sectors conclude that modernization projects are too limited if the rural masses remain a vast impoverished sector at the margin of a market or consumer goods.

The economies are stagnant not only for lack of a more extensive market, but also because the national enterprises can't compete in their own market with the foreign importations or capital. Thus free trade goes by the boards as the entrepreneurial sector makes a significant effort at import substitution and, further into the century, the nationalization of key sectors of the economy. All this implies an expanded capacity for consumption, the effort to bring at least greater national sectors (including rural and at times even indigenous groups) into modern life as part of the overall transformative process. Corresponding to these concerns on the political level, authoritarian liberalism (first of the *caudillos* and then the *señores presidentes*) begins to combine with what will become Latin American populism, in which the state claims it speaks for the people, taking on a popular voice, even when state power and its economic and intellectual representatives may in fact be acting in ways that will do violence to the people.

Rowe and Schelling (42) point to the psychological effects of the modernization process from the early years of the 20th century in which the ex-colonized subject experiences an ambivalent identification and rejection of the identity both of the former colonizer and the original native; the subject interiorizes tensions resulting from the project of civilization and the differential construction of the idea of nation.

In the 1920s, modernization led to the development of industry, migrations to the cities and the appearance of new social classes-including an urban middle class-who would eventually break the great landowners' monopoly of power, and help usher in a state more favorable to their interests. But in Brazil and many other Latin American countries, social change was achieved less through a radical break with the past than through a conciliatory accommodation of divergent interests and moderate social reforms introduced by the state.

Capitalist development and modernization often accompanied the creation of a heterogeneous mass society, and an urban population with fluid class, regional and ethnic identifications whose participation, essential for the legitimacy of the state, was nevertheless controlled from above. In this period "the people" became a major political, literary and ideological category. Popular cultural forms became important sites where traditional ethnic, and local identities were articulated by the state within the project of national integration and development. And they became a means through which subaltern groups struggled to participate in the formation of the new urban social order, using popular cultural forms to represent their new identity, to make their presence as citizens felt. Modernity contains a "multiplicity of concepts, themes and realities both new and old in which different cycles and periods intermingle in a unique kaleidoscope of realities and imitations" (*Ibid*.: 44-45).

Developmentalism was the Latin American bourgeois dream of the century; and it has gone through various stages important to note. But the end result of course has been deception, depression, and at times at least attempted revolt, although it should be added that Marxist developmentalist projects have also collapsed as the costs of development have virtually drowned developmentalist illusions. As peasants become salaried field workers, as workers are forced to move to the city, Latin American national bourgeoisies develop a new project involving an anti-imperialist, anti-oligarchical populist coalition or alliance between themselves and more popular sectors. This is the project of the Mexican revolution, as well as the project of Venezuelan and Peruvian politics in the 1930s, the Guatemalan Revolution (1944-54), and even such radical processes as the Cuban and Nicaraguan revolutions and many other failed efforts throughout the century. The various vicissitudes of this project constitute the background for the social novels of the 1930s-the novels of the Mexican Revolution (Azuela, etc.), the novels of state formation, like *Doña Bárbara* or *Canaíma* by Rómulo Gallegos, the Quechuan inflected, utopian novels of Arguedas in Peru and so many novels in Argentina, Brazil and elsewhere (cf. Beverley 1987: 104-114).

In this context too we can understand the varying *vanguardista* modes in poetry, whether the left wing varieties of Neruda and Vallejo or the right wing ones represented by the Nicaraguan anti-liberals, Coronel Urtecho, Pablo Antonio Cuadra, etc. As the early developmentalist dreams reach their first crises with the worldwide economic crisis of the 1930s, various sectors of the intelligentsia envision powerful centralized governments as fomenting indigenous cultural movements in the creation of new nations.

In sum, the transition to modernity is the main theme of Latin America since the late nineteenth century; and with the transition, the political and cultural intents (including the formation of left political parties, such counter melting pot ideologies as negritude, and transformations in music, visual arts and every day life), to oppose modernization's powerful force constitute the primary resistance narrative of the period. In the final decades of the nineteenth Century, the state begins to displace the dense network of local relations; industrial working conditions and worker struggles take on a mass character. Symbols and practices arise that start becoming homogenous over a large territory, as intensive capitalist growth and urbanization generate culture industry and mass media development. *Vanguardista poetry* and the social novel are responses to these processes.

To be sure, my account of these transformations underplays the question of left and right populisms as a political force and the relation of cultural and literary production to them (cf. the treatment in Laclau 1977, as well as Moraña 1984). Here I wish should simply note how, during the 1920s, in many countries, the urban and rural poor begin to organize and politicize, only to be set back by the depression. Apparently the 30s crisis marks the watershed of Latin America development, when under modernized centralized governments, and then with the help of World War II, many Latin American countries began a new phase of modernization which led to the massive rural to urban movement in waves that continue to this day. In fact, given the problems and failures of Latin American modernization and oppositions thereto, it may well that postmodern contexts may prove more hospitable for successful Latin American outcomes than most of the nay-saying Latin Americanist critics may believe. But a more comprehensive view of these matters waits upon an analysis of cultural processes from the 1940s to the end of the twentieth century.

E. From World War II to the Boom

The military dictatorships and strong populist governments exercising centralized control in the midst of economic crisis mark the thirties and provide the context for continuing social realist texts throughout the Latin American world. But World War II and the postwar period are the context for the continual veering toward more modernist techniques as in the labyrinths of a Borges, the magical realism of an Asturias or the *real maravilloso* of an Alejo Carpentier, as expressing a need to transcend the immediate circumstances of history to posit solutions which cannot be found with an epiphenomenal empiricism or in the application of European, positivist-based "realism" to the complexities of Latin American time and being. Indeed, if we think of the great short fictions of

Borges or Cortázar, the larger narrative structures of Asturias and Carpentier, (to say nothing of the larger poetic structures of Neruda and the young Ernesto Cardenal), we may well recognize how, at least in the more developed and cosmopolitan sectors of Latin America, the convulsions of Latin American historical time and the failures of most developmental projects led to writers seeking a space apart from myths of historical becoming in the realm of the imaginary in labyrinthine fictions and games. It is in this regard that Gerald Martin makes his significant contribution to our understanding of Latin American "boom narrative," its antecedents and subsequent developments.

If Borges may be posited as the writer who more than any other points to European traditions which undermine the positivist and realist currents as "cultural dominants" in the early part of Latin America's twentieth century literature, then Asturias and Carpentier in narrative (and Neruda in poetry) are seen by Martin as constituting the macro-narrative, epic/mythical structures establishing the transition from social realism to more complex narrative modes. While anticipations of these developments may be found in the naturalistic and existentialist urban narratives of successive generations (in Arlt, Mallea, Onetti, Sabato and the Asturias of *El señor presidente*, the early Fuentes, etc.), the key transitional narratives are *Hombres de maíz* and *Los pasos perdidos*, as well as other works by their authors, and novels such as those by writers like Joao Guimaraes Rosa, José María Arguedas, Roa Bastos, and Juan Rulfo. The transition may be termed as one from Borges's Latin American Kafkaesque structures to the appropriation of Joycean high, urban "Ulyssean" modernism with its mythic and surreal structuration, its narrative and linguistic experimentalism (Cortázar, but also Fuentes), especially in its more Faulknerian variant involving combinations of and conflicts between urban, modernizing trends and more traditional ones drawn from the rural, more archaic American mores and conflicts-e.g., miscegenation, racially inflected divisions of labor and status in agrari-aristocracies (cf. Martin 1989: 171-172).

What, then, were the specific circumstances which led to the extension of the experiments of Borges, Carpenter, Asturias and others of the so-called pre-boom to the emergence of the new Latin American novel and the writers of the boom-Cortázar, Fuentes, Donoso, Vargas Llosa, García Márquez?

In his most dependency oriented stage as a critic, Vidal (1976) sees the boom as the reaffirmation of the crisis of the epic tradition, inasmuch as it emerges from the post-World War II diffusionist economic modernization stage involving the hegemony of multinational conglomerates with their new communications and information technologies, as well as their development of cheap-labor satellite industries. Thus the boom's symptomatic economistic anglo name: it corresponds to the new phase which brought hitherto marginalized sections of the Latin

American population into a consumer culture; it both creates a broader reading public for the literature of the elites and a greater demand for artistic and cultural forms for the broader mass; it also leads to newer art forms in part produced by certain relatively more privileged sectors among the broader mass. These changes affect literary and overall cultural production at basic levels, impacting the dimensions of what is permitted or not, the elaboration of genres, the transmission of given representational forms.

The boom writers are the products of the new period. They attempt to provide a radical critique of the effects of dependency, but their critique remains inauthentic, since it does not come from a position which truly attacks the socio-economic roots of the system. Thus the ideological distortions of the social reality created by the system into which their discourse enters-ironically, the very creative, fantastic play that would probably be lost through "authentic representation." The critique for Vidal is intra-liberal, based on ideological attitudes, thematic and symbolic complexes and conceptions of the social role of the writer that tend to reinforce rather than attack or undermine the social order.

The idea of the boom as a kind of discursive rupture is born from the vision produced by this literature as an aesthetic universalization of the American cosmos, leaving the more provincial literary forms behind. But the idea is also due to the coincidence with the cultural and political effervescence that the Cuban Revolution brought to Latin American intellectual life in the 1960s. Thus the case of Cortázar who identified the literary action of the writer with the guerrilla *foco* (cf. Collazos, Cortázar and Vargas Llosa 1970). However, the social and psychic space of the boom is not socialist Cuba, against which most of the boom writers eventually turned, but Latin America's historical past in the stages of its formation. The taste for boom literature works corresponds to the crisis posed for traditional ideologies in the face of rapid modernization. And in this sense, the literature is not the surpassing of the Latin America's cultural past, but maintains within the ideological coordinates of bourgeois romantic liberalism (cf Vidal 1976).

For Beverley (1987), the general boom novel context is precisely the crisis of the social democratic project announced in a social realist novel like *Doña Bárbara* or a pre-boom experimental text like *El señor presidente.* The key symbolic space of the new narrative is no longer the countryside-the whole world of *costumbrismo* is seen as a boring, tired; Asturias's hope in a rural solution has been displaced for the most part by visions of the new capitalist city. Unlike the European novelistic city which functions as the focus of civilized forces, the boom narrative city is a world of multiple distortions and games (*Rayuela*), while the countryside which appears is often a site of mutilated bodies and death. The boom novel is an apocalyptic narrative; the predominant vision is one in which strange and inexplicable forces have taken over the space and the will to action. The structural cliche is the apocalyptic finale, in which the text in its moment of apotheosis plunges into a kind of black well.

There is the tragic-comic inversion of the liberal epic of national foundation (*Cien años de soledad*) or numerous avant garde fictions in which broken continuities and circularities proclaim the death of linear historicity, progress and even future. This is why *Cien Años* is perhaps the great novel of the boom, the book which defines the genre, because it expresses the failure of the nineteenth century historical project and of bourgeois modernizing projects in general. The collapse of Macondo, the sense of historical trauma with its attendant sense of loss, decline and decay, are all part of a Latin American world which is losing hope in transformative projects, at least to the degree that they emanate from traditional sources of transformative action. This last caveat may help to explain the fact that politically progressive figures like Cortázar and García Márquez write such pessimistic fictions. To be sure, by virtue of its inscribed ideology as a discursive mode, the new narrative is pessimistic in essence; often more beholden in its fundamental paradigm to Borges than to the other more historicist predecessors, Carpentier and Asturias, it is the apotheosis of dependent liberal discourse out of which even the most progressive writers can only project melancholy defeats for each posed project of solution.

Trapped in the conservative ideology of the instruments of literary communication that they use, and in the ties of these instrumentalities to a new technocratic (postmodernist) universe that is beginning to dawn, they cannot escape the social and economic compromises of their class situation in the midst of their dependent social formations of origins. Rather, their very efforts to transcend or escape their social formations lead them to expressing the structural parameters of those formations in their sharpest form. As Beverley notes, in their great majority, these narrators belong to the middle sectors of professionals fed by the project of modernization. Their books, articles and interviews circulate through the new means of mass communication and commercialization, of books dominated by transnational capital. Their work is not an object of consumer society and bears the traces of the new technocratic order.

Thus one of the consequences of the reified "Boom period" was an aesthetic-ideological modernization of the Latin American bourgeoisie that prepared them for the new repressive atmosphere of the 1970s and the "postmodern world" of the 1980s and beyond. As formulated by Carlos Fuentes (1969), the new novelist ended the dichotomy of civilization and barbarism but also the class struggle, the veritable end of history-at least as we had know it. The new novelist is a privileged subject able to synthesize his nation's past and future in a new Latin American mythos that is utopian and demonic at the same time; his work is a magical fetish able of producing a catharsis that is constituted by the sudden presence of modernity.

This position, much criticized by Fernández Retamar (1974) and Carlos Blanco Aguinaga (1975), leads Vidal to suggest that we are dealing with an ensemble of irrationalism and infiltrating technocratic ideology. The boom remains within the coordinates of aesthetic formalism; the writers seek to emulate the great European and U.S. writers at a time when the novel as a literary form is in crisis in the advanced countries. It renews the bourgeois illusion of the writer as the maximum expression of the free individual. Of course all the writers are different in their overt politics and also in their literary discourse structures, etc. But they cannot transcend their mode of production and its inscription in Latin American colonial and neo-colonial history. Reflecting the problems of dependence, the works of the boom cannot free themselves from their dependent structure, and are limited by their situation, and especially their mode of literary production. Having its correlatives in the poetry of Octavio Paz and in the technocratic criticism of Emir Rodríguez Monegal, the new novel becomes the mediational medium for the transition between past modernization projects and more recent phases of Latin American dependency.

Finally to round out this picture, we should also note that the "new novel" cannot simply be seen in a mode which reduces its qualities to just a mirror image of capitalist modernization, in part because the process has produced contradictory effects: on the one hand the integration of much of Latin America in the reified utopia of U.S. consumer society; for another, the demographic disaster of rural displacement and lumpenization in the shantytowns and favelas of the major cities: sites of polution and social disintegration.

The boom not only coincides with an epoch of economic growth and democratic hope in Latin America, but also with a generalized political tendency to suppress the contradictions emerging in the process of modernization through one form or another of technocratic order, whether backed by military dictatorship or some populist governmental form. Finally, boom narrative even when fully identified with American modernity, remains a post-epic discourse without positive heroes. Indeed, as Moraña (1984) observes, the new novel thematizes Latin America as peripheral to the world capitalist system, as an area in which developmentalist projects and thus modern Eurocentric history as we know it collapse into a series of labyrinths and fictions. In this sense, the new novel, which begins, in Martin's graphic phrase, as a "watershed of modernity," becomes, "after the illusions of the 1960s... a dam-manmade?-" in relation to a new postmodern fictional phase which arrives in the 1970s (Martin 1989: 9).

In his study of Donoso, Achugar (1979) notes a double process of masking and revelation in the new novel by which the apparent negation of the concrete social referent leads to seeing prior historical frames as ideological constructs which are now replaced by ones that, by being no less, but now obviously, imaginary, challenges historical reconstitution. It is certainly true, as Beverley (1988) and Larsen (1990) have argued, that the boom novel as a product of elites (whether "progressive" or not) failed to portray actively those social sectors which according to Laclau and others are at least potentially the prime social actors or subjects in any future transformative efforts in Latin America. Perhaps, it is sad to suggest today, this failure of the great, cultivated imaginative thinkers of Latin America represented class "ideological limits," but since revolutionary transformation of Latin America would inevitably depend on an alliance of the progressive elites with the other social sectors, then this failure may well be an expression of the fact that revolutionary or even successfully transformative/ reformist possibilities were simply not ripe in primary period of boom writing. This is a matter we should consider as we enter into a discussion of those alternative discourses which begin to emerge with force in the late 1970s and 80s even as the boom writers and their successors continued to churn out their novels.

F. The Post Boom and New Literary Forms

It is perhaps with the year 1967, the death of Che Guevara, and the appearance of *Cien años* that the failure of the Latin American bourgeois project fully emerges in boom discourse. This is this great moment of Latin American narrative, Franco (1973: 76), which is also the moment of historical confrontation with print culture itself at the moment when print was no longer the main instrument of domination and reading and writing no longer privileged tools of cognition." Certainly the period going from 1967 to the mid-1970s marks the watershed period involving the collapse of Latin American revolutionary projects, the emergence or reassertion of new dictatorships in Chile, Argentina, Uruguay, Brazil and elsewhere, and a severe economic crisis in Mexico and other countries. The *foco* theory dies, dependency theory rises, the writers keep writing, but no longer expressing any strong turn to revolutionary consciousness or possibility.

The effects of the technological-industrial stage of development-mass immigration into the cities, industrialization, the homogenization of culture, the creation of a consumer consciousness- were particularly extreme in Latin America both because of the rapidity of changes, especially in the 60s, and because these changes involved the destruction of well-rooted regional, tribal and national cultures. The Cuban revolution, the rural and urban guerilla movements, the Chilean experiment of the early 1970s, the Central American movements of the

1980s, represent peak transformational trends which met terribly repressive setbacks. As for predominant cultural modes, we may invoke Cuban conversational poetry, the Chilean new song movement and the new poetry and testimonial trends connected with the Central American revolutionary movements. The new conversational, committed poetry of Cardenal and Dalton and their efforts, drawing on boom discourse, but also on Cuban conversational poetry, to create post-Nerudian collage epic forms able to express and explore the possibilities for effective action among left-tending workers, new liberationist peasants, and the lumpen, dispossessed and exploited of their respective countries. However, whether we consider the performance of protest songs, the new social poetry of Cardenal, Dalton, Antonio Cisneros, etc., the narrative of the sixties or early seventies, or the New Theater and cinema, these need to be seen as elements of a counterculture which faced direct repression and the monopolistic control of consciousness by the mass media.

From the 1980s on, with over 60% of Latin Americans now living in cities, the popular must be distinguished from the products of the culture industry and mass media (Rowe and Schelling: 97). Popular culture, with oppositional implications, comes to include rural culture, urban mass culture and the culture industry. Mass society is not produced by the "culture industry," Martín-Barbero says (1987) "or from the media's degradation of culture, but "from the long slow process of prior establishment of mass cultural experiences through the constitution of the single national market, the consolidation of the state and the making of unified national cultures."

Whereas Adorno and Horkheimer (1973), saw the culture industry as inducing mass deception and consensus resting on blind and opaque authority, Rowe and Schelling note that in Latin America the culture industry, and above all TV, marks technological and economic changes involving the creation of a single national market for all cultural products, often aided by the state, along with the military and the publicity industry.

Cultural migrations, instabilities and reconfigurations flowing from urbanization continue. The shanty towns reveal the failure of industry to absorb the peasantry and create an urban infrastructure. Urban space is restructured both for corporations and favelas. The cities are invaded, including central plazas. In the major cities (Mexico City, Lima, Rio), there is a middle class psychosis of those who find their sense of city under threat. But the poor suffer their psychosis too. And they disrupt working-class living patterns, the relationships of neighborhood, extended family and rural origin. The struggles of the poor are now mediated less by unions, parties, traditional organizations. The people mobilize themselves in struggles for light, sewage. The emergence of a mythic figure like Superbarrio in the Tepito section of post-earthquake Mexico City was a sign of the growth of base community organizing as the way to deal with problems. Debt crisis, urban economic austerity, the failure of the state to provide basic services lead to an increase in structural violence suffered by urban populations: malnutrition, high infant mortality, unemployment, drugs, the informal economy.

There is no question of simply copying or 'catching up with' the cities of the advanced countries. The rapid and multiple cultural transitions and juxtapositions brought about by the urbanization process produce a unique mixing, a simultaneity of forms. The juxtaposition of technology and tradition-religious icons on the TV set or dashboard, magical objects involving handicraft and industrial production-pervade living space, as older rural symbols are transformed in but also impact urban and national frames (Rowe and Schelling 104-105).

As the question of mass and popular culture came to the fore, many intellectuals like Ariel Dorfman and Carlos Monsiváis began to focus on these themes looking for signs of reaction and hope; as new, more popularly inflected writers like those of the *onda* appeared, and as new feminist and testimonial production began to emerge throughout Latin America. It is in the context of the dominant mass media that the new variants of the novel and poetry, as well as new emergent forms, must be considered. Unlike the European novel which develops when print culture was both the instrument of domination and dissent, the Latin American novel developed technically at a time when books are super market commodities and when the social construction of reality is dominated by the media.

Like oral performance during the colonial period, the novel and poetry drew their strength by representing zones of resistance. By producing new educated middle class sectors, this phase of development had the paradoxical effect of creating a larger potential readership which did not accept their environment as eternally given. This was the readership that interpreted the boom writers in function of dissent and liberation. Increasingly, however, it became clear that novelistic dissent was in no sense equivalent to political resistance, and that resistance to commodity consumption did not release the novels from the domination of the commodity form or the state which sought to oversee or guarantee continued export-centered reproduction and distribution. In this sense, the new novelists elaborated articles of consumption and pacification for the educated elites. Indeed, one of the major themes of much boom writing from the early 1970s had to do with the impact of the media and mass culture, in the works of Manuel Puig, Mario Vargas Llosa, José Agustín, Gustavo Sáenz and other Mexican *onda* writers, as well as Puerto Rican novelist Luis Rafael Sánchez.

Related to these writers, we should mention the emergence of major women fictional writers, like Isabel Allende, Luisa Valenzuela, Ana Lydia Vega and Elena Poniatowska. The first two surfaces in the wake of revolutionary defeat, exile and estrangement; they, as well as Vega, Marjorie Agosín and others develop their discourse in relation to postmodernist and feminist trends in U.S. as well as Latin American cosmopolitan contexts. Finally, we may also note Poniatowska's continuing relation to new popular currents arising from Mexican crises since 1960s, starting with her testimonial reconstruction of one of the crucial episodes in the repression of the Latin American left in the 1960s, *La noche de Tlateloco* and reaching a high level with her subsequent text, *Hasta no verte, Jesús.*

In Poniatowska's book and other recent works, novelists have turned to testimonial forms to achieve more authentic portrayals of subaltern sectors. As Rowe and Schelling note (227), the popular and ethnic, the precapitalist and primarily oral enter fully into literature as a process of virtual reconquest. Most novelized testimonios don't confirm a fixed set of symbolic hierarchies, but narrate transitions into modernity marking the end of particular experiences of older pre-modern cultures, in which fragmentation and dispersal are accepted without the professional nostalgia or romanticism of intellectuals. The genre whereby a member of the dominant culture interviews a member or members of the subaltern is as old as the sixteenth century and may indeed go back to the Conquest. Nevertheless, if the cultural world of our "informants" is premodern, "it is nevertheless heard within modernity."

It is in the context of Latin American social developments in the late 1960s that the submerged testimonial dimension, so rooted in the past, comes forward in the next several years as a major mode of resistance within a literary system deeply inflected and networked by popular and elite, autochthonous and cosmopolitan impulses. We enter, then, the terrain that will be referred to elsewhere in this book-and especially in relation to Central America-testimonio as an important juncture between Latin American literature and popular culture very much identified with the project of Fernández Retamar in the 70s, and the relation between the new "Calibanesque" testimonial forms championed in Cuba and a post-boom discourse seen as signs of the emergence of postmodernist culture in Latin America. It is here that we extend from the testimonio as a current or popular base in poetry, novel and other modes in Antonio Skármeta, Eduardo Galeano, Hiber Contreris, Arturo Arias, Manlio Argueta, Claribel Alegría and many other recent writers, to the question of testimonio as genre-and all this in relation to the recent debates over postmodernism and the place of third world and Latin American literary forms and movements.

3. Testimonio, Boom, Postmodernity and Globalization

Testimonio is generally defined as a first-person narration of socially significant experiences in which the narrative voice is that of a typical or extraordinary witness or protagonist who metonymically represents others who have lived through similar situations and who have rarely given written expression to them. Testimonio is then the "literature of the nonliterary" involving both electronic reproduction, usually with the help of an interviewer/editor, and the creative reordering of historical events in a way that impresses as representative and "true" and that often projects toward social transformation. In the 1970s and 1980s, many testimonios appeared throughout Latin America, including narratives of indigenous representatives and labor and guerrilla leaders. In the 1990s, testimonios shifted toward representatives of NGOs and broader social movements that favored human, women's, and gay rights, as well as ecological and anti-global movements. *I, Rigoberta Menchú* became the most famous of many testimonios, and the recent attacks against this text by David Stoll (1999) and others have problematized testimonio as a viable expressive form.

Testimonio suggests testifying or bearing religious or legal witness, and the overall narrative unit is usually a life or a significant life experience. Many critics have seen the form as an expression of those marginalized by capitalist modernization. Testimonio was also seen as involving the intervention or mediation of a lettered intelligentsia. Elzbieta Sklodowska (1992) gave the most nuanced treatment of testimonio as a literary form, but John Beverley (1989) presented the most influential interpretation of testimonio's social dimensions. For Beverley, "testimonio [was] usually a novela or novela-length first person narrative recounted by the protagonist or witness to the events recounted" (1990: 173). Furthermore, testimonio signaled an overall transformation in social and literary formations and even in transnational modes of production (178)

Noting that testimonio-like texts had long been at the margin of literature, Beverley argued that genre was marked by its conflictive relation with established literary-aesthetic norms and with the institution of literature itself. Testimonio could be defined as "a nonfictional, popular-democratic form of epic narrative, since the narrative has a metonymic function which implies that any life so narrated can have a kind of representativity" evoking an implicit "polyphony of other possible voices and experiences" (175).

Testimonio emerges not as the creation of a Miguel Barnet, but as a series of extra-literary discursive practices with deep roots in Latin American history (cf. Lienhard 1990 and Smorkaloff 1991) recently crystallizing as the expression of new processes in the overall social struggle. The practices emerge, for example, in relation to the development of base community religious groups, feminist consciousness raising groups, as well as groups of guerrilleros, disappeareds, prisoners, etc.-as forms of subaltern opposition to state or other repressive entities. The art of testimonio involves its anti-literary character, supposedly without stylistic elaboration. Nevertheless, the testimonio, in spite of its ancient roots, constitutes a new genre of cultural and literary narrative produced by those groups which are marginalized and exploited by the previous development of cultural institutions in Latin America. As Franco notes, an emphasis on economic theory (in this case, the old dependency construct) helps to foreground the contemporary problems of Latin America in function of the technology of domination and forms of resistance. In this context, testimonio emerges and goes through several transformations as a prime expressive form.

To be sure, there have been many ways to consider testimonio and its relation to dimensions of popular and elite cultures. Jorge Narváez (1986: 235-79) distinguishes between literary and reportorial testimonio and defines the former as an aesthetically rich and generally linear first-person narration of socially and collectively significant experiences, in which the narrative voice is that of a typical or extraordinary witness or protagonist who metonymically represents other individuals or groups that have lived through other or similar situations and/or the circumstances which induce them. By virtue of its collective representativity, testimonio is, overtly or not, an intertextual dialogue of voices, reproducing but also creatively reordering historical events in a way which impresses as representative and true and which projects a vision of life and society in need of transformation.

Considering the origins and development of the form, Narváez, while acknowledging its pre-Colombian presence in the Latin American literary tradition, nevertheless argues that testimonio achieves its particular characteristics with the development of capitalism and the emergence of a radical fraction of the bourgeoisie able to appropriate their own history, or at least narrate from their own dissenting perspective. Once the conditions for the appearance of the genre emerged, other groups and classes could seek to appropriate it, or the radical sector could seek to assimilate these groups and their discourse to it; but in either case it was a genre marked by its status as a subaltern discourse, which came to speak from the perspective of middle or lower sectors frustrated, repressed, marginalized or exploited under capitalism.

By the late nineteenth century, Latin America was the site of national struggles generating cultural innovations and mutations among dissenting bourgeois sectors that could be adapted and transformed by more popular social elements in later historical stages. Furthermore, Latin American workers, peasants and lumpen, under pressure or uprooted in the countryside, and attempting to adjust to modernization processes in rural and urban situations, could generate their own forms in music and even basic literary modes (sayings, jokes, short annecdotal narratives, song lyrics, actual poems) which could present the basis for, or actually serve, as testimonial expression. The seeds for modern testimonio, secured in the early phase of the century, were spurred on by the depression and then by the transformations and pressures throughout Latin America in the wake of the Cuban Revolution.

While the great Latin American novelists at times tried to represent popular sectors in their works, testimonio, often involving the use of the tape recorder, prior to the submission to print technology, provided the basis for their self-representation even if ultimately there is a mediation of writerly discourse of the mediating editor/writer. The testimonio, then, is the genre which best expresses the resistance to domination in Latin America. As opposed to the polyphonic and super-realistic forms of the boom, the testimonio is a document in the first person, in which a narrative "yo" begins to emerge as the voice of lived and real popular experience. It begins (consciously or not) to stand against the fictions, labyrinths and games of boom fiction, as well as the totalizing effect of mass culture in much post-boom literature-matters of crucial importance in understanding and dealing with the dominant forms, tensions and resistances in Latin American postmodernity and globalization.

There is indeed an important sense in which what we have tended to consider as forms of cultural resistance themselves rise up on a Latin American postmodern terrain. The ideological and political significance of testimonio depends on its ability 1) to function in the historically constituted space which separates elite and popular cultures in the region; and 2) to generate a new post-colonial, non-Eurocentric narrative of historical space and destiny. If that narrative has been largely Marxist in inspiration, it has also been concerned with redefining an inherited European Marxist tradition to respond to the very different dynamics of Latin American society and history. In these senses, this literature is coincident with postmodernism, rather than its other.

It is clearly no coincidence that those countries severely impacted by the recent crisis of the agro-export model (including repression, revolt, debt crisis, narco and *maquiladora* capitalism) have generally been the ones where resistance and testimonial writing have most flourished. In this context, where the testimonial current has been especially compelling, the view is often set forth according to which testimonial writing is seen as a counter-hegemonic response to dominant (capitalist) postmodernist discourse as it exists in the metropolis and as it extends to Latin America.

One of the first people to establish this perspective, Yúdice (1985), noted that "First world postmodernism feeds off [and is at the expense of] an occulted third world warrant." Yúdice claims that the inclination among critics to identify Latin

American "boom" culture and literature with postmodernism "(supposedly because it is decentered, fragmented, carnivalesque, unrepresentable, marginal, etc.), is a ruse which facilitates greater material-symbolic penetration and colonization by transnational logic." His case is for "the viability of the counter-hegemonic projects of popular culture vis-à-vis late capitalism."

As early as the 1950s, Octavio Paz had pointed to marginality, invisibility and such characteristics as complexly mixing temporalities as typical of a third world and Latin American sensibility which first world writers were beginning to approximate. Symbols of progress were becoming as dysfunctional in the first world as they had in Latin America, which had experienced the failures of modernization and developmentalism. Latin Americans had always been at the periphery, but now the center was disintegrating. Every one, even in the advanced capitalist countries was living at the margins. As for the arts, where surrealism and European high modernism had been the models for new Latin American writing, later the deconstructive fiction of Borges, Cortázar and company would become the models foreseeing Latin American literature in poststructuralist, postmodernist terms. However, Yúdice notes, by the early 1970s, Latin American literature had "broken with the high canon and splintered into various trends-realist, nationalist, regional, historical, testimonial, feminist, ethnic-which are counter-hegemonic projects" of representation and identification.

For Yúdice these new discourses are conceived as resistance and struggle against capitalist and oligarchic oppression and the "transnational penetration of culture." They bespeak a break with the modern, individual subject, but also a turn toward a new collective subject living through each individual voice (a writer, a narrator, a character, a persona) which represents a new solidarity putting into question and resisting late capitalist projects and postmodernist visions. In sum, for Yúdice the postmodern is the cultural arm of a global system of domination, in relation to which myriad cultures define themselves in their particular struggles and in the context of their material and symbolic practices. In this view, he draws on García Canclini's view of popular culture in terms of a struggle for hegemony not only with metropolitan mass culture as it pervades the media, but also the Latin American variants of postmodern culture as they emerge in literature, even when it is progressive in content.

The flux of capitalism celebrated by postmodernists as liberating is an even greater form of oppression for third world peoples. Capitalism doesn't extinguish but restructures and re-semiotizes their cultures. Popular sectors struggle against the reorganization, resignify their patterns of production and consumption, ethnic customs, culinary and religious practices, etc. As in Fanon's vision of colonial struggle, culture in Latin American countries will suffer from imperialist and oligarchic domination, and cultural traditions may become unstable and overrun by centrifugal currents; but cultural despoliation is not complete, and new cultural forms emerge which struggle in solidarity against the forces of terror, "abjectification" and domination. Here then, is the place for grasping testimonial.

Yúdice's perspective is extremely valuable for the argument developed here, especially since it places new Latin American writing in a global political perspective and because it posits a relation and differentiation between recent Latin American literary and poetic discourse and that which is found in the area's past, especially during the "boom" period. However, this valuable perspective (which Yúdice 1989 and 1991 was later to modify, towards a view closer to the one enunciated here) tends toward a misleading, romantic dichotomy between the complex, anti-representational, value-leveling and predominantly bourgeois forms of postmodernist literature and the simple, lineal, representational, value-affirming and pro-revolutionary forms of popularly inflected testimonial literature. From this perspective, the first literature is almost completely imported and imposed and is seen as a form of spontaneous and authentic creation of "the people" in the midst of conditions of underdevelopment and exploitation.

My own perspective, developed with John Beverley (1989) questions the dichotomy and raises questions about the status of testimonial discourse in its relation to or relative autonomy from more globally-based postmodernist modes as they developed in and out of the Latin American boom period. Instead of resorting to a clear dichotomy between a pure popular culture of resistance and a pure high, oligarchical and/or neo-colonial culture, Latin American literature in general has involved from its origins in the colonial period a series of changes and transformations that intermix with and reconstruct elitist and popular cultural forms. Testimonial literature is involved in, and constructed in the midst of, and in the last analysis tries to surpass, an already existent discourse system based on a dialectic of oppressor/oppressed, negotiating between the terms of its dichotomies: literature/oral narrative and song, metropolitan/nation, European/creole, ladino or mestizo/ Indian, elite/popular, urban/rural, intellectual work/manual work.

In sum, the very nature of the perspective presented here implies that any particular piece of writing or semic expression in Latin America is constituted in the midst of an already existing discourse system. The apparent simplicity or linearity of a given text must be mediated by its place in a larger total system. In Latin America, that system is constituted primarily during and after the great narrative boom period, more often than not by writers who were of the same general social class and involved in an aesthetic project clearly internal to the contradictions of boom discourse itself. These literary transformations stand as epiphenomena for deeper structures and transformations which have to do with the effort to forge national constructs in weak and dependent social formations. Ironically, in relation to this view, we see, as Doris Sommer had already pointed out, that the apparent simplicity, linearity and easy referentiality of many testimonios is illusory, and in fact, Alegría, Argueta and others have worked to create the polyphonic, Bakhtinian testimonial texts that approach the density and complex structuration of the Boom's most polyphonic collage theories. In this sense, too, we may note effort like Eduardo Galeano's *Memory of Fire* to project a global, post-Nerudian, testimonio-inflected collage history of Latin America-not to mention (but yes mention) my own efforts to fulfill and update the epic efforts of Dalton, Cardenal, Zea and Cardozo y Aragón in my *Central American Quartet* (Zimmerman, ed. 1980, 1985, 1988 and 1993).

If Jameson is right in seeing the third world quest as one emerging in response to postmodernism as an effort to recapture an epic unity broken by imperialist history, then it is also an effort in Latin America to displace a narrow elitist modernism, however penetrated by popular currents, with a variety of cultural and literary processes that give expression to particular voices from various social sectors and perspectives, voices that were virtually marginalized, which then came to the fore and which provide the kinds of articulation necessary if the struggle to remake the Latin American reality is going to respond to the varied needs and perspectives of those most needing representation.

We have a process by which pre-conceived totalities (the rightwing ones are obvious, but we also mean monolithic left totalities-as in Neruda's *Canto General*) are displaced by more fragmented perspectives which, while each claiming and straining to express the whole, do so in metonymic rather than metaphoric ways, and imply a reality that is rich, complex and virtually untotalizable. In this sense, discussions of political poetry as a form which joins poetic and rhetorical functions, which breaks down metaphor and internality, etc. serve as useful orientations for understanding the transformation of Latin American literature and its role in what, from the perspective of the current crisis period in the area, may be said to constitute the politicization, testimonialization (and we should add, "*feminization*") of discourse systems (cf. Beverley and Zimmerman 1990: 193).

What we have is a literature in which popular representations of workers, women, ethnic groups, etc., emerge with great force. The texts in question don't necessarily transcend the dichotomies indicated; but they do constitute new possibilities of articulation and efforts to define new paradigms of the relation between the intelligentsia and popular classes. This literature has served not only as a political recourse if not also a model for the political. And in this sense, we should note, that the view of testimonio as a radical albeit integral part of an overall semic and reproductive system involving many variant socio-political systems and stances in relation thereto. Latin America, as Yúdice asserted (1991), is a place of multiple postmodernisms, variant models, simulacra, copies that may or may not fully copy. Standing within and not outside the overall system, mediating between varying social and cultural sectors, testimonial feeds off of, opposes and sometimes even integrates with other modes of discourse as a popular and democratic dimension of systemic functioning.

If Latin American writing involves an appropriation and development of avant garde techniques in a mix with indigenous traditions as a means of entering into cultural and literary modernity, then what are we to make of this endeavor when the advanced capitalist world has moved on to its encounter with postmodernity? What can we make of attempts or lacks of attempts to construct grand narratives or national, master narratives when such modes of high modernistic totality which (whether in function of developmentalism or Marxism, imperialism or anti-imperialism, populist nationalism or liberation theology, etc.) are severely compromised today?

Within the frame of these such perspectives, I have tended to agree with Beverley (1987, 1989) that contemporary testimonio signals a transformation of literary production that may well symptomize at least those forces tending toward an overall transformation in national social formations or even (at the extreme) modes of production. But in this regard, I have tried to incorporate my own understanding of Skodowska's view of testimonio (1992) as another form of literary discourse, meriting literary analysis. Nevertheless, I have also come to see the form as the last narrative stand of a radical national narrative which has now been overrun by the forces of modernization and globalization-a position recently taken by Beverley in his introduction to his key articles on testimonio (2004).

From this point of view, testimonio is a form which emerged and took its place in supporting and opposing revolutionary struggles in the 1960s and beyond. Consciously or not, testimonial narrators and their interlocutors sought to foster new, subaltern national narratives; they sought to deconstruct limited and excluding national constructs. Testimonio by the 1980s became the symptomatic site for the effort to merge exploited Indian and mestizo, elite and popular, male and female, Marxist and religious, urban and rural sectors in a movement that was ultimately far more broadly based, multiple and potentially forceful than any prior phase of political opposition and resistance in Latin American history. However, the interest in Latin American testimonio has for all too many years over-stayed its centrality. It is not so much that positive critiques of testimonio are incorrect but that the forces they have pointed to have been met and challenged by others which are instances of intervention and domination but also, sadly, have become part of popular realities.

The presence of the "real," popular voice in testimonio was, in varying degrees but always and ever, an illusory or indeterminate "reality effect" that could be readily challenged as David Stoll (1999) and others did in their effort to discredit Rigoberta Menchú and her book, but the effect's persistence helps to explain testimony's special force. A testimonial text simultaneously represents certain perspectives and questions supposed verities, but it is never "the truth."

Testimonio may well have symptomized dynamic transformational energies; but, given international, regional and national forces, testimonio could not guarantee any definitive change. Inevitably the form has declined in recent years, along with the social upheavals that produced its key examples. However, as an expression of gender and other identity-shaping differentials, testimonio on its own, and in its use in novels, poems, and plays, will long remain part of Latin American and global literature as a discursive mode available to individuals related to subaltern sectors and social movements. The form will continue into the future, always serving to present subaltern perspectives; but whether it will again surface in a predominant way, now as an expression of the: "multitude" or a significant fragment thereof, is a matter of the relation between the broadest systemic processes of globalization and the overall working of an ever expanding and globalizing discursive and cultural system of which testimonio is and will be a part.

4. Other Recent Post-Testimonial Developments

Literature and society, literature and social reference, literature and history-then, more particularly, literature and politics, literature and revolution, literature and exile. These themes were central in studies of Latin America until very recently and almost always invoked another: violence. And again almost always these themes were correlated explicitly and directly with violence of the state and especially its military branch, as well as violence of groups or movements organized against violence.

Many are still speaking and writing about these themes. But is it certain that they have the same resonance today as they did years ago, before the supposed democratization of Latin America, before the death of Marxist revolution? Is it certain that after Esquipulas II, after the accords over El Salvador, the elections in Guatemala 1985, Nicaragua 1990 and Guatemala once again in 1991, that things are as before or that the writers from these countries (sometimes the same writers about the violence) write in the same way? Or that the literary genres have the same function, or that literature still has the same function as in other decades? And what should we make of the Peruvian experience and other experiences during the decade, before and after Fujimori, before and now after the crises in Argentina and Venezuela?

In the steps taken toward the configuration of a new constellation of the world that some call postmodernity, we witnessed a transformation of relations, of forms, of connections. To meditate on the relation between literature and society/ literature and violence today is not the same as doing so ten years before, or before 1989. What should we do today with the theme of violence? How do we understand the theme in concrete social formations of Latin America- as one theme or many? And the relation between the theme of violence, the social in general and these two with literature and more amply, culture? Can one generalize from one place to another? Perhaps writers like the Chilean Dorfman in literature and the Guatemalan Aguilera Peralta (1971, 1988) in the social sciences theorized the theme in relation to the 1970s, at least in relation to certain left-right struggles. But I think we have to theorize the matter in another way today. I think we have to rethink them. We can easily spin out theories about Latin American violence in the fragile and formal democracies of Latin America's peripheral postmodernity, of the Andean and Central American areas, or the indigenous zones, etc. We can recur to the social science texts of FLACSO, CLACSO,-of Fernando Calderón, José Joaquín Brunner, etc. Or we can seek new theories over the theme in culture and literature, through García Canclini, Sarlo, Richard and company.

With respect to the development of narrative culture, the literary and cultural forms developed and refunctionalized in Latin America in relation to the Cuban, Chilean, Nicaraguan and other insurrectional movements, stand as instances of the effort to maintain memory and resist domination in the face of actualized or threatened violence. Given the many cultures that have disappeared in Latin America as a result of the struggle for domination of territories, resources and populations, the need persists to historicize memory and continuity.

Without doubt, the new poetry of Central America, especially as it developed out of Cardenal and Dalton in the 1960 and 70s, and above all testimonial literature, as represented by Domitila Barrios de Chungara, Rigoberta Menchú, and others have stood for important literary currents that have had an impact that is as great as such high modernist narratives as those by Márquez, Fuentes, Vargas Llosa and the rest. To be sure, the traditional writer as the leader of the people has arrived at the limit of the liberal or even Lukácsian conception of literature in which the writer is seen as a kind of bourgeois hero speaking for the masses. But testimonial discourse, and those forms drawing thereon, are in as precarious a situation as more canonical literature if only because the difficulties of any form of success in Latin America are clearer than ever before.

If testimonio emerged in relation to popular struggle, but also, and perhaps above all, its repression in the 1970s, it reached its apogee in the period of debt crisis and democratization in which we have been living; and it clearly speaks to a reserve of popular energy which may come forth in different ways if the current crises can find no mode of resolution. Of course, they may also represent a dying flame to be swallowed in the new forms of integration and cooptation emerging in our present historical juncture. In this context, with the older Cuban model of resistance culture is fading, testimonial, rather than speaking to the emergence of new modes of production and social organization in Latin America, may be speaking to those elements which will be suppressed in the emergence of a new phase of the new historical phase.

If we live in an era in which socialism has failed, we must also add that the same may be said for capitalism, at least in the Third World and Latin America. But in these circumstances, the new writers and literary modes confront the problems emerging in the new Latin American reality: the impact of mass media, of U.S. mass culture, the crisis facing the old publishing system in Latin America, the new religious waves, but also the new repressions, the collapse of developmentalist dreams of the left as well as the right. The writers of the post-boom, such as some of those figures we have mentioned, but many others as well (including the new young writers of *post-onda*, post-earthquake Mexico, the new generation in Puerto Rico, in Argentina, Uruguay, etc.) represent a new problematization of the Latin American narrative in their declining concern with the "great novel" and their effort to recuperate testimonial and popular forms. The question is in one sense whether the new popular and testimonial dimensions in their literature genuinely signal possibilities for social change in ways positive to the long-suffering Latin American poor, or whether the new narrative discourse means the exhaustion and cooptation of popular and testimonial energies in the new stage of Latin American dependency.

These questions come forth with even greater rigor if we look at some recent Latin American tendencies in the novel to retreat from even sophisticated and oblique boom-style social referentiality to a portrayal of small, subjective and fragmentary worlds. Thus, in his brilliant Puerto Rican-style *Ulysses*, Luis Rafael Sánchez presents the stream of consciousness patterns of people caught in a traffic jam, mixing commodified language with new song tunes and beats in ways that express, compensate for but also trivialize the colonial complex in which they live. Thus, many writers retreat from even expressing their national realities at all.

In this latter regard, let's take the temperature of current developments by drawing on Jorge Marcone's study of Peruvian narrative (1993) -a study which approaches the question of literary non-expressivity with very direct and rigorous correlation to non-literary discourse modes. First Marcone argues that "the absence of a literature and specifically a narrative related to violence and subversion, while there is an abundant social science literature over the themes." Afterwards, he notes that although there is a quantity of works which in one way or another treat the historical conditions of the country that establish something of the context for the violence, "there is little which approaches it in its totality" -and that, as Cornejo Polar (1984) had noted, "the historical omissions made the referential frame flagrantly incomplete." In this respect the least treated theme was that of migration.

Marcone's logical approach the question of the social functioning of Peruvian literature may remind U.S. readers of the polemic recently launched in this country in relation to Tom Wolfe's *Bonfire of the Vanities*, when the conservative writer charged that U.S. novelists were afraid to touch the "great social themes" and wrote little novels about little subjects. It seems that in the third world like the first one, the idea of the novel was no longer that of Balzac, Dickens or Dostoyevski. In post-boom narrative, the macro-novel (including intents like *Terra Nostra* by Fuentes, or *Jaguar en llamas* by the Guatemalan Arturo Arias) is longer in fashion. We live in the time of retreat, of mini-structures, of micro-struggle, of local matters, personal (though some subjectless) matters... The form most faithful to Latin American being in postmodern times, says Nelly Richard, is the fragment. So, the fragment-novel, or even the collage-ensemble of fragments in relation to various angles and degrees of referentiality, simulacra of the Latin American context now when the illusions of possible narratives and worlds has all but disappeared... at least-and here of course a key point-in the mentality of those who have received the formation that gives them as a vital option (and within the evolving canons of the discourse of their country) that of narrating.

Do the writers have to focus on social themes? Can and should they do well with a problematic that lies outside the norms of their formation and the discursive formation itself? Were the chroniclers able to narrate the Conquest, describe the people, and capture the American world and the colonial process? Were the writers of the nineteenth Century capable of narrating their world? To what degree were they able to transcend their classist, sexist, and racist prejudices to portray a world richer than that structured by their ideological limitations and those inscribed in the literary conventions upon which they could draw and transform? Writers are always able apparently to do what they do and little more. Where are the limitations? The limits? In their consciousness, a Lukácsian or Goldmannian would say; in the discourse itself, would say those who approach literature from more recent theoretical perspectives.

Some years ago Argentine investigator Nora Bonin (1998: 110) complained rightly or wrongly that Beatriz Sarlo's otherwise brilliant work on Argentina reduced the country to nothing more than a pretext for Buenos Aires. And does the Buenos Aires of Sarlo exist? For Mexican novelists and even for the filmmakers, whether it be el Indio Fernández or Buñuel, the harshness as much as the hope in the Mexico City of the 1940s and 1950s was worth serious work. Buñuel anticipated the processes of disintegration that he saw in the new society. But could he sketch out the disaster which is Mexico today? Mexican cinema as an expression of hope in social mobility, modernization, the whole myth of existing possibilities in modern life, fell into the historical dustbin. *La onda* sketched out the decline. And what about Mexico today? Monsiváis and others tried to point toward new possibilities in post-earthquake activities, in Super-Barrio, the Cardenista movement. But can Monsiváis, Roger Bartra, and Enrique Krauze-any of the brilliant chroniclers, analysts, poets and novelists of contemporary Mexico, left or right-really portray the Mexico of today? And who can capture the Lima, Guatemala City, the changes in the highlands and in the most Ladino zones of the country? How can writers narrate a world which cancels the very source of the discursive resources developed in earlier times?

Marcone notes "the difficulty of the very object, so changeable and in continual growth, which goes beyond the capacity to process it in literature and the difficulty of a generation of narrators to pass from the short story (fragment) to the novel (the ordered collage of fragments). What we have is "fragmentary vision and the impossibility to exercise a reflective as opposed to an affective sensibility." Further on Marcone indicates the disarticulation of fiction from the social sciences and supposed social realities. He explores Lauer's view (1983) with respect to a "mental block in national consciousness" as much as in the synthetic discourse of the narrators, symptoms which are found in the popular classes in which negation would form in the migratory experience in itself: the wish to erase the process of uprooting. At bottom, doesn't the failure to novelize this experience (and all the pressure it places on ethnic, land and gender identity sources, etc.) stem from the unconscious incapacity or rejection of the changes that this implies in the discourse system? The novelists find themselves facing hybridization, the destruction of their world, the exhaustion of the paradigms and perhaps of the social sector from which virtually all of them have sprung. Peru's new, precarious modernity has destroyed the Peruvian world in relation to which the modern literary discourse (let us call it vanguardist) took form. The incapacity to capture the new forms of social being haunts postmodernity. In this there is some hope, for example, in Orin Starn's appropriation (1992) of Edward Said's orientalist model to plot divisions between *urbe* and *campo*, *indio* and *mestizo*, and other dichotomies as the basis of an imaginative and discursive structuration of previous generations, and the sense that with the migration whatever organizational validity that this dualist thought held exhausted itself-of course without developing another paradigm, another narrative.

Marcone is quite correct in pointing out that Peru's structural crisis has created an intellectual one whose clearest expression is the lack of full expression, and in fact a change in literary functioning which indicate that literature is now more distanced than ever from any representation of social realities. On the one hand, journalism, social analysis and the most literary of these discourses, testimonio; yet even when testimonio enters novelistic discourse, it doesn't let us see or approach totality. And we arrive at the conclusion, suggested by Lauer (1983), that not only today but not even before was literature the mode by which Peruvian society narrated itself. Here, the end of Lukács-and Jameson with him. And what else could we make of the suicide of Arguedas?

But if literature doesn't narrate the new reality, why are we led to think it never did? Well, perhaps some works yes, others, no. And maybe to some degrees yes and some no. Perhaps we consecrate those that do, or do we force ourselves to see the works that were we think quite good in such a way that we believe the illusion that they captured the social?

If there is indeed now a new literature that doesn't narrate the social, can we study the way in which this literature leaves out the not narrated? Can we constitute the narrated from the not narrated? This would be, I believe, a way of approaching the question or of trying to overcome the impasse between literature and society. In this, one enters fully into an analysis of discourses, structurations, and language in itself as the basis for configuring, approximating and appropriating the world. A microanalysis of the supposedly not social (the search for a Jameson's political unconscious or cognitive map, the processes of transcoding needed to grasp shifting, nomadic relations) is the order of the day. Also something of general focus: Why and in what manner does Vargas Llosa approach totality, when seemingly more radical writers can't? What relation is there between Vargas Llosa and his politics, between his politics and what Fujimori and his successors have actually implemented? And what about those post-boomists in this sense?

As I suggest elsewhere (see Chapter V in this book), migration itself must be considered a fundamental aspect of Latin American being was an inadequately explored dimension in its effect on literary and critical discourse. Clearly migration (including exile) and the urbanization of Latin American populations and consciousness (as well as the ontological and "epistemic" violence attendant thereto) are essential dimensions of Latin America's entry into post-modernity, pointing to the destruction of old identifications and, hopefully pointing to new ones, including intensified feminist ones, able to transcend social anomie. If it is not registering fully in Peruvian literature and if Peruvian literature is not atypical and exceptional in this regard, then we are indeed pointing to a crisis of representation in Latin America, not unrelated to but not simply subsumable to the implications for all representation involved in the full emergence of feminist discourse in Latin American literary studies.

In effect, feminism and migration processes and identifications (and these involve return migrations as well) are part of a larger modernization pattern implicating all the major issues of Latin America that have been underground in Latin American literature and now moved central stage in what García Canclini had already designated as our nomadic deterritorializing critical work: questions of ecology, homosexuality and alternate, hybrid sexual identities, the informal economy, new hybrid religious, mystical and at least claimed revolutionary movements-all of these related, finally, to questions of power in its dispersion and re-articulations in function of internal and global processes.

It is in the increasingly complex relation between literature and society/ literature and violence where we might wish to return to the question of the function of testimonio and testimonial-inflected forms in a post-boom/ postmodern period when the macro-collages and macro-novels are not the prime order of the day, when literary narrative may be entering into a full scale crisis of representation and when the emergence of other cognitive maps indicate the existence of sectors whose consciousness, not to say "political unconscious," requires expression and analysis.

5. Concluding Thoughts

In an article on postmodernity in Latin American literature (1990), Jorge Ruffinelli confirms our view of recent writing by pointing to three main areas of innovation which are part of a contemporary, postmodern landscape in Latin America: (1) the explosion of new feminist writing and its effect on all literary production, as well as our view of the literary past; (2) the development of various modes of testimonio and the incursion of testimonio into other genres (his examples being recent novels) and (3) the enrichment of narrative style and form, notable in the *onda* writers and above all in Luis Rafael Sánchez, through an effort to recuperate popular language and perspectives (Ruffinelli 1990: 38-40). To these new trends, I would wish to add the explosion of overtly gay literature and its implications for a reconsideration of the overall literary canon and its periodization (cf. David Foster 1991), as well as implosion of U.S. Latino literature, which, even in English, has come to relate to and become a matter somewhat internal to Latin American cultural and literary functioning-a matter which Ruffinelli's California-based *Nuevo Texto Crítico* acknowledges in its thematic coverage, and which is the subject of a volume of mine (Zimmerman 1992), as well as Chapter VI in this book. With respect to the new trends Ruffinelli does specify in his article, he observes:

These are... some of the new avenues that Latin American literature has been opening-or widening-... in the 1980s: they are, in effect, new territories in the space of our writing, with specific strategies with relation to other discourses ( ).

Furthermore, Ruffinelli adds, while these three dimensions (above all the feminist one) are clearly part of international processes, still they are uniquely Latin American in their contours, and "constitute the best example of a growing independence of Latin American writing from European paradigms, as well as of the possibility... of constructing models... which even influence central and hegemonic cultures" (40-41).

Some years ago Angel Rama designated as transculturation the process by which Latin American literature worked over the influences it received modifying and processing their very forms until achieving the original expressions which emerged in the 1960s. In the same way we can say that our postmodernity is not only an epiphenomenon of Europe or North America; it doesn't just respond from an elitist literature which grew from the developed sections of our society; it is in great measure an expression of the progressive middle classes, of their popular contact, of a series of preoccupations generalized and immersed in the class struggle itself. Our postmodernity is, in effect, part of the unachieved modernity, an important stage of crisis (41).

For Ruffinelli, this Latin American postmodernity is the child of the innovative avant garde that produced a boom literature "expressing not the absolute negativity of a European postmodernity convinced of the disappearance of the great narratives, but rather the melancholy of a romanticism that never took off in our literature and continues accompanying its passage through time" (ibid.). It is precisely here that Ruffinelli situates Latin American postmodernity with respect to the paradigms of developed and post-industrial societies-its rootedness in its own historical and cultural problematics that ultimately recycle the contemporary overlays which can affect but cannot obliterate them.

Where all of this is leading in the future of Latin American societies, cultures and literatures is not fully clear. Surely much pain and violence will indeed be part of the process; and the need to record, remember and find roads to transcend violence will continue to be part of Latin American literary processes for years to come-though perhaps with comic strategies and ruptures that seek to propel Latin American literature and life beyond the labyrinths of repetition-compulsion born of the traumas of conquest and colonial, as well as neo and now post-colonial oppression. Unless violence in Latin American is remembered and registered in some way, warn Rowe and Schelling (228), proper historical understanding become impossible and cultural history runs the risk of becoming a comfortable exercise.

> *Part of the violence produced by global homogenizing trends is the illusion that there is only one history, an illusion which suppresses the differences between the different histories lived by different groups of human beings. Historical memory is a vital cultural action in making and preserving those differences, and the destruction of memory is a prime means of domination. Such memory is not just continuity and unchanging identity, it is also memory of destruction and discontinuity. Nor is it appropriate to speak of a single popular memory: there are a variety of differentiated memories (*ibid.*)*

The recent military dictatorships, which depended on obliterating the normal areas for the work of memory made the matter of social memory more urgent than ever. And so we must ask, how far will it be possible to reconstruct a history of the anti-somocista and anti-contra struggles, the Salvadoran years of war and destruction, Guatemala's thirty years of civil war, contemporary struggles in Colombia? The dead live along with the living. But so does the need to forget, so does the fear of remembering. Of course, as Rowe and Schelling point out, we have to distinguish the processes of popular memory from official, state and class-dominated ones. One of the basic aims of the Sandinista poetry workshops was to weave memory and everyday life, so that the war against Somoza would be recalled not in the idealized official versions, but as personal, lived experiences. Much of Central American revolutionary poetry was written in this spirit-involving concerns with individual memory and creativity, involving attempts to reverse the oppressive role of the written word in Latin America. The poetry remains valuable, even if we conclude that they inadequately figured ethnic, gender and other dimensions into the equation and even if we admit that as in other cultural processes, institutionalized or not, formal or not, this poetry is highly selective and exclusive in its memories and their treatment.

The same concern with preserving popular memory is at the heart of testimonial forms perse. The fragmented old culture becomes reformulated through a written narrative, itself disengaged from the pressure of dominant values. Testimonios contributed to Latin America's expression and understanding of contemporary experience. Even if involving the mediation or intervention of a professional writer or editor, testimonios were able to get at cultural dimensions and levels rarely accessible in the fictional projections of the writers working through their own imaginative capacity for empathy, identification and creation (230-31).

Rowe and Schelling note, finally, that many more people watched telenovelas than read testimonial texts. The mass media is a crucial area of study in the past thirty years-how far they destroy and stultify, but also how far they preserve, recall, reanimate. Although transformed, practices of popular memory can continue, even in relation to the mass media. Music spread through radio and record industries retains older life patterns; bolero and other forms are shore up collective memory. The telenovela may have some positive value in that, even in this market product the conflicts portrayed oppose market reduction. If Jameson is right to assume that the video, more so than literary narrative, film or even TV, is the art medium par excellence of postmodernity, then it is in part because it functions as a simulacrum of fragmented, collage construction, in part because it points to newer, uncharted identities and relations. Is this then the case for Latin America as well? Is video the preferred medium of contemporary representation, just as the novel and film were at previous modernizing phases?

It is also true that the working tools of many Latin Americanist critics for viewing potential patterns of transformative resistance are still honed in function of older, primarily literary categories (alienation as rediscovered in the early Marx and developed in relation to everyday life by Henri Lefebvre; reification and world views as developed by the early Lukács and his disciple Goldmann; structural Marxism as developed by Althusser and applied in Latin America by Perus and others; dependency theory as developed by Gunder Frank and company and applied to literature by Franco, Vidal and so many others, etc.). Are they adequate for explaining social phenomena and their relation to the authors under study? Clearly today we require more complex, contemporary models, ones that correspond to a modified sense of the nature of our situation in postmodernity in its Latin American and more global dimensions. Feminist perspectives, poststructuralist ones, comparative studies involving North American majority and minority literatures, other third world literatures, (e.g., Asian subaltern, post-colonial studies, etc.) -all these and other dimensions will come into play, as will the relation of these dimensions with broader cultural ones.

In this sense, and thinking of postmodernity as a periodizing concept (Jameson 1984), we should note that the periodization of Latin American postmodernity in fiction suggested by Martin, Ruffinelli and many others (Javier García Méndez, Nicolás Casullo, Alberto Moreiras, Ricardo Gutiérrez-Mouat, just to cite a few from Issue 6 of *Nuevo texto crítico [1990]*) does not completely correspond to periodizations based on other cultural and political phenomena either in different areas or in given countries; the discrepancies lend credence to the idea that literary transformations indeed anticipate rather than reflect changes at other social levels. In the continuing expressions and silences of Latin American literary and cultural discourse, in all its new and emergent forms and processes, we may find symbolic patterns which not only anticipate but also help forge a Latin American future in which some of the most important, best and nearly forgotten dimensions of Latin America's past live and find fruition.

6. The Briefest Post-Script: New Latin American Literary Syntheses and Against Against Literature

In concluding this chapter, mainly drafted in the early 1990s, I wish to mention some of the many ambitious projects that have transformed our sense of the history and relatedness of the Latin American literary field. First, Ana Pizarro's *La literatura latinoamericana como proceso (1985) marked a new síntesis which affected work throughout the 1990s; second,* Roberto González Echevarría and Enrique Pupo-Walker's three-volume *Cambridge History of Latin American Literature* (1996); and of course the former's pathbreaking book, *Myth and Archive: A Theory of Latin American Narrative* (1998) began to consolidate the field of study in new ways. *Literary Cultures of Latin America* (2004), edited by Mario J. Valdés and Djelal Kadir, is perhaps the most ambitious effort of synthesis in recent years constituting an valuable survey of Latin American literary cultures involving history, texts, cultural institutions, and social, political, and other contexts of the writing. Imbedding their study in a Braudelian vision of historical processes, the editors touch on geographical, demographic, and linguistic dimensions of the literature; they then explore the production of literary cultures, "literary access and participation"; Latin American literature's "institutional modes and cultural modalities'; and questions of "socioeconomic, racial and ethnic alterity"; gender and sexuality; religious, scientific, and political discursivity; as well as transformations in popular culture and cinema.

Such recent works as those by Neil Larsen (2001), Jean Franco (2002) and others-as well as the growing body of work on Afro-Latin American, gender, women's, queer and other perspectives-emerge to create an ever richer frame for Latin American literary study. But in this context of recent production which threatens to unsettle every dimension of the field set forth in this essay, we should must now ever briefly reflect on the controversy stirred by some of the ideas of John Beverley, mentioned here and given a new enunciation in *Against Literature* (1993) even as I was completing the rough draft of this text. There, as noted, Beverley effectively argued that Latin American literature, far from representing an alternative to, was indeed in collusion with, colonial and post-colonial creole state power, and could in no way serve an emancipating or progressive role. While sympathetic to many of Beverley's views which indeed stemmed from postions we developed in *Politics and Literature in the Central American Revolutions*, I nevertheless have generally wished to take a less radical tack and point to Bakhtinian textual contradictions and multi-voices in texts which point to how literature, even in its determined role, has become a repository for symbolic and imaginary resources which go beyond their initial inscribed relation to established power. As the place of the subjective and the imaginary, more distanced from commodification and political mimesis than are film, architecture and other expressive forms, literature remains a space for possibility even in the new world [dis]order that some call globalization and others call "Empire." It is in this light, that the new emergent literature, the literature of McOndo and the "Crack" and other tendencies should be examined today as we work in the somewhat bleak terrain of post-911 literary studies.

Works Cited

Achugar, Hugo. 1979. *Ideología y estructuras narrativas en José Donoso, 1950-1970.* Caracas. Centro de Estudios Latinoamericanos Rómulo Gallegos.

---. 1985. *Poesía y sociedad: Uruguay, 1880 – 1911.* Montevideo. Arca.

Adorno, Rolena. 1982. *From Oral to Written Expression: native Andean chronicles of the early colonial period.* Syracuse. Maxwell School of Citizenship and Public Affairs, Syracuse University.

---. 1994, 2000. *Guaman Poma: Writing and Resistance in Colonial Peru.* Austin, TX. University of Texas Press.

Adorno, Theodor and Max Horkheimer. 1973. *Dialectic of enlightenment.* London. Allen Lane.

Aguilera Peralta, Gabriel Edgardo. 1971. *La violencia en Guatemala como fenómeno político.* Mexico: Centro Intercultural de Documentación.

Aguilera Peralta, Gabriel Edgardo; Ricardo Córdova Macías; Francisco López Rodríguez. 1988. *El Salvador: límites y alcances de una pacificación negociada.* México. CINAS.

Anderson, Benedict. 1983. *Imagined Communities: reflections on the origin and spread of nationalism*. London. Verso.

Arias, Arturo. 1989. *Jaguar en llamas*. Guatemala. Ministerio de Cultura y deportes.

Beck, Mary Ann, Lisa E. Davis; José Hernández; Gary D. Keller; Isabel Taran, Isabel, ed. *The Analysis of Hispanic Texts: Current Trends in Methodology*. Jamaica. Bilingual Press, York Coll. 191-205.

Beverley, John. 1987. *Del Lazarillo al Sandinismo: estudios sobre la función ideológica de la literatura española e hispanoamericana*. Minneapolis. Institute for the Study of Ideologies and Literature and Prisma Institute.

---.1993. *Against Literature*. Minneapolis. University of Minnesota Press.

---. and Marc Zimmerman. 1990. *Literature and Politics in the Central American Revolutions*. Austin. University of Texas Press.

---. Michael Aronna and José Oviedo (Eds.). 1995. *The Postmodernism Debate in Latin America*. Durham. Duke University Press.

Bhabha, Homi, ed. 1990. *Nation and Narration*. London, New York. Routledge.

Blanco Aguinaga, Carlos. 1975. *De mitólogos y novelistas*. Madrid. Ediciones Turner.

---.1976. "Crítica marxista y poesia: Lectura de un poema de Julian del Casal" In Beck, et al.:191-205.

Bonin, Nora. 1998. "A star is Born: Action Groups, Power and Di Tella in Argentine Modernization. In Piazza and Zimmerman: 101-114.

Bourdieu, Pierre. 1984. *Distinction: a social critique of the judgement of taste*. Cambridge. Harvard University Press.

Collazos, Oscar; Julio Cortázar and Mario Vargas Llosa. 1970. *Literatura en la revolución y revolución en la literatura*. México. Siglo Veintiuno Editores.

Cornejo Polar, Antonio. 1984. "Sobre el 'neoindigenismo' y las novelas de Manuel Scorza" *Revista Iberoamericana*. Apr.-June; 50 (127): 549-557.

Cueva, Agustín. 1977. *El desarrollo del capitalismo en América Latina: Ensayo de interpretación histórica*. Mexico. Siglo Veintiuno Editores.

Fernández Retamar, Roberto. 1974. *Calibán y otros ensayos: nuestra América y el mundo.* La Habana. Editorial Arte y Literatura.

---. 1975. *Para una teoría de la literatura hispanoamericana.* La Habana. Casa de las Américas.

Foster, David William. 1991. *Gay and Lesbian Themes in Latin American Writing.* Austin. University of Texas Press.

Franco, Jean. 1973. *Spanish American Literature since Independence.* London, Ernest Benn Ltd. New York, Barnes and Noble.

---. 1988. "Beyond Ethnocentrism: Gender, Power, and the Third World Intelligentsia" In Nelson and Grossberg: 503-515.

---. 1989. *Plotting Women: gender and representation in Mexico.* New York. Columbia University Press.

---. 2002. *The Decline and Fall of the Lettered City: Latin America in the Cold War (Convergences, Inventories of the Present).* Princeton, NJ. Princeton University Press.

Fuentes, Carlos. 1969. *La nueva novela hispanoamericana.* México. J. Mortiz.

-- 1975. *Terra Nostra.* México. J. Mortiz.

García Canclini, Néstor. 1982. *Las culturas populares en el capitalismo.* La Habana. Casa de las Américas.

---. 1987. *Políticas culturales en América Latina.* Mexico. Grijalbo.

González-Echevarría, Roberto. 1998. *Myth and Archive: A Theory of Latin American Narrative.* Cambridge, England. Cambridge, England. U.K. Cambridge University Press.

González Echevarría, Roberto and Enrique Pupo-Walker, ed. 1996. *The Cambridge History of Latin American Literature.* Cambridge, England. U.K. Cambridge University Press

González-Stephan, Beatriz. 2002. *Fundaciones: cánon, historia y cultura nacional: la historiografía literaria del liberalismo hispanoamericano del siglo XIX.* Madrid: Iberoamericana. Frankfurt am Main: Vervuert.

Jameson, Fredric. 1984. "Postmodernism, or, the Cultural Logic of Late Capitalism". *New Left Review*. 146: 53-92.

Laclau, Ernesto. 1977. *Politics and ideology in Marxist theory:capitalism, fascism, populism*. London. New Left Books.

Larsen, Neil. 1995. "Posmodernism and Imperialism: Theory and Politics in Latin America." In Beverley, Arrona and Oviedo: 110-34.

---. 2001. Determinations: Essays on Theory, Narrative and Nation in the Americas. London. Verso.

Lauer, Mirko. 1983. *Los exilios interiores: Una introducción a Martin Adán*. Lima. Hueso Húmero Ediciones.

Lienhard, Martin. 1990. *La voz y su huella: escritura y conflicto étnico-social en América Latina (1492- 1988)*. Ciudad de la Habana. Casa de las Américas.

Marcone, Jorge. 1993. "Beyond the Andes: An Introduction to the Rewriting of the Amazon in Contemporary Peruvian Fiction". In: Wright, Will; Kaplan, Steven (ed. and introd.). *The Image of Nature in Literature, the Media, and Society*. Pueblo, CO. Soc. for the Interdisciplinary Study of Social Imagery, University of Southern Colorado, 350-55.

Martin, Gerald. 1989. *Journeys Through the Labyrinth: Latin American Fiction in the Twentieth Century*. London; New York. Verso.

Martín-Barbero, Jesús. 1987. *De los medios a las mediaciones: comunicación, cultura y hegemonía*. Mexico. Ediciones G. Gili.

Menchú, Rigoberta. 1984. *I, Rigoberta Menchú: An Indian woman in Guatemala*. Elizabeth Burgos-Debray (Ed. and Intro). Ann Wright (Trans.) London. Verso.

Mignolo, Walter D. 1997. *The Darker Side of the Renaissance. Literacy, Territoriality, & Colonization*. Ann Arbor. University of Michigan Press.

Monguio, Luis. 1968. "En torno al 'El reino interior' de Rubén Darío" *Revista Hispánica Moderna*. New York. Columbia University Hispanic Studies. 34: 721-28.

Moraña, Mabel. 1984. *Literatura y cultura nacional en Hispanoamérica (1910-1940)*. Minneapolis. Institute for the Study of Ideologies and Literatures.

Narvaez, Jorge. 1986. "El testimonio 1972-1982: Transformaciones en el sistema literario". In: Vidal and Jara, eds.: 235-79.

Nelson, Cary and Lawrence Grossberg, eds. 1988. *Marxism and the Interpretation of Culture*. Urbana. University of Illinois Press.

Ortiz Fernández, Fernando.1978. *Contrapunteo cubano del tabaco y el azúcar*. Caracas. Biblioteca Ayacucho.

Osorio, Nelson. 1977. "La nueva narrativa y los problemas de la crítica hispanoamericana actual". *Separata de Revista Crítica Literaria*. Lima: 1er Semestre, Año III, No. 5.

Pastor Bodmer, Beatriz. 1983. *Discurso narrativo de la conquista de América: ensayo*. La Habana. Casa de las Américas.

Pérez Firmat, Gustavo, ed. 1990. *Do the Americas Have a Common Literature?* Durham. Duke University Press.

Perus, Françoise. 1976. *Literatura y sociedad en América Latina: el modernismo*. La Habana. Casa de las Américas.

Rama, Ángel. 1970. *Rubén Darío y el modernismo (circunstancia socioeconómica de un arte americano)*. Caracas. Ediciones de la Biblioteca de la Universidad Central de Venezuela.

Rama, Ángel. 1982. *Transculturación narrativa en América Latina*. México. Siglo XXI.

Rama, Ángel. 1984. *La ciudad letrada*. Hanover. Ediciones del norte.

Ramos, Julio. 1989. *Desencuentros de la modernidad en América Latina: Literatura y política en el siglo XIX*. México: Fondo de Cultura Económica.

Rodó, José Enrique and Leopoldo Alas. 1967. *Ariel*. New York. Las Americas Pub. Co.

Rodríguez, Ileana. 1984. *Primer inventario del invasor*. Managua. Editorial Nueva Nicaragua.

Rowe, William and Vivian Schelling. 1991. *Memory and Modernity: popular culture in Latin America*. London; New York. Verso.

Ruffinelli, Jorge. 1990. "Los 80: ¿Ingreso a la posmodernidad?" In Ruffinelli (ed.) *Nuevo Texto Crítico*. Año III No. 6. *Modernidad y posmodernidad en América Latina,* I: 31-42.

Sarlo, Beatriz. 1988. *Una modernidad periférica: Buenos Aires, 1920 y 1930.* Buenos Aires. Ediciones Nueva Visión.

Sarmiento, Domingo Faustino. 2003. *Facundo: Civilization and Barbarism.* Berkeley. University of California Press.

Sklodowska, Elzbieta. 1992. *Testimonio hispanoamericano: historia, teoría, poética.* New York. Peter Lang.

Smorkaloff, Pamela María. 1991. "De las crónicas al testimonio: Sociocrítica y continuidad histórica en las letras latinoamericanas". *Nuevo texto crítico.* 4 (8): 101-116.

Sommer, Doris. 1990. "Plagiarized Authenticity: Sarmiento's Cooper and Others." In Pérez Firmat, Gustavo: 135-155.

---. 1990b. "Irresistible Romance: The Foundational Fictions of Latin America" In Bhabha.

---. 1991a. *Foundational Fictions: The National Romances of Latin America.* Berkeley. University of California Press.

Starn, Orin. 1992. "Missing the revolution: anthropologists and the war in Peru". In *Rereading cultural anthropology.* Durham. Duke University Press.

Stoll, David. 1999. *Rigoberta Menchú and the story of all poor Guatemalans.* Boulder. Westview Press.

Vidal, Hernán. 1976. *Literatura hispanoamericana e ideología liberal, surgimiento y crisis (una problemática sobre la dependencia en torno a la narrativa del boom).* Buenos Aires. Ediciones Hispamérica.

---. 1985. *Socio-historia de la literatura colonial hispanoamericana: tres lecturas orgánicas* Mpls., MN. Institute for the Study of Ideologies and Literature.

Vidal, Hernán y Jara, René eds. 1986. *Testimonio y Literatura.* Minneapolis. Institute for the Study of Ideologies and Literature.

Viñas, David. 1971. *De Sarmiento a Cortázar.* Buenos Aires. Ediciones Siglo Veinte.

---. 1982. *Indios, ejército y frontera*. Mexico. Siglo Veintiuno Editores.

Yúdice, George. 1985. *Alterando historia, alternando historias*. Caracas. Museo de Bellas Artes.

---. 1989. "¿Puede hablarse de postmodernidad en América Latina?" *Revista de Crítica Literaria Latinoamericana*. 15 (29): 105-128.

---. 1991. "El conflicto de posmodernidades". *Nuevo Texto Crítico*. 4 (7): 19-33.

Zimmerman, Marc, Ileana Rodríguez, Edward Baker and Bridget Aldaraca (eds). 1980. *Nicaragua in Revolution: the Poets Speak; Nicaragua en Revolución: Los Poetas Hablan*. Minneapolis. Marxist Educational Press.

Zimmerman, Marc et al., ed.. 1985. *Nicaragua in reconstruction & at war: the people speak: a collage of chronology, analysis, poetry, etc. portraying insurrection, reconstruction, cultural revolution & U.S. intervention*. Minneapolis: MEP.

---.1988. *El Salvador at War: A Collage Epic*. Minneapolis: MEP.

---.1992. *U.S. Latino Literature: An Essay and Annotated Bibliography*. Chicago. MARCH/Abrazo Press.

---. y Raúl Rojas; Patricio Navia (eds.) 1993. *Guatemala: Voces desde el silencio: un collage épico*. Guatemala. Palo de Hormigo and Oscar de León Palacios.

Notes

1 In this account, our prime model is Darío in relation to capitalist/imperialist developments, as constructed by Monguío (1968), Fernández Retamar (1969), Rama (1970), Perus (1976), and Blanco Aguinaga (1976). For an alternative and less Darío-centered view of *modernismo*, see Ramos (1989). .

2. For an English-language version of his key essay, see Beverley 1989.

Chapter II
Culture and Literature in Central America

1. Introduction

Until recently, and with obvious exceptions like Rubén Darío, Miguel Angel Asturias, Roque Dalton and Ernesto Cardenal, Central American literature had been a forgotten or neglected dimension of Latin American literary history-a marginalized and minor literature even in the context of general Latin American marginality. Of course, one could beg the question and ask if there is such a thing as a regional literature; one could point to the illusions and distortions involved in attempting to forge or promote a national literary system. Even when overtly trying to write a national "foundational" narrative or poem, writers often achieved aesthetic ends which diverged from or were not in direct relation to their overt intentions. Nevertheless, the focus on nation-building, on imagined national communities, supposedly harmonizing class, ethnic, gender and other differences for the sake of some false and falsifying concept of national identity, nevertheless led, indirectly or directly, to the tensions out of which emerged literary movements, currents and works of importance that others considered somehow representative of the Central American turf and specifically Central American contributions to Latin American and world literature.

This essay will seek to study the development of cultural and literary processes which were part of what some of us thought were revolutionary, but turned out instead to be abortive insurrectional, conjunctures in Central American history. Here, I will consider the socio-economic, political and ideological forces in which those cultural and literary processes should be studied. However, it is important to carry out this analysis within the frame of an overall theoretical and historical grasp of the world under consideration in relation to, but also beyond, questions of revolutionary nationalism and the effort to construct a new literature in the wake of post-revolutionary neo-liberalism. In order to accomplish this analytical operation, we need to explore further the socio-economic, political, cultural and ideological backgrounds which would set the stage for the literary phenomena to be considered.

2. Central American Socio-Economic Backgrounds, Similarities and Differences

In one of his key essays, Edelberto Torres Rivas (1983b: 1-34), the most important analyst of Central American socio-economic development, outlines the key similarities and differences that characterize the different countries and cultural complexes which constitute the Central American region. For many, he notes, it seems difficult to understand that the Central American isthmus, with an area of only 431,000 square kilometers, could be a site for such diverse national historical and cultural patterns. The countries share a situation of underdevelopment and thus a "basic, structural homogeneity." The Central American agrarian economies fulfill like functions in an industrialized world market, and that leads to certain common pressures affecting internal socio-economic, political and cultural patterns. Central American similarities result from the manner in which the region was articulated to the great currents of international commerce and from the ways in which capitalism was implanted... in the nineteenth century, as well as the role the military was to play, especially after during and after the world wide depression of the 1930s. Central American differences correspond to varying pre-colonial situations, dissimilar colonial experiences (during which present-day political and cultural traditions were shaped), to the particular forms that social and economic structure adopted as the export economy developed, and to the relations and conflicts between social groups and classes (Torres-Rivas 1983a: 2).

My primary concern in what follows will be to draw on Torres Rivas, Sergio Ramírez and many other writers, to trace the development of Central American ideological and cultural processes which were part of what some of us thought was a revolutionary but instead turned out to be an abortive insurrectional conjuncture in Central American history. Here, I will consider the socio-economic, political and ideological forces in which those cultural processes should be studied. But I think it important to carry out this analysis within the frame of an overall theoretical and historical grasp of the world under exploration. What is the theoretical basis for understanding particular Central American historical phases and conjunctures and the role of ideological and cultural phenomena in relation to broader contexts? How can we understand post-insurrectional processes without understanding the 1970s and 80s? But also of course, how can we study prior periods without some grasp of processes today? What is required is some examination of Central American history to set the stage for the remarkable developments marking the period from the 1980s to the present. For those knowledgeable, this summary will seem a rehearsal of the known and obvious, lacking in nuances and precision-they may modify or diverge from the text in their future efforts. For those relatively new to the field, this summary will provide the foundation which makes possible the minimal contextualization necessary for the comprehension of Central American literary developments and works.

3. Colonial History and the Independence

The Central American region was not the object of a unified European conquest. The activities of the European conquerors varied in the places that became the present countries of the area. In what became Costa Rica and Honduras, colonists tended to settle and work the land. Guatemala, on the other hand, became a commercial center. A bit of both were found in what is today El Salvador and Nicaragua. These separate outcomes were the result of different attempts at conquest, sometimes quite bloody, that originated in Mexico, Santo Domingo, and Panama. Only after 1560 was a rough border drawn for what was called the Kingdom of Guatemala, covering most of contemporary Central America. Until 1743, this area was also under a unified religious command as well.

Modern Central American history begins in 1524 when Pedro de Alvarado conquers what is now Guatemala, but pre-Conquest roots persist in varying forms and mutations as an integral part of the area's historical development. The heirs of Mayan culture, bearers of a rich tradition, endured; they conditioned the long colonial period and have survived throughout the republican phase and up to the present day. The strength of the indigenous culture was not uniform. The physical and human locus of that culture reached only as far as Guatemala and part of Honduras. In Costa Rica the indigenous population was smaller and resisted more, and was as a result decimated and then pushed into a marginal corner. In Guatemala the indigenous population still constitutes a demographic majority. The process of racial and cultural mixing was intense especially in El Salvador and Honduras, where racial homogeneity was produced through *mestizaje*. The Indian populations of Nicaragua retreated into the mountains along the Atlantic Coast, mixing to a degree with the Nicaraguan component of an African aggregate which was brought to the coast area extending from Belize to Costa Rica.

Poor in mineral wealth and other economic resources, the isthmus has had a geographical position which bequeathed it a geopolitical destiny that it has still not overcome. As a result, the colony had only administrative and political significance, but this was particularly strong in Guatemala, headquarters of the captaincy-general of the Kingdom of Guatemala and seat of the colonial authorities. Here settled a ponderous civil, ecclesiastical, and military bureaucracy, and here the *encomienda* (an arrangement involving a system of personal services and tributes that the conquered aboriginal population had to pay or give for long periods of time to conquistadores who were favored by the king of Spain) prospered beyond its legal limits.

While the colonial experience marked out different destinies for the five provinces, a characteristic feature of the period which the provinces shared was not permanent stagnation but cycles of boom and depression alternating inexorably. Ephemeral successes for a mining economy (gold and silver) were replaced by the modest agricultural production of tobacco, cacao, and indigo. Only a select minority of Spaniards and *criollos* (American-born children of Spaniards) profited from agricultural production in this region, and the export-import trade was restricted to those who lived in Guatemala City. The monopoly exercised by the principal families of Guatemala through the Consulate of Commerce gave them legal control over the flow of trade from all the other provinces after 1790. The prosperity of an aristocratic elite in Guatemala has always contrasted with the permanent difficulties endured by the small groups of landholders and businessmen in the provinces.

With respect to cultural questions in the colonial period, as Severo Martínez Peláez has shown (1971: XIII and 549), the reproduction of a metropolitan cultural model in the Kingdom of Guatemala responded to characteristics etched by the colonial mode of production that was installed over the dominion of land and the Indians. A unity of behavior develops, which is never conceived as a generator of internal cohesion, as a form of realizing power.

The dominant groups will retain a peninsular version of Spanish culture involving diverse transplants: educational institutions, philosophical norms, urban and architectural models (including central plazas, etc.), house design, furniture and decorations, musical instruments, dances, songs, etc. With the dominant *criollo* pattern coming into play, the ruling groups act to preserve or promote those cultural dimensions which serve or at least do not enter into contradiction with the order necessary for reproduction of the economic system or its supportive apparatuses. Pre-colonial languages, cosmologies, myth patterns, song, weaving, pottery, etc. survive to the degree they serve the system, modified of course in essential ways. Granted, many songs and stories of "Uncle Rabbit" and "Uncle Coyote", many forms of theater, including Guatemala's *Rabinal Achi* and Nicaragua's *El Guegüense* retain and develop their contestatory force. But even those forms that seem critical of the system may ultimately function to reinforce and represent successful modes of social containment. The emerging cultural complex was policed by both the colonial state and perhaps most importantly by the Inquisition, which was frequently used against *criollo* enlightenment impulses even more than indigenous ones. Rebellious, liberal concepts began to emerge in the eighteenth century; these concepts fed Creole justifications for independence and established the bases for ideological strains which would be crucial to nineteenth century political and cultural developments.

Through the colonial period and on into the era of formal independence, there is little development of an autonomous regional or national intellectual life in Central America. The Central American Union crumbled before the struggles between dominant sectors wanting local hegemony; and these fights led to new fragmented national contexts for further struggles between "Liberals" and "Conservatives" over who would dominate in exploiting and selling off lands and products, to say nothing of the people themselves. In this context, some universities and newspapers were founded; there are treatises on law, histories and odes justifying or praising Liberal or Conservative interests, etc. But we are still in what Mariátegui called the colonial stage of intellectual development.

4. From Independence to the Emergence of Coffee and Bananas

Civil war was a consequence of Central American independence, which was a bureaucratic operation executed by Guatemala City *criollos*. Gradually, the provinces put the solidity of the "Kingdom of Guatemala" to a test, through a series of conflicts in which disintegrative forces nurtured in the colonial period now won out.

Guatemalan liberals supported a federation concept (the Federal Republic of Central America) to re-establish authority in the area. Central America's famous "period of anarchy" (1823-40) ended by destroying the federalist program, as members of the Central American bourgeoisie split into liberal and conservative factions each seeking the adequate degree of relative autonomy and unified action to foster their ability to exploit their lands and workers for greater profits increasingly available to be made on a world market. Liberals began by championing the ideal of regional unity, the idea of a nation large, strong and rich enough to be able to "modernize" and "progress" and deal with new economic forces alive in the world. Conservatives also spoke of unity, but ultimately their orientation was toward maintaining and building their local power, often posing as friends of the Indian populations in their struggles against Liberal programs in which progress often meant the destruction of Indian communities and culture.

Once Spanish authority had been broken, the main issue became that of a revolution against Guatemala, and then, within each country, a rivalry between liberals and conservatives, a conflict sometimes complicated by local loyalties. This struggle- which lasted months in Costa Rica, years in Guatemala and El Salvador and decades in Honduras and Nicaragua- yielded multiple results. The Central American nation that was being formed fell apart, and from it came five projects for nation-states, which foundered in stagnation for over half a century, were subject to foreign rapine (Iturbide's effort to establish an American empire, William Walker's pro-slavery incursion into Nicaragua, English efforts to take over parts of the region, the designs by the U.S. and other powers to establish a canal through Nicaragua, etc.), and were to experience from that time on a difficult individual history.

Central American forces united one final time in the 1850s to defeat the incursion of William Walker. But now, the dream of unity put to one side (though never forgotten), each nation set out to map out its own destiny. One thing they shared in varying degrees during the second half of the nineteenth century was their achievement, through external action and local political conditions (and in spite of the sometimes heated Liberal/Conservative divisions), of building an export economy. Indeed, the earlier struggles between liberals and conservatives receded before new forms of struggle by which nascent merchants merged with their landowning producers and consumers to form a new oligarchy tied to the international market. Before, Central American export products included *añil*, indigo and balsams. Now the region became permanently linked to the world economy, expanding from the impact of the industrial revolution; internally, commercial agriculture with coffee and then bananas as its focus permitted the establishment of an increasingly important economic structure. Between 1850 and 1870 Central America exported on the average 11 percent of the world's coffee; in 1916 it accounted for 58 percent of the world's banana production.

The experience of forming agro-export structures was different for each of the national societies. These differences express precisely the particular character of economic growth, and political domination that was adopted as a solution in each setting. This provides a good example of how the "colonial past" conditioned later local history. For instance, Costa Rica established its coffee plantation economy on the basis of the family plot. The peasant smallholding, established through the relative independence of the direct producer, fulfills the egalitarian dream of the *campesino*. Here the concentration of wealth was organized through the monopoly on coffee processing and marketing rather than on production.

At the extreme opposite from this unique experience is the rest of Central America, particularly El Salvador and Guatemala. Agrarian capitalism developed on the basis of large landholding property and the accumulation of land was carried out to the direct detriment of the indigenous communal lands. Political violence presided over this operation in the name of progress.

Again and again, the "civilizing mission of coffee" brought about an opportunity for consolidating political power in function of "oligarchic domination" -that is, the social predominance of key agrarian sectors (large plantation owners and merchants) who controlled foreign trade. The authority of this class grew along with the expansion of the export economy, and it afforded an opportunity for advances in the building of the national state. Clearly the opportunity was not uniform. Costa Rica is a case of political stability and gradual economic consolidation. A miniscule oligarchy was able to control the power of the state and then create a structure of domination based on hegemonic manipulation. This system remained stable until the 1940s.

In Guatemala, violence was the only way to destroy *criollo* privilege. The *criollos* sought to maintain their rule through the political power of the church and the economic force of the Consulate of Commerce and the low-productive *latifundios* of a fading dye economy. Only the "liberal revolution" of 1871 made the development of commercial export agriculture possible, but again, the cost was an intensification of Indian exploitation.

Liberal reformism in El Salvador had a similar vigor but did not confront a *criollo* sector by force, and the separation of church from state was not a painful matter. The coffee planters' predominance, mounted on a peculiar form of agrarian capitalism, was based upon opposing forms of land ownership: *latifundios* burgeoned, forcing many peasants into a family subsistence economy linked to the new landowning class through archaic forms of rent expropriation. The fact is fundamental for understanding El Salvador and Guatemala. Coffee comes to stand for progress, the means for establishing a class's authority and for making some transformations of lingering colonial patterns. Where in Costa Rica, El Salvador and Guatemala, agro-export interests became the national interest; in Nicaragua and Honduras, monocrop production and its relation to the world market met with violent problems. These two backward countries provided no basis for the emergence of class forces able to exploit international trade possibilities. Honduras had an opportunity with banana export, but national interests were soon swallowed by a system dominated by modern, foreign-owned plantations. Agricultural production for local markets and commerce stayed with modern, capitalist, foreign-owned plantations. Liberals in the 1880s failed to bring prosperity and unity. So the creation of a national state was greatly impeded.

Nicaragua's phase of anarchy was prolonged for several decades. The Liberal/conservative split invited William Walker's adventure of 1854 and the failure of the liberal revolution and U.S. intervention (1911), which lasted until 1933.

Those rivalries explain the emergence of Sandino's resistance and also the Somoza dictatorship, which is the direct result of foreign military intervention. Nicaragua was not a stranger to the modernizing cycle of coffee in the 1870s, but the productive structure that came with it did not achieve sufficient stature to become the axis of social and political change. The conditions the country offer for an inter-oceanic passageway may still constitute its greatest wealth.

Honduras and Nicaragua entered into the world market haphazardly and largely by way of forms of the foreign "enclave," in the paradigmatic examples of the banana in one case and gold and silver mining in the other. In Nicaragua a true export economy was built upon the basis of the cotton plantation only in the early 1950s.

For Ramírez, the point of departure for bringing and relating national and regional attributes in Central America is "the rupture of the unity of cultural norms imposed by the Spanish colony, a rupture which fully materializes not with the 1821 independence proclamations, but in the second half of the nineteenth century, through the expansion of the world capitalist system and the place assigned Central America in the international division of labor by the entry of coffee and other products in the world market."

The subversive ideas which had circulated clandestinely in Central America in the last phases of colonial rule not only helped legitimize the call for independence, but became the basis of Morazanic liberalism and the ideological orientations that emerge in the early national and regional histories, as well as some of the novels-even in the historical writing of a conservative like José Milla. Naturally the emergent ideologies and the new cultural forms (novels, symphonies, etc.) which appear with them have their more immediate bases in the struggle for Central American unity, the struggle against William Walker, the effort to promote a Nicaraguan canal, etc. Such matters fed into a process involving the importation of French and English liberal ideas (including progress, free trade, modernization, etc.) that had begun during the previous century. But liberal ideas have little radical force when they become the legitimizing justifications for the coffee producers as they rise from the middle sectors to take power through armed revolts, installing military dictatorships that impose an order of civilization and progress, transforming existing systems of land tenure, abolishing the colonial property regime, the indigenous communal lands, etc., and restructuring state and social relations for the sake of coffee production and distribution (Ramírez 1983: 22). Presented with a great rhetorical aura, these "liberal" reforms became the basis for the political rule of a new class but had no effect in modernizing, let alone substituting, the traditional configuration of Central America which continued to be rural and archaic, with an exploitation of a servile *campesino* workforce and with the hacienda as the center of power and, in effect, as the true republic. Liberal ideology emerges in new laws which, in spite of their high-sounding and sometimes radical words, end up by doing no more than legitimize the concentration of land in the form of *latifundios* which will pass to the hands of the generals and their henchmen.

As coffee is exported, products manufactured in more advanced capitalist countries come into the region and begin to determine the cultural attitudes of the groups tied to agro-export. And the dominant ideology returns with greater force, bringing with it the metropolitan imposition of the desire for all things foreign. Above all the wish of the dominant groups is to be part of the metropolitan bourgeoisie, a wish that comes to determine their permanent frustration: their inability to articulate themselves as a bourgeoisie with clear attributes -e.g., with the ability to advance the project of the national state. All that is foreign becomes deified for the colonial bourgeoisie, so that they themselves are alien to the national identity they seek to champion. They pass laws that leave the native population on the margins of their own history. They design European-style buildings; decorate their European-style homes, their churches, their state and business buildings, their clubs. And to maintain their world, they must maintain the exploitative relations that assure the adequate concentration and appropriation of productive lands.

The imposed culture is nothing more than an ensemble of elements that assure the reproduction of relations of domination. Thus bourgeois liberalism is quickly no more than a facade for power. The dominant minority enters relations in keeping with its aspirations to be part of the metropolitan bourgeoisie at a moment in capitalist development when the modalities of internal rule are not modulated from outside, since the metropolitan countries will be distant from the process of local production until after the appearance of the heavily capitalist banana industry. In this pre-banana phase, international bourgeois ideology is represented by a subject colonial version whose characteristic differences from its model may be defined precisely by virtue of its being tailored to the reproductive capacity of a pre-existent internal system which is in turn a subordinate part of the overall system of international domination.[1]

The foreign comes to be the most closed ideal of the dominating minorities. So almost every institution, educational pattern, and artistic norm, etc., derives from Europe. This nineteenth century ideal of being a kind of "Little Europe" obsesses the ruling classes and has a great effect on civic architecture and other visual dimensions of Central American urban life. Of course, the imitation of Europe would take on different modalities depending on where it was imposed. But in general, positivistic French impulses would receive legitimation in function of Central American religious norms; the role of Central American workers in the international division of labor is legitimized not only by Ricardo and Smith but by racist forms of social Darwinism which tend to justify existing patterns of exploitation. The view also flourishes in this context that Central America's role is to provide Euro-proletarian stimulants (coffee, sugar, tobacco, etc.) and to remain in the agricultural sphere, using its agricultural profits to purchase goods manufactured with the help of its stimulants.

5. Economic Development in the Age of Imperialism and Beyond

With the age of imperialism, Central America is more deeply penetrated by international capital, and takes its place in a global division of labor as a producer of agricultural goods and a consumer of imports. This situation brings forth the emergence of a more cosmopolitan cultural and intellectual life. Indeed, the area's first important literary movements occur in the epoch of coffee production and liberal reform (1880-1927).

Modern imperialism implied an unequal intensification of commercial interchanges, and a socio-economic and political re-structuration to permit these changes. The entire transition to imperialist status was carried out according to what some commentators have identified with Lenin's "Junker route" to capitalist development (cf. Perus). An initial phase of modernization was underway. While older socio-economic relations were not eradicated, they were sufficiently disturbed to generate new political, social and cultural tendencies. To the degree that these tendencies fostered or did not interfere with imperialist relations, they were tolerated. When they led to strong opposition to the new order, intervention and interior repression and foreign intervention was the response. This meant that there was little transformation of the technical relations or forces of production and only adjustments in social, political or ideological structures.

A realignment of dominant sectors is achieved that is adequate to the intensification and systematization of labor exploitation. Thus certain fractions of the existing dominant classes regroup to form powerful oligarchies of landowners and merchants who serve foreign interests. While raising agricultural productivity, the oligarchy concentrates farm holdings in their own hands; they create a cheap mobile labor force of salaried workers out of dispossessed peasant sectors and a corps of penurious civil servants and "professionals" from the leavings of a "rural gentry" and an older urban bourgeoisie.

As the nineteenth century drew to a close, the oligarchic states had consolidated their power. The oligarchs dominated large areas of Guatemala and all of tiny El Salvador. In Honduras, the U.S. companies dictated; in Nicaragua and other areas, constant U.S. military interventions were required. But in all instances the mode of development fostered involved exploitation, penetration and overall dependent imperialist relations. This situation both responds to and creates an ever-growing sharpening of class contradictions and confrontations between dispossessed peasants and the local Junker landowners. There are a series of peasant uprisings in El Salvador between 1872 and 1900; there is a rising wave of popular resentment against the U.S. presence in Nicaragua. The inevitable confrontation occasioned by the original accumulation of capital marks, along with the intensification of class struggle, a growing recognition of armed struggle as the only way to overcome the problems posed by the new order, and the effort to establish a more equitable one. Workers, peasants, students and other "middle sectors" will participate in this struggle, which reaches its first peak of development in the early 1930's and, through a widening range of vicissitudes, continues into the 1970's and 1980's.

By the turn of the century, each of our future revolutionary countries had its direction fairly set. In El Salvador, coffee made the region the most intensely settled in Central America, and all that was needed was an adequate labor force to secure coffee development. That force was secured with the passage of laws in the 1870s which prohibited communal land holdings and the development of a state and military apparatus that would fend off any resistance to a process which led to the proletarianization and *mestizaje* of the nation's workforce.

In Guatemala, coffee production developed throughout much of the country, leading to an unsettling and pauperization of Indian communities and a growing Ladino domination of the highlands, so that traditional enmities were only intensified even as new capitalist forces controlled and transformed the country with the support of the government and its military.

In Nicaragua, the coffee bourgeoisie never obtained full hegemony over the merchants from Granada, and the export plantation only fully developed after World War II with the emergence of cotton growing. A coffee oligarchy never entrenched itself in Nicaragua as it did in Guatemala and El Salvador. But that in itself was a source of national instability and structural polarization between dominant sectors and foreign (i.e., U.S.) supporters that could only foster divisions, resistance and, finally, the installation of a repressive apparatus.

Indeed all three countries were subjected to strong, military-backed governments as a means of maintaining social power relations even as varying sectors struggled to maintain or transform the economy. El Salvador increasingly came under governmental-military control from the 1870s on, and, from 1913 to 1927, under the rule of the Meléndez-Quiñones family. The only counter to this was the emergence of a growing labor movement, including a strong Communist sector, which rose up in 1932 against the army's overthrow of the nation's freely elected government, only to be pulverized as the new Hernández Martínez dictatorship came to power and solidified an anti-modernizing pro-coffee oligarchy dictatorship which enduring until 1944. It was then succeeded by governments representing or opposing modernizing or liberalizing sectors, achieving no clear stability until entering into full crisis with the coup of the "military reformers" in 1979.

During the first part of the century, Guatemala was ruled by the Cabrera Estrada dictatorship, which presided over the growth of coffee production. But the key to modern conflicts is the dictatorship established by General Ubico (1931 -1944), which supported the coffee bourgeoisie by replacing debt peonage with a free (and continually impoverished) labor market, repressed labor and peasant organizations, and did everything in his power to appease the powerful United Fruit Company. As in the case of El Salvador, this dictatorship was overthrown by modernizing, reform forces in 1944 -in this case leading to a radical reforms and overall effort to remake the Guatemalan economy and social order as a whole. This effort, supported by new artisans, professionals, business people university students and industrial workers, and led by the governments of Arévalo and Arbenz, were subsequently overthrown by a CIA-led coup in 1954. The next thirty-five years were marked by strong military government controls and projects and waves of Ladino/Indian resistance, culminating in the intense crisis which began to develop especially in the highland areas between 1977 and 1980.

Finally, in Nicaragua, the traditional Liberal/Conservative struggle for power was overturned as a second U.S. intervention was set back, and as Sandino's resistance was followed by the installation of the U.S.-backed dictatorship of Anastacio Somoza García and his National Guard. Going through several transformations over the years, the Somoza dynasty survived and learned to live with the modernizing pressures which toppled Salvadoran and Guatemalan governments in the 1940s. However, under the third Somoza, the dictatorship was unable to appease the modernizing cotton sector and still satisfy its own narrow social base and so was unable to withstand the accumulating pressures which emerged in the late 1970s. With a weakened liberal tradition (and with the Liberal alternative in fact assassinated by the Somoza faction), Nicaragua had only one effective channel for the gathering consensus that Somocismo had to end. A divided bourgeoisie ended by backing a radical revolution which they hoped to control but which, until 1989, they were unable to control.

6. Efforts at Economic Integration and Common Market Formation

Without entering into all the reasons why the three countries emphasized most here experienced revolutionary upheavals, while Costa Rica, Panama, Belize and Honduras did not, we should note Torres-Rivas' frequent reminder that the upheavals were experienced by those countries which most benefited and advanced under the aegis of the Alliance for Progress. It was precisely these countries which most experienced the development of new middle and bourgeois sectors, as well as new groups of more advanced, proletarianized workers. Actually, the crises in these countries emerge as the immediate economic benefits seem to go into temporary decline (the price and debt crisis of the 1970s), and this would suggest that a shock to expectations and setbacks to the modernizing bourgeoisie, as well as the overall sense of setback felt by those sent upward, proletarianized, lupenized and radicalized by the processes spurred on by the Alliance are largely responsible for the upheavals which are central to our analysis. The repercussions of this period, even with the seemingly overwhelming setbacks suffered by the existing revolutionary forces of the three countries in the late 1960s, were to be felt in the subsequent decade and are directly tied to the revolutionary crisis.

Clearly the effort to develop the area-wide Common Market in the 1970s played a key role, so that the countries most deeply involved in the Market became the most revolutionary. The world economic crisis deflated the already low real wages of workers and drove each nation into a balance of payments dilemma that displaced and aggravated sectors of the middle and petty bourgeoisie and created a virtual alliance of disparate classes and class sectors all under attack by the new developments. But like conditions existed in many places without a revolutionary uprising occurring so that we are still left with the question: Why Nicaragua? Why Central America?

Part of the reason is to be found in the ideological contradictions fired by developmentalist strategies (a seeming justification for right wing hatred of such efforts). For example, we might readily see problems sponsored by AID and the International Monetary Fund as apparatuses of imperialist control and penetration. But if such programs send Central American students to foreign metropolitan centers where they integrate themselves with international left currents, then the apparatuses are in fact creating revolutionary intellectuals. Obviously the repressive functions of Central American dictatorships have themselves played such a role. But this role has been compounded by those structures established to mediate the dictatorship's force. So, in the sixties, the limited but real space opened for Central American universities and such influential projects as the publishing house EDUCA (the very programs developed to spur Central American modernization in tune with Common Market plans) contributed to the formation of an ideological front which would reach to and act upon the oppositions generated by economic crisis and political repression.

The displacement of rural workers and the growing marginalization of middle sector groups created a context for the breeding of new revolutionary groups in Central American churches and schools. The new revolutionaries could begin to identify with and elaborate variants of already existing nationalist and anti-imperialist cultural traditions, exemplified in such figures as Sandino and Farabundo Martí, but sustained through the generations and leading to the insurrectional processes which emerged in the late 1970s.

Racist and Euro-centric attitudes emerge with respect to the importation of black and then Chinese labor, but of course above all with respect to the Indian populations. So in 1894, debate rages over the question: What would be the most efficacious means to civilize the indigenous race, in the sense of teaching them a sense of progress and the habits of cultured people? Of course civilizing would mean providing the Indians an education adequate to and in harmony with the needs of their efficacious use in production. There would of course too be a concern with preserving and "protecting" their identity, so that they would thus (one can only assume) be preserved too as a workforce that could be called upon as distinct from the rest of the population. But as Ramírez notes, this concern for the indigenous population extended to the emergent urban *mestizo* masses. They were urged to work, to overcome antipathy and passivity, but not so as to fight for their rights or in any way to disturb or endanger the peaceful and lawful conduct of commerce or the potential tourist trade. "Should the Indian population and broader uneducated *mestizo* masses learn to read and write? What would they gain? Economic advantage, power over those who didn't learn, the ability to make trouble for productive landowners." In this context, then, "the dominant classes in the nineteenth century, imitators of metropolitan models, were unable to create a unified national culture, because such a development would clash with their economic and ideological interests. Even for themselves, their imitations of Europe were not strong or creative enough to evoke a national style of culture," because that would require a disseminating and promotional function, while the maintenance of their domination required the passivity of their servile population which mitigated against any serious liberal program of educational or cultural development. "We cannot even speak here of a... 'clash of cultures' [within given national territories]; for we have two general trends that barely converge: the dominating classes' imitation of the foreign and what we can call popular culture-a circumstantial...ensemble of elements that stem from oral transmission and thus [constitute a kind of] 'illiterature'" with pre-colonial roots, but subject to great transformations in various phases of colonial and post-colonial history (Ramírez: 42- 43).

From the point of Central America's entry into the world market, the area will become economically and politically subject to the U.S., and non-Spanish European, as well as U.S. cultural models (French positivism, social Darwinism, musical, artistic and literary forms, etc.) begin to impose themselves over previous colonial models (whether directly Spanish or Mexican, etc.) and establish basic modes of domination and (in the many instances of resistance) divergence. Central American cultural phenomena are to seen in relation to the determinations of dependence and their local elaboration on the part of dominant groups and those dominated, including those who, drawing on pre-colonial, colonial and/ or other models, seek to develop a fully oppositional culture.

As part of their effort to maintain and legitimize their rule, the oligarchs sought to establish institutional apparatuses which fostered democracy and free trade. Above all the "liberal" oligarchic reforms seek to "modernize" Central American states to serve the economic process by which the mainly rural economic base is consolidated into large readily cultivable economic units. They seek to legitimize their project by rejecting a local perspective and fostering a "universal," European model, which parallels their overall concern with the reception and consumption of finished products from the metropolis. The role of the ideologues is to legitimize this order. However, there are contradictions in the ideologues and their ideologies, just as there are problems with the rural peasants who balk at submitting to a process which dispossesses, uproots and impoverishes them. Even in its most developed trade centers, Central America was more backward than many parts of Latin America. The Central American economy could not sustain a highly specialized division of labor, so that professional intellectuals and poets were also politicians, bureaucrats, newspapermen, etc. Many poets emigrated to escape poverty and provincialism and develop a more cosmopolitan, universal perspective. The hegemonic ideological current of the period (paralleling political liberalism) was a watered down version of European positivism tailored to the "Junker route," though at times straining against it in terms of inconveniently modern conceptions and relations. Normative Central American positivism championed the myth of progress and science as standards to be achieved by a Central America intent on catching up with Europe and the U.S.

But the very ideologues who fostered the positivistic world view were often poets who found that world view too limiting and at times abhorrent to their creative work. Thus in their poetry, they mildly opposed certain aspects of the new order in the name of a higher, better world based on an idealization of the past as a time of harmony and beauty, or in the name of some future transcendence of the crassness, vulgarity and commercialization which came with the new imperialist relations.

As Sergio Ramírez puts it:

> *The inscription of Central America as a zone of monoculture in the concert of marginal territories incorporated in world capitalism through coffee, leads to two visible results with respect to the colonial model: the sudden access of European forms of artistic expression which, contained or retarded a long time behind the wall of incommunication, will be presented in synchronic form, to give a sense of anachronism to local forms, from which they can only separate themselves and transcend with great difficulty; and the ideological coloration emanating from the sense that the foundation of a culture incorporating modern values such as freedom and progress can only occur by means of Europe (52-53).*

The wealth of imported art forms animated by metropolitan ideology would come to Central America, with science and civilization in general along with commerce among its multitude of possible emulations and emanations. The imported forms of art, science, religion, politics, etc., were designed to show that Central Americans (that is, the elites) were progressing, that they were transcending the lethal atmosphere of the colony. This ideal can be seen in architecture and decorative art. But it stands out most in literature, in struggles over *costumbrismo* and modernism, "boom" narrative and testimonial discourse, "exteriorist" poetry and the "high art of metaphor."

According to Ramírez, the first manifestations of a literary art of importance in Central America emerge in the nineteenth century; there were only isolated cases of literary creators, many of them from Guatemala, such as Antonio José Irrisari (1786-1868) and the romantic poet, José Batres Montúfar (1809-1844). More than anything else, the colony had produced very orthodox religious poetry, mainly written in Latin; and the post-independence plagued by civil wars consumed writers in proclamations and discourses, newspapers and pamphlets, that they never freed themselves from the rhetorical norms of the epoch, or made rethõric approach poetry.

In effect, two literary systems developed, *costumbrismo* and *modernismo*, both of which drew from and variously opposed the positivistic current which dominated the historical writing and journalism of the period. These two seemingly contradictory tendencies (one highly urban and imaginative, the other at least superficially rural and realistic) both draw upon European cultural ideals. The lack of dynamism in Central American society, even in its transition in relation to world economy, means that the two currents are installed as public taste and official art. Darío's modernism will pursue the European ideal of transcendence as an instrument of formal rupture; and to achieve it, Darío has to stand apart from the circumstance of Central American literature, to which he will return with his instrumentality now elaborated. Narrative literature which turns inward toward national and regional perspectives will affirm itself in this very ideal and in a cultist pretension before going into decline.

The first *costumbrista* narration belongs to the final period of the work of the Guatemalan Milla, who was the founder of modern Central American narrative (historical novels, *costumbrista* novels, etc.), and also the first Central American historian of the century. The Costa Ricans, Manuel González Zeledón (Magón) and Aquileo Echeverría, developed *costumbrismo* in poetry as well as prose. In these writers, the same ideology dominates: it is the conception of a rural world as a foreign and romantic territory, kingdom of happiness which as a tropical Arcadia has no complications and should not disappear. This image is so executed at times with the very vital absence that we would expect in a Harlequin romance, so bookish is the Arcadia presented. The Central American reality closest to the image is Costa Rica's, a fact which helps explain the writers mentioned, as well as the *costumbrista* playwright Thomas Francis Meagher. As Ramírez explains it, *costumbrismo* saw the countryside from the balcony, that is with great cultural distance, as a quaint and sometimes savage space, where there is a real question as to whether the people can really enter civilization and (in sentimental versions) whether they should. In 1894, a polemic began in San José over the kind of literature the Central American writer should write: one that refers to local (meaning peasant) or national themes or one "that sought a more transcendent perspective." As Ricardo Guardia put it, "nationalism doesn't attract me... My humble opinion is that our people are deprived of all poetry and originality that could give birth even to a poor artistic sensation (cf. Castro Rawson 1966: 112).

But on both sides of the debate, the terms are European. Because even those who support *costumbrismo* do so from the perspective of a Chateaubriand, a master of appropriating vernacular as art, of forging artistic material out of what is not generally considered promising. The impulse toward idealized worlds transcending the limits of Central American provincial life, which emerges in modernism is ever paralleled by the fascination with localism, an insistence on finding the universal in the limits of a milieu. To the degree that writers throw off the European artifices of *costumbrismo*, they develop a genuine regionalism, as in the Salvadoran writer Salarrué, or the Nicaraguan Adolfo Calero Orozco, to the point in fact, that they lay the basis for a Central American narrative discourse that is genuinely rich and complete.

But apparently the detour of modernism was necessary to the movement from *costumbrismo* toward a fully developed Central American literary art in prose as well as poetry. In effect, *costumbrismo* is a more or less direct expression of oligarchic interests, which colonizes, falsifies and stereotypes the national reality. *Modernismo* is a more complex and contradictory phenomenon. But what is important to note here, by way of anticipation, is how, during and after the age of the *modernistas* and post-*modernistas*, as Central America began to enter into the crisis of the Depression, new modes of oppositional ideologies developed which went far beyond the tired European-based dichotomies of liberalism and conservativism to project more radical solutions and possibilities. So, Darío integrated elements of theosophy, Bergsonian creativism and other counter-positivistic motives into his own writing and the overall modernist system. So various modes of Rodó's elitist anti-Anglicism and distinct anti-imperialist, nationalist, and indigenist philosophies develop in the area. So, as El Salvador proletarianizes, a political activist like Farabundo Martí brings dimensions of third international Marxism into the heart of the Salvadoran labor movement. So, instead of imbibing no more than what Ramírez once referred to as "cheap theosophy that went running frenetically throughout Latin America in those days," (Ramírez: 75). Sandino combined various modes of anarcho-syndicalist communist thought with dimensions of theosophy, spiritism and spiritualism that provided a multi-valent basis for the various sectors who would later claim his name (cf. Hodges 1986). And so, other radical modes of thought, including early forms of Christian socialism and distinct forms of corporate Fascism (e.g., in the Nicaraguan vanguardists) became part of the intellectual atmosphere corresponding to depression and dictatorship. Only as these ideas take more modern form in the 1950s and 60s, only after the Cuban Revolution and the Medellín conference bring forth new radical modes Marxist and religious/socialist thought. Without question, U.S.AID projects directly tied to the Alliance for Progress seek to implant forms of developmental liberalism for the conformist, integrated intelligentsia, and forms of existentialist cynicism for those not so integrated and potentially dangerous. But these orientations had to compete with Che Guevara, Regis Debray and even such thinkers as Fanon, Marcuse and all the international superstars of the student rebellions of the 1960s in the formation of new left intellectual patterns-patterns which took on their own contours in the contentious centers of Central American modernization.

Intellectual Life in Modern Central America

A. The Views of Rafael Helidoro Valle

Against a backdrop of indigenous and other ethnic questions that are crucial and often poorly seen in the Central American turf a sketch of the region's intellectual life, primarily Ladino, up to the present period would seem to be well in order. In the preface to his book of 1960, *Historia de las ideas contemporáneas en Centro América*, Honduran Rafael Helidoro Valle complains bitterly of the impoverished and fragmented atmosphere in which Central American intellectual life has developed:

> *The best intellectuals have been set back there, finding any echo or silenced by the mediocrity pervading the bureaucratic ambience in which they have had to live... Teachers who form generations have been lacking. Each regime establishes laws and regulations which make it difficult to carry out a well-planned cultural program, and the little that has survived they have achieved in archives and libraries that all too quickly disappear or that are in disorder or have fallen into rapacious hands, or have succumbed to the action of natural elements. (Valle, 1960: 8).*

Writing at the time of the Cuban Revolution, after the Guatemalan coup, but prior to the Alliance for Progress offensive that would pressure economic and intellectual changes, Valle is worth citing to achieve a view of the intellectual atmosphere of an area whose subsequent transformations would unsettle long-prevalent structural relations.[2] So he tells us:

> *One of the cruelest enemies of the man of ideas is the ambience, sometimes for the hostility of those governing who hate freedom of expression; others for their existing interests which make the development of ideas impossible or which frustrate the purposes of the thinkers and investigators to the point of making them emigrate in search of a more breathable atmosphere; others through poverty, taking account of the fact that many intellectuals fail to encounter a publisher, or even a hand that offers support, or a bureaucratic office that would permit them the indispensable time to devote calmly to their authentic vocation (Valle: 10-11).*

Valle speaks of the corruption, the nepotism and the personalism, etc. which determine who gets grants, scholarships and minimal jobs. He speaks of the poor quality of schools, book publishers-all the apparatuses and institutions necessary to produce a rich intellectual and cultural life for a people. Many Central Americans with intellectual pretensions or interests were forced to emigrate to develop and find an audience for their work. They sought breathable air and stimulus, or, as in the case of that exemplary Central American intellectual, Don Edelberto Torres, and so many radical intellectuals after him, political asylum. On the intellectual environment, Valle cites poet Juan Ramón Molina as suggesting that escapism into intellectual clouds or even suicide might constitute understandable responses to an environment characterized y "deaf aggression and indifference." (Molina, 1913: 123, cited in Valle: 12). And going back even a few years earlier, Valle cites the famous words of Darío:

> *Poor republics... It's hard to say that in that land, known only for its canal and its coffee, there is absolutely no air for the soul or life for the spirit. (Darío, 1909: 78, cited in Valle, 13)*

And, in the same vein, Valle cites Manuel José de Arce y Vallardes speaking of Central American intellectuals and writers as being

> *... suspended between heaven and earth in an obligatory state of doubtfulness having always had to choose between the virtue of the middle way or that of remaining in the clouds. And they can't even live in the clouds. Material urgencies continually reclaim them and the harshness of realities punishes the hypersensitivity of their spirit. Their immediate and natural reaction is flight, or climbing into a world of fantasy. But humans after all, they have not been given the wings of gods and the wax melts with the sun. (Arce y Vallardes, cited in ibid).*

All of these comments invoked by Valle may be summed up in the lapidary formula of Alfonso Orantes, referring specifically to his own country, but having application to much of Central America throughout much of its modern history: "The fate of the Guatemalan intellectual is this: burial. Or if not, prison. And if not, exile." (ibid.).[3]

It is indeed a commonplace to say that intellectual life in Central America has been impoverished, unstable and "underdeveloped." Traditionally promising intellectuals have without doubt been forced to leave the zone in order to develop in relation to foreign centers. In the midst of indigenous structural weaknesses, varying colonial and neo-colonial powers have penetrated, maintained, cultivated, and even created Central American educational and cultural apparatuses, to breed a conformist or developmentalist intellectual ambience tied to the needs and projects of the metropolis. The goal, certainly since the Alliance for Progress, has been to train a kind of buffer intelligentsia of technicians who keep the system going by mediating between dominant sectors tied to international capital and an illiterate and semi-literate mass which is the object of exploitation. An alien institutional grid has been imposed which degrades national or area culture and its own organic growth.

It is certainly true that Central American intellectuals have lived in circumstances hostile to intellectual production. The division of labor, the distribution of goods and services, and the overall evolving function of Central America in the world capitalist system have prevented the development of the institutional infrastructure necessary to the advancement of a coherent intellectual life. The repressive regimes necessary to maintain and extend the penetration of existing markets have left a very narrow marketplace for the exchange of ideas, to say nothing of the elaboration of systematic modes of specialized discourse needed for a genuinely developing and ample intellectual culture. In a narrow market flooded by foreign imports and with local elites imposing these imports as the models for internal consumption, it is very hard to transcend the cult of imitation and to achieve a synthesis which surmounts the contradictions posed against its realization.

Such a perspective as presented by Valle has scarcely anything new to tell us; it has been offered on all too many occasions. But when we articulate it, do we find it to be the whole truth?

Historical events of the past decade suggest that we must know where to look to find our ideas and our intellectuals in Central America, and that as in other underdeveloped areas we may not find these ideas in the same place as in the metropolitan centers. Indeed, even the word, "intellectual" needs a Central American valence, if not a redefinition. If there is a general synthesis of intellectual production in Central America, it finds its actualization (its authentic nexus of international and national concerns) not in a formal philosophical system nor in an ethical theory, but in a political and cultural frame fed by manifestos, tracts, letters, testimonials and memoirs, and above all by poetry, which takes its most recognized and controversial form in relation to the quintessential Central American revolutionary, Sandino.

The Nicaraguan revolution and the revolutionary crises in El Salvador and Guatemala, as well as the intense squabbles over the diverse ideological origins and projections related to these phenomena, imply a prior intellectual and cultural tradition. The reason why this tradition went so long without recognition is because metropolitan definitions of "intellectuals" and "intellectual production" were based on dominant models inapplicable to the uneven development of a dependent area with large-scale illiteracy and intellectual life centered on synthetic cultural forms and modes (notably poetry, song, and dance) tied to oral and popular traditions. In sum, it is to be expected that given the fragmented history of Central America, her intellectual life would be dominated not by the development of a conceptually rich milieu nor the technological thought proper to advanced social formations. The significant ideas and intellectual constructs in Central America have not developed in function of scientific studies or philosophical treatises. Even the positivist turn generated by nineteenth century oligarchic control hegemony produced feeble results, and the significant body of thought in Central America, the richest intellectual expression is found in oppositions to the metropolitan positivist system-in political writings of course, but above all in the poetry of those men, and increasingly, those women whose literary production, wittingly or not, became tied to the socio-economic and political structures dominating their oppressive and dependent societies. If talented people are unable to develop in technical and scientific areas, or if those meagerly developed areas are only inhabited by those willing to serve an oppressive political apparatus, then intellectual energies will be displaced to other realms. This is a way of saying that however cosmopolitan given intellectual expressions may appear, intellectual life of any lasting significance from the nineteenth century on has been very much tied to the question not of developing world scientific knowledge, but to the question of oppressed national cultures-the languages, rhythms, visions and dreams of mainly illiterate groups which escape from or react to forces of domination as they experience them in their daily lives.

The very fact of recent revolutionary movements, as well as the fact that so many groups with so many divergent historical projects came to identify with those projects and struggle in function of defining the nature of revolutionary ideology indicates that the intellectual achievement, that of forging complex ideological-cultural patterns of identification, was far deeper than has been formerly imagined.

The fact is that since colonial times and most specifically since the inroads of the modern world economy, an anti-imperialist and radical intellectual tradition had been developing. This tradition had been fed by diverse social classes and sectors with diversely contradictory ideological orientations, which achieved varying syntheses in Darío, Sandino, Farabundo Martí, liberation theology, and a whole series of ideologies and ideological strands which emerged in different times and places and among different sectors in Central America. Ever newer intellectual developments, often spurred on by exile to foreign left intellectual centers (Mexico, Vincennes or Nanterre, Havana, Moscow, etc.) led to more comprehensive theses, as foreign oppositional ideologies were recast in terms of indigenous currents to constitute new constructs. Finally, in the wake of the Cuban Revolution, the limited but real space opened for Central American universities and such influential projects as the publishing house, EDUCA (indeed many of the very programs pushed by AID and IMF to spur Central American modernization in tune with Common Market plans) served to promote an ideological front which could react to and act upon the oppositions generated by economic and political setbacks. The displacement of rural workers and of whole petty bourgeois sectors created a context in which new Church and university-bred radicals could forge a revolutionary orientation and élan.

Somehow, we must account for the fact that in such a sterile and difficult atmosphere of conformist education for elite sectors and illiteracy for large numbers, so many significant intellectual figures have appeared. Are they merely elitist exceptions tied to external forces, or are they somehow condensed expressions of a deep indigenous movement?

Is it false to speak on the one hand of a sterile, corrupt and thoroughly dominated environment for the development of intellectual life and on the other hand speak of so many important intellectual figures? Or is there a richer dialectical unity which explains the contradictions, a long hidden tradition by which through exile in one form or another, through distancing from the patterns of cultural and intellectual domination, certain Central Americans have forged a rich intellectual corpus which is simultaneously a force in the emergence of Central America's revolutionary conjuncture?

Clearly the majority of active, significant "standard intellectuals" in Central America have bourgeois or petty-bourgeois roots. Some came from conservative opposition-as children of the older oligarchs, embittered by an imperialist penetration that began marginalize and at times dispossess their families, turning them toward various forms of opposition to a given regime. Some are members of the ruling party who nevertheless feel that the current regime is betraying their party. Much of the significant opposition generally came from these two sectors. But in the 1950s, the basis for a swelling opposition came from petty-bourgeois backgrounds and had their main institutional ties with the universities in their home area or in other parts of the world. In general it may be observed that those intellectuals who eventually radicalized tended to be those whose intellectual activity was more tied to questions of culture than to those of "civilization" -i.e., those whose concern with a national culture is such that even if they start as reactionaries, their insertion in national life will leave them ultimately with no other way to realize their project than by identifying and joining with a growing revolutionary movement whose ultimate consequences might even threaten or negate their projects if they cannot at some point achieve hegemony over the movement.

The fact is that in Central America, the greatest number of intellectuals not directly and strictly tied to technocratic and technical areas and even many whose relation to production meant serving the existing regime in one way or another were gradually carried off in programs whose consequences went beyond their own subjective projects and came to imply participation in, collaboration with, or sympathy for organizations bent on revolution. And the fact too is that many of these people came to share in a counter-cultural sphere which gave great weight to the production and reception of literature and poetry which increasingly embodied a revolutionary valence.

There were of course writers and intellectuals in each of the Central American countries who were part of national and international apparatuses which are far from revolutionary. But even here we find contradictions and even rival apparatuses: those tied to repressive apparatuses; those in keeping with a developmentalist frame which would involve loosening the unproductive and opposition-generating stranglehold of a given regime, and those who while often dominated by the second frame, finally become disillusioned, break loose and veer toward a radical or even Marxist frame in response to their national problematic.

It would be an error to underplay the role of foreign religious institutions and universities in forging radicalized intellectuals. Darío, Asturias and Dalton are only three of countless examples of intellectuals who forged their creative armatures after the experience of realities quite different from those forged in their own nation. Cardenal and the Trappists of Kentucky, Eduardo Contreras and the Althusserians of Vincennes are only two recent examples. It is unquestionably true that many of the left intellectuals of Central America developed in the more advanced capitalist countries where there was space for left perspectives. And countries such as Mexico, Costa Rica and Venezuela, as centers of growing Latin American exile communities often provided the seedbed for Central American revolutionary currents. Of course, there were always those who were educated at West Point.

Crucial to an understanding of the radical intellectual tradition in Central America, in the context of our effort to understand ideological and cultural developments of dependent social formations is the emergence of bourgeois ideology in the nineteenth century both as a justification of bourgeois modernization projects, tied initially to the question of "Civilization and Barbary," and as a force in continuing liberation and then especially anti-interventionist and finally anti-imperialist orientations. The frame for such perspectives was bourgeois liberalism and positivism, subsequently attacked or valenced by varying forms of dialectical, spiritual, radical and clearly non-positivistic modes. (The roles of Bergson, Krause, etc., etc., are perhaps as important to explore as Proudhon, Marx and Sorrel).

In this sense, consciously or not, Sandino's thought is an early response to twentieth century-style imperialism and its cognate ideological justifications in positivistic orientations toward "scientific development" and "progress" that were central to questions of Latin America's future from the mid nineteenth century on. How strong this tradition was in Central America can be measured by analyzing several chapters of Valle's book. Francoise Perus discusses the reactionary implications of positivism as received in the more extremely underdeveloped Latin American countries such as those like Nicaragua in her controversial book on Darío (cf. Perus 1976). But she and also Donald Hodges fail to see the relation between the emergent dominant ideology and an intellectual rebellion that can find little space in science, technology and the like and will variously find expression, separately and in varying combinations (especially given the structural weaknesses and displacements, as well as the resulting historical frustrations, repressions and the like, which, as we noted, are to be expected in social formations deeply marked by combined and uneven development) in modes of mystical, spiritualistic and religious thought, political radicalism, including many curious right and left wing varieties (particular modes of Marxism just being some among them), and also varying sometimes explosive cultural forms which accompanied the developing revolutionary situation in Nicaragua.

Sandino's project and struggle, Sandino's idea of the nation is a response that the structure of intellectual life in Central America was one which left space for radical, revolutionary production, and that space was one shared with religion, poetry and other forms of cultural production. By the late 1970s, revolutionary activities almost simultaneously expressed the needs and will of large and largely uneducated social aggregates and those of a small but strategically important intelligentsia. This conjuncture marked the synthesis of varying radical intellectual traditions once thought to be in absolute contradiction, but now contributing conjointly to a moment of great potential consequences.

Indeed, behind the epiphenomena of the period in question were a series of socio-economic and political mutations that have their necessary complement in Central American intellectual life. Behind the Sandinista Revolution and other Central American movements was a deep anti-imperialist and nationalist tradition that for its political, social and ideological contradictions, found its conjunctural moment as the effects of the economic and political order brought about the displacement of peasant and also petty-bourgeois and other sectors whose interests can no longer find even a semblance of expression or satisfaction in the existing state of affairs. Behind the words and pronouncements of the leaders was a cultural tradition which achieved its cutting edge in revolutionary poetry and in other cultural manifestations of social sectors attempting to forge their own history. That ideological construct would reach its culmination in the 1970s and 1980s; it would virtually collapse in the 1990s.

From the 1970s to the Possible Point of Rupture

Probably the theory most generally applied (though in modified form) to the revolutionary conjuncture of the 1970s and beyond was that put forth by Jeffrey Paige (1975) just before that period emerged.

To follow Jan Flora's useful summary,

> *Paige espouses an agrarian base for revolution, and stresses export agricultural development and concurrent shifts from land to capital and wages, to argue that a system in which the principal source of wealth for agricultural non-cultivators is land is inherently unstable since it requires direct political control of labor rather than the exercise of economic control through the market place. Such systems are economically and technologically weak, and those controlling these systems perceive a zero-sum game involving repressive political and military force over agricultural workers. (Flora 1987:1)*[4]

The Central American crisis of the 1980s confirmed Paige's view of the importance of understanding the situation in export agriculture countries where great pressure comes to bear on the workers, who then become rebellious. But the crisis also points to limits. As Flora notes, the prime point to make is that the strong repressive apparatuses generated by export agriculture come to act upon not only the workers, but also many other social sectors, and on society as a whole-including those involved in or tied to the state structure, or those bourgeois and middle sectors (business people, but also teachers, service workers, students, etc.) who have reached a certain level of development under the repressive government, but who now are balking against its limits.

> *If control of production and export are in the hands of a domestic elite, a stronger state will develop than if export agriculture is controlled by foreign firms. In states in which domestically-controlled export agriculture is important, and particularly in which one crop is the dominant export (export monoculture), the relatively strong state will seek to maintain absolute political control. Such efforts are likely to lead to repression. Such repression can lead*

to rebellion or insurgency, particularly when the economic reality approaches a zero-sum situation (e.g., in times of shrinking export values) and/or when, with diversification of agricultural exports and growth of industrialization, shifting alliances develop among peasants, workers and new urban elites who have not been allowed a share of political power (Flora 1987: 1).

Flora specifies four generalizations on the "roots of Central American insurgency":

1) Insurgency is more likely to develop in countries where productive forces of capitalism have developed sufficiently so that there is a significant agrarian working class, at least an incipient industrial working class, and perhaps a threatened artisan sector.

2) The development of a domestic export-oriented agrarian oligarchy results in the strengthening of the role of the state, increasing its capacity for repressive action and for exclusion of the poorer classes from the political dialogue.

3) As the economy diversifies (particularly the export portion of the economy), interests of the different class fractions of the bourgeoisie diverge.

4) The growth of foreign controlled export agricultural production tends to keep the state weak, making it difficult to exclude the poorer classes from the political dialogue. (Flora: 36-38).

Above all, Flora argues that the form of export agriculture, in particular whether it is controlled domestically or by foreign firms and whether the dominant form of production is petty commodity (peasant smallholder) production or plantation agriculture, determines how strong the state becomes, which in turn has a defining impact on the development of revolutionary movements.

If an agrarian oligarchy, which derives its wealth from plantation agriculture, develops, it will attempt to suppress popular movements when it has control of the state apparatus. This exclusion of the poorer classes from the legitimate dialogue will, given appropriate conjunctural conditions, lead to insurgent movements. If they are to be successful, they must involve alliances among urban workers and marginal groups, peasants and/or rural proletariat and other parts of the bourgeoisie. [In societies dominated by agricultural export], I would argue... for the agrarian roots to... revolutionary activity, without

> *suggesting [as does Paige] that only an agrarian class is the revolutionary class. I would place more emphasis on a revolutionary situation and an alliance of classes or groups- rural and urban- in support of revolutionary change. (Flora: 36)*

This model would seem to apply to El Salvador and Guatemala with some precision; it would seem to explain Nicaragua, with its smaller peasant and field worker population, if we take to heart Flora's insistence on the social whole and see how a repressive state attempting to build an stronger export agriculture (but still attempting to satisfy its base and limit the expanding modernizing bourgeoisie) can inflame enough social sectors to make revolution possible. As Flora attempts to show the same model could go far to explain why Costa Rica and Honduras have not had revolutionary crises, the first because neither country has not been dominated by large-scale export agriculture and the second because its export agriculture has been in foreign hands, so that, for different reasons, neither country has had the structural situation which has been conducive to long-term powerful dictatorships (Honduras had Carías in the 30s, but found its way to a more participatory government form in the 40s), and thus, prior to the heavy U.S. intervention of the 1980s, had no structural basis for strong revolutionary movements.

Nevertheless, even in Flora's necessary modification of Paige the explanation would seem to be too narrow, objectivistic and mechanistic to get at all dynamics involved in the Central American processes. While the theory does place the Central American crises in global perspective, linking Central America to other third world struggles, especially during the increasing inflation and debt crises emerging from the early 1970s on, the theory is not fully adequate to what transpired in Central America (e.g., Indian/Ladino dynamics in Guatemala, the power of ARENA and the sectarian struggles within the Salvadoran left, the role of middle sectors and even supposed *lumpen* in the Nicaraguan revolution, etc.); nor does the theory fully explain why insurrections occurred in some countries fitting the bill, but not in others.

Here the perspective of Edelberto Torres Rivas is most useful, especially since it is Torres Rivas who Flora himself most follows as he points to how the crisis of the late 1970s is the result of the convergence of the interests and projects of the various social sectors proliferated but also left discontent by the economic growth and diversification spurred on in the 1960s. But Flora stops short of the stress Torres Rivas lays time and time again on the fact that the socio-economic and political roots of the crisis are not adequate to understanding what has happened in recent years. Instead, Torres Rivas, in harmony with post-Gramscian theorizations developed by such thinkers as Bourdieu and Laclau and Mouffe, consistently seeks an antidote to extreme objectivism, by a focus on the emergence of ideological and cultural spaces to which oppositional energies have been displaced and from which new revolutionary energies are engendered.[5]

In sum, Torres Rivas insists on the need to understand the state of consciousness of the social actors involved, the cultural and institutional patterns crucial to the emergence and subsequent development of this consciousness, and also the new and unforeseen "spaces" for the realization of the political. The questions of "political space" and consciousness Torres Rivas raises take us to matters which are fundamental to this study and which we must address. For our purposes, the question is the spaces of ideological and cultural processes in the development of the Central American crisis as it manifested itself in Guatemala, El Salvador and Nicaragua. What were these spaces in Central America and how were they realized? Let me schematize the historical and cultural development of the three countries in function of the theoretical orientation informing these pages.

The relation between economic and political factors suggested by Paige and Flora takes us to the kind of perspective first opened by Althusserian theory with respect to how economic structures may "position" politics as a "structure in domination." By the mid-70s, this perspective was already incorporated into advanced dependency and world systems theory analyses. So, seeing the crisis as the pivotal point between past capital formation and future socio-political crises, Cardosa and Faletto (1979: 32) note that the key to modern social formations depends on the variations that occurred with respect to the passage from the exploitation of development toward the exterior from the middle of the nineteenth century on. According to Cueva (1977), this situation conditioned the development of the countries in contention to the crisis caused by the Depression (the moment of transition). In countries where there was local control of the means of production, a dominant class with economic and social roots could maintain control; establish an internal market for the substitution of importations, etc. In enclave economies, where the means of production (mines and plantations) were controlled by foreign capital, the dominant class was by definition relatively inorganic-that is, it served as a political intermediary for an insulated sector of exporters, with few economic, political or social ramifications. In such cases characterized by an absence of diversification, the impact of the Depression was extremely sharp, while the bases for responding to the crisis were less resilient. Thus the consequences were more determinant. Again Cardoza and Faletto explain:

> *Where a certain degree of control by financial and commercial sectors had created new middle and urban classes, these classes established a significant presence in the relatively autonomous state apparatus. Where this hegemony*

> *did not exist-e.g., in the plantation economies [including states tending toward monoculture domination], the crisis of the depression resulted in a generation of dictators. The post-war trajectories of different Latin American countries were structured by these historical situations-i.e., by the forces capable of determining the new modes of organization, dependence, and oppression that may come to the fore. Such are the determinations of the means of production, with their consequences for the specificty of internal capital accumulation and the resulting state and class formation. Why does politics dominate these formations? The economy of exploitation is disproportionately subject to the external market; so the economic factor is absent from the social formation. And so, by default, politics (or the military apparatus) becomes dominant-the dominant class governs disproportionately through the mechanisms of its political relations with other classes, rather than through economic mechanisms which it doesn't control. Control and its reproduction depend on extra-economic matters. The capital which modulates the dominant classes independently of whoever controls it is merchant capital and so the social relations of production in the export sector tend to be non-capitalist (and almost feudal, at least apparently) in diverse ways. Political domination is a different matter. In the agricultural countries, the relations of production are reproduced largely by political and ideological forms rather than the economic forms. (Cardosa and Faletto 1979: 33)*

To put all of this in other, Althusserian terms, the weakness of the economic mode of production in Central America (the fact that its contradictions and inadequacies constantly threatened its continuing viability) created the necessity for the domination of the political structure (and specifically the repressive apparatus of the state) as the basis for the reproduction of the system. Lacking internal governmental strength, or even adequate, deep-rooted and long-lasting class consensus (capitalists fighting with each other) the system was maintained by an externally imposed and funded political police state as the structure in domination at least in Nicaraguan, Salvadoran and Guatemalan state formations. So, whenever the governmental/military state could not get adequate backing from sufficient internal sectors, there would be an appeal for external support to give strength to the political apparatus. When internal opposition became too strong for normative modes of external support, then extra-normative support (more direct intervention) might become necessary to avert or (as in the case of contra aid) counter revolutionary victory.

As the political structure imposed its heavy domination on all other structures, including the ideological and the cultural, so a politics of opposition became the basic counterweight. And almost all significant and effective modes of political opposition, no matter what form they might take (Marxist, populist, religious, liberal, etc.), tended toward becoming macro-structural and totalistic-bringing together all major modes of opposition in an all-out struggle for control of the nation, for an end to the political regime and the socio-economic and ideological structures it sustained.

Here we find the place for such Althusserian concepts as "displacement," "condensation" and "over-determination," especially as they come into play in the neo-Gramscian and Laclau-Mouffean terms which return us to the question of "spaces of opposition," suggested by Torres Rivas. So repressed political energies condense in ideology and literature until they re-emerge in active opposition the nature, time and place of which can rarely be reduced to the economic and political contexts which gave them their potential force. So, the contours of the opposition at each stage of struggle were largely determined by a combination of residual and emergent cultural and ideological dimensions whose resultant character was conditioned by (but also conditioned) the status of the struggle itself. Prior stages of struggle and the ideological and cultural forms which crystallized provided reserves that could be drawn upon in newer stages. And when direct phases of extreme, repressive dictatorship blocked political and military modes of opposition, the spheres of ideology and culture tended to radicalize even as they brought together a wider range of disparate forces and tended to grow all the more powerful.

In varying degrees, in each of our three countries to experience revolutionary convulsions, an ideological macrostructure emerged that could encompass the various modes of opposition to the repressive regimes. The clearest and most extensive instances were Sandinismo, liberation theology and accumulative de-sectarianizing tendencies among Marxist-Leninist organizations. But as these macrostructures were elaborated over the years, and as they took on ever broader and more inclusive form in the 1950s and beyond, as the dictatorships intensified and reasserted their control through the Alliance for Progress and other mechanisms, political and ideological opposition grew and was often displaced to the cultural realm, where political and ideological perspectives could find new articulation. In this realm, dictatorship meant the imposition of commoditization and alien metropolitan forms on more indigenous cultural patterns. For the middle sector intelligentsia, this meant an inclination toward literature than toward other forms of intellectual pursuit and to a kind of literature that for the sake of its very right to aesthetic integrity, for its very right to relative autonomy, had to champion human and social values that implicitly and more and more explicitly had to be political. This is not to say that all cultural modes became completely conditioned by the political context; but the fact that powerful dictatorial apparatuses affected all cultural production meant that most overt and influential cultural expressions (those stemming from the rising middle sectors and their "organic intellectuals") become the most politicized. Furthermore, the economic and cultural life of the area was deeply marked by the lack of a developed infrastructure, especially in the crucial period after the emergence of the dictators in the 1930s.

There were no clear signs in the early 1970s of what was to come. Throughout the decade the ruling sectors grew weaker and less able to control popular forces without illegitimate power and force. The decade began with a sense of defeat for popular forces that had developed throughout the 1960s. The Guatemalan guerrilla was almost completely dismantled and would have to start all over again; the military had assumed direct control of the state to prevent a return of reformist rule. In 1972, in El Salvador, a reformist coalition won the election, only to be turned out by the military which reasserts its power with greater force than in the previous years. In Nicaragua, the *Frente Sandinista* had been set back severely, and the Conservative opposition had signed a pact with Somoza in 1971. Only the socio-economic transformations brought about by the earthquake of 1972 would begin to galvanize a growing massive opposition which would eventually have no other recourse but to armed struggle under Sandinista leadership. Only in Costa Rica was there a relatively successful reformist opposition in the government of Figueres (1970-74), and the formula "democratic reconstitution and development" showed great promise. In Honduras the military was seen as defending popular interests against the stronger Salvadoran invaders, and so a dynamic peasant movement was structured in relation to "a reformist space" which could not last for long (since economic needs could not realistically be met under the existing structure), but which would not reach its logical conclusion because the crisis in neighboring countries would lead to the militarization and social restructuring of the entire area.

According to Torres Rivas (1983b), the crises which emerged resulted from a large process of disequilibria and problems created by economic growth and unfulfilled needs and expectations deriving there from, and especially from repeatedly disappointed vindications, violated rights-in sum by pacific and legal social and political struggles made illegal and repressed by the state. In the 1970s, the Central American bourgeoisie renounced once more any search for national consensus in relation to accumulating problems and opted once more for a military dictatorship which, in spite of sometime democratic trappings, fundamentally constituted a form of state terrorism.

The local bourgeoisie and international capital were unable to resolve the social and political problems created by the type of economic growth they had championed. But if this reality (and the resort to military force as a resolution) has been a constant of recent history, why should we see it as a situation of crisis?

The reason was the "autonomous eruption of the popular masses into the political scene," and their willingness to resort to the most violent means to meet their needs. The masses can include religious sectors, peasants and street urchins in Nicaragua; they can include Quiche Indians in Guatemala. What is important is that the economic processes fostered y Central American Economic integration produced a situation of growth and rising expectations, displacements and transformations which in relation to persisting and reinforced dictatorial rule and intra-bourgeois schisms, led to revolutionary upheavals in the late 1970s in three Central American countries. The equilibrium maintaining the socio-political structure could not hold. The repressive governments were pushed to reinforce even more repression; the dissenting middle sectors merged their concerns with groups directly representing more popular sectors. By the late 1970s, a radical polarization had developed in which violent repression was met by those ever more keyed to violent revolution. The emerging political crisis of ungovernability appeared to be a rejection of continuity the sufficient objective cause of which was the eruption of subaltern sectors whose political practice broke all possibilities of contention, including state terrorism, and led to a "collective impatience" which was seen by the ruling classes as a "great popular disobedience." Clearly this situation was not necessarily revolutionary. Even if bourgeois power were divided or weakened, everything depended on the organization of the dominated sectors. The crisis, however, was indeed total, in that it was produced in the space where the ruling classes constructed and executed their direction of society.

The power of the military in this period was an institutional materialization of the crisis because it meant that the governments had seen themselves obliged to forego democratic pretenses (only with U.S. intervention would the governments seek out democratic facade once again in El Salvador and Guatemala). The extreme form of repression, the killings, massacres, etc. that took place in the late 1970s and especially in 1979-81, were indications of a critical rupture which apparently only foreign intervention prevents. The rupture marked the end of previous (though not new) reformist illusions, of earlier forms of political organization of the dominant classes; furthermore, the rupture pointed to a new combination of forms of struggle, the discovery of new places to make politics. All of this projected from the present of that time to a potentially different future-this of course depending on the international context and the way the forces of intervention might impact the development of the area. (Torres Rivas, in Diskin: 29)

Central America in the 1980s was affected not only by a significant economic crisis, which had diverse effects in the countries of the region, but also by political processes that represented possible historic ruptures. After the triumph of the Sandinista revolution, Central America could not remain the same. The collapse of the Somoza dictatorship was less important than the total systematic crisis that its fall introduced into the core of Nicaraguan society, a result that undoubtedly obeyed structural factors found in the way capitalism functions in the region.

The profound political crisis in El Salvador -with all the signs of civil war- and the politico-social breakdown affecting Guatemala for years were factors that cannot remain outside analysis. We are dealing with national processes in which what was being questioned was not a matter of the replacement of one arbitrary and incompetent military dictator by another-or by the emergence of democratically elected "centrists" who must sooner or later turn right and accept the military-dictated parameters or fall. In sum, in the countries considered here, it was the whole system that was being challenged as a system of domination, incapable of resolving the elementary problems of living together in a civilized way but also, perhaps, incapable of achieving any easy "revolutionary" solution as well. The political crisis being expressed in state terrorism and in revolutionary struggle represented a total confrontation that each day came more and more to resemble that contradiction between the state, in the hands of an armed minority, and the nation, represented by millions of workers, and peasants, and other social sectors.

Whatever the perspective used, it is impossible to keep from thinking that the problems posted for economic growth and the political crisis that was violently disturbing the life of several of the region's countries were placing Central America at the most difficult crossroads in its history (Torres-Rivas in Diskin: 29-30).

Some Further Reflections on "The Indian Question" and Other Ethnic Dimensions

There has been no unity of views on the part of the Central American Ladino intelligentsia with respect to the "Indian question." In this regard, matters related to Guatemalan indigenous identity generally take center-stage in Central Americanist discussions, in spite of the fact of a great diversity of non-Mayan indigenous groups still existent throughout the Central American area. Indeed as Arturo Arias notes:

> *When we speak of indigenous groups in the Central American context, we run into [a]... conundrum: in Guatemala alone there are 22 different Maya groups, and their own rivalries can be fierce. El Salvador has Lencas and Pipiles who are Nahuatl speakers and, by extension, not descendants of the Maya; thus, Maya history does not apply to them. Nicaragua has Miskitos and Ramas, who are not Maya either. Costa Rica had the Chiriqui, Chorotega and Chibcha, who were culturally closer to the Incas and related to the Rama of Nicaragua. Panama has the Kuna of San Blas. Though Mayas are clearly the largest indigenous population in Central America (close to 6 million at present), the most powerful economically, and have come the closest to asserting their own rights and even dreaming of their own nation-state in recent years, their experience is not shared by other groups. Thus, when speaking of Central American indigenous groups, we also run the risk of homogenizing their identity. (Arias 2003: 170).*

Taking this overall perspective into account, my discussion here nevertheless concentrates on the Maya Indians as the largest and most studied ensemble of indigenous groups in the Central American area. In this regard, we face a long, complex history of claims and counter-claims.

Reflecting their trade union base, Guatemalan Communist Party intellectuals looked to ladino field workers and the urban working class as the basis for their support. Other left and liberal intellectuals roughly following perspectives laid out by Mariátegui have argued that the separation of an Indian and ladino peasantry was a colonial inheritance, and that the future development of the country rested on processes of land and social reform tied to processes of acculturation, or Indian-ladino *mestizaje*, which would result in the Indians becoming part of a modern multiethnic proletariat that struggles for its rights and emancipation as such. Severo Martínez Peláez, in his now-classic work, *La patria del criollo* (1971), argued that indeed even the existence of groups defined as "Indians" was largely a survival of feudal arrangements implanted by the Spanish colony and reinforced by the developing agro-export economy, so that therefore Indian-ladino differences were purely ones of imposed ideology and culture.[6]

A special, somewhat quirky variant in the class-ethnicity debate in Guatemala emerges in the exaggerated, over-polemical postures of sociologist Humberto Flores Alvarado, in his critique (1968, revised 1973) of the positions with respect to Indian ladinization or cultural *mestizaje* developed by U.S.-based social scientist Richard Newbold Adams (1956). Flores Alvarado coined the term *adamscismo* to characterize Adams's theories as an imperialist construct that obliterates class analysis in function of an ethnic- centered orientation positing the essential polarities of Guatemalan social organization in function of the existence of two social groups (Indians and Ladinos) whose future unity is to be found in a process of ladinization within the framework of modernization theory postulates. In making his case Flores Alvarado further argues that *adamscismo* drew on and indeed replicated the earlier views of Mario Monteforte Toledo, Ricardo Falla, and (implicitly) Miguel Angel Asturias and Luis Cardoza y Aragón as well. In this sense, Flores Alvarado would seem to represent a radical version of Martínez Peláez's position, although one which even seemed to deny the Indian question as an ideological mediation worth consideration.

The criticisms of such positions grew among left historians and sociologists in the 1960s and 1970s (cf. C.F.S. Cardoso 1972). Julio Castellanos Cambranes (1977) showed how Severo Martinez's thesis about the situation of Indians in what he characterizes as the period of "colonial feudalism" is seriously flawed by what leading Guatemalan historian Julio Pinto Soria had characterized as "a mechanistic conception of Guatemala's history, that emerges in the static and undialectical form in which he portrays the development of the relations of production in Guatemalan agriculture" (Pinto Soria 1993).

As Castellanos Cambranes's major work (1985) shows, Martínez Peláez imputes Indian domination so completely to the colony that he fails to recognize that the colony helped to preserve as well as transform Indian identity, and that the real effort to obliterate Indian "otherness" was a nineteenth-century Liberal modernization project. Hence, Martínez fails to understand Indian support for Conservatives. Like most "old Marxist" thinkers, and even those breaking with orthodoxy (the parallel would be Roque Dalton's historiography in El Salvador; cf. Zimmerman, ed. 1985), Martínez holds onto a mechanical and linear stage theory of history that causes him to overvalue nineteenth-century Liberals as forerunners of future progressive movements. This leads to the question raised by some Guatemalan "New Left" historians of the 1970s and subaltern theorists of recent years: Is Liberalism's treatment of the Indians as objects the forerunner of the problems facing Marxist, as well as capitalist, modernization projects?

Influenced by dependency theory and the emerging critique of Eurocentrism and modernization assumptions in the social sciences, the most representative New Leftists, Jean-Loop Herbert and Carlos Guzmán Böckler, argued for an "ethnic" perspective which emphasized indigenous cultural specificity, difference, and resistance, insisting that the Indian question could not be reduced to class categories and rejecting both modernization and transculturation models.[7] There is no question but that the new perspective had a strong influence on the strategy of the armed struggle in the late 1970s.[8] However, at times it may well be considered as simply another polarization that fails to put matters in an adequate light. José Mejía schematizes the opposition involved: for Martínez Peláez, "the

Indian doesn't exist"; for Guzmán Böckler, "only the Indian exists" (Mejía 1970, 10-11).[9]

In the light of growing signs of Indian resistance (as well as the criticism he had received), Martínez Peláez (1973), without surrendering his previous position, sought to modify and deepen it by a study of indigenous rebellions and resistance patterns throughout the centuries. And for his part, Arturo Arias (in Camacho and Menjívar 1985: 118) was to modify his views, affirming that the indigenous population had become crucial to the future of the revolutionary movement, but warning also that an overemphasis on ethnic identity and separatism-representing the interests of rich and middle income Indian producers and encouraged by anthropologists and agencies and programs linked in the last instance to U.S. counterinsurgency policy-may constitute also a danger to the revolutionary movement, as in the case of the CIA's manipulation of the *Miskito* autonomy movement in Nicaragua.[10] Nevertheless, with respect to contemporary left critique of class reductionism, the ethnic issue still remains. Thus, in what is perhaps the most striking critique of the issue, Carol Smith notes that "if Marxism is to become truly the theory of liberation in Latin America it must break free of the dogmatism that reduces age-old cultures of resistance and ethnic identity to mere epiphenomena [of]... objectivized class categories" (1987, 217).

In an article with Jeff Boyer (1987), Smith argues that ethnic formations, as they developed in Guatemala, significantly undercut and question purely international or local economic and class considerations; so, in a prime instance for this essay, Paige's dependency theory view (1975), that "revolutions are most likely to occur in capitalist export economies, where conflict centers on ownership of the productive resource (land) such that reformist solutions are not possible to either...seasonal plantation workers who lack land...or plantation owners who monopolize the land," is shown as unable to withstand the test of concrete circumstances (Smith and Boyer 1987, 209-10).

Smith's views achieve their richest articulation in the book she edited, *Guatemalan Indians and the State* (1990). Here she points to Guatemala's enormous diversity, which she sees as "a long-standing phenomenon, a result of differences in pre-Hispanic heritage, or various and changing economic options, and of historical experience" (1990, 18); and she goes so far as to suggest that the common pattern of community identification feeds cultural diversity (enforcing differences of dialect, dress and custom), which "has been a protection against state power."

> *What might be an attractive state agenda in one area is almost certainly unattractive in another, so the Guatemalan state has rarely been able to persuade Indians to follow any general state policy. Thus, out of diversity comes*

> *unity: what Indian communities generally share is their tradition of acting as corporate units in political struggles with the state-despite the fact that they may have different economic and political reasons for those struggles... While the Guatemalan state has almost always acted against all Indians as a class, Indians have rarely acted as a self-conscious class (i.e., a united political group), more often reacting to their oppression as separate communities. At the same time, economic conditions in the western highlands, from the turn of the century to the present, have created the conditions for class differentiation among Indians, even among Indians from the same community... Why, under these conditions, does a sense of community identity remain strong among most highland Indians, suppressing the expression of class interests in these communities and preventing class unity between Indians and non-Indians...? [ibid., 18-19]*

Seeking an adequate theoretical model to answer her questions, Smith, like many other anthropologists, has turned to the conception of "the closed corporate peasant community" introduced by Eric Wolf in 1957 and refined and elaborated over the years. According to Wolf, Indian identity is seen as rooted in a *municipio*-based and land-based "sense of community" which in fact has suppressed pan-Indian, tribal, political, or class identifications while enabling indigenous peoples to maintain strong bonds with their community and thus survive as Indians in the face of centuries of colonialism and encroachment.

To be sure, Wolf's initial conception does not apply well to Guatemala's seventeenth century, nor to this one. Wolf did not deal with peasants who were also wage laborers, not to speak of artisans and petty merchants, nor with Indians whose labor and extended relations were transforming them into ladinos; nor could his view deal with the complex relations that emerged between the Indians, the colonial state, the landowners, the church, and other sectors. Wolf's concept emphasized closed micro-societies relatively unresponsive to economic and political pressures; and yet the Guatemalan model, persisting from colonial times and into the twentieth century, was based on state relations with, and possible control of, such pressures in function of other conflicting interests central to economic and political reproduction at global and state levels.

Nevertheless, while she stresses the Guatemalan differentials from Wolf's initial and subsequent interventions, Smith concurs generally with the corporate community model in arguing that both the repressive Guatemalan state in its role as an instrument coercing Indian consent to given land and labor relations, and the left attempting to win Indian support for a war against the state and those it serves, have seen the Indians as a social class, when in fact the core relation of Guatemalan history has been that between the power of the state and the Indian communities.

Rather than pan-Indian or class identifications, the Guatemalan Indians have identified more strongly with their local *municipios*. Indeed, strong community identity suppresses class expression, and Indians rarely act as a self-conscious class. They have resisted Spanish, Creole, and ladino political, economic, and cultural oppression; and while their supposed lack of class consciousness has been viewed as a negative force that must be overcome, they themselves have sensed, correctly, that it is precisely their strong bonds to their community that has allowed them to keep a separate Indian identity in the face of centuries of colonialism and encroachment.

Whether one variant or another of Wolf's initial formulation is evoked in relation to Guatemalan history, the essential thesis that municipal-based corporate Indian identifications are central to colonial and subsequent periods, seems virtually indisputable today. Furthermore, this perspective affects how we consider Indian exploitation and resistance, as well as Indian and ladino identifications, interrelations, and possible alliances. Nevertheless, no matter what precise perspective on the "indigenous question" is found to be the most adequate, still, clearly no theoretical frame worth considering with respect to Guatemala and Central America as a whole can negate the existence, or avoid conceptualizing crucial characteristics, of the Indian population, no matter how transformed their identity by forces of domination and class stratification, or by hybridizing forces related to contemporary globalization processes. In effect, what has happened to the indigenous peoples and their cultures, however hybridized, and what the role of indigenous peoples might be in the future of Guatemala constitute a major preoccupation facing Central America and its researchers to this day.

Of course, it has been argued that Indian resistance functioned quite well during the colonial period to impact and at times redirect or reshape Spanish or Creole rule. By this count, colonial Creole hegemony was a matter that was indeed negotiated in the full Gramscian sense, to such a degree that on hearing of Indian demands placed on the Creole rulers, I was compelled to comment at a conference on the theme in Guatemala: "Those poor Creoles who had to deal with those Indians" ("Pobres los criollos que tenían que tratar con estos indios").

Finally, then, the point is not that the Indians were completely dominated; Martínez Peláez's view dangerously tends toward one-dimensionality in this regard. While anthropological studies such as those by Kay Warren (1998) and John Hawkins (1984) provide sophisticated versions of Indian subordination, still, as John Watanabe (1992) has noted in his recent book, the briefest historical overview reveals how through nearly five hundred years of colonial domination,

Indian customs, arts, and cultural values have been repositories of resistance even as they became modified to conform to or synchronize with that domination. In all the stages of conflict developing throughout the twentieth century, Watanabe argues, unevenly maintained dimensions of Mayan culture have persisted as the bases for any and all transformations.

But the danger of stressing Indian resistance is to romanticize it, to overinflate its efficacy. As often noted, much Indian opposition would be "retrogressive"-in function of often-divisive concessions and privileges achieved in a structure of domination. In spite of qualifications projected by James Scott and his followers, all recent Indian achievements of opposition and more radical resistance, including those of Rigoberta Menchú, the CUC, and so forth, have taken place within the context ultimately of hegemony-and it is the dialectical relation between hegemony and resistance within a Wolfian view of Gramscian negotiations that we can best understand the Indian situation through the centuries and down to our present day.

To be sure, figures such as David Stoll (1998) and Mario Roberto Morales (1998) raise important questions in this regard. With the qualifications noted and explored, however, the basic image still stands in its overall validity-the view that, super exploited and dispossessed over and over again, the indigenous population has suffered from high illiteracy, infant mortality, and alcoholism rates; it has been subject to cultural despoliation and commoditization; and the population has sought various modes of resistance. Repressed and all but crushed during the military regimes which have dominated this century, seriously considered on a national level only during the Revolutionary period of 1944-1954, the various Mayan peoples both accommodated and resisted in a multitude of spontaneous and systematic ways; however, it was only with the national crisis of the late 1970s that Indian opposition became a major force in Guatemala's revolutionary struggles, even if only for a brief period. Even if set back by the mid-1980s, at least sectors of the Indian population, especially through their articulation in new organizational forms, will be a key to future developments in the 1990s and beyond.

Finally, of course, "the Indian question," or questions of Indian identity, are only one major ethnic dimension among others, which include the role and place of Central American Caribbean populations, of Indian-African-Ladino and other mixed groups, of foreign enclave dwellers (Chinese, Germans, Spaniards, Cubans, U.S. citizens, etc.) and others in the constitution of regional identifications and contradictions, relations and conflicts. The core question of *mestizo* and Ladino identifications themselves (so important obviously for dominant cultural and intellectual patterns) is itself understudied as an ethnic phenomenon, with ideological, gender and other dimensions that are certainly essential to the study of Central American "high" culture as well as overall patterns of intellectual and social development.

The Place of Literature in the Past and Now

A. Poetry

Our consideration of Central American socio-economic, political, intellectual and cultural contexts has prepared us to consider the historical role of poetry and other literary or discursive forms and currents as they developed as dimensions of Central American insurrectional and post-insurrectional culture. We turn, then, to certain enigmas we have noted and must now confront and understand. First, while poetry has been a dominant mode of literate cultural production throughout Latin America and, it would seem, in every underdeveloped part of the world, in few places, even in Latin America, has poetry played such a dominant cultural role as in Central America. Second, the importance of poetry has not remained in the cultural sphere alone, but extends to a significant impact on the total social formation and onto the political realm in particular.

As John Beverley had noted, "Poetry has a different specific gravity in areas like Central America, which is the same as saying that it has a different class referent, a different relation to history" (1983: 129-130). And on this question, Alfonso Chase (1985: 3) asserts that an examination of Central American poetry as a whole proves the existence of a basic unity and coincidence among the diverse problems affecting the overall socio-geographic area and also the emergence of a common language by which area poets seek to portray and articulate these problems. Of course each country and region has its particular realities, its language, beliefs, etc.; but Chase points to how especially the work of contemporary poets demonstrates a common Central American framework for the thought and expression of difference.

> *Central America exists as a historic and social reality in the contemporary world. For this reason, a Central American literature exists centered... on the intellectual attitudes and artistic production stemming from the factors which draw together area writers. (Chase ibid.)*

Chase argues that the existence of this literature based on regional concerns brings new dimensions to universal literature as a whole. True, the global character of Central American socio-literary development... has still not been defined by researchers. But at the heart of this question of the special role and systemicity of Latin American poetry is the point on the close relation of writers and their writing to politics and political action-or, as Chase would have it, "the social value" of the poet and poetry "in the creation of a new world and of a new culture that... presents a new mode of seeing the world. In sum, he is concerned with the area-wide and global parameters defining "the writer's place in the transformation of the world" (Chase 1985: 4).

Central America proliferated a group of poets who, while focusing national struggles, nevertheless forged a region-wide mode of literary and cultural production which according to the variants generated by the concrete differences in each national poetry, came to represent an active front in the revolutionary struggle of the area. The emergence of this system had anticipatory moments even in the cosmopolitan modernism of Darío but it has its virtual "takeoff" in the vital, nationalistic, radical and sometimes even reactionary poets who emerge in the late 1920s in Nicaragua, El Salvador and Guatemala at the time of imposed dictatorship and emerging popular resistance. Here, we need to comment on the overall Central American importance of Darío and the transition away from him and his *modernista* aesthetic. Darío brought to Central American poetry cosmopolitan currents developing European and Latin American countries and thus helped to move the area's literary expression away from a stilted and rhetorical provincialism. According to the famous formulation by Mariátegui the cosmopolitization of what a narrow national perspective can be the first stage in the development of a national language and code that transcends democratic and national (that is, bourgeois) liberalism, towards a solution that is socialist. Thus, contrary to the thesis of most Marxist critics, who reduced Darío to an expression of the oligarchic order, the perspective suggested in the Sandinista Revolution placed him and his valence of modernism in function of a poetic system whose most positive values played an important role in the development of a national culture. While the oligarchs and the later dictatorships in Central America would attempt to use modernism as a justification for their own order, other aspects of modernism and Darío's work would be absorbed even by those poets and poetic traditions that will nominally oppose him in the formation of a new poetic system that will dominate Central America.

As Salvadoran poet Roberto Armijo puts it:

To speak of Central American poetry one must speak of Darío. In his work vibrates, in a mature and limpid realization, the renovating accent of contemporary poetry in Spanish. In his incessant effort to revolutionize our language and to approach unsuspected domains of our Hispanic identity, Darío prefigures the greatness and originality of Central American poetry. When we immerse ourselves in the transparency of his language, we sense the world which nutrified his expressive force; and in some of his most perfect pieces we can sense his preoccupation for with the social crisis through which he lived, the persistent presence of foreign powers and for with the selfishness of the oligarchic groups which have exercised absolute control over our peoples. The important point is to testify how the great poet, author of Cantos de Vida y Esperanza, expresses in his writing the outstanding traits and prefigures the directions that will animate afterwards the inheritors of his words (Cf. Armijo 1983: 7).

And speaking of the direction of Central American poetry after Darío, Sergio Ramírez notes,

Darío succeeds in creating his own universal American stamp, so that the pattern of valorization could be American for the first time...But those who follow Darío in attempting to bring the modernist revolution into the internal Central American cultural process tend to fetishize imagistic and sonoral qualities, developing a modernist poetry and even a prose which is all too "poetic," "literary," "bookish." Even Darío was able to recognize this and to stress the need for other dimensions to constitute a valid national culture. And indeed it would be outside of the dominant tendencies of the modernist revolution that poetry would constitute a major cultural force in Central America and that one of the area's most important cultural currents, that is, modern Nicaraguan poetry develops (Ramírez 1983: 57-59).

In effect, the important space that poetry was to map out for itself in Central America was to occur not in conformity with but in direct opposition to at least the active Central American modernist tradition as received from Darío. Thus, while the Nicaraguan *vanguardistas* will establish their own national poetry by attacking Darío, they have more continuity with him and modernism than they will admit to for several decades. Subsequent generations will realize this, and in the wake of the Sandinista Revolution, articles appear tracing the lineage between Darío and Martí, Darío and Sandino, Darío and Carlos Fonseca Amador. And the new *Ministerio de Cultura* will take on the task of etching out a

Darío who fully feeds into the formation of a drive against imperialism and for self-determination (cf. Darío 1983).

For the decades after Darío's death, Central American poets in Nicaragua, El Salvador and Guatemala elaborate a body of poetry which has intense connections with ever more intense political, social and specifically class struggles. These struggles have been important in the generation of what Iván Uriarte has described as a transformation in literary aesthetics and the development of a realistic aesthetic which changed the direction of poetry (and through this hegemonic mode, other forms of discourse as well) leading to a reinterpretation of national history and a new platform of historic action codified or conceptualized by Cardenal as *exteriorismo*, but constituting in effect a revolutionary poetic of regional as well as national significance.

According to Uriarte, there are three key moments in the Central American political struggle after Darío which condition subsequent developments, including those in literature. First, there is the guerrilla, anti-imperialist war of Sandino (1927-1934); second, the peasant insurrection of El Salvador in 1932; and third, there is the October Revolution in Guatemala (1944-1955). These three moments were not only important historical nodal points, they led also to ruptures in the existent poetic systems and sub-systems of the area; they led to the poetic system of *exteriorismo* which was to develop in the 1960's and that continues to rule in the area, finding its maximal expression in Otto Rene Castillo, Roque Dalton and Ernesto Cardenal. We will look at these three moments and their relation to the developing hegemony of a certain mode and system of political poetry as a force in Central America. But in doing so, we must realize that the matters involved cannot be understood according to strict chronology or strict national borders. Sandino's moment finds contradictory expression in the new *vanguardista* poetry of Nicaragua, but it also becomes the basis of a political poetry and a cultural/ideological force which affects poetic production throughout Central America. Local factors influence Ernesto Cardenal's own rupture with *vanguardismo*, but so do the Salvadoran and Guatemalan experiences, as they generate their own poets and as these poets influence not only Cardenal but the young Nicaraguan writers who, though influenced by the *vanguardistas* and Cardenal, then affect them. Without question, many of the younger poets were to be influenced by the poetic movement best known for Cardenal and summed up most adequately by the conjunction of *exteriorista* poetry and Sandinismo.

In the effort to apply general theory to the development of Central American poetry, we may elaborate upon Uriarte's view to posit the following stages of development out of the modernist frame established for Central American poetry at the turn of the century:

1) Nicaraguan *vanguardismo* in relation to Sandino's campaign;
2) El Salvador, 1932 and the early development of political poetry out of this conjuncture;
3) Guatemala, 1944-54 and the emergence of *la generación comprometida*
4) The emergence of El Salvador's *generación comprometida* and *anti-somocista exteriorismo* in Nicaragua during the 1950s;
5) The radicalization of Central American poetic systems, with the full development of Guatemalan and Salvadoran left poetry and the emergence of *Frente Ventana*, Rugama, Ricardo Morales, a more revolutionary Cardenal and the young Solentiname poets in the 1960s and 1970s;
6) The full emergence of liberation theology, feminism, etc., in Central American combat poetry and in the poetry of Nicaragua's Reconstruction in the 1980s;
7) The growing domination of testimonio as current in poetry but as the primary force in Central American prose as a symptomatic characteristic of the crisis of the 1980s.
8) In the post-revolutionary period, a decline of political and testimonial dimensions and the re-emergence of metropolitan, "universalist" models for local literary production, increasingly affected by de-nationalizing and de-regionalizing processes of globalization and the effect of the global as opposed to local literary market-though also with patterns of regional assertion.

Here I should reiterate that I am not merely seeing literature as the expression of left revolutionary currents, but as an active force invoking past revolutionary impulses and as an active forger of new revolutionary trends. Our view is of literature and piety not as a mere reproducer but as an active producer. Dialectically, this involves us in the question of poetry as part of cultural consumption-i.e., as a phenomenon whose consumption (or "reception") takes on a productive role and becomes an active, cultural, ideological and political force. In this regard we must recognize that even texts whose intention and formal configuration are not revolutionary may feed into a cultural process which is predominantly insurrectional and which transforms the significance of those texts in terms of its own functionality. This is to say that the process of cultural and ideological reception has been so keyed and attuned that it is able to transmute texts in terms of the most radical or revolutionary interpretation of its images and impulses. But this receptive process (and the overall elaboration of a revolutionary "horizon of expectations" in the sense of Jauss [1974] with regard to poetry) feeds back on poetic production itself so that the poet may very easily create works whose implications are far more radical than the poet's own overt ideological position.

Thus we may perceive literature and ideology as relatively autonomous "modes of production." But we must recognize that in Central America the ultimate implications of these modes were subject to a cultural productive and receptive process which established their objectively functioning relation and significance. All of this was the result of the particular weak and dependent structure of Central American social formations; but it is also the result of the particular historical circumstance which those social formations have experienced in the course of their historical development.

In Central America, where productive differentiation never reached the degree common to the advanced countries, intellectual production is poorly developed and fails to constitute itself as a distinct region. Indigenous cultural modes struggle for hegemony with overt metropolitan intellectual impulses; new ideas and idea systems are largely displaced to the realm of culture and remade in function of hegemonic relations. Culture itself lacks autonomy and is under the constant pressure of political and ideological structures. Literature has little relative autonomy and yields to the cultural-political hegemony that pertains.

Obviously we are speaking of a reactive process, and the cultural sphere is one opposed to structures of overt socio-economic and political domination. We are dealing with the formation of a revolutionary counter-culture. Ultimately we witness the condensation of all tendencies and contradictions in the privileged cultural and literary mode, poetry. We see the politicization of a zone in which the recently forged hegemony of modernist aesthetics is threatened. We see structures of metaphoric and imaginative expressivity veering toward the metonymic and testimonial.

Like literature as a whole, poetry fails to achieve a significant degree of relative autonomy. Even modernism, the most extreme effort at autonomy, was a reaction against the inroads of social life and history into aesthetics and literature. Darío had to defend his pure modernist perspective at every turn; the armature of modernism broke down under the incursions of the imperial culture which it sought to elude. But modernism secured poetic expression as a dominant mode of cultural production.

The breakdown of the modernist system and the development of nationalist poetic movements in Central America resulted in the contradictory situation whereby the very basis of literary systemicity was dependent on the integration of poetry with national problematics. What were the specific conditions that enabled culture and ideology, as already hegemonized by poetry, to assume a major role in oppositional politicization in Central America? To answer this question most specifically, we must understand how in the 1930s, internal and international socio-economic contradictions led to the military dictatorships which "positioned" politics as a "structure in domination" to which all other dimensions of social and cultural life had to respond.

In sum, the Central American poetic mode of production secured its relative systemicity by the act of internalizing the conditions of form and content as pressured into place by a growing cultural resistance to military-political and imperialist hegemony, as the resistance crystallized in *sandinismo* and other national variants of anti-imperialist resistance in Central America. As noted, *sandinismo* and other forms of Central American radicalism served as cultural macrostructures, embodying popular anti-imperialist resistance throughout the area's history and projecting that resistance into the present historical moment. It thus had the capacity to transform itself constantly as each new present moment generated a reconstruction of the past in a new light; it was also able to absorb a wide variety of contradictory ideological positions in function of a popularly rooted cultural project that was forced by necessity to become political. This is not to say that all cultural modes became completely conditioned by the political context; but the fact that powerful dictatorial apparatuses affected all cultural production meant that most overt and influential cultural expressions (those stemming from the rising middle sectors and their "organic intellectuals") become the most politicized. It thus served the function of relating continuity to discontinuity, of bringing together the most disparate, class-based perceptions, visions and projects.

The degree to which pre-existing Central American poetic modes felt the pressure of this macro-structure and the degree to which this macro-structure ultimately became the basis of a new politically and culturally attuned poetic system that made subsystems of other poetic modes, was in some measure an indication of the force of revolutionary nationalism not only in poetry but the world view and possible active life of Central American peoples. The further fact that the politicization of the poetic system was in function of realistic, documentary and ultimately testimonial trends provided one of the means by which testimonio as a variant, anti-hegemonic discursive mode came to dominate not only prose but poetry and the entire literary-cultural system as a symptom of the crisis period of the 1980s. *Sandinismo* provided a broad, ideological, cultural and political basis for real dissatisfactions. Within its framework of *sandinismo*, many very distinct social class and sector projects could find a conjunctural unity. Clearly, after July, 1979, the future of Nicaragua would in many ways be in function of what groups and perspectives would achieve hegemony in defining and elaborating, or as it turned out, opposing *sandinismo*. One of the problems for El Salvador and Guatemala might well have been in the lack of a broad, indigenously rooted ideological "macro-structure" such as *sandinismo*. Even if, in varying degrees, they elaborated some equivalent-e.g., liberation theology-the question of the times was if groups representing broadly popular needs and aspirations could win hegemony, especially given international pressures and internal polarizations which, even more so after the Nicaraguan Revolution, tended to pervade and dominate the zone. And the question would also be what roles ideological, cultural and literary dimensions (including poetry and testimonial) would play in these national processes. In the end these dimensions failed as did the revolutionary processes they sought to represent. In the end, too critics such as those represented in the Latin American subaltern group came to question their capacity of representation.

It is clear, as Nicaso Urbina and Douglas Salamanca argued in 1991, that it is impossible to think of Central American poetry exclusively in function of revolutionary processes, although the was undoubtedly the case during the Central American and World wide historical conjuncture of the 1980s. In this sense Urbina is right to argue (1991: 914) that the post-insurrectional conjuncture implied the emergence of a new poetry in which repressed and obfuscated elements of an epoch of crisis and war now become visible and even hegemonic. Equally one could generalize the perspective of Salamanca with respect to the present and future of Nicaraguan poetry to the present and future of poetry in other Central American countries:

> *The era that begins now brings with it a return to the bitter reality of underdevelopment, in moments in which such small, dependent and super-indebted countries like Nicaragua seem less viable than ever..... Now, a new period of searching begins for literature, marked by the specter of precariousness and weekly illuminated by the hope of building democracy. One thing at least is for sure: the renovation of our letters will not emerge from* sandinista *stances, nor even less from rightwing sectors. The best hopes appear to be concentrated-once again-in a curious constellation constituted by dissidents, skeptics, renegades and apostates (Salamanca 1991: 858-59).*

Without a doubt, the social changes of the last several years come not only from the internal development of the countries in question. And, therefore, in spite of Salamanca's words, we can hope that the changes in poetry will not always, ever and without contradiction in sync with rhythms of history that will come so conditioned by the exterior World-as some recent experiences tell us, it is easier to change the socio-economic and political structures of a country than change its cultural, ideological and discursive practices. It is hoped, therefore that for good or bad, Central American poetry will continue as an expression of the events and struggles for which the writers and the most popular and widest sectors that, at least certain of the poets will try to represent.

B. Central American Novelistic Discourse since 1989

The novel developed in Central America as the area became integrated as a periphery in the world economy. Romantic and custombrista novelists, modernista and vanguardista novelists developed in each country, each seeking to reach an audience inside and outside of national borders. In Guatemala, there were so many writers prior and subsequent to Asturias that Seymour Menton could write about a virtual novelistic system in which Asturias was just the most significant representative of a group that included Montforte Toledo and culminated in the 1980s with the writing of Arturo Arias, Mario Roberto Morales and many others (cf. Menton 1985). El Salvador featured novels by Roque Dalton, Manlio Argueta, Claribel Alegría and others; Nicaragua gave us novelists like Lisandro Chávez Alfaro, Sergio Ramírez and Gioconda Belli.[11]

Where is Central American postwar and contemporary novelistic fiction in the new context in which we live? First, we can follow Arturo Arias in an article written from my book with Michael Piazza, *New World [Dis]orders and Peripheral Strains* (1998)-that the new time in the history of the zone changed also the symbolic framework of the Central American subject. Narrative discourses of the region are articulated as varied expressions and reactions to the processes of neo-liberalism, supposed democratization and globalization. In fact, the old represetations of social processes are substituted by new signs which evoke the imaginary concept of "the social" -and in fact the Central American.

The new phase after 1989 is a fluid moment in which the very identity of Central American being, of the supposed third world subject, of the supposed postcolonial subject, has grown complicated. The supposed benefits of globalization are confused with a sense of disintegration, disorientation and disterritorialization in which the majority of all the goods and communications received in each nation have not been produced in their own territory, they don't emerge from their own relations of production; and they don't carry signs which tie them exclusively to a given national community.

Now with the events of the 1990s, Central America and its literature has "exited from [their prior] history." The area has stopped being a key point of conflict; and excepting an occaisonal 1980s-style massacre, an environmental disaster, or, at the discursive level, the intent to discredit the testimonio (and person) of Rigoberta Menchú, the area has dissappered from the news in the first world. This implies that the peace has brought even the countries of insurrection to the level of obscurity reached by Honduras, while Costa Rica, Panama and Belice have lived their modes of cosmopolitan modernization (including ecological, narco-capital and sexual tourism). In the 1980s, Central America succeeded, at an extremely high cost, in capturing the attention of the world because we live the last struggles on the state level against the forces of modernization, developmentalism and all the processes that involved the transnationalization of production and immigration. But already in the 90s and thereafter, the wars ended, we arrive at a situation of acceptance and conformity with the macro-processes that characterized the pre-insurrectional stages-but now poorer and even more apt to integrate themselves well within the globalizing system. Now, as in earlier times, Central America counts very little, and to few, in the global and literary as well as the economic sphere. Nevertheless, the cultural, literary and fictional legacy left by the Central American crisis is enormous, and the recognition of that great legacy is only beginning.

The takeoff point for 1980s narrative (the celebrated fictions by Sergio Ramírez, Gioconda Belli, Manlio Argueta, Claribel Alegría and Carmen Naranjo) is the revolutionary experience lived in the region. The novels by younger writers in the 90s and after are unknown outside and even inside the country and area of origen. The fictions of Rodrigo Rey Rosa from Guatemala, Rosario Aguilar from Nicaragua, Mario Carías from Honduras, Jacinta Escudos and Horacio Castellanos Moya from El Salvador and still others are outstanding; so too are the writiing of several new talents who live outside of the zone. There is a new indigenous literature in Guatemala; new Afro-Caribbean narrators who emerge in Belice, Panama and other places. And nevertheless if the Central American conjuncture implied the end of macro-narratives on social and literary levels, what then can we expect from the new conjunctures or the supposedly representative new forms in the new century and milenium? And in this context, critics point to the lack of readers, and the lack of knowledge and interest in the texts in the rest of Latin America and the world.

In the past, "formal literature" attempted to create a national cultural identity and discourse as a means of problematizing the nation-state and produce ideological consensus among key social sectors. Until very recently, this role was filled by the testimonial genre, while "formal literature" inclined toward subjective matters of the libido and the imaginary. Many texts represented a rupture with traditional novelistic form based on a rationalist cause/effect model, with its schemes derived from formal logia. Feminist and gay literature represents an ideological and at time formal rupture that defies traditional notions of the subject and the marginality of women, homosexuals and others. Parody and pastiche as employed in contemporary Central American novelistic practice suggest new approaches to the subjects now identified as key inflections of postmodernity in its peripheral-globalizing turn. The ludic projection-games with linguistic y fictional structures are crucial for the new literature, with dimensions derived from testimonial and other documental modes providing the bases for the literary structures that are complexly related to social happenings.

One has to consider the formal transformations and qualities that are symptomatic of struggles over modernization in Central America's fragile and vulnerable social formations.and the basis they provide for Central American literary work in the context of transnational processes globalization flows, providing thereby a model for considering postmodern literary developments elsewhere in Latin America and the postcolonial Third World.

The 1990s point to the beginning of a new period in Central American history. This new period can be dated from the electoral defeat of the Sandinistas in February of 1990. The end of the guerrilla cycle and of the utopian dream of revolution changed the symbolic framework of the Central American subject, and it redefined priorities, identities and cultural projects. Common sense indicates that this should have also changed this region's literary narrative. If narrative texts are symbolic systems of representation that generate "truth effects" through their discursive practices, it is evident that they register these subjective changes in the perception of beingness; and their study should enable us to explore transitions in identity as well as in ideology.

Traditionally, period changes in Central America have always been marked by stylistic changes in which the challenge is that of redefining the writer/reader relationship through transformations in reading practices. In that process, old-fashioned representations of reality are substituted by new verbal signs that evoke or allude to a new imaginary concept of "the social".

The end of the 20th century is a fluid moment, in which the very identity of being Central American, of being from the Third World, and of being a postcolonial subject, can get lost in the strong winds charged with acculturating connotations. As García Canclini puts it:

> *For the first time in history, in the second half of the Twentieth Century, the greater part of all goods and communications received in each nation have not been produced in their own territory, they do not emerge from their own particular relations of production, nor do they carry signs that link them exclusively to a national community. Rather, they have other bearings that indicate their belonging to a deterritorialized system. [1992]*

Given these parameters, we are forced to ask ourselves if this scenario changes Central American literature. Or does it change rather the critical gaze over Central American literature itself? After all, part of the First World's insertion in

Central America implies a reflection about the nature of the critical instruments themselves. The adoption of postcolonial or postmodern conceptual tools force the critic to embrace a broader definition of literary studies.

To this one has to add the problematic of a Central America that, with the signing of the peace accords in El Salvador, the electoral defeat of the Sandinistas, and the recent signing of peace terms in Guatemala, has "exited from history." That is, it has stopped being a source of conflict -and by extension, it has disappeared from the news- in the First World. That means that peace has brought these conflictive, dynamic and destructive countries to the level of obscurity acheived by Honduras, while Costa Rica lived its particular mode of cosmopolitan modernism so near and yet so far from the areas of primary conflict.

As Arias puts it, the Central American drama is precisely that it concerns absolutely no one when it does not disturb the sleep of any super power.

In the 1990s Central America managed, at a very high cost, to capture the world's attention because in Central America we saw the last Latin American state-level struggles against the forces of globalization and maquilas. But in the nineties, it would seem as if we had returned to the previous situation. As before the insurrectional period, Central America still matters very little, and to very few, in the cultural sphere.

However, the cultural heritage that the Central American crisis left us is enormous and its recognition is only beginning. What is more, many of the traits celebrated in the First World as postmodern were already present in Central American cultural production since at least the 1970s. However, an absence of critical recognition of this postmodern presence combined with a singularly poor regional critical tradition has prevented the acknowledgment of these facts.

Nonetheless, as with the narrative of the seventies and eighties, the starting point for its critical recognition is the revolutionary experience lived in the region during these years The nineties are just as forgettable for their literary production as they are for their transitions to democracy. When we observe the overall picture we only come across the rise of Rodrigo Rey Rosa from Guatemala, the last novel by Honduran Julio Escoto, *King of Sunrise: Dawn* (*Rey del albor: Madrugada*) and the gradual emergence of Rosario Aguilar from Nicaragua and Magda Zavala in Costa Rica. After all, the texts with which the very scarce Central American criticism delights itself at this moment and the conferences of Central American literatue -the fictional works by Sergio Ramírez, Gioconda Belli, Claribel Alegría, or Carmen Naranjo, or else testimonial narrative- were almost all produced in the previous decade. We keep waiting for "the great Mayan novel," "the great Afrocaribbean novel," etc.; and perhaps they will never arrive as novels but as something else: testimonial, popular theater - perhaps even some other form of a hybrid genre that arrives unexpectedly. And yet the fact is that postmodernity implies the end of master narratives on the social and specifically literary levels. So what kind of forms, what can we truly expect as we approach the new millennium? As Arias puts it:

> *For whom does the Central American novelist write? Do readers exist for such texts? In Central America, textuality emerges from within the margins of marginality. In this particular region of the world, discourse is not only marginal in relation to centers of world power, but it is even marginal in relation to the smaller centers of peripheral power. (Arias 1998: 178).*

What has been happening in Central America goes beyond the fatigue of militant writers who felt the need to write about something else in order to preserve their sanity. In the recent past, "formal literature" attempted to create a national cultural identity and discourse as a means of problematizing the nation-state and producing ideological consensus among key social sectors. For some years, this was being done by the testimonio, while so-called "formal" literature was displaced towards the libidinal space, towards the space of desire, where it articulates discourses that reoccupy subjectivity but without a totalizing effort, nor a consensual effort either. In the novels of Honduran Mario Carias or Roberto Quesada, we observe a rupture with traditional novelistic form based on the rationalist cause-and-effect model becomes a delirious negation of the Enlightenment heritage, and of its narrow demands for always operating within the schemes of formal logic. With the recent fiction of Gioconda Belli and Arias himself, among others, we find an ideological rupture that defies traditional notions of the subject and questions the marginality of women. Then too, among many traits one can mention, parody as employed by contemporary Central American literature suggests important prying into the hyper-real, schizoid conditions of human subjectivity, now openly identified as key inflections, or infections, of postmodernity and globalization processes. In sum, ludic projection and playing with linguistic and literary structures is basic to the new literature, with dimensions derived from testimonio and other documentary modes providing the basis for new literary structurations and new, complexly mediated relations with social being. At this juncture, it remains unclear where Central American novelistic discourse will go under the continuing and growing weight of globalazation.

c. *El Testimonio*

It is in the relation between literature and society/literature and other discourses or cultural modes where we can confront the quesiton of testimonio and forms influenced by testimonio in a post-boom/postmdern period when the emerging cognitive maps indicate the existence of social sectors whose conscience, not to say their "political unconscious," require expression and analysis.

As noted in relation to Latin American testimonio (chapter I), the form emerged in relation to political and social struggles, as well as their repression, during the period extending from the 1960s to 1989. And nowhere was this emergence clearer than in the case of Central America. Modern testimonio may have begun with Jose Roman's interview of Sandino in *Maldito País*; or in Manuel Galich's account of the events leading up to the 1944 October Revolution in *Desde el panico al atacque*. Among prime Central Ameican examples are Roque Dalton's *Miguel Marmol*, Omar Cabezas's *La montaña es algo mas que una inmensa estepa verde.*, Mario Payeras's *Dias de la selva,* and of course Rigoberta Menchu's famous testimonio.[12]

Writing during the period of insurrection, Ileana Rodriguez argued that Central American testimonial literature was an important component of the study of popular insurgency in the region. She pointed to its value in revealing the "hidden secrets of popular tradition in relation to questions of resistance," providing access to situations and forms of thought unknown or poorly understood by officially sanctioned culture. In her view, testimonio is not only a form of representation of popular ideologies and cultural forms; it is also a means of popular- democratic cultural practice, closely bound up with the same motivations that produce insurgency at the economic and political levels (Rodriguez 1982: 85-96).

In our book, *Literature and Politics in the Central American Revolutions*, John Beverley and I concurred with Rodriguez in seeing the origins and evolution of testimonio in Central America as a cultural aspect of the overall struggle for hegemony, linked to the impulse to displace or overthrow both elites and elite cultural modes (including those represented by dominant models in literature) in favor of a more informal and popularly inflected culture. Inevitably we were led to the assumption that there was a relation between the crystallization of testimonio as a narrative genre and the crisis and corresponding revolutionary upsurge of the 1970s in Central America.

In principle, testimonio appears as an extra-literary or even anti-literary form of discourse. As noted in Chapter I, the form in Latin America represented both a rejection of and an alternative to the sophisticated boom narrative; but it was also incorporated to some extent within this narrative. In the Central American case, we encounter the following: (1) fictional novels that are pseudo-testimonios (Manlio Argueta's *Un día en la vida* and *Cuzcatlan*); (2) the incorporation of testimonial voices in complex boom-style narrative structures (Sergio Ramírez's *¿Te dio miedo la sangre?* and several subsequent works); (3) texts that fall somewhere between the authorial novel and/or autobiography and testimonio as such, like Claribel Alegría's *Luisa in Realityland*, Roque Dalton's *Pobrecito poeta que era yo*, or Tomás Borge's memoirs, *La paciente impaciencia*.

What happens, however, when testimonio is appropriated by or becomes itself literature? Does this involve a neutralization or attenuation of its peculiar aesthetic effect, which depends on its status outside sanctioned literary forms and norms? In the case of Nicaragua, this becomes an issue particularly in a post-revolutionary period where the situation of urgency, activism, and collective enthusiasm that informs the testimonio has abated. If testimonio persisted as a highly significant force in Guatemala into the late 1990s, this was an indication of a continuing social struggle that was inhibiting or refracting the impact of new globalization processes, but the impact of the new processes also accounts for the weakening testimonial effect, say in the books by César Montes (1997), or the second testimonio (or is it a memoir?) of Rigoberta Menchú.

Weakened in expression, questioned in effect (as in the David Stoll/Menchú controversy, testimonio persists in itself and as a current affecting Central American literary processes. If testimonio comes into being necessarily at the margin of the historically given institution of literature as a sort of anti-literature, it has also been in the process of becoming a new, post-fictional form of literature, with significant cultural and ideological repercussions continuing to insist on the local in the midst of global processes.

The Contemporary Conjuncture: An Extended Postscript

In recent years, Central America has been experiencing radical transformations marked by a new political era, which as emerged as a product of the participation of Central American countries in processes of democratization and the integration of Central America in the new world order or [dis]order. These transformations have required new structures, and it is possible to detect a new historical phase emerge, which will require new instruments and perspectives adapted to radically changed circumstances.

William I. Robinson's recent book, *Transnational Conflicts: Central America, Social Change, and Globalization* (Verso 2003) which, as the book blurb notes, "shows how capitalist globalization has thoroughly transformed the region, disrupting the conventional pattern of revolutionary upheaval, civil wars, and pacification, ushering in instead a new transnational model of economy and society." The full emergence of Central American postmodernity and its entrance into contemporary globalization processes can be dated not so much by the end of the Cold War as by the Central American peace processes -for example, the Arias Plan, to refer to a matter close to the heart- as an event symptomatic of the close of at least a phase of the contradictory and conflictive relations with capitalist hegemony at a worldwide level. Obviously, the new phase consolidates with Esquipulas II and the Sandinista defeat in 1989; the phase has intensified within the socio-economic and political transformations that affected and continue to affect the Central American area during the period of transition toward globalization, transnationalization and neo-liberal democratization. The revolutionaries of the 70s and 80s fought against these tendencies; their failure implied the end of the political opposition to the transition; but the struggles of these years implied that Central America lost time and opportunity, and remained behind other Latin American regions. Furthermore, the economic lag was in many cases accompanied by processes of cultural disarticulation or fragmentation that in themselves implied even further difficulties of transition. Under these conditions, Central American countries and peoples have needed a new infusion of study and theorization to help understand (and act according to) the area's situation in the new order. Particularly, what has been required is a theoretical corpus to explore the global, regional and local relations between socio-economic and cultural processes in relation to political processes which have to do with "regime change" and transformations of civil society in what some call the new "empire" and that the LACASA group has called, "the new world [dis]order" (cf. Piazza and Zimmerman 1998).

Nevertheless, the attempt to establish a theoretical frame to understand what has happened and what can happen in Central America is marked by certain particular ironies and difficulties. First, some of the primordial questions and contradictions that initiated the movement of Latin American cultural studies emerges from the Central American areas during its period of war and armed conflict. On the other hand, an outstanding gap in the construction of contemporary theory over Latin America has been a perspective on one of the major zones whose revolutionary failures gave way to a new socio-political and ideological era that without question greatly influenced post-Marxist theory when attention veered toward the crises of new processes of democratization and new struggles in Mexico, Peru, Venezuela, Colombia and other countries.

Central American revolutionary movements in the 1970s and 80s grew as a direct reply to the imposition of the agro-exportation model and the initiative for economic expansion and integration during the years of the Cold War and the Alliance for Progress. Then came the reaction of the middle sectors, the workers and indigenous groups who imposed unequal forms of modernization. The failure of the left opposition translated into the consolidation of a renewed subordination in function now of the attempts to revive regional commerce and accelerated the growth of *maquiladoras* and others forms of organization in the fragmented transnationalization of labor and consumption to give a new articulation with NAFTA and other emergent neo-liberal practices and trade agreements. The problem may well be, as in the case of Mexico, that other parts of the World had already conquered the markets that should have logically been Central American for the exportation of raw materials and goods whose cost of production meant that the area could not enter into competition in the global marketplace.

In this context, we can configure the struggle in Chiapas and in Mexico in general as part of a much larger Meso-American drama and as a sort of bridge between modernizing/post-modernizing, pre-globalizing/full-globalizing phases and tendencies of Latin American development. Of course this is a matter that requires a more ample consideration than what has yet been attempted in the terrain of postmodernist studies. To this should be added that these macro-contexts only put in place or prepare the field for the configuration of new historical subjects and constellations, for new social movements, and the new subaltern actions no longer tied to structures or narratives based in nation, state, class or caste. To arrive at a clearer perspective, however, one would have to consider Central American processes of economic, political and cultural modernization, hybrid and transnational globalization processes, and the implications of these processes for Central American literature in itself.

In particular, we would have to consier the transformations and cualities that are symptomatic of the struggles over modernization in the fragile and vulnerable social formations of certain countries formed in funciton of variants of an agro-exportation model-of café, of bananas and other products that are, so to speak, more dramatic-and the bases that these variants provide for the construction of cosmopolitan structures and the modernizing literary modes and genres that correspond to these structures. And this should be seen in the context of the fluxes and tensions created by globalizing processes and their effects on politics, religion. But above all, it should be noted that the attempts of resistance against the emergent globalizing stage left the region in a tetarded situation, so it has been unable to participate well in the taiwanization, dollarization, privatization and miamazation of all the other neo-liberal processes that have characterized recent years. With the partial exceptions of Costa Rica and Panama, Central America has remained behind in the globalizing processes-and this can consitute a certain advantage, althought the great disadvantages of advanzing poverty, of all-too limited development and social fragmentation are too serious and obvious.

The constant problems in Central America are matters of adjustment in the post-war period. Now the nations manifest infrastructures weakened by struggle and war and trembling in the aftermath of hurricanes, earthquakes and internal conflicts that lead them toward new levels of need. The post-war period implies continual out-migration although return migration occupies a major role that involves internal transformations as well as transformations in the typical out-migration zones. Costa Rica is becoming Nicarica or Costaragua. Among the *guanacos* who return are the East L.A. *cholos*, who have converted the center of San Salvador into a postmodern war zone. The remittances from migration transform homes, neighborhoods and hearts. Narco-capitalism continues on the rise, entering into every family structure, every pore of civil society. Meanwhile, the Honduran migration to the U.S. has begun to rival the Salvadoran and Guatemalan. And we find ourselves facing a situation in which the social, political, cultural and natural processes have combined to detour the advance of Central America within the globalization game.

It is a question of a period marked by the fall of revolutionary macro-narratives and nation-centered discourses; it is a question of radical changes in Central American economics, social structures and cultural processes.

In the wake of the end of the insurrectional phase and the turn toward the efficacy of a literary model for Central America has come into crisis, as Ileana Rodriguez and others pointed to the limits of literature as a mode of representing women, gays, indigenous groups and Afro or Caribbean Central Americans; and, as in the case of John Beverley's critique, literature was seen as presenting a narrow Creole vision centered on national integration and construction. Even leftwing Central American versions of Latin American arielism would be fraught with limitations that would make a literary-centered model untenable in a post-national globalized neo-liberal societies where the primary concern for any left seeking viable solutions would be subaltern political construction. Whether from the left, center or right, and even with the production of excellent new work, primarily, it would seem, in new post-insurrectional and post-testimonial fictional forms, Central American literature could only play a precarious, fragile and problematic role in the search for new directions crucial to Central America's future history.

Here it is important to point out the effects of neo-liberalism and globalization on Central American literary production. First, regional and national publishing infrastructures have declined and in many ways disintegrated. According to Jill Robin (2004), the publication of Central American books has been largely taken over by publishing houses in Spain. This new situation points to Spain's growing role in the European community and implies a rejection of Latin American third wordlist cultures in favor of an identification with the economies, cultures and governments of Europe. This Spanish reaction-resistance but also welcome to globalization/ nostalgia for economic colonization and the rejection of Latin America-has deeply affected which Latin and Central American works have been published by multinational conglomerates, as well as what works and authors receive literary prizes in Spain and elsewhere. What is more, it should be added, the globalization influences what local authors decide to write about and how they write-including the abandonment of local themes and modes of enunciation, the rejection of local, regional and national concerns-all in the name of a more international and cosmopolitan style and orientation. Clearly there are fine things produced in this vein, as there are also fine works resisting these processes. But it is also clear that Central American literature as regional and local expression is in great jeopardy as processes of neo-liberalism and globalization deepen.

As Ana Patricia Rodríguez (2004) notes:

> *Following the noted apex of the* testimonio *and the Marxist-Leninist revolutionary narrative in the 1980s, contemporary Central American cultural production is located at the crossroads of discourses on Central American regional cultures. Post-revolutionary movement literature shows the signs of recent historical and discursive transformations. Grappling with the legacy of armed conflict, post-revolutionary movement literature in Central America is in the process of constructing narratives produced under the duress of neoliberal cultural politics and the homogenizing trends of global economic and cultural capital. Major strategies of this literature include... the invention of a Central American regional imaginary across diverse texts, which propose utopic and dystopic visions and which seek to disrupt embryonic neoliberal master-narratives of the region. Many recent literary texts interrogate the effects of neoliberal politics and economies on the specific and diverse populations of the isthmus, and offer critiques of the general devastation of the* South, *including Central America. They engage in a rethinking of alliances forged among Central Americans and their displaced refugee / immigrant populations (re)located in other sites in the North and the South.*

In the midst of all this, the writers face a market that is so severely limited and under-developed that they seek a more ample and less local public. The begin to deprecate local and particular representations. They reject history, look for the universal-so that the globalization processes begin to affect if not distort regional production, with the result that there are few intents to represent key socail processes in contemporary Central America. On the other hand, the migration of soo many Central Americans in recent years has implied the intensification of the transnational theme within the thematic repertories of writers from the area; and the development of new latino writers of Central American origen who elaborate new forms of literature within the Central American context, and of course within the U.S. Latino literature context as well. How do we grasp the books of Mario Bencastro or the Chicano-Salvadoran texts of Rubén Martínez? Is the new Central American Latino Literature Central American or Latino or... something else? What happens if we decide that *The Long Night of the White Chickens* and the recent book of Héctor Tobar, *The Tatooed Soldier* (2000) suggests that literary representations of the newer imigration waves are grasping regional and national realities more fully than are the texts written from within the countries depicted which are perhaps so submerged in ungeneralizable regionalisms or globalized generalization that they evade the local. What does all this imply and where does it lead?

In general, this consideration of Central American culture and literature shows both the need for understanding the structures emanating from historical processes, and yet the inverse relation or relative autonomy with respect to of the literary from the over-determinations those processes would seem to imply. The continued fragmentation of Central American societies, now in globalized and transnationalizing phases, suggests a troubled history for the area and its dispersed populations. Human difficulties are often of course the source of the richest creation., especially if there is already a tradition to draw upon even as traditions erode. In this sense, Central American life and cultural processes will continue to be crucial in the years to come, as Central America's internal differentiations of ethnicity, gender, caste and class shift and intense restructuring occur throughout the region and the world.

These are among the matters that should prove important to the study of contemporary and future Central American literature, and especially the study of testimonial and novelistic production.

Works Cited

Acevedo, Ramón Luis. 1982. *La novela centroamericana*. Río Piedras. Universidad de Puerto Rico.

Achugar, Hugo. 1984/85. "Poesía política e interpelación populista: el caso de la poesía salvadoreña". En Vidal, ed. 1984/85: 313-32.

Adams, Richard. 1956. *La ladinización en Guatemala*. Guatemala. SISC.

Arias, Arturo. 1979. *Ideologias, literatura y sociedad durante la revolución guatemalteca*. La Habana. Casa de las Américas.

Arias, Arturo. 1990. "Changing Indian Identity: Guatemala's Violent Transition to Modernity". In Smith ed.: 230-57.

Arias, Arturo. 1998. "De-Colonizing Knowledge, Reformulating Textuality: Rethinking the Role of Central American Narrative." In Piazza and Zimmerman, ed.: 173-188.

Arias, Arturo, ed. 2001. *The Rigoberta Menchú Debate*. Minneapolis. University of Minnesota Press.

Arias, Arturo. 2003. "Central American Americans: Invisibility, Power and Representation in the US Latino World." *Latino Studies*, I, 1. March: 168-187.

Armijo, Roberto y Rigoberto Paredes. 1983. eds. *Poesía Contemporánea de Centro América*. Barcelona. Los Libros de la Frontera.

Armijo, Roberto. 1983. "Introducción: Reflexiones sobre la Poesía Centroamericana." Roberto and Rigoberto Paredes eds.: 5-10.

Balcárcel, José Luis. 1977. "Filosofía de la Filosofía en Centroamérica", in *Revista Filosófica*. San José. Universidad de Costa Rica. XV, 41: 197-200.

Beverley, John and Marc Zimmerman. 1990. *Literature and Politics in the Central American Revolutions*. Austin. U. of Texas Press.

Beverley, John. 1983. "Sandinista Poetics". *The Minnesota Review*. Ns 20 (Spring): 127-134.

Bouvier, Virginia M. ed. 2002. *The Globalization of U.S.-Latin American Relations: Democracy, Intervention, and Human Rights*. Westport, CT. Praeger.

Boyer, Jeff and Carol Smith. 1987. "Culture and Community: The Language of Class in Guatemala." In Mike Davis, et al., ed.: 197-217.

Cabezas, Omar. 1982. *La montaña es algo más que una inmensa estepa verde*. La Habana. Casa de las Américas

Camacho, Daniel, and Rafael Menjívar, eds. 1985. *Movimientos populares en Centroamérica*. San José, Costa Rica. EDUCA.

Cardoso, Ciro F.S. "Severo Martínez Peláez y el carácter del régimen colonial". *Estudios Sociales Centroamericanos*. Enero-Abril. 1972.

Cardoso, Femando E., & Enzo Faletto. 1979. *Dependency and Development in Latin America.* Berkeley. University of California Press.

Cardoza y Aragón, Luis. 1976. Guatemala, las líneas de su mano. México. Fondo de Cultura Económica (1st ed. 1955).

Castellanos Cambranes, Julio. 1977. "La tesis de Severo Martínez sobre el bloqueo agrario a los mestizos". *Estudios Sociales Centroamericanos.* Mayo-Agosto.

Castellanos Cambranes, Julio. 1985. *Coffee and peasants in Guatemala. The origins of the modern plantation economy*, 1853-1897. Institute of Latin American Studies. Universitet Stockholms, Sweden.

Castro Rawson, Margarita. 1966. *El costumbrismo en Costa Rica.* San José, Editorial Costa Rica.

Chase, Alfonso. 1985. "Prólogo", Alfonso Chase, ed. *Las armas de la luz. Antología de la poesía contemporánea de la América Central.* San José. DEI. Departamento Ecuménico de Investigaciones.

Comisión de la Verdad. 1992-1993. *De la locura a la esperanza: La guerra de 12 años en El Salvador.* San José, Costa Rica. DEI.

Cohen, Ralph, ed. 1974. *New Directions in Literary History.* Baltimore. Johns Hopkins University Press.

Cueva, Agustín. 1977. *El desarrollo del capitalismo en América Latina.* Mexico. Siglo XXI.

Darío, Rubén. 1980. *Nuestro Rubén Darío.* Intro. Ernesto Mejía Sánchez, Selección de Jorge Eduardo Arellano, Fidel Coloma, Julio Valle y Marc Zimmerman. Managua. Ministerio de Cultura.

Darío, Rubén. 1905. *Los raros.* Barcelona. Casa Editorial Maucci.

Davis, Mike et al., ed. 1987. *The Year Left.* London. Verso, 197-217.

Dawes, Greg. 1991a. "Hacia una rearticulación del posmodernismo en América Latina. El caso de la poesía nicaragüense". *Nuevo texto crítico.* Año IV. No. 7: 85-109.

Dawes, Greg. 1991b. "A Critique of the Post-Althusserian Conception of Ideology in Latin American Cultural Studies". Postmodern Culture. v. 1, n. 3. May.

Dawes, Greg. 1992. *Aesthetics and Revolution: A Historical Materialist Analysis of Nicaraguan Poetry, 1979-1990.* Minneapolis. Minnesota University Press.

Diskin, Martin, ed. 1983. *Trouble in our Backyard: Central American and the United States in the Eighties.* New York, Pantheon Books.

EGP, "The Indian People and the Guatemalan Revolution," in Fried et al. 1983, 278-84.

Flora, Jan L. 1987. "Roots of Insurgency in Central America," in Latin American Issues (Number 5): 1.

Flora, Jan L. and Edelberto Torres-Rivas. 1989. "Sociology of Developing Societies: Historical Bases of Insurgency in Central America," in Flora and Torres Rivas: 32-55.

Flora, Jan L. and Edelberto Torres-Rivas. 1989. *Sociology of Developing Societies: Central America.* New York. Monthly Review Press.

Flores Alvarado, Humberto. 1968. *La estructura social guatemalteca.* Guatemala. Ed. Rumbos Nuevos.

Fried, Jonathan, et al., eds. 1983. *Guatemala in Rebellion: Unfinished History*. New York. Grove Press.

Goldman. Francisco. 1992. *The Long Night of the White Chickens.* New York. Atlantic Monthly Press.

Guzmán Böckler, Carlos. 1975. *Colonialismo y revolucion.* Mexico. Siglo XXI.

Guzmán Böckler, Carlos. 1986. *Donde enmudecen las conciencias: crepúsculo y aurora en Guatemala.* Mexico. SEP/CIESAS.

Guzmán Böckler, Carlos, and Jean-Loup Hérbert. 1970. *Guatemala: una interpretación histórico-social.* Mexico. Siglo XXI.

Hawkins, John. 1984. *Inverse Images: The Meaning of Culture, Ethnicity and Family in Postcolonial Guatemala.* Albuquerque. University of New Mexico Press ,

Hodges, Donald C. 1986. *The Intellectual Foundations of the Nicaraguan Revolution.* Austin. University of Texas Press.

Jauss, Hans Robert. 1974. "Literary History as a Challenge to Literary Theory," in Cohen, ed. :11-41.

Lascaris, Constantino. 1970. *Historia de las ideas en Centroamérica.* San Jose. EDUCA.

Martínez Paláez, Severo. 1971. *La patria del criollo, ensayo de interpretación de la realidad colonial guatemalteca.* Guatemala. Editorial Universitaria de Guatemala.

Mejía José. 1970. "Guatemala, país desconocido". *Alero* (1. 1): 9-17.

Menchú Tum, Rigoberta. 1984. *I, Rigoberta Menchú. An Indian Woman in Guatemala.* Edited and introduced by Elisabeth Burgos-Debray. New York and London. Verso.

Menchú Tum, Rigoberta, con la colaboración de Dante Liano y Gianni Mina. 1998. *Rigoberta: La nieta de los mayas.* México, D.F. Aguilar.

Menton, Seymour. 1985. *Historia crítica de la novela guatemalteca.* Guatemala. Editorial Universitaria.

Molina, Juan Ramón. 1913. *Tierras, mares y cielos.* Tegucigalpa. Editorial Turcios.

Monteforte Toledo, Mario. 1972. *Centro América: subdesarrollo y dependencia.* Mexico. UNAM.

Montes, César. (Julio César Macías). 1997. *La guerrilla fue mi camino.* Guatemala. Editorial Piedra Santa.

Morales, Mario Roberto. 1998. *La articulación de las diferencias, o, El síndrome de Maximón: los discursos literarios y políticos del debate interétnico en Guatemala.* Guatemala. FLACSO.

Ordóñez, Jaime y Nuria Gamboa, eds. 1997. *Esquipulas, diez años después ¿Hacia dónde va Centroamérica?* San José. EDUCA/CSUCA/Asociación Hombres de Maíz.

Paige, Jeffrey M. 1975. *Agrarian Revolution: Social Movements and Export Agriculture in the Underdeveloped World.* New York. The Free Press.

Perus, Françoise. 1976. *Literatura y sociedad en América Latina: el modernismo.* México. Siglo Veintiuno.

Piazza Michel, Marc Zimmerman. 1998. *New World [Dis]Orders & Peripheral Strains.* Chicago. MARCH/Abrazo Press.

Pinto Soria, Julio César. *Régimen colonial 1524-1750. Sociedad Estatal Quinto Centenario.* FLACSO. 1ra ed. 1993. Madrid. Ediciones Siruela, S. A. Vol.Tomo II.

Ramírez, Sergio. 1983. *Balcanes y volcanes y otros ensayos y trabajos*. Managua. Editorial Nueva Nicaragua.

Robin, Jill. 2004. "La producción editorial centroamericana en el proceso de globalización". In Zimmerman and Ventura, ed.

Robinson, William I. 2003. *Transnational Conflicts: Central America, Social Change, and Globalization*. London. Verso.

Rodríguez, Ana Patricia. 2002 "Wasted Opportunities: Conflictive Peacetime Narratives of Central America, 2002". In Bouvier, ed.: 227-247.

Rodríguez, Ana Patricia. 2004. "Central American Cultural Production Under the Aegis of Neoliberalism". In Zimmerman y Baeza Ventura, ed.

Salamanca, Douglas. 1991. "Literatura, sandinismo y compromiso". *Revista Iberoamericana*. Vol. LVII, 157. Oct.-dic.: 843-859.

Smith, Carol. 1987. "Central America since 1979: Part I". *Annual Review of Antropology* 16: 197-221.

Smith, Carol. 1990. *Guatemalan Indians and the State: 1540 to 1988*. Austin, Texas. U. of Texas Press.

Stoll, David. 1998. *Rigoberta Menchú and the Story of all Guatemalans*. Westview Press.

Tobar, Héctor. 2000. *The Tattooed Soldier*. New York. Penguin.

Torres Rivas, Edelberto. 1983a. "Central America Today: A Study in Regional Dependency," in Diskin, ed.: 1-34.

Torres Rivas, Edelberto. 1983b. *Crisis del Poder en Centroamérica*. San José, Costa Rica. EDUCA.

Torres Rivas, Edelberto. 1983c. *Interpretación del Desarrollo Social Centroamericano: Procesos y Estructuras de una Sociedad Dependiente*. San José, Costa Rica. EDUCA.

Torres, Edelberto comp. 1989. *América Central Hacia el 2000: Desafíos y opciones*. Caracas. Editorial Nueva Sociedad.

Urbina, Nicasio. 1991. "Palabras de silencio hablado: introducción a la poesía nicaragüense". *Revista Iberoamericana*. Vol. LVII, 157. Oct.-dic.: 891-913.

Uriarte, Iván. 1980. *La poesía de Ernesto Cardenal en el contexto histórico-social centroaméricano.* Ph.D. dissertation, University of Pittsburgh.

Vallardes Arce, Manuel José. 1950. *Diario de Hoy.* San Salvador, 17 de enero.

Valle, Rafael Helidoro. 1960. *Historia de las ideas contemporáneas en Centroamérica.*

Vasconi, Tomás Amadeo. 1969. "Dependencia y superestructura" in *Revista de Economía y Ciencias Sociales* (Caracas), vol. III, núm. 3: 99.

Vidal, Hernán, ed. 1984/85. *Literature and Contemporary Revolutionary Culture I.* Minneapolis. Society for the Study of Contemporary Hispanic and Lusophone Revolutionary Literatures.

Wolf, Eric. 1957. "Closed Corporate Peasant Communities in Mesoamerica And Central Java. *Southwestern Journal of Anthropology* 13: 1-18.

Warren, Kay B. 1998. *Indigenous Movements and Their Critics: Pan-Maya Activism in Guatemala.* Princeton. Princeton University Press.

Watanabe, John M. 1992. *Maya Saints and Souls in a Changing World.* Austin. University of Texas Press.

Zimmerman, Marc. 1995. *Literature and Resistance in Guatemala: Textual Modes and Cultural Politics from El Señor Presidente to Rigoberta Menchú.* Athens, Ohio. Ohio University Press. 2 tomos: Volume I: *Theory, History, Fiction and Poetry.* Volume II. *Testimonio and Cultural Politics under Cerezo and Serrano-Elías.*

Zimmeman, Marc, ed. 1988. *El Salvador at War: A Collage Epic.* Minneapolis. MEP.

Zimmerman, Marc and Gabriela Baeza Ventura, coord. 2004. *Estudios culturales centroamericanos en el nuevo milenio.* Special edition of *Istmo: Revista virtual de estudios literarios y culturales centroamericanos.* Núm. 8. Invierno.

Notes

1 On the dynamics of the Central American bourgeoisie, see Vasconi 1969: 99-131.

2 For a similar perspective see Lascaris 1970.

3 The Spanish original is much better: "El destino del intelectual guatemalteco es este: el entierro. Y si no, el encierro. Y si no, el destierro" (Valle: 13).

4 See also his article with Edelberto Torres-Rivas, in the book they co-edited (1989): 32-55.

5 Torres' main text is his seminal volume (1983a). However the perspective to which we refer here most readily emerges in the articles collected in Torres Rivas 1983b), as well as in subsequent publications.

6 For a sophisticated semiotic reinterpretation of Martínez Peláez's orientation, see Hawkins 1984.

7 See Guzmán Böckler and Jean-Loup Herbert 1970; Guzmán Böckler 1975, esp. 256-57; see also Arias's critique of the PGT position in Arias 1979c. For a sympathetic but critical critique of the first volume in comparison with Flores Alvarado, see Mejía 1970a. The Guzmán Böckler and Flores Alvarado texts are the ones that Arias uses to construct his critique of Monteforte and left-liberal Guatemalan literature (1979). However, Arias later rejects this perspective as "petit-bourgeois" indigenismo (cf. Arias 1990.). See note 10.

8 See, for example, the "Theses of the EGP" in Fried et al. 1983, 278-84.

9 For a review of the issues, see Castellano Cambranes 1977.

10 As Arias softened his stance, Adams seemed to move away from his earlier developmentalism (see his views as set forth in Smith 1990 and in Zimmerman 1995, chap. 5), as the two came closer together in the 1980s. For Guzmán Böckler's subsequent views, see his *Donde enmudecen las conciencias* (1986).

11 For a compendium of Central novelistic production see Acevedo 1982.

12 For a far more complete area list of Central American textimonial and testimonial-inflected texts, see Beverley and Zimmerman 1991, Chapter VI. For a very complete survey of Guatemalan testimonio up to 1995, see Zimmerman vol. II (1995).

Chapter III

The Unity of the Caribbean and its Literatures

1. Theoretical Parameters and Perspectives

A. World Literature and Fernández-Retamar's Problematic.

The question of a Caribbean literature must be seen in function of a broader concern for the eventual constitution of a general literary theory as related to a global theory of culture under the spread of capitalism. Accordingly, Marx's view of how capitalism generates a world literature finds specificity in terms of extensive systemic relations but also in terms of the international framework embodied in individual works. In this framework, Western metropolitan literature predominates because its historical domination accompanied that of the capitalist mode of production over all other modes. However, the focus of attention falls not only on the forms dominating but on the ones dominated: it involves "tradition," literary influence and "quality literature," but also oppositional forms generated by different peoples, groups and classes, even as capitalist commodity production and its superstructures set up their varied configurations of domination, submission and sometime transcendence.

On the basis of similarity and difference, literary systemicity and those tendencies finding their way beyond system would begin to achieve adequate conceptualization, and we would have the means for developing a coherent, differential theory of an emerging world literature, a theory able to grasp the conformative or oppositional functionality of regional and local structurations, at given historical moments throughout the course of capitalist development and decline. In this way, we would find the proper basis for grasping, relating and ultimately historicizing the myriad phenomena constituting the written and more broadly expressive systems, which characterize the modern world.

One of the problems inherent in the elaboration of this totalistic theory is that of "wholes and parts": We cannot have a total theory of literature until we have a theory of the different literatures: we cannot have that theory until we have at least the basis for a generally applicable global model. The resolution of this problem may be in a progressive oscillation of wholes and parts, the wholes themselves seen as subsets of still larger totalities. But this resolution waits answering the question of the specific units which constitute those adequate partial structures that operate most significantly in terms of the larger synthesis. Latin American or Hispano-American literature is one of these potential units: Caribbean literature is a possible (though incommensurate) sub-unit.

The question of a globally oriented theory of Latin American literary history has been growing concern since the Cuban Revolution and the not unrelated emergence of the Latin American literary boom. Many critics have attempted to formulate the basis for such a theory, but for our context, the most important effort is that of Roberto Fernández-Retamar (1975: 55-108). Coming from a Caribbean writer with a clear international orientation, Fernández-Retamar's ideas point toward radical problems, which resist easy theoretical integration, and yet which must be faced before any adequate new history of Latin American or of Caribbean literature may be written.

Fernández-Retamar stresses the need for a specific Hispano-American literary theory as the basis for a new literary history or any eventual theory of world literature. He stresses the "ancillary, hybrid, extrinsic and instrumental" nature of Hispano-American literature-its unique system of literary genres and socio-generic functionalities: he argues for a literary history based on literature, but tied to the specific conditions determining what in Latin America literature is and what is not. Fernández-Retamar emphasizes also the historical standards by which Hispano-American literature has been judged-the reasons why certain kinds of works or genres did not emerge, how certain European genres were transformed in form or function in the process of their transmission, how certain literary phenomena from certain social sectors which did emerge were excluded from the transmitted cannon; how new historical circumstances led to their reappearance or reassessment in relation to current tendencies of literary production which regenerated earlier forgotten or obscured developments.

In effect, Fernández-Retamar asks that we distinguish between a general Marxist approach to literature and a more particular approach, which respects historical particularities. His project has historical roots, which must be historically transcended before it loses efficacy. He insists that a world literary system is not a fact but a tendency, which capitalism first generates and then blocks, and which only a world socialist transformation can make a final reality. But in the long capitalist epoch preceding Fernández-Retamar's socialist world, we require a theory able to generate adequate comparisons and contrasts, relations and discontinuities.

And Fernández-Retamar, for all the help he offers us in specifying the need for a literary theory based on actual literary practice, leads us into a seemingly blind alley in one significant way. For the very notion of a Hispano-American literature which becomes a totalistic unitary object of study runs up against the concrete possibility that the ultimate object is rooted in socio-historical realities that tie the literary production of, say, his own native Cuba to the production of Jamaica or Haiti, as much as it would to the production of Chile or Peru.

Fernández-Retamar, Cuba's writer-spokesman for a general "Third World" drives for liberation, for Latin American and Caribbean unity in struggle under the sign of Calibán, does not map out the parameters of his theory in ways adequate to the constitution of a unified differential theory that includes Hispano-American and non-Hispano-American literatures in the Americas.

In the course of a conference on Latin American Ideologies and Literature, Ileana Rodríguez[1] indirectly focused on this veritable contradiction in Fernández-Retamar's perspective, and thereby generated the problematic around which the present essay is organized: "An integral view of Latin America," says Rodríguez (1978: 1), "has to... include up to now neglected areas, has to redefine concepts, has to theorize about certain urgent problems. ...I propose, then, to begin with, that we include within the theoretical consideration of an integral vision of Latin America the area of the Caribbean and Central America." While expressing her concern over whether the area she designated constituted two regions or one, Rodríguez bemoaned the relative neglect of the Caribbean, and its fragmentary study in terms of nation states or linguistic blocs. She insisted on a global ensemblic definition of the area, which comprehend the American mainland, Caribbean coasts, and the islands, including "without doubt, the French, English and Dutch islands that have been marginalized up to now."

By following the spirit of the Cuban Revolution and, we believe, Fernández-Retamar's deepest impulses, Rodríguez called Fernández-Retamar's focus into question. The issue at stake may emerge clearly when stated as follows: Without a proper definition and integration of the Caribbean, there can be no total view of Latin American literature. With a proper definition and integration, our object of study undergoes a mutation: Can we speak of a Hispano-American literature that includes English, Dutch, French and diverse Creole languages? Can we speak of a "Latin American culture" in the sense, even, of Calibán, when extensive sectors of the Spanish Caribbean may relate more significantly to plantation societies in Brazil, or in Ceylon, or to certain societies in Africa or the Balkans?

The purpose of this essay is to resolve or at least refocus this problematic in an effort to forge a differential but unitary vision of the Caribbean and its literatures in relation to Latin American and, I would argue, the larger world totality to which Fernández-Retamar and others ultimately refer.

B. Criteria for Regional Literary Unity

The socio-historical analysis of literature would be a relatively simple matter if literary systems could be construed on international, national, regional, political, cultural or linguistic bases-or in function of modes of production, concrete social formations, social classes, etc. But literary systems, while influenced by such determinations, tend toward more complex relations with all of them, sometimes submitting to one valence, sometimes another, depending on patterns of hegemony had hierarchy (as well as resistance and capacity for inverse action by generally subordinate elements) prevalent at given historical moments.

The question for general literary theory, and for any proposed theory of Caribbean literature, is whether at any given time or times, a geographically designated totality can have such structural efficacy as to constitute the principal or dominant determinant (transcending national, linguistic and even strictly literary valences) that characterizes the various cultural or literary expressions of the totality. This question involves others: the circumstances under which such structural dominance may or may not be achieved; the specific effects of such dominance on the other sub-totalities dominated in themselves and in their inter-relations; the specific resultants of such time-bound dominations when and if their moment passes: the specific ways and mediations by and through which this new domination asserts itself on literary production; the particular effects of past dominations on the character of the literary system now subject to a new configuration; the mode of incorporating, accommodating, reconstituting and negating these past effects; the present and future effect of the new configuration on literary (including critical) production, on the new social totality which has affected it, and on the literary, cultural and social totalities from which the new configuration is distinguished and to which it is now newly related.

In general, we may say that a geographic zone may provide a basis for tendencies of literary unity when the diverse sub-regions found to constitute the zone are marked significantly by a common series of intermediate factors which link with, pressure and measurably determine literary forms and expressions. Such points of unity include similar historical characteristics and modes of elaboration establishing relatively commensurate social totalities with relatively commensurate relations among the regional sub-totalities: similar socioeconomic and political determinations; similar national and group divisions, problems, projects and interrelations with similar relations to external, intra-regional and internal forces, but also with a similar syncretic dynamism: similar patterns of reception, disposition, synthesis and reproduction of all elements.

In sum, for us to speak of the potential regional unity among literary products, there must be enough general unity to constitute the region as a historically determinate socio-cultural block, with its own distinctiveness from and relatedness to other such regional blocs or totalities. And essential to this definition is the assertion that this unity must of necessity emerge at the level of similar cultural composition and process built upon a facilitating commonality of geographic, socio-economic and political features. Needless to say, the question of ideology is crucial in this context: the degree to which diverse regional groups become conscious of the real and potential tendencies toward unity, the degree to which circumstances generate unifying will and action. But only with a commonality at the level of a regional, as opposed to a national or ethnic, culture can we posit even the potential unity of a literature. Only on the basis of a common regional culture (characterized as differential object and process), built out of concrete historical submissions and resistances, conformities and constituent variables, can we begin to map out the dimensions of a common regional literature able to incorporate and transcend sub-regional socioeconomic, political and linguistic differentials which inevitably mark each and every concrete social formation on the globe.

Obviously all of this carries the provisional qualification that the totality thus achieved is not demarcated on so abstract a basis that concretely significant internal differences are homogenized, negated or so reduced to the lowest common denominator that the totalistic definition becomes applicable to any number of other totalities (Caribbean literature as capitalist, dependent, "Third World," "Afro," "Latin American," etc.), or that it can account for neither variations nor external relations. The value of unification is that it provides a means for relating a range of diversity among the elements conceptualized, and among other ensembles from which the elements are distinguished and disengaged and whose own unity the unification process serves to redefine. A viable abstraction must embody the concrete determinations able to account for and facilitate the reconstitution of the diverse particularities it embraces and distinguishes.

Finally, it follows from the above that a general theory of regional literary unity as a socio-historical tendency, reality or possibility must provide a basis for incorporating and "gauging" constituent variables, differentials and "exceptions" which challenge any conceptual abstraction: such a theory requires a basis for determining not only what generates but what opposes degrees of unity: what historical processes or conjunctures might have determinate weight in promoting or impeding, propelling or blocking unifying inclinations and tendencies: what "factors" might lead to a reordering of literary systems in relation to different regional or extra-regional constellations, according to other hierarchies among socioeconomic, political, linguistic, cultural and literary forces; and what factors might lead to any reassertion of the initial regional focus.

C. Caribbean Unity / Literary Unity: a Problematic.

According to José Antonio Portuondo, "The peoples of the Caribbean, in spite of their geographical and historical unity, lived unknown to one another, and it is hardly a quarter of a century since they have become aware of their physical and cultural contiguity... The Caribbean still is not our sea: its colonial status, its diverse flags and its languages maintain the division despite geography. But the idea of unity persists. Starting with geography, it begins to assert itself by reason of the coincidence of interests and ideals, which motivate a conscious cooperation of endeavors. This is already happening in the political and economic spheres and it is, happily, foreseen in literary themes." (Portuondo: 257).

A theory of Caribbean literary unity would have to correspond to the general framework specified above. It would of necessity rest on a conceptualization of the Caribbean itself as a potential unity, and it would have to set forth (and ultimately demonstrate) how, through a series of socio-historical and cultural mediations, this general Caribbean unity creates the parameters for a literature which corresponds somehow to it, and which is both linked to and differentiated from other literary systems representative of other regional and broader totalities.

To be sure, even the wish to establish the bases for such theory must rest minimally on a felt or randomly empirical sense that such a unity exists and is subject to conceptualization. There must be material and ideological pressures demanding the specification of Caribbean and Caribbean literary unity. The very fact of the conference and book for which this paper was written and the preoccupations uniting conference and book participants are symptomatic in this regard. Since the Cuban Revolution, tendencies toward Caribbean unity have registered on eye and mind. In the sixties, awakened energies among U.S. and African Blacks helped stir local hopes for a socialist Caribbean, while, subsequently, intervention in Santo Domingo, the survival of Duvalier's dynasty, the interminable crisis over Puerto Rico's status, the grotesque incursions from Miami and the sinister counter-insurgency projects in Panama signaled difficulties for the future. In varying degrees, the governments of Williams, Manley and Torrijos bespeak an era of ambiguity; but Cuba's role in African liberation struggles (though still not fully won), the Panama Canal Treaty (though still leaving much to be desired) and the mass risings in Nicaragua (though not on the *Costa de Mosquitos*-and still without happy results) at least suggest that Caribbean unity is still on the agenda.

Throughout the Caribbean, U. S. economic, political, military and ideological penetration preys on integral cultures, immiserates rural sectors and drowns urban dwellers in the dredges of commercialism, opportunism and disaffection. But the very pressures of commodification, deracination and exploitation set off a chain reaction of anger and disgust-in the fields, in the streets, in the offices-that only awaits the maturation of deeper historical forces of unification (in the world and in the islands) to link up in a process that leads toward a new world.

The meeting and jostling of hopes and disillusionments have galvanized practical energies in politics, culture and the arts, and they have ultimately produced a moment of synthetic theorization -a taking of stock, as the energies toward fragmentation and integral reassertion vie for dominance. Caribbean writer-critics like Fernández-Retamar, Edward Brathwaite, Sylvia Wynter, Iris Zavala and Roberto Márquez recharge strains from Martí, Betances, Carpentier, Depestre, Césaire and Guillén; and then, with resurgent powers, they turn to the task of forging the possibilities for a Pan-Caribbean socio-cultural synthesis as a guide to the future.

Concrete historical circumstances and their articulation by those critics who seem to capture the aspirations of Caribbean peoples give us sufficient confidence to say, offhand and prior to systematic analysis, that our effort to conceptualize Caribbean and Caribbean literary unity is an action upon a real or at least potentially real object of study. In a sense, the effort contributes to the further materialization of the object. And yet the obvious challenge, which the enterprise poses, should be acknowledged.

First, this area itself, while constituting a geographic unity and while sharing certain crucial historical characteristics because of its ecological and geographical circumstances in given junctures of capitalist development, is nevertheless highly diversified according to politics, language and degrees of cultural mix. Thus, with respect to literature, the differences between Spanish, French, English and Dutch Caribbeans, in terms of inherited, and continually renewed ties with, European political and cultural traditions, are a major basis of cultural differentiation. This crucially affects literary structures, especially since written expression and literature have been and are still mainly the province of social sectors distanced from Caribbean realities and more likely to grasp them through the discourse, cannons, conventions, language norms and overall cultural signifying systems of those European literatures which exert hegemony in the totality of world literature.

This phenomenon can have positive or negative consequences for diversely developing national and pan-Caribbean literary tendencies. To the degree that literatures embody traditions imbedded in language-culture complexes, and that Caribbean sub-regions share a differentiated but generally common history of colonial dependence. Caribbean literatures will most emphatically relate to (even become sub-categories of) the literatures of the European mother countries: Jamaica and Barbados will follow England, then, possibly the U.S.: Cuba and Puerto Rico, Spain, and then other parts of the Spanish-speaking world. Though obviously linguistic and cultural proximity or affinity have their measured effect, all the island literatures will inevitably be subject to the hierarchical ordering of influences determined by hegemonic literary tendencies which will generally (though never completely) exhibit configurations or options set up by one of the dominating capitalist national cultures. Thus, in this century, U. S. influence vies with French, English, etc. Inversely, island literature expressing opposition to hegemonic capitalist tendencies will draw from or relate to the opposition literatures either by ethnic minorities in the metropolitan centers or by groups in other "underdeveloped" or colonial enclaves-though again, linguistic-cultural affinities will have their determinant effect, and special circumstances may also intervene e. g., Cuban influence on mainland Latin American literary production, or (especially with the Angolan conflict) on Jamaican or Haitian literatures.

In mapping such possibilities, we should recognize that the effect of external literatures is mediated by the unconscious mental structures of writers from the perspective of their social group, by "medium-deep" internal political structures, and by the profound, ever-adjusting and hence long-enduring structures of cultural core values which, we will argue are broadly, but also exclusively Caribbean. The question of actual, potential and hoped for reading publics, and the shaping of literary discourse in terms of determinate perceptions of potential public "expectation horizons" also play a role in conditioning the utilization of available literary traditions. But in any event, these and like factors suggest the multiple variables at work in attempting to establish any unitary basis for Caribbean literary production, as well as any easy unitary correlation between this production and even national social totalities. Even if we adhere to a deep cultural core process such as "creolization" Caribbean literary production, as one of the most Westernized modes of Caribbean Westernization, renders up no ready cultural or societal homologies.

Again, this is because of the weight of Western literary traditions over preliterate Caribbean cultural forms, in determining the character of Caribbean literature, especially since so many of the writers are at least structurally marginal to the Caribbean masses. To be sure, the very sectional position of writers may enable them to overcome certain of the most pernicious aspects of the

West, and to align their works with tendencies that are more progressive than ones directly dominating the macro-economic production and consumption patterns of Caribbean life. Caribbean literature may leap ahead as well as lag behind general historical processes- sometimes accomplishing both simultaneously. But at this historical juncture, progressive trends in Caribbean literature can only exert a counterweight of a certain commensurate force on the Western front. This force can be powerful enough to de-center any easy conformity with dominant Western genres and genre relations: it can even lead to a progressive creolization of supposedly "universal" topic and symbolic patterns, and generate new forms and systemic mutations. But, probably for some time to come, the capacity of this force to become fully hegemonic and to feed back into social life with efficacy is highly problematic.

In spite of these and other qualifications, the Caribbean area and its literature merit examination in relation to their patterns of unity, as an essential step to grasping the systemic processes governing and struggling against the force of modern capitalism in its regional and global dimensions. It is apparent that this area is one of the world's most directly international zones-with the weight of the European powers at their peak moments of worldwide expansion-and with peoples, religions, institutional structures and cultures representing Amerindia, Africa, China, Java, India. Within the Caribbean, these multiple forces were subjected to the implantation of successively modern capitalist patterns over an earlier mercantile capitalist synthesis. Thus, while the Caribbean may emerge as distinct from all other areas, it is nevertheless a differentiated microcosm-a veritable laboratory for a study aimed at global socio-historical and literary dimensions.

One of the issues to be resolved in probing the unity of Caribbean literature is how to establish the criteria by which this literature is unified in itself and in relation to potentials for Pan-Caribbean unity-this in the face of the fact that Caribbean unity is, like all regional unities, of a tentative historical nature, and that, in some crucial ways, as constituted by forms related to group ideologies, it may simultaneously register, contribute to or impede, anticipate or falsely promise, a unity only realizable fully in concert with more powerful material forces. The only way we can even begin to establish our concrete criteria, is to seek a substantiative definition of the Caribbean, and some basis for determining commonality and differentiation in the area. We must link these determinations with a historical analysis of the development of Caribbean cultures in their unity and diversity, in their modes of interaction, disposition and elaboration; and finally we must relate such matters to the specifically literary.

What is needed for such a project is a synthetic history of the Caribbean comparable to Fernand Braudel's *Mediterranée*: a grasp of Caribbean complexities and vicissitudes out to the global patterns set forth in Braudel's *Capitalism and*

Material Life and Immanuel Wallerstein's *Modern World System*. Short of this, we will have to make do with the splendid partial efforts thus far produced, recognizing that any grasping project of Caribbean literature in relation to the totality of Caribbean society will remain partial and limited, suggestive and programmatic.

2. Caribbean History and Culture: A Synthetic View[2]

A. Historical Bases.

Caribbean unity is grasped by seeing the area as constituting a bloc of societies resulting from parallel historical experiences during five centuries of European capitalist development and influence. The Caribbean is distinct even among underdeveloped blocs because its extant characteristics embody the full elaboration of capitalization and westernization (including the effort to dehumanize workers and ethnic groups-and the struggle against these efforts-) from the beginnings of European expansion to the present.

The Caribbean is a "planetary area," a cluster of small-scale, lowland westernized societies sharing ecological, geographical, socio-economic and other patterns and problems: patterns of colonization, immigration, peonage or slave production for export: problems stemming from pre- and post-slavery social integration patterns-from phenotypic class divisions, limited social mobility, contradictory national and cultural identity struggles. The Caribbean communities are part of a single geographic area designed to function and functioning in specific ways in relation to European metropolitan centers, to adjacent American mainland areas and to the world, with characteristics, which both distinguish these communities as a bloc from other areas and establish their mode of global insertion.

The Caribbean was the base for Latin American exploration and conquest, for the imperial designs of diverse nations, for the virtual decimation of indigenous populations, the construction of plantations societies on the basis of massive forced worker migrations, for the seasoning of diverse African peoples to produce cheap food commodities for European workers: for cultural and national developments affected by mix of distinct European "master cultures" and those of the initial and subsequent immigrant groups. All these elements, as modified by the specific circumstances of their historical insertion, and the socio-economic conditions in which they developed, led to the formation of distinctly heterogeneous multi-racial, multi-cultural societies.

As an object of "manifest destiny," as gateway to the Panama Canal, as U.S. defense bulwark and investment center, as target for Venezuelan sub-imperialism, as cheap labor source both at home and in the U.S., and yet as core area for emerging Afro-America, for liberation struggles, for potential socialist development-the Caribbean maintains its unity in the midst of rampant diversity.

Of course, there are similarities in agriculture, in the structure of local markets, in cuisine, in music, in folklore, religious cults and other traditions. There are also similar divisions, similar weaknesses in local organization, in patterns generating and struggling against these debilities. The regional Caribbean differences of habitat, economy, population mix, language, political history and status, etc. distinguish the different islands. But Caribbean differences stem from the fact that the diverse societies have been subject in different degrees to the very forces that have made them similar. The interrelated effect of the various common factors (working in different proportions and degrees according to historical and cultural differentials) establishes the basis of unity.

To be sure, the unity produced by diverse factors acting on varying cultural mixes is more societal than cultural. As Sidney Mintz has noted: "The diverse origins of Caribbean populations, their divergent European cultural impositions, and the absence of any firm continuity of the colonial culture result in a heterogeneous cultural pattern." (Mintz 1966: 2A). But the societal frame itself generates a basis for the syncretization of new cultures, new literatures, sublating, past structural elements. Peoples of different origins but similar presents jostle each other in new social settings, resisting each other, but inevitably intermixing; developing heterogeneous and innovative patterns, conflicting, struggling, but hopefully moving toward some synthesis that does not drown creative differences. The issue is to see how past patterns generate not only the divisive world of poverty, exploitation and inter-group struggle; the conflictive, partial core values and symbolisms: the fragmented and compartmentalized group and community structures we find today-but also the basis for a future, more harmonized and dynamized world.

B. The Plantation Structure.

The core of Caribbean societal unity (for its diverse political and cultural divisions and struggles) is found in the structures generated by the early definition of the area as a sphere of European overseas capitalism based mainly on the organization of slave labor in sugarcane plantations. Amerindian decimation blank-slated the islands for the refashioning of diverse European and African heritages in relation to the local and international factors affecting the various subtypes of the plantation system and the societal forms they engender. Indeed says George Beckford, "Modern Caribbean societies display forms that are a direct legacy of the slave plantation system, so that even after abolition the basic structure holds". (Beckford: 7).

The plantation is a production-centered social organism with interpersonal relations reflecting the authority structure governing economic organization: high degrees of coercion, control and centralized authoritarian decision-making. This structure, along with the not unrelated diversification among workers, acts against their uniting in production and fosters a fragmented model for social relations. We have parallel segmented societies with incomplete organic unity, a shared language based on acceptance of difference and authority, and an acculturation process largely determined by accommodation to these patterns.

Initially, there is the imposition of mono-cultural export economies based on family own plantations and a social organization by rigid class and racial distinctions: a mass of black workers organized and controlled by white owners, with peasant, commercial and professional sectors (poorer whites, mulattos, etc.) in the interstices or on the fringes of the central formation. After emancipation, the structure is complicated by multiple factors: the plantations merge to become factories in the field; the dialectics intensify between corporate and small farm holdings, island and international interests; worker groups diversify into agro-business field workers, peasants, city workers, etc; new immigrant workers of varied ethnicities enter several countries and compete with the earlier immigrants. And there are also the various turns of overall capitalist penetration as they affect given social areas and levels.

But the colonial ambiance persists. There is still unequal bipolar class-race rigidity; still limited access to education, social mobility and power; still a divisive cultural plurality; still separate plantation-based sub-area hierarchies; still fragile community and family structures. Existing opportunities merely went to expanding intermediate "mulatto" buffer groups tied to dominant sectors, rather than to changing the social structure in any radical ways. We have societies imbedded in the material and ideological patterns attendant to their formation -societies girded with internal tensions and rifts, too lacking in a united focus of identity that could foster nationwide (not to speak of pan-Caribbean) ends.

C. Unity and Disintegration.

The central drama of the Caribbean is the play of tendencies toward unity and integration, as it develops historically on the basis of the plantation structure and its modern mutations. This drama actualizes itself most crucially in relation to the linked issues of nationhood and culture.

The forces of disintegration stem from the "syndrome" which social scientists have labeled "social pluralism" in which "there are two or more distinct or rival complexes of social demand." (Beckford: 9-10).

Groups tend toward integration by their sharing a place in production, similar achievement motivations for services and benefits that favor survival and advancement, and national aspirations. But in the Caribbean, there is rivalry for jobs and advancement in a basic productive pattern arranged according to castes; and there is an increasing social sectionalization of demands, as each group concentrates on certain aspects of the social whole. The dominance of this basic productive structure on all of social life intensifies this problem. In this divisive class-race context, Caribbean nationalism as adherence to ethnic identity or adherence to a pseudo-metropolitan model intensifies social alienation and group tensions.

"The development of a coherent national identity in the Caribbean has been slowed down by the lack of a homogeneous host population with a homogeneous culture developed in situ" (Mintz: 921). Caribbeans have a national identity to the extent that they feel themselves to form a distinct community. Obviously, the persistent plantation structure mitigates against this. Whether national identity emerges early in history of a particular society, very much affects the subsequent process of assimilation of new immigrants and the overall process of national identification. Thus there is a "negative correlation" between the force of colonial plantation regimes as instruments of international capitalism and the growth of national identity. Those nationalisms, which have developed (including certain of the Afro-Caribbean movements using anti-imperialist rhetoric), have tended to be populist ideological expressions of intermediate intellectual groups seeking a broader base for the pursuit of a bourgeois national development ultimately beneficial to them.

Nevertheless, the forces for social integration can be successful. Heterogeneous societies can have a degree of national identity as long as people can be aligned on other than ethnic or caste lines. The divisive pressure of imperialist penetration may generate new bases of ideological and cultural unity in the very seat of production and community life. All Caribbean groups have remarked the inaccessibility and alien character of norms governing the behavior of dominating sectors. U.S. power exerted from without and within the Caribbean, may create national and even Caribbean movements of great unity. But so too may the force of Cuba, of Nicaragua, of Africa -not old Africa and her diverse cultural legacy, but new Africa, and her revolutionary élan, and the new relations her liberation may bring to the external forces which enter and become internal to

Caribbean life. When social movements take on a class character, when they begin to unite masses along class lines, then the door opens to revolutionary possibilities.

State ownership of production could lessen Caribbean group tensions, cut into class divisions -even if old privileged sectors grumbled or found their own Caribbean unity in Miami. Caribbean society can move toward a just existence for its people only if its plantation foundations are undermined and then destroyed (Beckford: 20-21). The solution of Caribbean divisions is not in complete genetic intermixture, but in a system that respects, maximizes and then overcomes group cultural interests and divisions and then projects them in relation to socio-economic equality. In this sense "the Caribbean peoples are very much peoples of the future."

But how, in the midst of current divisions (and still lacking the achieved social form that would create the unity sought after) can Caribbeans build on those tendencies toward unification spurred on by imperialism and external anti-imperialist struggles, when the immediate complex of socioeconomic structures seems to preclude a viable move toward liberation?

The key to this may be in cultural processes as they relate to the complex noted. That is, national and pan-Caribbean identity reposes on the question of cultural processes as they flow into and relate to broad-based political movements that galvanize repressed impulses into active forces of transformation.

D. Cultural Process and the Creative Movement from the Given to the Possible

For Mintz, "Culture constitutes a repository of historically derived beliefs, values, modes of behavior, on which societies may draw for symbolizing integrative purposes," and as the basis for secure individuation. (Mintz 1974: 324). The origin of cultural elements is not as crucial as their felt and understood references, as cues to communication and concerted action. Thus the issue in Caribbean culture is not one of African authenticity, but African and Afro-Caribbean development in the specific constitution of the factors indicated in this essay.

More important than cultural forms and survivals is cultural functionality, both in practice and potential. (M. C. Smith 1957: 34-46). Caribbean cultural content takes its importance from the ways it has been creatively adopted by the Caribbean peoples to changing needs. Masters were no more able than slaves to transplant ancestral cultures intact. Much of the transferred content lost its former symbolic meaning in the absence of traditional social frameworks. Where masters came to stay, legitimized their unions with women of inferior status and recognized their estrangement from Europe, and innovative Creole culture began to emerge. In most cases, for slaves, bringing diverse traditions from West Africa, the process of creolization was uneven, depending in part on the creolization of the masters, the degree to which they presented an assimilation model embodied in social structures and values, the degree to which master-slave offspring participated in social core values and possibilities. In most cases, master core values were fully alien, and there were resistance efforts to maintain Afro-cultural links. But most of what appears to be African in Caribbean cultures has been distilled, reworked and re-synthesized to fit new life conditions after revolting against or submitting to slavery and oppression.

The key to the culture of the Caribbean peoples, then, is the creative and innovative capacities of cultural maneuver and symbolization, to adapt to and yet fend against values that were oppressive and dehumanizing. The key to the future of the Caribbean ties in how global and local socio-economic and political transformations are creatively registered in the developing cultural process-toward greater division and defeat, or toward greater united assertion.

An indication of Caribbean possibilities emerges through a closer look at those cultural processes and the model they offer for liberating (and literary) activity.[3] For Edward Brathwaite (1974), Caribbean creolization is an ambivalent acceptance-rejection syndrome consisting of adjustment or acculturation (an overt process whereby the subordinate conforms to or imitates the super-ordinate) and resistance of indigenization (a more subtle process whereby the subordinate reorganizes values to withhold and preserve distance). The results are seen in mimicry charged with an irony that alienates the slave from the master's value world and unites him with his peers. The results also appear in the fact that the master's creolization, while dominated by resistances (through stereotyping, censoring, etc.) to Afro norms, involves influence from the slave as well. The basic form this dual process takes for the slave is a kind of psychic maroonage, leading to the preservation and development of the "little traditions" -i.e., the elaboration of a syncretic vision of African performative patterns, symbols and communicative canons (modes of walking, eating, working, interrelating; musical, artistic and other practices) which the subordinate maintains in everyday life even in the course of submitting to large-scale socio-economic pressures of dominance. That is, creolization enables the subordinate or subaltern to preserve some bases for a totalistic, humanized view of social life.

In spite of the unequal terms involved in creolization, the blacks were able to blend their diverse tribal traditions and foster a Creole identity. Against the greatest external pressure, they even succeeded in countering European capitalist influences in acculturating whites to certain of their norms.

For Brathwaite, the basic Afro-Caribbean core values were integrated before emancipation. The failure of West Indian society was that immediate hegemonic class and racial interests prevented whites from entering more fully into creolization, so that they submitted to the increased force of neo-colonial metropolitan values, and became even more alienated from the Black masses than ever before. Many favored blacks and "mulattos" also rejected the Afro-Caribbean core: and later, other groups entered and underwent a similar but separate process of oscillating between their own norms and those imitations of metropolitan values. The potential movement toward cultural wholeness was halted and the internal divisions of West Indian society deepened. This process intensified with the entry of modern mass media and tourism, especially for blacks enrolled in metropolitan industrial and service sectors. But even in these circumstances, Brathwaite sees signs in art, literature, politics and everyday life (involving "lateral creolization" between the diverse ethnicities) that the core values of the "little traditions" persist.

The Caribbean for Brathwaite cannot be defined, then, as Plantation America. The notion of a national society, of "one people out of many" (deriving unity from the lowest common denominators of the various cultures) strikes him as submission to capitalist commodity fetishism. Neither does he hold with a hopeless pluralistic model (each group held in its place) nor an interculturation model (each group struggling for hegemony). Opposing too the totalistic syncretic ideal according to which a new racial type will eventually emerge, Brathwaire opts for a "folk maroon orientation model," which holds that a specific cultural root or vision based on "inner plantation maroonage" could come to be seen as the norm uniting the diverse whole.

Brathwaite struggles to integrate the Indian, Japanese and Chinese situations to his model; he is concerned too about Caribbean differentiation, the dimensions of imperialism, of class and class-consciousness. Recognizing that his view of creolization may seem alien to groupings that are crucial to cultural unity and liberation, he argues that the process must be seen in its historical continuum of movement/ interruption, of dialectical, progressive synthesis/solution, and that the various Caribbean castes realize "their section authenticity" as a necessary step toward giving their values "residence" and embarking on genuine social integration. Insisting that his orientation model is no mere populist ideal, he asserts that it is not apart from but endemic (though submerged and "submarined") in the lives of that population which forms the worker core in the Caribbean. So, he concludes:

> *For the Caribbean, as elsewhere, the basis of culture lies in the folk-not acculturated static-groups, giving little, but a people who from the center of*

an oppressive system, have survived, adapted, recreated; have devised means of protecting what has been gained (miraculous, precarious maroonage) and who begin to offer in return some of this experience and vision. (64).

3. Perspectives towards a Theory of Caribbean Literature.

The Caribbean conceived as a unity does not exist in our literature. There is not a single poem or novel of the Caribbean as a whole. (Portuondo: 258).

A. Creolization and Totality.

Brathwaite's view of Caribbean cultural process may be transposed to establish the criteria for evaluating Caribbean literature and its different stages of development-to determine degrees of creolization, different degrees of Caribbean and extra-Caribbean emphasis. At stake is the potential construction of a historically calibrated acculturation model, able to measure degrees of adherence to dominant Caribbean patterns and degrees of adherence to international, national, class or other patterns, which are not in conformity with a totalistic Caribbean conception. Such a model would be useful for the diverse island sub-areas in their patterns of internal and external, centrifical and centripital relations; but the model would also be crucial for the ambiguous littoral areas which turn both toward the Caribbean and toward their distinct internal national formations. Thus, we would be able to gauge tendencies in Darío, Gallegos and García Márquez, which turn toward or away from specifically Caribbean problematics; we would be able to determine the ways in which general literary movements and currents take on or resist a specifically Caribbean character and articulation.

In effect, we might eventually be able to construct a veritable poetics of Caribbean literature in relation to Brathwaite's conception of a historically evolving somatic norm, realizing itself in function of totalizing, world-historical forces as they are filtered through Caribbean frames and as they achieve synthesis in the mentality and activities of Caribbean peoples.

Clearly this poetics would stress Caribbean "creative innovation" in a literature that not only registers but also contributes to the creolization process. Clearly too, then, this poetics would provide a basis for ever constructing and re-constructing a synchronic and diachronic totality, so that our normative standard is a literature that has within it the generative structural coordinates that are able to transcend local and class constraints and relate to all of Caribbean development as expression and praxis. The "ideal type" of such a literature would draw on Caribbean linguistic and cultural resources to play upon and transform those varied international forces contributing to Caribbean configurations. But while grasping the totality of the Caribbean, this ideal type would have to go beyond it, to portray as well the degree to which the Caribbean synthesis acts back on the Latin American, European and worldwide forces which condition it.

Finally, the norm for evaluating specific Caribbean literary works, movements and genres would be one which, from a given historical moment of socio-historical development, portrays that moment in its totality and as an expression of Caribbean history in its movement from a divided colonial past to a united future which is socialist.

It is of course too much to ask that any literary work, opus, genre or movement fulfill all the terms implied in our ideal type, especially given the forces of fragmentation and disintegration which have marked Caribbean history. To paraphrase Martí: "There is no expression if there is no essence to express in it. Nor will there be a *pan-Caribbean* literature until there is a *Pan-Caribe.*" Caribbean unity remains only a tendential reality, and our conception of a totalizing literature is just a model. Both are distant goals against which we may measure actual developments. They provide us with the general parameters for constituting the more specific criteria to be used in the evaluation of texts and larger literary processes in relation to the totality of Caribbean literary and social history.

B. Guidelines and Questions for a History of Caribbean Literature.

A Marxist study of Caribbean literature might well begin with a comparative analysis of the dominant phenomenal forms of each concrete social formation in relation to the development of the general mode of production figuring the area and relating it to other productive configurations. With respect to literature, we should begin with the dominant literary phenomena, the dominant genres, currents, expectation horizons, etc. -i.e., the ones that have been placed in dominance. But we should provide an analysis of the material basis on which the dominant expressions arise, point out contradictions and problematics that place these dominant tendencies in a broader scope, which involves other forces that do not find even limited expression. We must never assume that dominant works genuinely totalize a given historical period: we must always bear in mind that given group projects distort historical realities in function of specific ideologies and interests, also that a great part of Caribbean history has been one of exclusions. Thus, within a general Marxist perspective of regional and cultural determinations, differentiations and unities, we should examine dominant Caribbean literary movements and currents in relation to dominant stages of capitalist development as registered in the material and political life, in the consciousness and activity of social groups. Caribbean literature should be seen as the mediated but expressed praxis of social groups, to be related to the cultural and overall praxis of other social groups that do not find literary expression. Investigations must be sensitive to what is and what is not expressed in literature, between an epoch's total literary expression and what is consecrated, between the groups that find literary expression and those that do not, between the expressions that become institutionalized and those that do not. We should study the criteria for institutionalization in their distinct social functionality. We should study cultural ensembles and processes-the relation between cultural, oral, pre-literary and literary traditions, between traditions crystallized in the lives of workers, and those crystallized in cultural or literary groups, in literary schools, etc.

In examining these dimensions, we will have to deal with the difficult problems posed by uneven development-problems which peak in relation to the complexities of regional and sub-regional periodization. A comparative history based on chronological slices fails to account for the Caribbean "relay system," whereby, according to Rodríguez's analysis, sugar production, and then cultural and literary production, moved at varied unequal rhythms from island to island, encountering diverse patterns of acceptance, resistance and synthetic integration. (Rodríguez: 3). This would suggest that the best mode for the comparison and integration of Caribbean literatures is not chronological but structural-i.e. in function of relatively similar totalities achieved at different chronological times. Accordingly, a history of Caribbean literature would first require the integration of various sub-regional periodizations. But, while chronology is not the best measure for such a history, structure can also be misleading, if only because special circumstances may enable forces emerging in one context to act in and on other contexts which are contemporaneous but distinct (e.g., the effects of abolition, the Spanish American War, the Cuban Revolution, Angola, on the politics and literature of areas not directly involved). Thus, we must study the bases for the reception of extra-literary and literary influences emerging in one social formation on other, very different social formations. We must study resistances to such influences posed by socio-economic, political and cultural forces, and the final transformation of these influences in form and function resulting from specific patterns of literary promotion, consumption and exclusion-from the tension and tussle between acceptance and rejection.

In addition to these general guidelines, we may point to specific questions which must inform any attempt to particularize Caribbean literary history: To what degree are local, national, Caribbean, Latin American or international literary and extra-literary forces determinate in given moments of Caribbean literary production? What is the history of literary consumption in the Caribbean? To what degree do writers write for home consumption? For export? To where? What are the effects of real and hoped-for reception on the character of literary production? In effect, to what degree do Caribbean literary products respond to extra-Caribbean or intra-Caribbean concerns? Towards the formation of a pan-Caribbean literature or towards integration with international forces-of the capitalist metropolis, the Socialist countries, "Third World" revolutionary centers, etc.? To what degree does literature in the literal American mainland areas reflect Caribbean as opposed to centralist national interests? How can we distinguish what is Caribbean and what is not? What is Caribbean literature and what is not? What is the relation between literary production and other aspects of Caribbean culture-especially the culture of the working masses? What is the weight of common socioeconomic circumstances in determining relations among the various national literatures of the Caribbean? How and to what degree do different political, ethnic, linguistic and other characteristics subject to varying degrees of creolization affect tendencies generated by common socio-economic circumstances? What is the weight of these characteristics (of national political structures, of related linguistic and literary traditions, etc.) in differentiating, characterizing and relating the various literatures? To what degree do the different class, ethnic and racial groupings and their historical situations shape the literatures of the Caribbean? To what degree do these groupings constitute integral national or regional literary systems, or do similar groupings in different islands constitute literary subsystems which have more in common with their counterparts in other islands than they do with the literature of other groupings in their own? To what degree do literary works represent the vision of more than one or two groupings throughout the Caribbean? What is the relation between the literatures produced and the real or potential consciousness of the working masses who constitute the Caribbean peoples? What is the relation between the writer-sectors and the masses? To what degree do the circumstances of Caribbean literary production and the vocational and class interests of writers impede the ability of Caribbean literature to reflect and contribute to the progressively beneficial development and unity of the Caribbean peoples?

C. Towards a Periodization of Caribbean Literature.

In a very schematic way José Carlos Mariátegui establishes the basic steps for the development of a "dependent" literature:

The normal process of the literature of a people distinguishes three periods, colonial, cosmopolitan and national. During the first period, the people are nothing other, literally, than a colony, a dependency of another. During the second period, it simultaneously assimilates elements from diverse foreign literatures. In the third period, its own personality and sentiment achieves well-modulated expression. (Mariátegui: 214)

Mariátegui had in mind Peruvian and Latin American literature; but, in applying his steps, we may recall that Fernández-Retamar has since made a distinction that contrasts all the dependent literatures of the Americas with the literatures of other colonial blocs:

Latin America finds itself in a particular situation. While the West is a mere intrusion in the major part of the colonies that have taken root, in the New World, it is one of the components, and not the least important, that will give place to the mestizo *(not only the racial mestizo, of course). If the "Western tradition" is not the entire tradition of Latin America, it is also its tradition. There is a more delicate counterpoint in the case of Latin American thinkers than in the thinkers of other zones. (1965: 55)*

Brathwaite's analysis of Caribbean culture process points to the ways, in which a Caribbean literature and culture, distinct even in the Americas, gradually emerges. Of course, only Caribbean specialists can deal with the concrete complexities of Caribbean literary history, but the following partial perspectives come to mind: 1) Caribbean literature starts as a "tropical European" colonial planter literature on the basis of little internal market or indigenous identity, as British capital rises it becomes mainly anti-slavery, vaguely liberal and urban Euro Creole literature. (1970: 47-48). 2) After emancipation, and with the gradual imperialist integration of Caribbean countries into a world productive system, Caribbean literature becomes a cosmopolitan literature, separated from the mass cultures and assimilating local realities to hegemonic (and therefore universal) European literary values (Darío's modernism); or it becomes a nationalist literature attempting to give voice to the masses, assimilating whatever can be garnered from European literary traditions to the project of expressing present and possibly future Caribbean realities (Martí's modernism). (Perus: 1976). 3) Because of the heavy weight of U. S. power, especially after 1898, the Caribbean alternates between metropolitan and national (often populist) literatures -between efforts to creolize surrealist and other European avant-garde strains, or to Europeanize "Afro-Creole" and other indigenous tendencies, sometimes for genuinely national, sometimes for genuinely imperialist, ends. 4) But writers like Carpentier, Depestre and Guillén transcend even the nationalist tendencies and anticipate a fourth, pan-Caribbean, Creole-socialist stage (one implied, of course, throughout Mariátegui's work), which now a few progressive writers (including many in Cuba) seek to follow.

1. Colonial Literature. The Caribbean element in early Caribbean literature may be measured by the extent to which writers "had intimate knowledge of and were in some way committed" to the area. "Given the origin and... education of these writers, we cannot expect to find examples..." of Caribbean writing as we understand the term today." To have produced Caribbean literature, writers "would have had to have possessed a far greater knowledge of and interest in the society they were writing about... the very structure of... their work would almost certainly have been affected by the cultural patterns" of the area. But their models were the European baroque and romantic masters; and they drew on existing metropolitan genres, which were ill-equipped to grasp, and hence distorted, Caribbean reality. (Brathwaite 1970: 47-48). Thus much of this writing reflects an ideological distortion of Caribbean reality, and even of the power, which dominant groups imposed on the population. Even when anti-slavery, these writers only rarely and feebly reflect the counter, resistant forces that would work on and even modify the stance and very culture of the older oligarchic plantation owning sector.

2. Modernism. Progressively nineteenth Century Caribbean writers, representing liberal and conservative wings of a small middle sector tied to nascent comprador oligarchs, focused on Caribbean life. After slave emancipation, increasing imperialist penetration pressured the growth and diversification of middle sectors. As a small but expanding internal market develops, so does newspaper and periodical production for a growing reading public able to consume this production. Increasingly fictional and essayistic prose forms seek to follow the contours of Caribbean life mainly (though not always) as ideological support to prevailing developments. In this context, however, the contradictions between material and spiritual growth, and between rich and poor, seigniorial and merchant norms, let certain poets (who were journalists as well) to identify with an alienated bohemian Western discourse that distanced them from Caribbean realities even as it sublimated and hence enforced them. Only in Martí and a few others does the force of the imperialist conjuncture lead to a situation in which metropolitan modernist discourse is subjected to a creolization process in the name of an anti-imperialist national expression. (Blanco Aguinaga 1976).

3. Nationalism. The nationalist, populist and Afro-Caribbean tendencies among twentieth Century Caribbean writers express and even foment the unfolding of the creolization process in conformity with and beyond its concrete materialization in social life. Fully emerging after the crucial U. S. interventions in the Caribbean area (the occupations of Santo Domingo, Haiti, Nicaragua, etc.), these writings mark a creative synthesis of world historical and literary currents galvanized by indigenous and mainly Afro-Caribbean dynamism. But, as the expression of intermediate social sectors constrained under prevalent forms of colonial domination, the negritude and even the Marxism of many of these writers may be (consciously or not) as readily serviceable to a developmentalist national capitalist ideology as to a vision transcending capitalist relations toward socialist future.

4. Pan-Caribbean Socialism. Only certain writers like Guillén and Carpentier transcend the ambiguities of a national literature toward a pan-Caribbean Creole vision, in which, as the Cuban Revolution sends out its signals, even an Argentine like Guevara, a Nicaraguan like Cardenal and an Uruguayan like Mario Benedetti may join.[4]

D. Caribbean Literary Themes and Modes.

In his article on Caribbean literary unity, written some years before the Revolution, Portuondo noted three recurring themes. First Caribbean unity is expressed in landscapes and seascapes -i.e., in the topology of a world that is politically and economically alien to the people that inhabit it. Second, unity is expressed in the people themselves -the diverse groups who may find common cause in their oppression and their vision of the oppressor. "Against an identical curtain of tropical background...men spend themselves on soil which does not belong to them and drag themselves about with their spirits broken or burning with rancor, like phantoms shaken by storms of the Caribbean." (Portuondo: 264). Above all, then, Portuondo sees the unity of Caribbean literature in a hatred of imperialism. "Poets and novelists continually point to the sadness and bitterness which has never left the Caribbean. The literary themes continue to be, as before, an orgy of rhythm and color... and of pain and protest among men of all races who hunger and thirst for justice on land sold to some foreign enterprise." Thus imperialism "determines the growing expression of... unity; it is the danger which every moment brings (the Caribbean peoples) together, provoking clamorous and unanimous reaction." (Ibid: 265).

The particular force and nature of imperialism in the Caribbean, as it acts against and in the process of Caribbean creolization, shapes the specific nature of Caribbean literary themes. But such external-internal interplay of economic, political and cultural forces also affects given modes of Caribbean writing in themselves and in their systemic relations as they elaborate a diverse but growingly unified literature. On this subject, we only offer a few limited and unsystematic observations.

The very openness and apparent disarray of modern metropolitan poetry had favored the development of distinctively Caribbean poetic forms uniting elements of every day life with broad cosmic vision, as the sentient realities of capitalist oppression are subjected to the distinctly Caribbean transposition process. The novelist is, by that very choice of literary mode, caught in a dominant metropolitan tradition, but the novel's openness to generic differentiation allows an Alejo Carpentier to incorporate indigenous and Latin American as opposed to rigidly European elements, and to generate new hybrid Caribbean novelistic forms. Aspects of the European tradition are progressive here-realism because of its grasp of the objective sources and textures of lived experience, its portrayal of different social groups in action: surrealism, because of its projection behind the reified given. Theater should be the site for materializing the action of creolization as ritual and spectacle, for projecting the very essence of creolization as it reaches from symbolic gesture toward concrete realization, expressing and creating community through patterns of song, dance, act and word that may communicate even to those who cannot read a program. But the historical institutionalization of the theater has generally made it a sacred precinct of those sectors most closely tied to metropolitan values, for which anything Caribbean is exotic. The theater has thus tended to be the most colonial of all modes of literary representation, except for the work of Césaire and a few others. Thus René Marqués draws on and is judged by his ability to produce a Puerto Rican version of García Lorca. Even after the Cuban Revolution, Triana offers us a revolutionary theater modeled on Genet, even if his play's problematic is to grasp the new Cuban reality by breaking through the metropolitan prism. The development of new theatrical modes (workers' theater, *campesino* theater) in today's Cuba may show the way to the future. But clearly it is the cinema, as a mass dramatic-narrative mode, which has already broken through to new dimensions: Cuban directors forging an innovate Caribbean art which grasps Cuban history in relation to the generative and receptive forces which constitute the totality of Caribbean reality as we have attempted to define it. Finally, we should point to the existence of an intermediate, hybrid genre: the prose-poem/ dramatic/ monologue/ manifesto/essay best represented by such works as *Nuestra América*, *Retour au Pays Natal*, *Calibán* and *Contradictory Omens* (not to mention the speeches of

Che and Fidel, the books of Fanon), which simultaneously explore, promote and exemplify the process of creative creolization as it moves toward dynamic cultural and political synthesis.

Other themes, modes and specific genres might be mentioned, but the essential point should be clear: Caribbean literature does not fully emerge until received metropolitan extra-literary and literary materials are minimally transformed in relation to the given play of socio-economic forces existent in the area, until new genres and sub-genres are generated which, while respecting local differentials, express Caribbean unity. Those who write Caribbean literature continue to represent a narrow band of intermediate social sectors. But the writers who succeed in generating a progressively Caribbean literature are those who transcend their social positions to incorporate the verbal and cultural languages of the Caribbean working masses. With respect to literary form and content, then, the question is not just one of equivalence with, or "reflection" of the given-but of a projection, a contribution to realizing liberating potentials. The matter is one of a class transformation of the modes of literary production in function of a less exploitative future.

4. A Summing Up

The question of unification is not one of undifferentiated social homogenizing, but one of giving the fullest measure to particular areas and peoples in their cultural configurations. Unity is no fixed reality, but a process, which refuses to leap over differences, but rather works through them toward a commonality among diverse and irreducible totalities. On this basis, a truly Caribbean literature should represent the full proportionate play of differential forces and interests in the past, present and future of Caribbean history. The measure should be totalistic literary-social correspondence in relation to the moment of literary production and to past and future totalizing tendencies. A proper view of this literature would evaluate literary works not only by their socio-historical fidelity, but also by their immediate and continuing contribution to the process of making the future. This future is one of form-making: the creation of unity. Art is both exemplum and anticipation of larger human processes. Thus our criteria for Caribbean literature are simultaneously historical and aesthetic.

As a unity, this literature remains one of creative action against imperialist and capitalist oppression. It is, in effect, the literature of Calibán -of the Caribbean Calibans who must first learn the master's language before fully learning their own, and who must then, out of the extremity of their expressed authentic differences, become one to break the staff of Prospero. On that day of Caribbean unity, a firm and deep literary unity may begin to emerge. Since that day may well depend on the ability of Latin American Calibans to achieve their victory, we may then be able to speak of the determinate but intertwining relations between Caribbean and Latin American literatures as differential objects in a truly world literature expressive of a liberated and united human world.

Postscript

The necessary, extended postscript to this text is the next one in this collection.

Works Cited

Beckford, George L. 1971. "Plantation Society: Toward a General Theory of Caribbean Society." In *Savacou*, 5 (June) 7-21.

Blanco Aguinaga, Carlos. 1976. "Del Modernismo al Mercado Interno," in Franco, et al.: 35-83.

Brathwaite, Edward. 1970. "Creative Literature of the British West Indies during the Period of Slavery," in *Savacou*. I June.

----1974. *Contradictory Omens: Cultural Diversity and Integration in the Caribbean*. Mona, Jamaica. Savacou Publications.

Fernández Retamar, Roberto. 1975. "Para una teoría de la literatura Hispanoamericana," in *Araísa: Anuario del Centro de Estudios "Rómulo Gallegos"*. Caracas. 55-108.

----1965. "Martí en su (tercer) mundo," in *Cuba Socialista*. Enero, No. 41.

Franco, Jean, et al. 1976. *Cultura y dependencia*. Guadalajara. Departamento de Bellas Artes, Gobierno de Jalisco.

Mariátegui, José Carlos. 1963. *Siete ensayos de interpretación de la realidad peruana*. La Habana. Casa de las Américas.

Mintz, Sidney Wilfred. 1966. "The Caribbean as a Socio-Cultural Area," in *Journal of World History*. Vol. 9, No. 4: 912-937.

----1974. *Caribbean Transformations*. Chicago. Aldine Publishing Company.

Perus, Françoise. 1976. *Literatura y sociedad en América latina*. México. Siglo Veintiuno Editores.

Portuondo, José Antonio. 1951. "Caribbean Literary Themes in the Last Fifty Years," in Wilgus.

Rodríguez, Ileana. 1978. "Modelo de trabajo para la integración del Caribe dentro de una visión total de la Literatura de la América Latina." Paper presented at the *Quinto Taller de Ideologías y Literatura*. Minneapolis. Institute for the Study of Ideologies and Literature. April.

Rubin, Vera D., ed. 1957. *Caribbean Studies: A Symposium*. Jamaica. Institute of Social and Economic Research, University College of West Indies.

Smith, M. C. 1957. "The African Heritage in the Caribbean" in Rubin ed.: 34-46.

Wagley, Charles. 1957. "Plantation America: A Cultural Sphere," in Rubin. ed.: 3-13.

Wilgus, A. Curtis, ed. 1951. *The Caribbean at Mid-century*. Gainesville. University of Florida Press.

Notes

1 Here I wish to note the considerable debt, which my paper owes, both in orientation and detail, to Professor Rodríguez's ongoing work on the Caribbean (her reading and lecture notes, her papers and presentations) during the 1970s. I am of course responsible for any errors or problems here.

2 Synthesis, that is, of readings specified in notes 5-13. Also like Beckford (see note 6), Wagley sees French, English, Dutch and Spanish Caribbeans as belonging to a sphere distinct from those to which mainland Latin and Anglo America's belong.

3 From this point on in 2-D, we follow Edward Brathwaite 1974.

4 Fn 4 should read: For Guevara as a heir to Martí's tradition, see Fernández-Retamar 1975: 9-101.

Chapter IV

Caribbean Literature and its Theorization: A Latin Americanist Perspective

1. Introduction

A few years before he died in a plane crash over the Caribbean, Alejandro Losada noted that the question of the area's unity was one of the most difficult matters to grasp in relation to an overall view of Latin American and Caribbean literatures (Losada 1980: 77-81). According to Losada, the area's unity derives from the "the fragmentation, disarticulation and dispersion of a social formation... founded upon the liquidation of the aboriginal population; the transplantation and enslavement of vast numbers stemming from diverse cultures; the organization of a regressive system of exploitation articulated in relation to the needs of the most modernized capitalist sectors; dependency with respect to multiple metropolitan poles; the permanent replacement of the dominant poles; the persistence of the colonial situation; and finally the dominant hegemony of North American imperialism over... 'national' societies that have not achieved any... marked degree of density, ...or development." But, says Losada, the unity discernible among Caribbean literatures speaks to the "subteranean unity of a vast socio-historical heterogenity"; and, he suggests, that unity can be conceived in function of characteristics which emerge from the area's absences, "its lack of homogenity, its expanding process of degeneration the more it has depended on dominant societies in... an accelerating, centrifugal process of capitalist modernization, the inability of the archipelago's diverse components to articulate themselves, by virtue of their dependence on diverse hegemonic centers that don't permit the system to explode or organize itself.

It is a system that acquires its differential traits from the impossibility of constituting itself, that is situated in negation and that draws its historicity from the absence of a formative process, since all the events that have decided

> *its fate contributed to avoiding any type of social structuration and cultural autonomy. If this view were found to be correct, we would confront a series of cultural ensembles dependent on dominant metropolitan centers until the abrupt process of de-colonization began; and we would confront a literature of exile, which is totally internationalized, and whose central problem goes back precisely to history, converting negativity into a principle of positivity and formulating an identity which could only be realized in a revolutionary future. In a society that is disperse, regressive, dependent on multiple international poles of. hegemony, and which has what is probably the most conflictive sense of identity in contemporary social experience, a literary system has developed from José Martí to today, that takes its point of departure from a situation of alienation as much with the popular masses as with dominant groups-a literature that can only constitute itself in exile... from their societies of origin, whose future capacity to create their own history and their own action on nature is only expressed in the anticipatory patterns found in that literature (Losada 79).*

Ultimately, Losada argues, the affirmative dimensions of Caribbean societies are beginning to emerge in consciousness before they surface in reality. And this process takes place first in literature. Referring to the writings of Roger Bastide, Roberto Fernández Retamar, René Depestre, José Luis Méndez and Jan Carew, he stresses the impact of surrealism, the development of magical realism and *"lo real maravilloso"* as inherent to a literary system which projects beyond the given; and he points to the processes of immigration and exile as fundamental to understanding the growth of a social consciousness in literature which goes beyond what can be expected given the limitations of the social formations which propel these processes. He then concludes by posing his central question about "how one should elaborate a study of Caribbean literature as a unity":

> *I ask if it would be possible to work from the hypothesis that... it is possible to constitute a system which emerges as a social-revolutionary mode of production which by virtue of its marginalized situation with respect to its own people as much as with the dominant groups, by virtue of being produced in exile, by virtue of its effort to deepen and re-elaborate the serious problems and the consciousness of these masses exploited throughout so many centuries, by virtue of being able to overcome this situation by providing a revolutionary future that includes the entire region and is only fully given in the context of world revolution... for all these reasons, that is, for the predominantly internationalized system configured by works of writers closely tied to the struggle for a new international order and for the reinvention of the identity*

of their own people... And I ask if this literature doesn't receive its unity by responding to one and the same mode of production and above all,... by being referred, not to each particular small nation-society,... but rather to the social formation of the Great Caribbean which,... with the Cuban Revolution and the process of decolonization and the acceleration of anti-imperialist revolutionary agitation, begins to constitute a new global social formation and to determine its own history. And I ask if it is not the social function of the cultural production of the Caribbean writers to participate in the preparation of this new consciousness that will permit them to march to the encounter of an identity that, today, only can be presented in the future (80-81).

I have quoted Losada at length, because I take his position to be a superior but representative synthesis of views common to Marxist and Left Latin Americanists confronting the question of Caribbean literary and broader unity during the late 1970s. Advances in literary sociology throughout that decade and the intent to bring the Caribbean into the advancing endeavor were part of the effort set forth clearly in the Cuban Revolution and especially in the work of Roberto Fernández Retamar, and also of critics representing such institutions as the Centro de Estudios Rómulo Gallegos, or Losada's Berlin Institute and Minnesota's Institute for the Study of Ideologies and Literature. Indeed it is no accident that many of Losada's views and orientations coincide with those found in the volume which was published by the latter institute and which I had the privilege to co-edit, *Process of Unity in Caribbean Societies: Ideologies and Literature* (1983).[1]

It has been many years since the conference was held which resulted in the volume; and while many such conferences were held before and since ours, it seems to me fitting that we take this opportunity to look back at that particular one and see where it came from and where we are going now, because of the particular impact the book has seemed to have had at least with certain Latin Americanists concerned with the Caribbean. The fact that the book was published by I&L, and that there seemed to be few prior texts in English that addressed the theme so much at the level of theory, is responsible for at least part of its impact, although the same reasons may contribute to the fact that it was not widely distributed among Caribbean specialists or specialists in Black or Afro-Caribbean studies." In effect, the book reflects its time of germination-the period prior to and after the Nicaraguan and Grenadan revolutions, corresponding first to the presentation of the materials and then (in June-September, 1980), the period of their decisive completion. More importantly the materials constituting *Process,* as well as Losada's commentary, reflect the views of Caribbeanists and Latin Americanists who still believed in the hopes in a revolutionary transformation of the area and drew their sense of unity in function of a vision of revolutionary struggle and hope.

Much has changed since Losada's words and the appearance of our volume; inevitably much has changed too in the ideological, cultural and literary spheres, as well as in our understanding of socio-literary relations both on global and region-wide levels. Indeed enough has perhaps occurred for us to be surmise that we may be living in a distinct epoch. So, while the theme of Caribbean social and literary unity was certainly on the table long before, the conference of 1978; and while many important interventions have occurred since, some confirming and some questioning the nature, the direction and the very viability of a concept of unity (and indeed many taking on the theme in a very different political light from our own-e.g., there are those who use the question of "Caribbean unity" to speak of strategic defense dominated by the U.S. to promote domino theories and then counter the dominoes through regional hegemony schemes), now some years into Latin American debt and developmental crisis, now after the collapse of Grenada, the relative stalemate in Guatemala and El Salvador, the changes in Jamaica, Haiti, and other places, now when international pressures are focused on Nicaragua, on talks in Santo Domingo, now after the Mariel, the Haitian boat people, rebellion and election slaughters, it is time to address once again the questions raised by the conference of 1978 and examine their relation to this conference of 1988, to this point in time from which we once again attempt to totalize past and future.

What in sum were the premises, findings and conclusions in our conference and conference volume? What major achievements can be ascribed to our efforts and what major errors may we have committed? What if any solid bases for future work? What forces stemming from the past led to the book's particular successes and limitations? How should we see the text now, in relation to what changes?

This essay is orientated toward the question of very recent transformations in Latin American-Caribbean culture itself, and then in the theoretical apparatuses used to examine them. In this regard, I will emphasize the emergence of recent forms and even of cultural systems which relate to new supposedly democratic and anti-dictatorial (but also non or even anti-Marxist) tendencies in Latin America and the Caribbean and speak to an incorporation but also partial negation of a Cuban influence which was once very strong indeed but is now experiencing great modification even by those with Marxist orientations. In this regard, I point to a left critique which is best exemplified in a recent volume by Ernesto Laclau and Chantal Mouffe; *Hegemony and Socialist Strategy: Towards a Radical Democratic Politics.* (London: Verso, 1985); Lacclau and Mouffe may help us to explain such phenomena but clearly point to a shift away from the kinds of orientations that are associated with the Cuban revolution, with the policies of Cuba's cultural producers and its Ministry of Culture, and of ideologues like Roberto Fernández Retamar, as in his well known essay, *Caliban*.

What I will attempt here is to point to current theoretical orientations being accepted by many critics who have been impacted by, but who in certain ways are now greatly modifying, the heritage in cultural orientation and theory provided by the Revolution. I will take a critical stance visavis what I suggest are standard and normative Marxist ways of looking at Caribbean cultural production as represented by Losada as well as by virtually all of us who were involved in the Caribbean conference and the conference volume in question. Thus, the theoretical orientations stemming from Laclau and Mouffe are shown to raise questions about and counter the standard ways of viewing cultural production- most specifically, perhaps, as formulated by Nestor Garcia Canclini, whose work clearly bears the direct weight of Cuban orientations to popular culture and whose early work indeed won the Casa de las Américas prize several years ago and is considered by the cultural establishment to be modelic in surveying and theorizing cultural questions with regard to capitalist processes, state policy and everyday life, as well as relations between so-called elite, popular and folk cultural dimensions.

2. The Book's Major Achievements and Limitations

At its best, *Process* constituted a synthesis of perspectives that had been developing over the years on the theme of Caribbean socio-literary unity, and an effort to move to newer levels of conceptualization and applications. What was going to make possible any advance was the fact of the prior years of work by many social scientists, including Franklin Knight, who was a prime conference participant, and of course by many literary critics and theoreticians represented among others by Roberto Márquez, Maximillian LaRoche, Lisa Davis and my co-editor, Ileana Rodríguez.

It was Rodríguez who in fact planned and organized the conference and who was largely responsible for its orientations and achievements. Clearly her perspective as a Latin Americanist (and a Central American Caribbeanist) served to orient discussions toward seeing the Caribbean in Latin American contexts. The other Latin Americanists brought their varying linguistic backgrounds and specializations to the discussion; and I suppose my own role was to provide perspectives stemming from my dual background in comparative literature and migration studies.

Knight provided a unitary view of Caribbean history in terms of the imposition of varying degrees of plantation structure on one or another varying degrees and combinations of original forms of social orientation established by European conquest patterns. Discussants built on Knight's perspective by raising questions about the relation between the historical dimensions he specified with linguistic, aesthetic and literary phenomena, coming to the conclusion that such factors of differentiation as varying forms of colonial and neo-colonial domination, distinct languages and language mixes, aesthetic and literary determinants and traditions were themselves subject to patterns of similarity and identification stemming from the basic economic structuring and the political forms which emerged to secure the reproduction of Caribbean socio-economic relations. Thus, attention went to labor force development, structural parallels in movement out of and beyond plantation societies, and in this context, patterns of cultural resistance and transformation, in relation to patterns inducing immigration, growing national and pan-Caribbean consciousness and political organization aimed at promoting, neutralizing or repressing various forms of opposition.

Common literary themes, forms and movements were identified and differences were projected in function of varying modes for dealing with similar problems and similar modes of dealing with divergent problems. And here I can boast to my own effort to establish a basis for evaluating literatures in a regional context, for synthesyzing past perspectives on Caribbean societies and literatures in a world context, and for attempting a critical application of Edward Brathwaite's concept of creolization as a model of cultural process for relating socio-cultural and literary dimensions of Caribbean life. Provisional, preliminary efforts were made at a thematic survey and a historical periodization of literature (perhaps the most suspect aspect of my own contribution came here), and sample analyses were offered and evaluated, primarily centering on Cuba, Jamaica and Haiti as representative cases. Clearly a key failure of the conference was to deal adequately with the Dutch Caribbean, and for some reason not intended by the editors, a key paper on post-revolutionary Cuban literary development was left out of the published volume. But these major absences aside, perhaps the most valuable aspect of the proceedings was the overall rejection of an analysis centered on chronological analysis in favor of one which combines an emphasis on structural (or systadial) phases with allowance for certain key determinate, "nodal" moments or conjunctures (e.g, the Haitian Revolution, 1898, 1959, etc.) that were so forceful that they tended to level structural and productive differences to produce certain cultural parallels in diverse social formations. In addition, the volume took a significant step, I would argue, in the almost quixotic effort to conceptualize the impact of migration and exile in the generation of Caribbean literary production and pan-Caribbean consciousness (Rodríguez and Zimmerman, ed.: 121-124).[2]

Obviously the text was very uneven and had innumerable shortcomings. But whatever weaknesses or strengths may be ascribed to individual papers and presentations, it is interesting to note how willing participants were to criticize each other and themselves, to call attention to the tentativeness of analyses and conceptualizations, to suggest matters to be explored that might totally alter their orientations and findings. In this respect, considerable attention went toward the imprecision and mainly rhetorical emphasis given to political analysis-i.e., to the struggles for state power and also to the political apparatuses and organizations that mediate between economic and cultural dimensions. Such an orientation to comparative study would have required the most careful tracing of patterns. It would perhaps have put too much reductive pressure on political/literary correlations (tying given literary structures to given political groups or strategies and perhaps limiting the possible range of significations that a given literary work, genre or movement might actually embody), but it would have had the virtue of moving discussion beyond generalizations based on dichotomies such as "progressive/regressive" utopic/dystopic elements, etc. At another level, and here we may be getting to the question about the conference and the volume resulting from it, the text is marked by (1) an attempt to include at least parts of Mexico, Central and South America in its definition of the Caribbean; and (2) a fundamental insistence (reaffirmed again and again in spite of all objections) on a core unity of the area. These two points make for certain core difficulties which, it should be noted, Alejandro Losada's text clearly shared.

First, while Vera Cruz, Puerto Limón, Belize and countless other littoral area towns and regions may be clearly Caribbean, or have strong Caribbean dimensions, Guatemala City and Managua cannot be so considered. One of the problems, perhaps, of the Nicaraguan Revolution in its early phase was the failure of the Sandinistas to distinguish between Caribbean and Central American dimensions of their nationhood, and also, it should be noted, to assume that Caribbean roots would be sufficient to guarantee a positive relation between Cubans and from Bluefields Afro-Caribbean Nicaraguans. With regard to the unity theme, a stress on common African roots blurs the diversity of African cultural patterns imbedded in divergent Caribbean polities, and the way in which varying modes of domination meant varying degrees and kinds of cultural resistance. Above all, then, the preoccupation with unity may erase significant differences which distort cultural and literary analysis. Indeed, to the degree that this preoccupation is constructed in function of anti-imperialist/anti-colonial struggles leading to some kind of socialist pan-Caribbean unity and to the degree that that orientation becomes the key assumption motivating our own conference volume (as well as Losada's text), we may be left ill-prepared to study Naipul and Wolcott, to grasp the transformation of a figure like Eric Williams, to grasp the problems of a Manley, to understand the kind of tensions that would undermine Granada-in effect to understand all the complexities of the Caribbean in the course of a historical development that would seem far less simple than what one can expect from the kind of linearity generally found in the more traditional stage theory orientations of Marxist analysis. Inevitably, limitations with respect to understanding the Caribbean's political and cultural past would lead to problems in anticipating the future. The transformations of Caribbean culture in the 1980s and beyond cannot be reduced to the conception of the area's emerging future that is articulated both by Losada and by most contributors to our conference volume.

3. The Cuban Dimension

It is obvious that the perspectives referred to stem from the ethos generated by the Cuban revolution and dispersed throughout the Latin American universe in the 1960s and into the 1970s; and it is also obvious that while this ethos persists, it has been modified by newer currents that have emerged in this universe and have come to dominate our times.

To speak of "change and a move away from," it would serve our purpose to attempt recapturing and articulating here what indeed the orientation was toward Caribbean culture embedded in the Cuban Revolution, what role culture and its theorization played in the revolution and its consolidation and what effect these matters had on Latin America and on those who would be called upon to characterize and theorize about Caribbean culture and literature. Then we would be in a better position to point to where things went in the late 1980s and where they are today-where the initial and subsequent dimensions of Cuban cultural production and theorization stand visavis more recent developments.

It is still not difficult to recall the effect of the Cuban Revolution on young, rebellious spirits throughout the Americas. The Guatemalan Reform Movement had been overthrown; the U.S. was still living the effects of the McCarthy years. Cuba reminded many young intellectuals of African cultural dimensions in Latin America, the Caribbean but also the U.S. and, of course, Africa itself. The young intelligentsia read Aimé Cesaire; discovered the Harlem Renaissance; discovered Amilcar Cabral, Albert Memmi and Frantz Fanon; discovered the critiques of colonialism and neo-colonialism-and then such constructs as Regis Debray's foco theory and Andre Gunder Frank's version of dependency theory. Through the Revolution, popular images (of Che, of Castro) became virtual icons of a new cultural orientation; the example of Nicholas Guillen, and his *poesía negra,* joined with the images of bearded revolutionaries as variant versions of *"el nuevo hombre."* The "New Song Movement," new political poetry, new popular theatre, new dance, new art, new narrative genres such as the testimonial, and above all a new cinema surfaced as part of an overall emerging system of Cuban and more broadly Latin American/Caribbean left popular culture that incorporated and yet challenged more exclusively elite cultural models and posited a pre-history that linked José Martí to Mariátegui and Sandino, to Cuban left writers of the 1930s and 40s, and to a wide range of writers, cultural producers and revolutionaries who developed in the fifties and on into the sixties. Indeed a genealogy of revolutionary culture and revolutionary ethos emerged linking *el nuevo hombre* to the indigenous struggle against the Spaniards, to moments and movements of Indian and Black resistance and then *mestizo, mulato* and overall worker and poor people's struggle throughout the centuries in the Caribbean and Latin America. Martí was heralded as the father of a modern movement that had roots in Tecum Uman, Toussaint L'Ouverture and Bolívar; and the Revolution's ideologues fought over his image against his liberal and rightwing champions and interpreters, to posit him as the forerunner of the Sierra Maestra revolutionaries who were in turn seen as heirs to Sandino and all prior liberation fighters, and as the predecessors of a veritable new wave of revolutionaries that would emerge very quickly throughout Latin America, the Caribbean and the Third World, and finally between Blacks and Latinos in the U.S.

Summing up this overall perspective in the cultural sphere (and then applying the perspective to his own literary specialty) was Roberto Fernández Retamar in his *Calibán* essay (1985 and 1989). Here, the Cuban critic overturns Rodó's old *modernista* identification of Latin America as a spiritual Ariel opposed to a materialistic U.S. Calibán in function of a view which takes on the colonial vision of Latin America as Calibán (a barbarous malcreant-indeed a Caribbean cannibal) to be "tamed" and controlled by white European civilization, and transforms the image to posit a future in function of the resistance and revolt of the oppressed African, Indian and "half-breed" or mestizo masses of Latin America. Fernández Retamar then traced the cultural expressions of this revolt seeing in them the bases for the emergence of a new revolutionary ethos through a creative cultural *mestizaje* in fulfillment of Latin America's particular nature as the most westernized sector of the colonial or third world.

Inevitably, Fernández Retamar sought to see all cultural forms and works in relation to his overall theory; he sought to develop his own work and that of other Cuban and Latin American cultural producers in this direction.[3] Indeed, even long before writing *Calibán* and as director of *Casa de las Américas*, he had made the values underlying this work essential dimensions and criteria in promoting and granting prizes to works submitted to his *Casa* journal and its annual literary contests. On the whole, *Casa de las Américas* joins with the overall Ministry of Culture program in promoting the specific developments in new song and the new film industry and the institutionalization of all these advances in function of international competitions and festivals, as a prime force in the generation of the cultural image fostered by the Cuban Revolution for internal and external consumption.

This orientation has much to tell us about the importance of cultural production and theory for Latin America as a whole. To the degree that revolutionary ideologues were able to go beyond orthodox paradigms, they projected a long-term situation in which Cuba's underdeveloped economy would not lead the way in transforming consciousness; rather, cultural and ideological structures and their institutionalization would have to provide the concrete practices that would in turn sustain revolutionary élan through hard times and would in fact help in the ultimate socio-economic and political transformations required by the revolution. Since resistance to powerful structures of domination had frequently been centered in, or displaced to, cultural and ideological expression, and since, then, cultural resistance could also become a mode of opposition to the Revolution itself, great attention was given to these aspects of social life as essential to the revolutionary process. Culture became a prime site of struggle against resistance to the Revolution.

At first, Cuban cultural production was pluralistic and explosive. In painting, sculpture and photography, the older artists were encouraged; and new artists working in new media with a wide range of techniques, were helped along. In poetry, the Afro-Cuban forms of Guillén were heralded, and taken up too by a new generation of writers like Nancy Morejón. But Black revindication and recuperation, so central to Guillén's work, were not promoted as the only national way. Non-Marxist Catholic "progressives" such as Cintio Vittier and Fina García Marruz were promoted; and a kind of "conversational poetry" more indebted to Vallejo and Nicanor Parra than to Neruda or Guillén was championed by Fernández Retamar and became the prime model. As for narrative, Alejo Carpentier was seen as the national model, though many continued to recognize Lezama Lima as the nation's greatest writer, and his views about the Revolution, and his relation to the process (including questions of his sexual orientation) became the subject of continued commentary. Among the younger writers, Herberto Padilla, Roberto Desnoes and Antonio Benítez Rojo won praise, even, for a time, when their work showed some severe questioning of the Revolution. As policies began to tighten up, when Padilla was jailed and his work censored, when Vargas Llosa and other Latin American Boom writers began to question Cuba's cultural policy and the Revolution as a whole, the official response was to point toward the generation of more "popular" modes as essential to the needs of the people.

Miguel Barnet's *Autobiography of a Runaway Slave* launched the new testimonial genre, which, as theorized by Barnet, Margaret Randall and others, came to be seen as a literary form expressing the oppressed and subaltern (the black slaves, the abused Indians, women, workers, etc.) opposing the modern boom novel in essential ways and having a certain traditional base in the Caribbean. Then of course there were the developments in song, theater and film. The new song movement foregrounded older artists and musical forms obscured by commercialism, and opened the door to new poets, musicians and singers in the creation of the new Latin American music. In addition to reviving older Afro-Caribbean musical traditions, the musicians also sought new fusions of jazz, tropical, popular, classical and other musical modes, creating some of the more exciting experimental music work in the hemisphere.

The cultural ethos of the revolution led to institutional efforts promoting the discussion and creation of new plays and theatrical forms. Yet, while many agit-prop plays developed, it should be noted that one of the first acclaimed plays, dealing with problems of domestic adjustment to the revolutionary process, *Noche de los asesinos*, by José Triana, was modelled more on Jean Genet than on Bertolt Brecht, and that the kind of theater most encouraged, the kind which developed in the countryside by the Escambray theater group, drew on a wide range of popular and "high culture" forms in trying to find dynamic ways of portraying and participating in the new social process that was under way.

Along with the literacy program and other forms of popular outreach, the film industry developed, producing not only a wide range of educational and propaganda films of high quality, but also new feature film forms seeking new ways to link history and narrative, collective and individual experience. From the documentaries of Santiago Álvarez, to Humberto Sola's *Lucía,* to masterpieces like *Memorias de subdesarrollo, La Ultima Cena, La Muerte de un Burócrata* etc. Cuban filmmakers working with low budgets and under often primitive conditions followed the lead of a few others in Latin America (Buñuel in Mexico, a few key directors in Argentina, Brazil, etc.) in linking popular indigenous traditions with elements of Italian neo-realism, surrealism and the world revolutionary cinematic tradition to further the development of "the new Latin American Cinema."

Of special relevance was the film industry's concern with national history and culture, with some special emphasis on folk traditions and slavery. In productions such as *El Otro Francisco,* the film industry sought to present and critique previous Cuban ideological-literary constructs; Sara Gómez's *En cierta manera,* shows various dimensions of transformed African and Spanish culture to be in conflict with the Revolution's social and productive ethic, and the film remarkably projects a series continuing and future conflicts that will plague the Revolution over the years.

The impact of Cuban cultural developments and their institutionalization had a marked impact on Caribbean cultural production throughout the sixties and into the 1970s-partially through imitation, partially because national social forces dictated parallel developments and partially because young revolutionary artists saw the situations as similar or wished them to be so. In art and theater, many radical young artists followed the Cuban lead; and in some cases, they developed forms paralleling Cuban "models," but speaking to distinct national contexts and possibilities. For many, the Revolution and revolutionary cultural achievements constituted a new phase in a long history of Caribbean struggle and resistance. The institutionalization of the prizes of *Casa de las Américas,* the promotion of Caribbean cultural conferences and investigation, the development of international cultural competitions created vehicles for spreading Cuban cultural influences. Revolutionary poetry, testimonials and new novels appeared throughout the area, often showing the Cuban impact. Musical forms like salsa and reggae at times captured or reflected on certain dimensions of criticism, protest and rebellion that had been given new life with the Cuban experience. In the Caribbean, as in much of the third world, and even in the U.S., among counter cultural sectors, and especially among radical Latino cultural workers, what was understood as the Cuban example was a constant dimension of cultural life. Cultural expression and aesthetic criteria became overtly politicized; radical artist groups developed; new journals sprang up; on several islands, there were even efforts to follow the Cuban lead and produce socially-oriented feature films.

4. Changes in Latin American and Caribbean Cultural Production

Changing circumstances in Latin America, the Caribbean and in Cuba also led to great changes in political and cultural spheres. From the economic crises of the early 1970s, a new order began to emerge involving renewed efforts at revolution or other modes of social renovation, structured in part by the now inexorable costs of development, the overwhelming reality of debt crisis, and the search for alternative economic and government models, especially in the wake of the renewed ambition by the U.S. government, under Reagan, to restore and maintain U.S. hegemony throughout what was considered to be the "U.S. sphere of influence." Meanwhile, Cuban cultural development seemed to have reached structural limits. Television fare was less experimental, and the most important new narrative experiments involved the elaboration of a socialist detective genre. The Cuban film industry seemed to flag (the failure of *Cecilia*

Valdez, seems a turning point), and the drive to carry out a revolution at the level of "people's culture" seemed to lose considerable momentum. The Mariel raised questions about the revolution and its relation to the "masses," and even the role of Caribbean syncretism as an oppositional force against the Revolution's production ethos. Efforts to institutionalize the film industry through the establishment of a festival and institute, the appearance of new films and new directors in the past few years, signal efforts at renovation whose ultimate direction and impact was not yet clear. (Though, curiously, the successful film, *Lejanía,* with its intense focus on interior domestic and familial space, seems a filmic throwback to Triana's early study of the revolution's impact on family dynamics).

In the meantime, with the exception of countries like Nicaragua and El Salvador where revolutionary movements nurtured on the Cuban image continued to live and grow (though even here the national dimensions and strong religious emphases generated crucial differences), new transformations occurred which no longer strictly reflected old left/ right dichotomies and which pointed to the emergence of a new order. In the Caribbean, dramatic governmental changes in Jamaica, Grenada and Haiti simply were the most sensational dimensions of an overall process involving profound socio-economic and political transformations.[4] Part and parcel of this change was the new interweaving of Caribbean and U.S. dimensions, as reggae, salsa, and jazz, for example, effected a series of roundtrip circuits, and as an island-based literature was impacted by bourgeoning U.S. Puerto Rican and Cuban literatures, now bearing strains from the U.S. mainstream, but also from U.S. Black and Chicano literature. In this newly emerging context, I believe it is safe to say that in cultural sphere, the Cuban model for the development of an anti-bourgeois people's culture is still a strong but now more indirect influence, and it seems to be less central in the cultural schemes projected by even by sectors that are considered radical or progressive. So for example, the transformations we may find from the early films of Sanjines, Glauber Rocha and Getino are now displaced by new, less radical modes of filmmaking by Equino, Diegues and Getino himself in South America. So too if we compare the few Caribbean films, the new novels, etc., we find less radical images, even as social problems such as marginality, drug addiction, exploitation and the like are portrayed. In one sense, the changes may reflect the fact that the radical model of political culture is just too extreme, too much opposed to immediate mass interests, which include a desire for forms of entertainment which revolutionary elites with populist orientations might well find as lacking redeeming social or even aesthetic value. In many places, conservative forces have won at least a temporary victory, as people begin to fear risking the little they may have (or think they have), and as their "democratic" government forms or political parties tend to involve a wide variety of bourgeois and popular groups and tend to generate cultural forms that signify broad alliances which submerge polarizing class interests.

So it was that the reality of the socio-economic and political order (including the fact of reasserted U.S. hegemony) clearly impacted the cultural sphere. But of course the reality was also an expression of people's ideology, the general discrediting of Marxist solutions and orientations, which affected the work of the most progressive cultural producers. In many respects, we witnessed the extension of the public sphere of progressive cultural production, less specifically revolutionary in content, at times more and at times less extreme and experimental in form. It may even be possible to speak of a throwback to the early stages of the Cuban revolution, before its specific "socialist offensive" and the implementation of more narrow party norms, etc. So it came to be that the less radical surface of most representative Caribbean cultural products pointed toward a new social and cultural ethos which would require new modes of thought and understanding in relation even to literary models in the years that were to follow.

5. Caribbean Literary Studies and Broader Conceptual Orientations in the 1980s

In the meantime, what studies appeared with respect to the Caribbean's evolving culture and literature and how did these texts stand with respect to the broader theoretical trends? Just to cite a few key texts published in the U.S. during the 1980s, we may point to the volumes written by Jackson, Cudjoe and Darthorne the collection edited by Minc and, as a sample, modelic monograph, the book by Sommer.[5] In effect, the relatively comprehensive published book-length studies have not been many; and, compared to the Rodríguez/ Zimmerman volume, they have not, I believe, explored theoretical questions very extensively. On the other hand, they have been decidedly more concrete, involving close looks at given themes and given works, bringing together dimensions of the Caribbean literary and cultural past in diverse combinations, treating Caribbean culture from a variety of Latin Americanist and Africanist angles. In this sense, the new books constitute sequels to the kind of work represented by G. R. Coulthard (1948 and 1962) in a previous generation.

Jackson's volume was a pioneering survey of Black writing throughout Latin America and thus, for its virtues, suffers from the rough empiricism that usually characterizes surveys. In the last analysis, Caribbean developments were subsumed to Latin American ones; and all the volumes are informed by a framework referring to Black History that informs U.S. Black Studies more than it does normative Latin American or Antillian studies orientations. Cudjoe's volume on the other hand is a very broad study of Caribbean resistence covering nineteenth Century Caribbean novels and presenting rich analyses of key novels from Jamaica, Haiti, Cuba, etc. In one sense, the volume might be said to concretize perspectives invoked by the Rodríguez/Zimmerman (and Losada) texts, but I believe that the author's own particular brand of Marxist-Leninist orthodoxy with respect the question of resistance and literary expression subsumes not only his Africanist and Latin Americanist orientations, but also other modes of left critique. Cudjoe too readily excludes works and writers that do not fit his paradigm of resistance, except when, as in the case of his analysis of Naipul, he can use the occasion to attack the author's colonial mentality and betrayal of what is for the critic a more correct Caribbean perspective.

For its part, Darthorne's book shows a substantial grasp of the multiplicity of African cultural strains in Caribbean writing. In spite of the sexist title to his text, he is very alive to the commodification and stereotyping of black women, as well as other dimensions of exoticism, racism and chauvinism, to be found in what of us have taken as "progressive" writing among Harlem Renaissance, *negrista* and *negritud* texts. Indeed, Darthorne's book is characterized by an analytical and critical sharpness that indicates a certain degree of authority. He has much to tell us about what is authentically African in a text and what could be its significance in given contexts. He is able to indicate the great failures of Palés Matos at the same time as it signals positives in his work. Nevertheless, Dathorne falls short in relation to our concern for a more integral analysis of Caribbean literature, which, as Cudjoe reminds, cannot be reduced to a few transformations of an African essence.

Minc's collection makes many valuable contributions and signals new orientations, especially those that are developing in the field of Latin American popular culture that are promoted by Jean Franco and her associates. But the virtue of the book's pluralistic analysis is partially limited by the unequal coverage, by the lack of rigorous parameters of organization and theory, and by the incomprehensible inclusion of Central American materials that seem foreign to the theme of the book. Finally, Sommer's study of the Dominican novel in effect signals new theoretical models that include questions of literary romanticism relation to advanced theories of populism, but I would argue that the book is constituted without an adequate Caribbean mediation.

If, in the last analysis, we find that these texts of the 1980s don't lead much beyond the efforts of Rodríguez/Zimmerman and Losada to express theories or perspectives adequate to the most recent Caribbean developments, we should not be surprised or overly critical. Jackson's book appeared very early to merit this kind of reprimand; and the woks mentioned previously were published before *Process* and therefore in no way reflect that text. Nevertheless, as publications focused on a summary of previous developments, these volumes, with the partial exception of the efforts of Minc and Sommer, partake of an ethos with *Process* (and also with Losada's book) that was common to a previous period, but that we can now find waning by the time of the book's appearance.

But where should we direct ourselves then to describe a synthetic, unified and adecuately differentiated conceptualization of Caribbean culture and literature that fits with our present realities? What more ample theoretical orientations have developed that explain contemporary transformations and signal new perspectives in Caribbean literature? How should we understand all that is at play, and what group of orientations can guide our understanding?

First we should examine general theoretical models that have developed recently in Comparative Literature that include criticisms of national literatures, theories of influence, questions of dependence, national minorities, uneven development, of "intertextuality," but also of relations betwen text and the broader cultural field.[6]

Nevertheless, to go beyond literary concerns, as the volumes cited suggest but don't totally realice, the energies of Latin American and Caribbean studies have centered on posing the question of the relations between literary and broader cultural systems. This tendency can probably find no more logical place for its application and elaboration than in the Caribbean, where, given the low levels of literacy and economic development, literature as such and written discourse, must relate to and indeed mesh with broader cultural configurations or die.

6. Broader Conceptual Orientations in the Early 1980s

Of course, whatever type of theoretical frames that we can invoke will have to be modified by particular regional analyses (like those of the Caribbean o any of this sub-regions), and also by the integration of theoretical perspectives that can question the mode by means of which the conceptual units are constructed. In the case of the Caribbean, questions obviously emerge about the relations between different policies and cultural processes, but also abut whether the units of comparison should be realized on the basis of genre, language, etc. Once again, the same questions persist over the decades, although they are formulated in different ways. In all this, it could be argued at that time that while respecting what Walter Mignolo would come to designate as the "colonial differnce," Caribbean culture and literature were best understood in relation to Latin America, the transatlantic and overall African diasporic experience, underdevelopment, imperialism, etc.. If we choose a Latin Americanist perspective (although we recognize that the Caribbean is part of "Black America" and possesses particular characteristics that for moments have more in common with other other African diaspora constellations than with other, specifically Latin American sub-totalities with which they also find themselves related), then, it seemed clear we should pay special attention to the recent Latin American cultural perspectives and especially those that provide orientation that, no matter how influenced by Cuban influences, they also respond to the political and socio-economic currents that had changed the cultural configuration of our hemisphere, and especially the theoretical constructions utilized to think about cultural aspects with other dimensons of social life.

There is no doubt that the transformations of the American hemisphere in this period, including the problematic of the so-called Caribbean Basin countries, and the general crisis of Latin America in function of its financial debt, developmentalism and "redemocratization" have been accompanied by largescale transformations in cultural theory, as in cultural production and relations. It seemed that we were on the verge of a new global theorization of Latin America and the Caribbean, as well as of new intents to conceptualize the Caribbean and its ideological/cultural production within this context.

In the 1960s, the critical models based on "modes of production," "dependency," "world systems theory" and other constructions had already extended beyond high Latin American culture or the so-called literary boom toward other forms of cultural expression. At a time when the debt crisis and tenative movements toward democratic agency in the contemporary hemispheric landscape, the new emergent cultural forms challenged dominant boom post-modernism or the many modes of a de-culturating mass culture. Many more women, working-class and otherwise subaltern producers had appeared, and theories emphasizing mass media, feminism, "ethno-poetics," "socio-semiotics" and "symbolic anthropology" joined in a radical critique which found a new articulation that rejects any inevitable "centering" on fixed truisms, developmentalist or Marxist.

The effort in dependency theory to displace the problems of normative national histories through a grasp of international forces was itself transformed by a questioning of the conceptual units used to think social reality and by a mode of analysis which refused any predetermination of social causality and coherence. Internal forces were respected as much as external ones. Points of social dynamism, questions of subordination and domination, were not automatic; variables were known to function nation to nation, region to region but even internally in each polity. Literature and culture were not themselves fixed in meaning or functionality, but came to be different things and play different roles in different social totalities. Above all, literature and culture were not seen as reflections or even mediated or relatively autonomous expressions of other social forces, but as variously and differentially functioning constituents (and sometimes even important, conditioning ones) of social processes whose "laws" of development were subject to shifting gravities and combinations. The new theoretical constructs induced by new phenomena and new circumstances caused a re-questioning of past literature and cultural life. A new sense of historical richness and possibility emerges in a view of Latin America in which elite and popular culture played important, intertwined roles, and in which non-Iberian Caribbean literature and a bilingual U.S. Latino literature were now integral parts. A Bakhtinian view of the carnival came to dominate literary studies, breaking down old categories, intertwining ever more complex and dialogical relations and making for an ever more complex, rich and world which could not be grasped by our older oppositional and categorical modes of thought, dialectical, positivist or otherwise.

In these circumstances, meta-theories such as "the unity of the Caribbean" or the "unity of Caribbean literatures" threatened to become a conservative and not a revolutionary critique. Such "unifying" or totalizing efforts came close to a fatal reductionism, in which specific and determinate differences, whether products of distinct origin, domination, resistance or some combination of these elements, came to constitute a dimension of analysis that could not be ignored. It was important to think through to the points of unity, but one should not assume as did Alejandro Losada and several of the contributors to *Process*, that Central America could or should be confused with the Caribbean, that an easy unity can be achieved over race difference (the frequent failure by Latin Americanists to underestimate racial tensions and enmities) or that racial unity could easily transcend class difference (the frequent failure of those who promoted national and ethnic pride). We had to learn not to confound Miskitas or Belizians with Ladinos, nor necessarily concur with Eric Williams or Derek Walcott, or V.S. Naipul, or Edward Kamau Brathwaite even if we recognized that they were key Caribbean thinkers and artists. Pride in autonomy did not, on the other hand, obviate the need for economic planning and integration if Caribbean polities were ever to arise above dependence. Clearly, if there were ever any illusions, we had to know now that the costs of development were simply too high to repeat models which worked problematically even in other, larger countries under other circumstances. A reggae by Pablo Moses or a salsa by Rubén Blades might have radical lyrics, but they might be neutralized by the music; in other cases, traditional music patterns were in fact dynamized by their lyrics. But no matter how radical the subject, we had to be careful not to make assumptions about its possible effect on a given object.

Ultimately, the collective work-in-progress over Latin American and Caribbean culture was meant to articulate a synthetic method for explaining cultural life in ways that pointed to those processes by which new possiblilities could come into being. But the contribution of our collective work was seen as having to extend from the Latin American/Caribbean foreground to more general theoretical, comparatist, cross-cultural and interdisciplinary orientations. Perhaps most generally work had to address pressing contemporary concerns such as the effort to plot relations between the high, postmodern culture of the elites and the various modes of popular and mass culture existing in various parts of the world; and the effort to establish the relevance of advanced theorizations to the variations of urban life and culture in the U.S., Latin America and the Caribbean and the Third World.

On the question of Latin American-Caribbean cultural studies, the main approaches to the subject had been based on dependency theory or semiological constructs. But the years had shown that neither approach gave much space or probability to compelling political dissent or revolutionary opposition. And many critics drew on the early work of Néstor García Canclini for definitions and orientations. For García Canclini, popular culture consisted of the practices and forms of thought that the popular sectors create by themselves to conceive, manifest and at times struggle against their reality and their subordinated place. Popular culture itself was "constituted in a process of unequal appropriation of the economic and cultural capital of a nation or ethnicity by its dominated sectors, and by the real and symbolic comprehension, reproduction and transformation of general and specific conditions of life and work" (1981:13-14).

These perspectives may have given off the impression that García Canclini's views were monolithic. True, for him, the cultural arena was a battleground. Popular elements existed, other forces sought to appropriate and coopt them; the people and their artists struggled back in a battle to semiotize and thereby dominate the world of representations. The basic Marxist scenario persisted in spite of some new wrinkles. But were there dimensions of his theory which lead to a more complex model? And where would that model be found?

On the question of Latin American-Caribbean cultural studies, the main approaches to the subject had been based on dependency theory or semiological constructs. Efforts to counter an overly external-directed dependency perspective came to imply too centralized an orientation or a top-down structuralist bent. Theoretically minded Caribbeanists like George Beckford sometimes lay down structures of domination and convergence so well, there seemed little space to explore possibilities for significant counter-practice. The question remained: Where had a theoretical or historical/anthropological space been mapped out for significant opposition? This question involved the adequate application of theory to the point that we were able to grasp authentic or spurious counter cultural forces and forms.

To be sure there was something uncritical about too many of left Caribbeanist studies about workers' and people's culture, about African roots, Caribbean identity and the like, about the portrayal of emerging oppositional forms. Did the emergence of a militant group culture lead to a broad front or to the kind of sectarian divisions that made a Reaganite victory all the more possible in Grenada? What were we to make of a subculture dominated by a single group or constellation of people? What happened when counter cultures became institutionalized and dominant either in the overall cultural sphere or in the society-at-large-with or without the conquest of state power? What we had too often were inadequate theorizations. The older models too readily depended on truisms about imperialism, exploitation, pan-Africanism, "the people" and their voice. Assumptions were made about the "revolutionary" nature of a popular form, simply because it was said to originate and express (again) "the people," or because some revolutionary government office or official claimed the work to be revolutionary. Often there was an inability or unwillingness to relate given cultural forms or moments to broader trends and movements. When Gramscian questions of "cultural hegemony" or "organic intellectuals" were raised, it became clear that these perspectives were not grounded in a theorization pointing to any underlying bases governing transformations in the broad syncretic process. With respect to, say, surviving elements of folk culture, even if we could establish to what degree they might be functioning as "emergent or residual," etc., we still had no clear sense of the "laws" or even tendential bases for their mode of operation. If we pointed to progressive tendencies or "utopian moments" in overtly conformist cultural forms, we really had no sense for how and in relation to what broader skein of characteristics and trends these tendencies and moments might in fact come to play a role in making some dimension of the future.

We were left with gestures toward theorization, more than full application and critique of theory; we had studies that were too optimistic in that they found authentic opposition and resistance everywhere or that were too pessimistic, since they found the forces of domination to be completely ineluctable. In the Caribbean, the survival of voodoo, *santería,* etc., could be an expression of submission or resistance; the appropriation of surrealism could lead to progressive or reactionary results; the most negative experiences of exile and migration could lead to positive creolization; the *carreta* could make a u-turn. All these possibilities had to be kept in mind, and the search had to be for a theorization adequate to foreseeable and even unforeseeable understandings and transformations.

In sum, once we attempted to enter a terrain beyond the theorizations tied to the Cuban Revolution, we could see that we were still very far from having an adequate theoretical framework. We were still very theory-poor indeed. We were still in the realm of dichotomizing frameworks: domination/opposition, reaction/revolution, structure/praxis, strategy/tactics, rulers/people. Even accepting that all conceptions impoverish reality for the sake of clarity, the most realistic of left critics had to agree, I think, that we were far from having a theoretical apparatus adequate to the complexity of a notion of counter cultural production that had a genuine impact in relating mass preoccupations and everyday life with revolutionary possibilities in Latin American-Caribbean and more broadly third world contexts. Where are we to find roots of such a theorization? Wasn't it about time that we confronted García Canclini's work fully, to see if it was minimally adequate or at least provided us with some orientations that would help us move toward a theory of popular culture in relation to capitalist domination and opposition? And, even prior to this enterprise, wouldn't we have to explore a more global perspective and see if there is some more global theory we can agree to and then apply to given places or historical moments?

Here is where theorists began turning to Ernesto Laclau and Chantal Mouffe; and in this connection we may note how approaches suggested by their work placed much more emphasis on the destructive/creative and some what structure-resistent flux of everyday life, rather than on the formal institutional and ideological forces which structurally oriented meta-theories such as dependency theory had emphasized. For example, it was not that Caribbean state apparatuses didn't attempt to structure and even permeate all, as in Althusserian or even Foucaultian constructs. Rather it was that the object of authoritarian control retained a grade of indeterminacy and possibility, maintained and developed its counter-spaces and areas which provided a sphere of possible contention and freedom. To give another instance, writers and intellectuals might well express the "potential or latent consciousness" of larger social aggregates; they might constitute themselves as the "organic intellectuals" of subaltern sectors. However they had to be ever viewed critically in this guise, and literary production had to be ever be viewed in relation not only to literary traditions, but in relation to the everyday life patterns of the larger social mass. Fluid representational forms developed, generated by the people or by the growing Caribbean culture industry, expressive of people's concerns or not, coopted or not, but ever modifiable into a force for change or repression by wider forces which foster and structure new events, relations and possibilities. Macho Camacho's *guaracha* might express the cooptation and submission of Puerto Rican culture, but it might also express that culture's triumph against the odds. And could not the same be said for Luis Rafael Sánchez's novel? The creative play, inter-relation and transformation of cultural forms and their political correlatives were complex and not always readily predictable. However, I and others believed, the space and nature of opposition was not so fluid that it could not be somehow conceptualized and codified and then perceived at another level. It is to efforts to achieve newer conceptualizations in the era of postmodernity and globalization that we now turn.

7. Postmodenity and Globalization in Caribbean Culture and Literature after 1989

There is no doubt that the transformation of Marxist discourse in function of post-Gramscian culturalist theory was most fully implemented in the work of Jamaican transplant Stuart Hall of the Birmingham School of cultural studies, although his direct Anglo-Caribbean effects have yet to be fully studied. In the meantime, the theme of postmodernity which became central to Latin American discussions in the 1990s and the theme of globalization which came to the fore in the last years of the previous century were important in the Caribbean area as well. Even in Cuba, there were intense discussions about the work of Fredric Jameson and then Hardt and Negri and their views that postmodernity and globalization were more than just new versions of cultural imperialism. In the Dominican Republic, these themes took on their particular contours in relation to zona franca industrial development, as well as questions of Haitian in-migration and Dominican out-migration. In Puerto Rico, the discussion of postmodernity became central to the break of a new generationn of thinkers who formed new journals and developed an overall publishing project centered on the application of postmodern theory to critiquing normative and left forms of nationalism, as well as exploring Puerto Rico's global, hemispheric and Caribbean roles (cf. Luis Felipe Díaz and Marc Zimmerman, coord. 2001). Furthermore, Puerto Rican scholars located in U.S. universities also had done much to develop postmodern and globalization perspectives relevant to the U.S. Puerto Rican population and its impact in U.S. and Puerto Rican contexts (cf. *Puerto Rican Jam*). Meantime, figures of the previous generation, like Arcadio Díaz Quinones and Ángel Quintero Rivera, from the group of CEREP, produced stellar essays like former's *Arte de bregar* and the latter's *Salsa, sabor y control*, reflecting on the effects of Puerto Rico's particular form of colonial modernity.

Of course when the theme of Caribbean postmodernity comes to the fore, no single work has done more to bring the Caribbean to the postmodern table than *La isla que se repite* (1989) by Antonio Benítez Rojo. In this work, Benítez Rojo had set forth an early pan-Caribbean postmodern vision tying Deleuze and Guatarri's rizomatic nomadism to Chaos theory as his theoretical base. According to Benítez Rojo the argument that Latin American postmodernity precedes rather than follows the North Atlantic phenomenon can be best maintained in the case of the Caribean, because the Caribbean is defined by the very heterogeneity of historical and times, rhythms and processes that has been a key dimension of the postmodern in general. Furthermore, the social sciences have constantly described Caribbean cultures in terms of fragmentation, instability, isolation, uprootedness, cultural complexity, dispersed historicity and impermanence-characteristics frequently used to distinguish postmodern tendencies For Benítez Rojo, Caribbean culture is synchretic, heterogeneous, acquatic, contradictory and performative-characterized by double and ambigous codes. In fact postmodern culture in the Caribbean is among the most heterogeneous in all of Latin America-derived from the complexity and multiplicity of its original roots, its colonial legacy and now its close and precarious relation with U.S. cultural elements leading to contradictory transformations in cultural forms and everyday life which only intensify in their manifestations and implications in the current historical phase dominated by intensified processes of globalization.

How should we consider the views of Benítez Rojo now several years after the publication of his path-breaking book? First, as one of his critics in Puerto Rico noted, this island which repeats itself is more Cuban than anything else. And indeed it is rather clear that Benítez Rojo's vision is Afro-centric, indeed Afro-Cuban-centric. His perspective, which in some ways seems a sophisticated extension of the views set forth in Rodríguez and Zimmerman, as well as Losada, suffers because it essentializes Caribbean identity by privileging the African and plantation-aspects which are clearly crucial but which can no longer (if ever) explain all. Benítez Rojo contradicts his own encounter with postmodern discourse by means of his essentialist bias and his dependence on chaos theory which only complicates but never transcends a anti-postmodern essentialism. In this, we may be witness to problems typical of white Caribbean efforts to obliterate guilt feelings by an over-reaching effort to embrace an Afro-centered vision of his own world. It seems that his notion of the Caribbean as a performance space in which Africanness and its transformations function as the nucleus of unity is overly based on concepts originating Ortiz, Mintz, Moreno Fraginals and others I discussed in Chapter III who would have us see the Caribbean as a series of plantation societies-reducing or criticizing recent Caribbean transformations from this perspective. No one would deny the importance of the plantation as a colonial structure and as a basis of postcolonial resistances in the Caribbean. But can Caribbean cultures still be reduced to this structure as essence, with all that has passed in the last hundred years? And now, especially, in the era of globalization? Strong elements from the past continue, but haven't the structures of Caribbean being and doing also changed, especially through the transnational immigration of people, goods, ideologies and cultural forms, through the development of drug trade, tourism, film and world music, etc.? Does the past continue to absorb and order the present? Or is it not that the present, while drawing on the past, transforms it? And why Benítez Rojo's emphasis on literature, as if literature were in itself the prism to see, conceptualize and give unity to all that is the Caribbean? But Benítez Rojo doesn't stop with this, but rather insists that Caribbean culture was formed as a performative and artistic critique of processes of economic modernization and cultural modernity, understood as occidental projects. This is to say that the cultural patterns formed through the colonial process were already poli-rhythmic, pastiche, performative-in sum, postmodern *avant la lettre*. As Román de la Campa says:

> *Modernity is... deconstructed... as the repository of pain and violence implicit in exploitative regimes (pantation machines) that failed to produce modern industrialized states; as the root of disillusionment and historical failure to which premodern rituals, rhythms and performativity become the antidote; and as the archive of texts whose major, if not only, remaining value lies in the possibility of unearthing their rhetorical and literary excess... Accordingly, the flow of Caribbeanness... swings back and forth from colonial to postmodern times... slipping above and beyond the narratives of state formation, anticolonialism, socialist and capitalist dependency, literacy campaigns, and other traces of social textuality that still pertain to modernizing needs in the Caribbean evev if they are now devoid of modernity's utopian legacy (1999: 101).*

For de la Campa,

> *A postmodern reading of the Caribbean would need to resist the tendency to lump the rich and multifarious history of modernity into an undifferentiaed chronology encompassing four hundred years. For the Caribbean, as well as for other postcolonial societies, the narratives implicit in modernization remain rich in the dialogic entanglements of postmodern socio-political as we as literary textualization... Cultural mapping can no longer... rely on... nation, patriarchy, party, class, race, and ethnicity... as modern foundational narratives, with their concommitant notions of fixed identities and subject positions. Yet, a certain utopian impulse also lurks behind a postmodernism that is strictly bound to a new celebration of literariness... and complacent aestheticism... The contemporary fabric of Caribbeanness remains largely abscent... and cultural mapping reline... on a largely antiquarian gaze that essentializes the premodern and erases the modern in its literary pursuit of the postmodern (102)... The Caribbean's... experience with modernity is re-*

> *duce to a literary archive... The narratives of emancipation, nationalism, cultural identity, developmentalism, political reforms, educational campaigns and revolutions,... all turn into profound errors... In the meantime, conjuring the idea of a living community from this theoretical cul-de-sace becomes unlikely, if not irrelevant. The people of the Caribbean engaged in ongoging life experiences are left with an invitation to levitate from the coffin of their modern struggles, to leave their bodies behind as relics of a sad case of mistaken identity, and to join the celebration of a newly found and largely premodern indeterminacy. (103).*

In the last analysis, in spite of his bases in Lyotard, Deleuze and Guattari, Derrida, De Man, and chaos theory, how can we call a theorical position post-modern when it seeks to reduce a cultural complex to an essence that continues to resist history? How can we approach the partcularities of Caribbean spaces such as Puerto Rico or Martinique which have not emerged from colonialism but have indeed entered a kind of modernity which readliy corresponds to most postmodernist criteria? How account for the globalized dynamics of these societies-the constant tropicalizations of rock, rap, hip-hop and other forms, as in regaton, the development of narco-criminality, and trans-identities of various performative mode and styles-the resultants of so many transnational migrations and connections, so many combinations and transformations?

From a contemporary perspective, how should we consider the degree and effect of what we used to call "capitalist penetration" in various areas and social sectors during the centuries of mercantilism and the industrial revolution? Can we still raise questions today about degrees of transformation and effect, and of course degrees of equal and unequal development? The studies of various investigators have explained much about the processes of Caribbean absorption and recodification, of mestizaje, of mulatez, of criolloismo and most recently, crealité-in function of processes of transculturation (cf. Fernando Ortiz and Angel Rama), heterogeniety (Cornejo Polar) or hybridization (García Canclini)-processes in which the dominated have a strong impact over the dominating. And one can register in this examination how processes which almost terminated in the nineteenth century in certain places have hardly begun in others.

8. The Emergence of Antillanité and Creolité

Perhaps the most important post-Benítez Rojo perspectives on the Caribbean have surfaced in the continuing work of Eduard Glissant, Patrick Chamoiseau and the other writers of Antillanité and Creolité. These tendencies emerged to affect all Caribbean studies from the mid-1980s but to become pre-dominant if not hegemonic at century's end. Glissant's reconfiguration of creolization as "Antillanité" urged Caribbeans to explore their cultural inter-relations and points of common cultural identity (their "Caribbeaness"), in spite of their different colonial histories and national fragmentation (Glissant 1996: 97-157)

As Roberto Márquez notes, Glissant's version of creolization "becomes a description of a cultural process, as an empirical outcome, and as still dialectically unfolding future possibility." From *Le Discours Antillais* (1981) *to Caribbean Discourse* (1989) and *Poetics of Relation* (1997), Glissant enlarges and amplifes his earlier notion of Antillanité. Juxtaposed and contrasted to Antonio Benítez Rojo's turn to chaos theory for explanation of the Caribbean's complexities, it is Glissant's more convincing rhizometic model that ultimately presides as paradigmatic exemplar" (Márquez 1997).

Glissant's rich theoretical work is perhaps best explicated by J. Michael Dash (1995), who points to Glissant's theory of landscape, which was to play a major role in the formation of contemporary subaltern studies as well as in Caribbean studies in particular (cf Rodríguez 1994, 2004). On this theme, Dash cites Glissant as follows:

For us, the inescapable *shaping force* in our production of literature is what I would call the language of landscape. We can say that the European literary imagination is moulded spacially around the spring and the meadow. [...] In European literature an intimate relationship with landscape is primarily established. From this has evolved a stylistic convention that has for a long time focused on meticulous detail, exposition "in sequence," highlighting harmony (exceptions or extensions constitute reactions to this rule). (Glissant 1996: 145-147, cited by Dash: 121).

This theme and "antillanité" as a whole exerted a special influence on Chamoiseau, one of the most important Francophone Caribbean writers of the postmodern period. Chamoiseau extended Glissant's work in function of his own transformative term, "creolité," which was meant to designate an effort to validate Caribbean popular culture, including popular music, popular religion, folk traditions, and folk tales-and perhaps above all, the effort to combine oral Creole with written French in a way which privileged the former. A theme that both incorporates but battles against Cesaire's homogenizing negritude and the "naïve models" of political resistance in Fanon, Brathwaite, Fernández Retamar and others, creolité writers soon took up Glissant's concern with landscape and also a recurrent motif in the literature of the French Antilles, folie, *or "madness," a defense mechanism, or as a splitting of an*

> *inner and outer self, used to show the difficulty of living in a society that has been controlled by outside powers and to dramatize the difficulty of expressing identity in a colonial language that does not value Caribbean cultural ideals.*

Nick Monk (1999) seeks to make essential connections between questions of antillanité, creolité, landscape and madness or disorder in his critique of Chamoiseau's best known book, the novel, *Texaco*:

> Créolité *is figuratively rendered in a form that is the antidote to the overwhelming notions of 'sequence' and 'harmony' characteristic of European styles of literary production. Ultimately, it may be argued, the sense of place dictates the world view; the profusion and entanglement of Chamoiseau's jungle aesthetic is, in itself, a challenge to the teleological, linear progression of the Eurocentric model of nationhood and history. In Chamoiseau's novel of fused and multiple themes and voices, the aesthetic reflects the ideal and the ideal reflects the aesthetic. As Dash observes of the father of* Antillanité*: 'Glissant's first meditations on a Caribbean worldview [are] based on a convulsive, unregimented ideal and not on the ordered symmetry associated with Europe (Dash, Introduction to Glissant 1976: xix). In* Texaco *the performative aspects of the novel and its willingness to allow the aesthetic to melt into the ideal function together to outflank the Eurocentric certainties that are under constant pressure in the text.*

In Monk's view of "*Texaco's* intellectual agenda," some dimensions of European culture are accepted, while others receive extreme critique. But Chamoiseau rejects "reductive oppositions in the creation of the ideals of *Texaco*/Texaco," using but also deconstructing tropes of jungle and city, Nature and Civilized order in ways which "recall... Glissant's 'language of landscape.'".

> *In Chamoiseau's fiction symmetry is refused a dominant role, as is the exclusive, regimented and ordered privileging of one element over another that is deeply characteristic of much European fiction and its associated colonial postures. The 'sequence' that, according to Glissant, is produced by an aesthetic of the tidy, symmetrical harmony of the 'spring' and the 'meadow' gives way to the wild, random patterns evocative of the tropical forest. The aesthetic and thematic result is a kind of euphonious dissonance. (Monk 1999).*

Opposing Martinique's situation as a colonial department of France, opposing Aymé Cesaire's negritude as a populist and one-dimensional mythos and seeking a Caribbeanness that refuses an Africanist reductionism, Chamoiseau and his friends, Raphaël Confiant and Jean Bernabé forged a mode of representation that soon won them followers and allies in his generation in the Franco-Caribbean world and even became a source of fascination in Spanish and Ango-Caribbean literary circles. Nevertheless, there were negative notes in the evasion of class perspectives and the construction of male-centered oppositions.[7] And it is not clear where the political and social agendas of creolité, not to speak of its aesthetic and literary dimensions, might lead (cf. Chamoiseau 2002).

Postscript

The Nobel prizes to Derek Walcott and V.S. Naipaul, as well as the Goncourt Prize to Chamoiseu, have brought new attention to the array of writers animating the field of Caribbean writing. With this growing recognition has come a broadening arc of critical and theoretical discourse that has enriched the field. One of the most ambitious projects charting Caribbean literature is the three volume work coordinated by general editor A. James Arnold with J. Michael Dash, Julio Rodríguez-Luis, Ineke Phaf-Rheinberger, Vera Kutsinsky and other associates developing and extending new totalizations of Caribbean literature (cf. Arnold, A. James, et. al., ed. 1997). Less systematically but with great elán, Lowell Fiet and Janette Becerra's provocative collection, *Caribe 2000: Definiciones, identidades y culturas regionales y/o nacionales* (1997), points to new dimensions of performativity as essential to understanding Caribbean realities and includes splendid performances by Benítez Rojo and Quintero Rivera focused on music and rhythms as essential dimensions of creolité.

Beyond these texts and ones mentioned above are several major Caribbean syntheses of recent years that begin to change the landscape and the frames for the field of study. Key recent volumes that should be noted include Silvio Torres-Saillant's *Caribbean Poetics* (1997), J. Michael Dash's *The Other America: Caribbean Literature in a New World Context* (1998), and Belinda J. Edmondson's *Caribbean Romances: The Politics of Regional Representation* (1999) and \o "Gertrud Aub-Buscher - search by author" \t "_top" Gertrud Aub-Buscher and \o "Beverly Omerod Noakes - search by author" \t "_top" Beverly Omerod Noakes' \o "The Francophone Caribbean Today: Literature, Language, Culture ISBN: 9766401306 - compare prices" *The Francophone Caribbean Today: Literature, Language, Culture* (2003). On the question of creolité, beyond Glissant's *Poetique de la rélation*, we can point to *Eloge de la créolité* by Bernabé, Chamoiseau y Confiant (1989); as well as Chris Bongie's provocative *Islands and Exiles: The Creole Identities of Post/Colonial Literature* (1998). Just in Puerto Rico, to choose a few among several texts of note we can cite Edgardo Rodríguez

Juliá's *Caribeños* (2002) and Quintero Rivera's *Vírgenes, Magos y Escapularios* (1999 y 2004).

Certainly these critiques and above all, those of creolité, drew on, but also questioned the theoretical work of Fanon, Beckford, Mintz, Fernández Retamar and Brathwaite and therefore the synthesis of their work represented in much of Chapter III as well as in this chapter. So it is signifcant that, speaking to the issue of creolization which he sees as implicit in current discourses of antillanité and creolité and as central to the books of Arnold and colleagues, Roberto Márquez (1997) sums up the continuing relevance of the term:

> *The nature, role, place, meaning, and implications of "Creolization" for a Caribbean poetics... necessarily has a certain pride of place as one of its major foci. Even before... Brathwaite's* Contradictory Omens *(1974) theoretically mobilized the concept for the anglophone Antilles as a less static, multivalent, non-hierarchical, lexically localized and "indigenous" alternative to the deficiencies... Fernando Ortiz's influential notion of "trans-culturation" and the less insightful, tendentious analytical terms (assimilation, acculturation, inter-culturation, pluralism) long in conventional vogue, "Creolization" had already begun moving to the center of contemporary Caribbean studies and discussions of a Caribbean aesthetic [; and] ...it will remain there for some time yet. "The Caliban Complex," by contrast, would appear to be receding from its once privileged position of allegorical authority in the era of the "postnational;" in the face of a sharpened critique of its masculine inflection; and what, in the "Spanish" Caribbean at least, Vera Kutzinski trenchantly calls "its problematic validation of mestizaje as a cultural discourse and national ideology..." The intricacies and connotations of race, racism, and racial discourse in so pigmentocratic, polychromatic a region, not unexpectedly, continue to be the inevitably central issues they have always been. A more broadly embracing idea of hybridity than the dyadic or triadic imagery that negritude, negrismo, mestizaje or marronage usually conjure up seems, at the same time, to be winning increasing favor as it simultaneously corroborates the constitutive centrality of black, mulatto, and white and yet argues for amplifcation of the traditional range of inclusions in our discussions of Caribbean culture and identity.*

Indeed, for Márquez, much contemporary work assumes "that multiple ethnic and cultural strains have contributed to the formation of contemporary literatures in the region and that they are... inevitably connected." (ibid.)

Certainly the writers of creolité raised questions about the age of Caliban; and it is also true that our older models marginalized questions of Chinese, Indian and other racial, ethnic, gender and sexual identities and reduced the Caribbean to a narrow masculinist binary of relations summarized in the Hegelian master-slave dialectic. Nevertheless, efforts to obscure those relations completely would make us blind historical, cultural and literary processes in the Caribbean. Márquez and I concur in believing that such processes require a still richer and effective brew able to forge connections which grasp the past and project the future. But we also concur that Caribbean inventiveness beyond structural determinations and theorizations will continue to characterize the varying modes of Caribbean performativity and identity in all cultural forms, including literature.

In this light, it is instructive to return to a document cited at the end of our preface, Quintero Rivera's meditation upon the death of Antonio Benítez Rojo. In his notes, Quintero Rivera indicates how in recent years the Cuban critic-writer/critic had advanced a schematic version of his vision of the future, above all in an article entitled, "El Caribe en el siglo XXI: un proyecto de trabajo,"where expanding Caribbean multiplicities and heterogeneities are seen as weaving their way throughout the world, back and out again in processes which we call transnational, transcultural and hybrid. As in his essay in the Fiet/Becerra collection, Benítez Rojo argues that Caribbean rhythm is the basis of the particular Antillan aesthetic that goes far beyond questions of sound and music to questions of the visual arts, literature, body movements (not only in dance, but also in way of walking with a certain swing) in the kitchen, in boxing and other sports. In this way, says Quintero Rivera, Benítez Rojo was heading toward a new totalization beyond *La isla que se repita* to finding "the best way possible to position oneself in the world of the future" in terms of a view in which "a contemporary version of a syncopated cultural creolité served as a way of participating in a rhythm (or ancestral root) that is fertile with meanings which fend against the apparent chaos of discontinuity, arbitrary power and chance."[8]

Works Cited

Arnold, A. James, et. al., ed. 1997. *A History of Literature in the Caribbean: Cross-Cultural Studies*; Volume 2: English- and Dutch-speaking regions; *A History of Literature in the Carribean;* Vol. 3: *Cross-Cultural Studies*. Amsterdam/Philadelphia. John Benjamins Publishing Company.

Aub-Buscher, Gertrud and Beverly Omerod Noakes, ed. 2003. *The Francophone Caribbean Today: Literature, Language, Culture*. Mona, Jamaica. University of West Indies Press.

Barnet, Miguel. 1994. *Autobiography of a Runaway Slave*. Willimantic, CT. Curbston Press. Trans. of Miguel Barnet. 1998. *Cimarrón: Historia de un esclavo*. Madrid. Siruela.

Benítez Rojo, Antonio. 1999. *The Repeating Island*. Durham, NC. Duke University Press. New version of *La isla que se repite*. Hanover, New Hampshire. Ediciones del Norte 1989.

Bernabé, Jean, Patrice Chamoiseau, and Raphael Confiant. 1993. *Eloge de la créolité/In Praise of Creoleness*. Paris, Gallimard.

Bongie, Chris. 1998. *Islands and Exiles: The Creole Identities of Post/Colonial Literature*. Stanford. Stanford University Press.

Chamoiseau, Patrice. 2002. Interview with James Fergusson at website http://www.patrickchamoiseau.cwc.net/index.htm;

Conference call for the 9th International Conference of the Association of Caribbean Women Writers (ACWWS), *Liberatory Poetics in Caribbean Writing: Gender and Nation Re-Configurations* (held in Santo Domingo, Dominican Republic, May 18-25, 2004) http://www.patrickchamoiseau.cwc.net/aande.htm

Coulthard, G. R.. 1962. *Raza y color en la literatura antillana* (Seville. Escuela de Estudios Hispano-Americanos, 1958. Translated as *Race and Color in Caribbean Literature*. New York. Oxford University Press.

Cudjoe, Selwyn R. 1980 *Resistence and Caribbean Literature*. Athens, Ohio. Ohio University Press.

Dash, J. Michael. 1995. *Edouard Glissant*. Cambridge University Press.

Dash, J. Michael. 1998. *The Other America: Caribbean Literature in a New World Context*. Charlottesville. University of Virginia Press.

Dathorne, 0. R. 1981. *Dark Ancestor. The Literature of the Black Man in the Caribbean* Baton Rouge and London. Louisiana State University Press.

de la Campa, Román. 1999. *Latin Americanism*. Minneapolis. University of Minnesota Press.

Díaz, Luis Felipe and Marc Zimmerman. 2001. Globalización, nación, postmodernidad (Estudios culturales puertorriqueños). San Juan. Editorial LACASA Puerto Rico.

Díaz Quiñones, Arcadio. 2000. *Arte de bregar*. San Juan. Ediciones Callejón.

Durisin, Dionyz. 1984. *The Theory of Literary Comparatistics.* Bratislava. Veda. Publishing House of the Slovak Academy of Sciences. Institute of Literary Sciences.

Edmondson, Belinda J. 1999. *Caribbean Romances: The Politics of Regional Representation.* Charlottesville. University of Virginia Press.

Fernández Retamar, Roberto. 1985. "Calibán y la literatura de nuestra América", presented and interviewed by Fidel Coloma, Ileana Rodríguez and Marc Zimmerman. Chicago. LASt Publications. Reprinted in Sklodowska and Heller, ed. 2000: 227-252

Fernández Retamar, Roberto. 1989. *Caliban and Other Essays.* Minneapolis. University of Minnesota Press.

Fiet, Lowell and Janette Becerra. 1997. *Caribe 2000: Definiciones, identidades y culturas regionales y/o nacionales.* San Juan. Universidad de Puerto Rico.

García Canclini, Néstor. 1981. *Las culturas populares en el capitalismo.* La Habana. Casa de las Americas.

Glissant, Edouard. 1981. *Le Discours Antillais.* Paris. Le Seuil. Republished by Gallimard 1997.

Glissant, Edouard. 1996. *Caribbean Discourse: Selected Essays,* trans. J. Michael Dash. Charlottesville. University Press of Virginia,

Glissant, Edouard and Betsy Wing. 1997. *Poetics of Relation.* University of Michigan Press.

Jackson, Richard. 1976. *The Black Image in Latin American Literature.* Albuquerque. University of New Mexico Press.

Laclau, Ernesto and Chantal Mouffe. 1985. *Hegemony and Socialist Strategy: Towards a Radical Democratic Politics.* London. Verso.

Losada, Alejandro. 1980. *La Literatura en la Sociedad de América Latina: Los modos de produccion entre 1750-1980. Estrategias de Investigación.* Berlin. Freiheit Universitat.

Márquez. Roberto. 1997. *Seeing Fragments Whole: "The Unity is Submarine"* Review of Arnold 1997. In *The Americas Society.* http://www.counciloftheamericas.org/as/literature/br58walcott.html

Minc, Rose, ed. 1982. *Literatures in Transition: The Many Voices of the Caribbean Area* Gaithersburg, Md.. Hispamérica.

Monk, Nick. 1999. "Fragile Monuments, Ambiguous Archives: The Nature of Resistance and Reclamation in Patrick Chamoiseau's *Texaco*". http://www.patrickchamoiseau.cwc.net/aande.htm

Motleyn, Langhorne A. 1984. *Democracy in Latin America and the Caribbean*. Washington, D.C.

Quintero Rivera, Angel G. 2002. *Salsa, Sabor y Control! : Sociologia de la Musica "Tropical"*. México. Siglo XXI Ediciones.

Quintero Rivera, Angel, ed. 1998. *Vírgenes, magos y escapularios: imaginería, etnicidad y religiosidad popular en Puerto Rico*. (San Juan. Fundación Puertorriqueña de las Humanidades.

Quintero Rivera, Angel. 2004. Letter in Homage of Antonio Benítez Rojo. November 6.

Rodríguez, Ileana. 1994. *House, Garden, Nation*. Durham, NC. Duke University Press.

Rodríguez, Ileana. 2004. *Translantic Topographies: Islands, Highland, Jungle*. Minneapolis. University of Minnesota Press.

Rodríguez, Ileana and Marc Zimmerman. 1983. *Processes of Caribbean Societies: I deologies and Literatures*. Minneapolis, MN. Institute for the Study of Ideologies and Literature.

Rodríguez Juliá, Edgardo. 2002. *Caribeños*. San Juan. Editorial Instituto de Cultura Puertorriqueña.

Sklodowska, Elzbieta & Ben A. Heller, ed. 2000. *Roberto Fernández Retamar y los estudios latinoamericanos*. Serie Críticas 2000. Instituto Internacional de Literatura Iberoamericana. Pittsburgh, PA

Sommer, Doris. 1983. *One Master for Another: Populism as Patriarchal Rhetoric in Dominican Novels* (Lanham, MD. University Press of America.

Torres-Saillant, Silvio. 1997. *Caribbean Poetics: Toward an Aesthetic of West Indian Literature*. New York and Cambridge. Cambridge University Press.

Zimmerman, Marc. 1986. Review of Durisn 1984. *ICLA Information AILC (Bulletin of International Comparative Literature Association*, 7-8 [summer-fall, 1986], pp. 14-15).

Notes

1 A further point we might as well mention has to do with the misnaming and the late appearance of the volume. These matters flowed from a set of circumstances which led to impaired communications between the editors and then between the editors, the contributors, and the publishers, the net result of which was the fact that the book bears an incorrect version of its descriptive working *(Processes of Caribbean Ideologies, Societies and Literatures)* as opposed to its projected publication title-a matter which perhaps impeded its receiving as much attention as it might have (what can you expect from a volume so badly and ungrammatically named?)-and also the fact that some of the book's reviewers didn't read the fine print and believed they were reading materials responding to Ronald Reagan's Caribbean Basin initiative. The situation of confusion is such that Losada, who was after all very much connected with I&L, did not know of our text until after he had published his remarks; and it was widely thought that we had drawn on his specific Caribbean meditation for our own work, when the fact is that our book manuscript was long complete when his book appeared and he himself began to use our manuscript in his graduate seminar long before it was published.

2 Republished as hypotheses related to the views of Roberto Márquez, in part 3 of Chapter V below. In this respect also, compare the perspectives developed by Losada 1980: 66-67.

3 For an explicitly Caribbean perspective on the critical intervention of Fernández Retamar, see his interview, "Calibán y la literatura de nuestra América" 1985.

4 For one of many points of reference, see Motley 1984.

5 Cf. Jackson 1976; Cudjoe 1980; Dathorne 1981; Rose Minc, ed. 1982; Doris Sommer 1983.

6 Here Dionyz Durisin's book (1984) can turn out to be very helpful, especially his perspectives on literary systemicity and on contract In his view of contactual and no-contactual literary affinities, in the role of reception in "interliterary continuity," as well as in the question of national literatures and interliterary communities. Cf. my brief analysis 1986.

7 So, on the gender issue, the conference call for the 9th International Conference of the Association of Caribbean Women Writers (ACWWS), "Liberatory Poetics in Caribbean Writing: Gender and Nation Re-Configurations" (held in Santo Domingo, Dominican Republic, May 18-25, 2004) raises the following provocative questions: "How does the literature of the Caribbean construct sexual and body politics along side discourses on national and cultural identity specific to the Caribbean? How does resistance politics textualize and perform itself on certain configurations of bodies and sex? [Maryse] Conde for example, has criticized the gendered textiomatics of Glissant's Antillanité and Chamoiseau's creolité,. What are the socio-historical axiomatics of the ways in which discourse and bodies are sexed, and sexual identities performed/constructed in the service of a discourse of the nation?" http://www.patrickchamoiseau.cwc.net/aande.htm

8 Quintero Rivera's letter on the death of Benítez Rojo, January 7 2005.

Chapter V

Latin American Literary Criticism and Immigration

1. The Advances of Socio-Historical Criticism

As many of us are quick to point out, great advances have been made in the past several years with respect to the socio-historical study of Latin American literature. New methodologies developing in literary studies have enmeshed with perspectives developing in the social sciences to create a new range of possibilities for historical and critical analyses of texts, movements and currents. The traditional canon of works has been questioned, and the doors opened to the study of a whole series of genres and modes of written expression, so that the very definition of the object of study has been questioned and transformed. Intensified work on countries and regions that have been neglected or given scant attention has enhanced our understanding of the richness and diversity of Latin American literatures, their varying rhythms of development, their varying relations with, and distances from varied social totalities. Studies directed toward the multi-lingual, multi-cultural Caribbean area led to a certain problematizing of our object, and of our overall theoretical apparatus, implying a need for grasping regional totalities and relations among works, writer-groups and larger social sectors before establishing a firmer basis for a comprehensive or reconstructed totalistic theory.

In terms of approach, we have participated in a shift from rather simplistic Marxist and historicist perspectives to an enriched focus on the relative autonomy of "literary practices" and the importance of "relative literary systemicity" as forces mitigating against any socioeconomic, ideological or even class reduction of literary phenomena; and we have carried out an application and then critique of dependency theory and Althusserian perspectives, ever in function of a more complex and adequate grasp of social formations and processes, as well as socio-economic relations. We have seen a gradual shift in emphasis, too, from a concern with the social explanation of the production of texts to a concern with their functioning in distinct social formations as part of a cultural or counter-cultural field.

Ultimately all roads have led to the bases for constituting a new history of Latin American literature in function of regional, historical and cultural differentiations, and in terms which see "literature" as the varied written expressions of social groups in varying degrees of conformity or opposition to the ideological and formal determinations of evolving local, national and international apparatuses which have acted to assure the extended reproduction of the relations necessary to the socioeconomic and political system in which these determinations are operative. And in all this there has been a shift from a focus on literature as a received phenomenon to a focus on all written and expressive forms-on a shift, then, from *belles lettres* according to dominantly European models, to "cultural expression," from institutionalized ideological and even cultural manifestations to those connected with everyday life, seen as a kind of creative cauldron of compensations, resistances, condensations of oppositions to forces of domination. Nevertheless, while the bases in method and knowledge for a new totalistic approach have grown, while a process of institutionalization has taken place which has made many of the advances noted possible, and while many of those who have participated in this movement have themselves become institutionalized and thus enabled to carry on their work, other forces have been developing which have raised questions about the value of the ongoing project and the functions it could serve, its overall impact on the social totality in which it operated and the social totality which it had as object.

Of course changes in the world economic and political order, as well as the place of the U.S. in the midst of these changes had much to do with both our advances in socio-criticism and our latest sense of uncertainty about its purpose, effect and future. Since the early 1970's, the capitalist countries have suffered stagflation, internal crisis and a series of realignments within their internal and external relations; meanwhile, underdeveloped nations have undergone nationalist, religious and cultural turmoil, so that the configuration of global power relations and possibilities has changed considerably. Many advanced countries have been crippled; underdeveloped countries oil rich or not, capitalist or not, have been unable to underwrite or attract the ever escalating sums required for modernization. The conflict between capitalist and socialist policies and powers, between advancing and declining capitalist states, between these states and multinational corporations on the one hand and developing national liberation struggles and established governments of national liberation on the other hand-all these have had a far-reaching impact on economic and political policies and strategies, on ideological and cultural structures and on the expressive artistic systems in which literary systems and specific literary expressions are born and operate; they have also had impact on the institutions and entities in which the study of literature takes place.

As for Latin America, the fall of Allende and the seeming collapse of many revolutionary movements led to the exile of many progressive scholars, critics and writers from the Southern Cone and other points. The entry into a period of reflux, paralleled, some would claim, by twilight in the Latin American narrative boom had actually helped to dynamize the new developments in Latin American literary studies. But the new order which emerged globally at the same time would not only facilitate but simultaneously put constraints on the whole process and eventually tended to neutralize much of its hoped for effects, even as a new revolutionary wave, this time from Central America, gave even deeper importance to literary-historical studies. At the very moment when socio-historical approaches to Latin American literature seem on the threshold of significant totalizations and applications in grand synthetic and national literary histories, we find ourselves questioning the value of such a field as a pedagogical and practical force. The decline of U.S. resources of education, the consequent pressure on academics, the elimination of many promising teachers from the academy, the scarcity of committed, advanced students to carry on the work, the erosion of the force of literature and literary criticism (or rather the neutralization of the space for such endeavors). All these and other dimensions come together to present us with a sense of uncertainty. Indeed, the need to delimit, neutralize and rechannel left-tending Latin American studies becomes even more crucial as Central American revolutionary movements are seen as a threat to U.S. hemispheric hegemony, at a time when a reduced global position makes "local" hegemony seem all the more important. Advanced Marxist literary studies as applied to Latin America has come to seem just an alternative academic approach in a vapid pluralistic democracy of discipline; the possible social effect of our work, indeed even our effect on most of the students we teach, is rendered quite minimal in the total constellation of forces affecting social consciousness and action.

At the same time, another not unrelated matter, too much ignored in our past efforts at theoretical totalization, the process of immigration and its implications for Latin American literary history studies and their effect, came to bear strongly on the very conditions of literary creation and analysis.

I. *Immigration, Latin America and Literature*

Of course immigration has long been an international phenomenon of great significance as both an effect and causal factor in the functionality and development of socio-economic and political forces and institutions. Obviously world economic tendencies as they impact specific regions and policies are essential in determining the flow and impact of immigration; and these broader tendencies then create new contexts for a whole series of problems which confront home base and host countries involved in particular immigration processes. A study of immigration causes and effects with respect to home-base countries is very important in plotting the future development of these countries and their international role; such study is also important in understanding the future of immigrant populations in host countries. Inevitably the consequences of immigration for the host countries and their particular constituencies are of vital concern, especially with respect to questions of economic, social and cultural adjustments, impact on pre-existing institutions and forms, technological and overall productive development, employment, housing and an array of issues affecting social dynamism, public policy, law and politics. Ultimately immigration related issues affect and potentially transform the very nature of host countries and the very world order of which they are a part. Thus, to the degree that immigration has become an essential dimension and expressive form of world socioeconomic development, it is a key issue for understanding all things, which are said to relate to that development. Indeed, the general normative observations set forth here are especially relevant to Latin America and the Caribbean in their relation to the U.S. While immigration is a global phenomenon, and while recent key migrations include the exodus from Southeast Asia and Eastern Europe, the movement of Mediterranean guest workers to Northern Europe, and such Latin America-related phenomena as the Japanese movement to Brazil, the Salvadoran movement to Honduras, the Guatemalan movement to Mexico and the more longstanding Columbian movement to Venezuela, still, for Latin America, the chief issue must be the massive and still growing movement of peoples to the U.S. These latter movement signals important and deep structural processes, which are important, even for literary studies.

Just as the decline in U.S. world hegemony led politicians and strategists to give more attention to Latin American and Caribbean social formations, and just as Grenada and Central American revolutionary currents broke lose, the rate of immigration from these and adjacent areas accelerated. Of course, these phenomena were not unrelated. To cite just one connection: As U.S. and homegrown Latin American capitalists invested heavily in capital-intensive enterprises, rising growth rates betokened new levels of immiseration and stirred new waves of revolutionary unrest and migration. As U.S. products became less competitive in the world market, more U.S. capital migrated to Latin America, and the immigrants who were increasingly forced to move north became subject to a process aimed at bringing down the price of labor to thus stave off the further export of industry and capital.

While the total process has been far more complex than can be grasped by any one pattern, still the overall implications of U.S. decline and its effect on large numbers of Latin American and Caribbean workers, as well as our overall hemispheric economic and social life, have not escaped notice. And yet Marxist literary critics were not in the forefront of considering this dimension of our times. Perhaps they were fetishized by their own objects of study, by their theoretical syntheses and above all by their concern for the literary movements in the Latin American countries they studied and, in many instances, with which they identified. It is not that they never mentioned the phenomenon, but we are speaking here of a real, operationally implemented concern. Even when we verbally acknowledged a need to include, say, Chicano literature as at least a problematic part of our Latin American object of study, even as more and more refugees and exiles, or their sons and daughters, began to write a literature of migration and exile, little attention was given to such work except to the degree that it could be assimilated to concerns with home base countries. Indeed, I believe that it was not until the Chilean literature of resistance in exile appeared, so qualitatively distinct in contours as to demand a mutation in critical frame that say, Chicano, and U.S. Puerto Rican or Cuban literatures began to attract an attention that could begin to impinge on the theoretical synthesis toward which we were heading.

The whole syncretic process of the internationalization of a specifically Latin American mode of literary production tied to the concrete circumstances of Latin America was slipping between our fingers. And only now, before a phenomenon that has been developing for any number of years, are we persuaded to consider that we can have no theory or a theoretically - guided study of literature expressive of Latin America if we do not pose the question of how Latin America and its literary expressions have extended north and of how Latin American literature however hybridized and mutant was part of a world which most of us had opposed to Latin America.

Suddenly, after several years of affirmative action, when Spanish Departments and Latin American Studies programs have held on and in some cases thrived in relation to the growing importance of Latin America and the Latin American presence in the U.S., we find ourselves saying (and this at a moment when affirmative action is dying) that the issue of immigration and the literatures of immigration may be a very important dimension of our work.

If we are saying that Marxist literary study extends now beyond the realm of traditional literary criticism and to deal with the contours of everyday life, then what more apt phenomena than the ones posed by immigration? The issue is no longer peripheral, parenthetical or tangential, but the very stuff of our work, because it is increasingly the substance of many Latin American lives. And clearly in this country the question is not simply that of Chicano literature (indeed that literature poses a particular problematic instance with relation to the question of totality, since it is both a literature indigenous to the Southwest and a literature of immigration And isn't it a coincidence that Latin Americans involved in our field bring up this subject just at a time when at the theoretical level they are talking about everyday life? Can it be that the subject of immigration encroaches on the everyday life of the researchers, and has been a business they have lived without ever wanting to confront it as a subject matter until, turning a corner; they find it staring them in the face?

For our proposed object of study, immigration and its culture and literature, is certainly one of the hardest objects of study for U.S. based Latin American Latin Americanists, if only because they are so very directly part of the object of study. And it is an object which the force of our socioeconomic system has perhaps made them want to stand apart from-as so many middle class Latin American immigrants (or those who have risen in class once here) have wanted to stand apart from those lowly economic refugees, those *mexicanos* and *caribeños* with their beaded curtains, and loud stereos, their dashboard Christs and macho crosses hanging from their necks-those people whose treatment in a racist country threatens the status and sense of being of the Latin American middle class, and the life experience of their children. The very value which Chicanos celebrate in function of *La Raza* are values which even Marxist Latin American Latin Americanists, as respectable members of the middle class, may instinctively seek to avoid. And yet, if as I have insisted elsewhere, Latin American socio-criticism constitutes a veritable mode of production interior to the literary system which Latin American literature, the problem for the critic is especially compounded, for the exterior object of study becomes a mirror.

So there, turning the corner, the critics see that even the literature of exile (of political immigrants after all!) may also be a literature of exiles who will never return and whose distance from home grows each day as they sit in one place dreaming of home. And this literature-it may, stylistically, structurally, somehow, have more in common with certain works of Chicano literature than of the literature in the home base. And so we begin to take note, and we must, simply because hardly any subject can be more symptomatic to Latin America today and to the situation of Latin American critics whose own lives and writings are the causes and effects of immigration. And if we are concerned about distances (between the critics and the reality they treat, between the literary texts and the people they however mediatedly express), the phenomenon of immigration as fact and object of study will provide many of the answers. And if solidarity work with Latin American struggles provides some extra-professional means for bridging the gap back to Latin America, and if in this work, we suffer perplexities and frustrations (as well as certain naive pleasures) when we try to work with other home base immigrants or other Latinos, are we not once again facing the same issue in another guise?

Reconstructing Latin American literary history, we come to realize that the issue has always been there (we think of Marti and so many countless others). But immigration and its context have undergone innumerable transformations, and never has the issue been so extensive and profound as it is today. Never has it affected so many; never has it been so much the expression of social formations in crisis; whole socio-economic systems, whole peoples and cultures.

If we are concerned about the practice of Latin-Americanist Marxists in this country at a time when the pedagogical function seems to be shrinking for even certain of our more advantageously placed colleagues to specialized studies for ever more tiny and elite elites and basic language skills for future technicians and low level technocrats, the question of Latin American immigration poses a whole area for creative and responsible activity in the very areas of everyday life, cultural expression, mass media, sex role transformations, etc..., with which we are becoming increasingly able to deal. And what issue confronts us more directly with domestic concerns and even the future of the U.S. working class in ways that connect so decisively with Latin America?

What are the implications of immigration for Latin America and the U.S. and for the particular areas of culture, ideology and literature in which our work as critics is situated? What are the parameters of our object? What are some of the problems and tasks before us? In what follows, we will look at just certain dimensions and possibilities of an enormous yet-to-be mapped out field.

2. Latin American and Caribbean Immigration – Population, Culture and Literature

In the context of the above considerations about U.S. Latino culture, and others I have developed in other more detailed papers (see Chapter VI), it would be valuable here to supplement the very impressive work which has been developing about the questions of Chicano and U.S. Puerto Rican literature with some observations and working hypotheses that would have reference to both Latin American and U.S. Latino literature in function of our focus on immigration. At a conference on the Caribbean sponsored by the Institute for the Study of Ideologies and Literature in the fall of 1978 (the basis for the book I edited with Ileana Rodríguez (1983), which is discussed in considerable detail in Chapter IV above), Roberto Márquez addressed himself to the impact of immigration on Caribbean writers in a way that is very valuable for our concern.

Since his comments were never published, I take the liberty of quoting him at length:

> *The problem of immigration... requires thorough investigation before it can be fully integrated into a theoretical schema governed by the notion of totality. Indeed the immigration issue pressures a more acute historical precision with respect to a totalistic orientation that could otherwise be too abstract, lax, romantic or unrigorous... My sense is that [many twentieth century Caribbean writers] share several characteristics with [a figure like] José Martí... Martí spent almost all his life outside the Caribbean area. Is he any less a Caribbean writer? Hostos is another example, so that even in the nineteenth century, the problem is not one that can be dealt with in terms of geographical location. Yet, when we come to the twentieth century, the problem seems to become more complex, for the fact of residence, say, in the U.S. even for five or ten years creates a veritable* problématique *out of the question of integral Caribbean identity. That is why the issue of immigration needs to be sorted out in a theoretical and historical manner, which affects our overall conception of Caribbean society and literature.*

While it is... correct to see Claude MacKay's Harlem as a transposed Caribbean setting, the precise coordinates of this transposition are difficult to define...Nevertheless, by seeing MacKay as a transitional figure between the nineteenth century and our present moment, we can begin to locate a significant dimension of the conceptual apparatus we require. A constant dimension of the immigration process has consisted in the fact that the immigrants have brought with them their entire sense of class structure into contexts that have not provided the social buttressing for this structure. In the capitalist center, the fact of class is generally superceded by national origin, and indeed "Caribbeanness" tends to outweigh and homogenize both class and national differences. The distinctions that existed in the home environment... between some anonymous sugar worker and a George Lamming are minimized by a foreign productive structure and by a social process, which says that both men are Jamaican or Caribbean or black.

> *It is more than a coincidence that the Negritude movement is at once a movement of immigration and a movement whose contradictions in terms of class perspective stemming from the immigrant situation did not prevent its being accepted by many Caribbeans at home and in foreign centers as an indigenous phenomenon. Immigration from the Caribbean was already becoming a general occurrence in the 1920's; even then it was more a phenomenon of push than of pull... And the fact is that the salient features*

> *and contours of negritude were determined by the immigrant push...It is also more than coincidental that it is in London that Caribbean immigrants whose native language is English come to realize that they are from the Anglophone Antilles, and not just from Jamaica, Barbados or Guyana. Indeed, within certain linguistic and cultural parameters, both national and pan-Caribbean consciousness are intensified by the push-out process... The writers are pushed out because they can't make a living, because they have no place to publish. Structurally their situation is similar to that of the field hands; the relation of both groups to the mode of production is untenable. Once outside their class differences are outweighed by their more or less common cultural* desajuste *in a new geo-cultural setting, where, we might add, racism cooperates with the needs for cheap labor to lump the two groups together. Thus features of their native mode of production and the ones that dominate the world to which they migrate both serve to define them as composite. And obviously the same composite crosses over distinct national identities. This composite typing in the immigrant centers inevitably poses a* problématique *for those who are its object; they must come to terms with it.*
>
> *For a countless number of reasons, then, the phenomenon of migration and what it means in its historical and geographical variations has to be looked at very carefully, because this phenomenon dovetails back and becomes central to the question of Caribbean identity... Recently Puerto Rican migration has vied with the migration of... Cuban middle sectors and exiles and migrant workers from all other parts of the Caribbean. Thus the class and political dimensions of immigration have multiplied; in addition, the dimension of lateral acculturation with dominant and minority groups... in the host country have become increasingly complex. These matters have greatly complicated Caribbean realities... Of course what is complication and fragmentation at one level may be the basis for greater richness and unity on another. But ultimately the question of immigration must be given the theorization it requires if we are to arrive at an adequate approach to Caribbean culture and literature (Márquez, in Rodríguez and Zimmerman: 121-123).*

On the basis of Márquez' comments, I offer the following hypotheses, which I believe helpful (though by no means sufficient) in the examination of Caribbean literature and in the overall effort to develop a theoretical perspective on the immigration process in relation to literature:

1. Caribbean immigration to the imperialist centers involves a transposition of cultural values and norms tied to one local mode of production, to the

values and norms of a second mode, which in fact conditions the very functionality and efficacy of the first.

2. The immigration process involves the immigrant's cultural and even psychological "de-centering" from imperialist contradiction to the more determinant contradictions of capitalism itself.

3. This shift derived from immigration tends to homogenize Caribbean class, national, cultural and today even linguistic differences in function of the core capitalist dichotomy of capital and labor, so that while some Caribbeans from the middle sectors may aspire to and succeed in maintaining or securing their nonworking class status, the force of the dominant host society's ideological and productive necessities will tend to displace large numbers toward the laboring (which often means unemployed or under-employed) sector.

4. In this circumstance, Caribbean immigrants, while perhaps attempting to assimilate white dominant class values, will often grasp those values through the filter of the oppressed group, which dominates the productive sphere to which they have been relegated.
   a. This historical and geographical variable conditions the process of lateral acculturation among immigrants and means that in New York, Caribbean peoples will tend toward "Newyorican" norms, which will in turn be conditioned by U.S. Black; in the Southwest, Hispanophone Caribbean norms will tend toward the Chicano, etc.

5. The immigration experience may lead to the most negative possibilities: unemployment, acculturation into lumpen patterns of drugs, prostitution, loss of viable cultural identity, etc.; it may involve the most radical *de-creolization*. However, it may, as in the case of the negritude movement, involve an actual intensification of positive creolization.
   a. The stereotyping, domination and concrete exploitation of Caribbean immigrants may have the positive effect of giving them a sense of class consciousness which they could not perhaps, have as easily acquired in the imperialist context of their home base; their lateral acculturation process is a dialectical one which involves a sharing of tendencies (though obviously in the center of domination)-which means that while they obviously remain Puerto Rican, Jamaican or whatever, they may become simultaneously "decentered" from their national core identity and incorporate more Pan-Caribbean and then international working class dimensions.

6. Given the large return rate of Caribbean immigrants from the U.S. (the Haitian, Jamaican and Dominican farm workers returning from Florida, the constant ebb and flow of Puerto Rican return rates), the negative and positive resultants of the hybridization process re-enter the Caribbean reality, and begin to modify it. Contradictions external to the islands not only penetrate through the importation of goods, through mass media and tourism, but through the returning Caribbean peoples, who bring along their new parcel of contradictions as integral elements of their identity to disseminate at home.

7. Obviously, a Marxist perspective seeks out the means for countering the negative developments and for intensifying and instrumentalizing the positive dimensions of this process. In this sense Marxist *literary* studies of the Caribbean require the full examination of several very important matters-for example:
   a. The degree to which immigrant and non-immigrant Caribbean writers are able to grasp the social processes involved in the immigration movement, especially those processes which relate to sectors other than their own.
   b. The degree to which immigrant writers, either by their pre-immigration or post-immigration formation, in fact (and in spite of their claims to shared experience with other immigrating social sectors) begin to distance themselves or relate themselves to a more totalistic Caribbean identity.
   c. The degree to which they take on metropolitan majority or minority patterns in literature-to undergo the influence, say, of dominant culture writers like Conrad, Faulkner or Pynchon, or an "internal minority migrant" artist like Wright or Ellison, or a more cosmopolitan minority figure like Ernie Gaines or John Williams.

8. We need to see what theoretical parameters we can establish, to specify the overwhelming complexities we have been describing: the degree to which the writers in fact say what the people are saying; the degree to which the cultural distance immigration or the very practice of writing implies ultimately dilutes or intensifies the capacity for totalistic Caribbean expression; the degree to which externally generated creolization has its reverberations on the metropolitan center (for immigration certainly means that Caribbean norms do influence the metropolitan norms- e.g. MacKay influences Ellison, which influences the Caribbean); and finally, then, the

degree to which the immigration experience, and immigrant literature act on the culture and literature of the Caribbean home base.

These hypotheses are only meant as general guides to future work in which the Caribbean focus here may be expanded to overall Latin American immigration. In such work we would have to reach the point of being able to deal with the question of immigration in relation to specific themes, modes and genres, and a whole series of formal considerations. In this direction, three further points with respect to Caribbean writers may help to articulate and refine the literary dimensions of our hypotheses:

1. Immigrant writers are not only a product of the class of value sets developed around two modes of production (as in hypothesis 1); to the degree that they establish themselves as writers, they are subject to the social relations of production pertaining to their particular productive sphere-this in spite of the fact that their Caribbean immigrant status makes them marginal to those relations in their new work center and in their home base.

2. Further, Caribbean immigrant writers are simultaneously installed in a specifically and historically determinate literary mode or sphere of production, and in one or more subdivisions of this mode. They may work in function of a Caribbean subset of literary production, or, say, in a U.S. dominant or minority subset-or in some hybrid context; further, they may work in one or more literary modes or genres of the literary "mode of production." However, whatever these writers produce in their productive sphere can only be a modification or transformation of what that sphere already contains or allows.

3. The degree to which that mode, then, is initially distanced from expressing immigrant concerns or Caribbean concerns will condition the distance which a given Caribbean immigrant writer must go to express the social groups basic to Caribbean identity and unity.

To be sure, the suggestions I make with respect to Caribbean literary modes and genres are ones which are very difficult to consider-especially if one wishes to sort out, and pinpoint the impact of immigration (as opposed even to imperialist penetration) on these complexly determined literary matters. Why is it, Márquez asks, that Caribbean poetry is more homogeneous in levels of achievement and forms of expression than is the Caribbean novel? And he adds:

Whatever the sociological and specifically cultural and literary reasons for differences between Anglo and Hispanophone novelistic practices, they are clearly multiple, involving the greatest complexity among interacting processes. Among these processes, immigration undoubtedly makes its contribution. But ultimately we must ask how we are to measure that contribution and how we are to elaborate a proper theory enabling us to trace the materialization of an effect.

All of these and other objections that could be raised have their validity. But as Márquez finally admits, the fact that we must acknowledge our current inadequacy on this score should not prevent us from applying those concepts and notions about which we feel reasonable sure, to carry on what we trust are more or less adequately scientific and useful studies of Caribbean culture and literature.

Again, I believe these remarks can be extended to Latin American literature, and I also believe it would be very valuable to carry out future developments along the lines of theory, compilations and analyses of Caribbean and Latin American immigrant literature within an overall framework of immigration studies. It is to certain suggestions in this regard to which I will now turn.

3. Suggestions for Work on Latin American Literature and Immigration

In an effort to explore the hypotheses raised as well as the difficulties cited above, I would propose that the phenomenon of immigration (as well as exile and displacement, as related processes) be one of the primary areas of exploration among Latin Americanists (and of course Latin American literature specialists) in the years to come. But I say this within the frame of a concern for the future study of historical, cultural and literary phenomena of the home base as well as the host countries. Indeed, I believe that by centering on the question of immigration and immigration culture (the expression of that experience), we can well justify more practically oriented examinations of home base developments, as well as their transformations in this society, their impact here and finally their impact back on the home bases. In many ways, immigration studies provide a particular locus for understanding cultural and literary developments in the context of overall transformations of international capital in which home base and host nations are implicated.

In order to carry out our proposal, we would ideally make use of such centers of immigration and of immigration studies as New York, Washington, Chicago,

Los Angeles, etc., with given specialists in given centers focusing on their particular priorities. Ultimately it would be necessary not only to work in our two traditional literary and Latin Americanist frames (MLA and LASA), but also in the frames of established general and specifically Latin American immigration institutional developments. Such organizations as New York's Centro de Estudios Puertorriqueños possibly offer us an expandable model. If no such institutions exist in other urban areas where we think they should be, then we should work with others to establish them. And here we should note that it is important that the centers be multidisciplinary, but that when possible, literary specialists should participate in their formation and development as early as possible, because if not, our concerns and what we have to offer will receive little space.

There is of course something extremely challenging in all this, because to the degree that we choose to focus on immigration literature in the context of immigrant cultural expression, then we must not only be investigators and analysts, but creative producers, promoters and participants in immigrant culture.

Our first task might be to establish seminars in which we work with students to survey community resources and issues. Out of the seminars could come more permanent interdisciplinary curricula and bibliography, as well as the beginnings of a library or archive of materials, which would include whatever holdings we could acquire and reference materials which would indicate other local, regional and national holdings, special and individual collections, etc. At a certain point in development of modest university-based programs and libraries, it would become valuable to utilize or set up a local consortium frame of universities and community based organizations (cultural centers, etc.) to develop a more coordinated city plan.

As the macro-organizational work is going on, our work with students in class is very important. We need to have students working on projects, which help to build our library and increase our knowledge at all levels; we need to form student cadres who will continue the work when their class-work ends. Projects could be as simple as clipping articles from local newspapers, developing a bulletin board of current happenings, etc. But more ambitious things have been attempted, even with undergraduates and have worked. Students have gathered materials from the community, done oral history projects, factual studies of community organizations, agencies, associations, groups, cultural producers, etc. Other projects suggest themselves:

1. A survey of daily life and recreation in immigration centers takes on special importance in a time of high unemployment. The organization of unemployed time as well as traditionally defined "leisure time" should yield special insights. What are the most popular songs in the cantinas?

What recordings do people pay to hear, to own? What requests do people make of strolling musicians? What do they sing when the spirit moves them? What kinds of books and magazines are available in libraries, grocery stores, etc.? What do people buy and read?

2. Oral history tape and also photograph libraries are relatively easy to develop, and represent great riches for studies of immigration culture; developing video libraries is also a not too expensive possibility.

Obviously, along with the library and curriculum components of our work we need to establish journals or other publication frameworks, which would disseminate our materials and our findings, offering opportunities for student and community research and cultural expression. These publications can be of the simplest nature (mimeographed, photocopied, whatever meant for classroom use, sharing among centers, etc., perhaps in the style of the Centro de Estudios Puertorriqueños monograph series. But from our point of view, perhaps the most important task would be to establish the means for placing, developing and publishing local and regional immigration cultural expression and providing a basis for analyzing it. In this context, our creative use of our critical skills is essential. The selection and editing of the cultural materials and fragments entail a series of ideological choices bound on the one side by our concern with historical accuracy (too narrow a selection aimed at highlighting a progressive trend may simultaneously distort its rather minor role in the constellation of immigrant tendencies) and our concern with cultural and ultimately political effect.

There can be no question but that the political is intimately involved in this project. For we would not simply be reflecting and expressing Latino immigration culture in its historical development and proliferation of expressive modes, but we would be playing on possibilities, affecting future production, if only by creating our own vehicles, and we would also be proliferating effects on those Latinos and non-Latinos who would read our publications, attend our exhibits, film showings, etc. The emphasis would indeed fall on our creative function in developing and promoting projects and collaborations, in writing grant proposals at a time of severe cutbacks, for one or another aspect of our total project. Also it would take a good deal of time before a mass of cultural expressions could accrue that would provide the basis for rich theoretical and critical elaborations, although from the inception of this work, we must be guided by a sense of theoretical frame, a sense of global processes, a sense of unity about the nature of processes in home base and host populations, because we would be trying to feed into the more progressive possibilities of the immigration population in their participation in this society and the effects this society has on home bases.

To the degree that our concern with regional and local phenomena results in products of a certain expressive richness, we will, in fact be helping to create a richer basis for the elaboration of the literature of immigration and U.S. minorities.

In the work on literature itself, of course distinctions must be made among three Latin American literatures being created in the U.S.:

1. A literature of "middle-class" Latin Americans who happen to live here for reasons of exile or transplantation as part of the "brain drain." Whether progressive or reactionary, this literature tends to integrate itself with dimensions of the overall "high literature" literary systems, the works standing as Caribbean, Central American, Argentine, etc. or even, as an effect, North American majority or "international." Relations between this literature and the phenomenon of worker immigration are very distanced and mediated, perhaps emerging in certain linguistic or stylistic transformations of varying significance in terms of internal dynamics of the work or its relation with the world. Here it is a matter of degree, for the Chilean exile poet from the Allende period, still thinking himself *chileno,* not integrating into a Latino group that functions as an ethnic minority, middle class in social status, a professional or intermediary between Latinos and the large rationalized structures of modem U.S. life, nevertheless can write more broadly and openly, less symbolically and restrainedly about the Chilean experience that they could if they were to approach similar materials in present-day Chile.

2. Another, less "*culta*" literature with form and theme dictated very much by the immigration experience itself, a literature that draws perhaps on other immigrant literatures but that grows out of the mass of Latin American workers in this country, even if the writer is basically a son or daughter of immigrants so that already sufficient distance exists between the writer and the mass so that the act of writing itself (whether in "mother tongue" or adopted language) can occur at a level of elaboration sufficiently high to constitute a relatively coherent text. The usual treatment of writers of such often crude and unschooled literature is to encourage them to "develop," that is, to take on what is seen as meaning for them to enter into the categories of those writers we note as belonging to the first literary mode, rather than seeing how their expressive experience may be enriched by a greater relation with a third mode:

3. This is the literature not even produced as literature, but as the product of oral history, as graffiti, improvised lyrics, etc. The raw material of the other two literatures mentioned, this literature involves the pattern of daily speech, the songs and variations of songs, the jokes, the very spontaneous creative, syncretic and dynamic reproduction of the experience of everyday life which remains then as part of everyday life in the creation of further patterns. One of our goals should be the recording of such materials and in critical practice, of making it available to the writers of literatures 1 and 2, so that they may draw upon it in the creative development of an ever-richer literature.

Implicit in all this is the creation of a literature and culture, which sustains its relation to broad numbers of people, and maintains and develops its creative possibilities, so that the prospects for a progressive culture are kept ever alive, though never imposed. Indeed, the effort to impose a sense of history and consciousness which does not grow out of the concrete development of a people can often lead to negative results. Pushing too hard, say, on the political dimension of a given question may create resistance in a Latino community not carefully prepared to hear the message.

The goal of our work is not the mere focus on local communities but on their role in a larger national and international totality, and their value as models for tracing the links between all phenomena subject to international and local determinations. We are not only interested in particular Latino subgroups, but their interactions with other immigrant groups, minority and dominant groups in the configuration of patterns existing today and the possible patterns (and alliances) for tomorrow.

Work along these lines is very much open to Latin American literature specialists who have already had a grounding in the history, cultural development and literature of home-base areas and who can then begin to develop a knowledge of immigration and acculturation effects which ultimately feed back into an enriched knowledge of the home base. Such work also gives Latin Americanists a local area of study and practice and provides those in remote places with very minimal immigration influx with a framework of ties to nearby regional centers where they can apply their and their students' expertise and intellectual interests. While much of the work involved feeds into the practical and implies an action on culture and ideology, it also implies a theoretical frame for action and the increased enrichment of that frame which ultimately remakes our conception of Latin American cultural and literary history, as well as our ability to understand it as it develops in the future. In this sense, the growing consciousness of U.S. Latino immigrant populations and of their cultural products feeds in and affects home base literary production, not only because some of the exiles and immigrants return, but because their works and experiences, as well as writings about them do. The full-fledged development of this dimension of Latin American and Caribbean studies suggest an actual praxis on literature, the kind of multileveled intervention of which Marxist intellectuals often dream. We cannot be sure of all the results; we can only hope that some of them will be roughly as progressive as the intentions. But the project I am proposing does provide a logical place for the insertion of U.S. Latino and other minority students in gradated studies and activities that can even begin in their early formative years. Hopefully we can develop projects that delving into local communities, others reaching out into the larger world. In this way, the object and subject of study come together in ways that propagate creation and hope.

Postscript

Now in the age of globalization, as many of the older exile writers have returned home or entrenched themselves in their new environments, and as immigration has become increasing transnational, Latino communities are experiencing new problems and tensions, as their composition changes and as the political winds shift.

In this context, even though many local projects have developed in the past few decades (the richest case being the Recovering the Hispanic Literary Heritage Project at the University of Houston, which has gathered materials on the discursive production of virtually every U.S. Latino community) still the suggestions for concrete work proposed in this essay seem more timely than ever, especially in view of expanded demographics and transnational cultural developments which continue to have multiple effects in every U.S. Latino community. We will consider some dimensions of the evolving problematic in the next chapter, which can indeed be considered an extended postscript to this one.

Works Cited

Rodríguez, Ileana and Marc Zimmerman. 1983. *Processes of Caribbean Societies: Ideologies and Literatures*. Minneapolis, MN. Institute for the Study of Ideologies and Literature.

Chapter VI

U.S. Latino Literature: Frames, Points of Entry and a Postscript

I. Introduction

In the past several years, with the remarkable growth and diversification of the U.S. Latino population, we have witnessed the emergence of a literature expressing Latino traditions, conflicts, and transformations. Contrary to common understanding, literature by Hispanics or Latinos, mainly in Spanish, but sometimes in English as well, has existed in what is now the U.S. since the sixteenth century; and a distinctly ethnic Latino literature has been evolving for well over a hundred years. With the emergence of U.S. Chicano and Puerto Rican social movements in the 1960s, a number of Chicano and Nuyorican writers also surfaced and synthesized the bases for new literatures which were consciously and specifically ethnic in character and function.

Characterized by nostalgia for a fading past, by a critique of racial oppression and negative acculturation experiences in the fields, in the city neighborhoods, the schools, factories and homes, by bilingualisms, schizophrenic goal conflicts and sex role confusions, by cultural tensions, affirmations and anger, and by calls for reform, rebellion, revolution or other forms of opposition, the emergent Latino literatures of the 1960s attempted to serve as laboratories for the expression and then reconstruction of transformed Latin American and U.S. Southwest Hispano-Indian peoples into "Mexican-Americans" or "Chicanos," into "Nuyoricans" or other Ricans, and ultimately, into the problematic and questionable but aggregate we know today as "Hispanics" or "Latinos."

Of course, few people knew of the literatures emerging among the *chicanos* and *boricuas*. Professional writers and critics (non-Latinos almost all) were slow to recognize and come to respect even their greatest early achievements. It was also common for budding Latino writers in different parts of the U.S. to be unaware of the existence of other Latino writers; and even when burgeoning

Chicano and Puerto Rican literary movements had emerged in relation to growing Latino national consciousness and action, few Latinos living in the U.S. were aware of the literatures. But what could one expect when millions of Latinos only had limited functional literacy in Spanish or English and when most Latinos were consigned to blue-collar or no-collar jobs, if they found work at all? It took the first relatively large-scale wave of Latino students in U.S. universities, in the context of the overall civil rights movement and the emergence of an anti-establishment, anti-Vietnam War counter culture, to produce both the writers and readers of these new literatures.

Where were the Latino writers in the sixties? Some were in colleges and universities, studying and sometimes even teaching. But others were in the countryside, doing stoop labor. And still more were in the cities, in their enclaves and *barrios*, in all the real and metaphorical jails and refuges provided for those marginalized by harsh and inhospitable urban circumstances. Of course some of them who could free themselves and grow actually found a way through the maze of bilingualisms and biculturalisms to express themselves, and indeed forge a new written language; and some of these writers even found their way into the few magazines and journals that would publish their work-or into the new publications they or friends created which served as outlets they otherwise had great difficulty finding in the U.S., in their own region or in the cities and towns where they congregated.

While starting as a "marginal, subcultural enterprise" whose promotion and study was restricted to small publications and small ethnic studies programs, U.S. Latino literature has recently received increasing attention in relation to the efforts to redefine and articulate the U.S. and Latin American literary canons, to deal with demands for multi-cultural curriculum and to explore the possibilities of cultural and symbolic, if not more direct, transformative opposition to the social systems in which we live. The study of these literatures and their pre-histories is important in itself; it is also important in understanding the U.S. and its literary culture, as well as relations to Latin America. What is more, the literatures may help in understanding the future of a significant sector of the U.S. workforce, as well as of the so-called "underclass," if conditions and prospects don't improve rapidly as we move toward the twenty-first century. While questions persist about the relation between Latino literature and the Latino social processes and cultural transformations they are supposed to represent, nevertheless it may said with some confidence that by projecting imaginatively and by not always respecting existing literary categories or fashions (to say nothing of respecting the normative grids applied in most social science research), at least some Latino literary works may come closer to expressing the deeper levels of Latino processes and transformations, Latino patterns of accommodation and resistance, than do most conceptually driven historical and sociological approaches. This may give special social value not only to the works, but also to the growing corpus of Latino cultural and literary theory and criticism which provides means for understanding the creative works.

This essay attempts to contribute to the understanding of U.S. Latino literature by exploring some dimensions of Latino culture-in-transformation, and then some historical and theoretical aspects of Latino literary production in relation to our overall concerns with Latin America's present and future developments from the perspectives of postmodernity and globalization.

But here we must specify a major caveat. The notion of a Latino emergence of the 1960s involves a mirage of newness-as if Latino literature were strictly a new generational phenomenon. Only the most erudite were aware of the fact that U.S. Latino writing might well be said to begin when the first Spaniards, *criollos, mestizos* and *mulatos* writing, in what we today call the U.S., show the first indications of the effects of their Anglo-American context in theme and style. Nicolás Kanellos' Recovering the Hispanic Literary Heritage Project at the University of Houston has been documenting centuries of such writings-finding, editing and sometimes publishing novels, essays, collections of poetry, etc. which reveal a historical range of subjects and orientations, etc., that belie the notion of an emergence of Latino writing in the 1960s. Nevertheless, I would argue that there was indeed an emergence in many ways distinct and discontinuous from the earlier writing and at times distinct and discontinuous with Spanish and Latin American literary roots as well, mainly because of its emphasis on Latino literature as an ethnic and minority phenomenon. I would also argue that the new literature itself triggered the emergence of the study of past roots, and an exploration of tendencies leading to the new Latino literature embedded in older traditions. I would finally argue that since the late 1980s, we have been seeing a re-emergence of older patterns as new waves of Latin American immigration have led to a new, growing mass of literary writing in Spanish, so that U.S.-based Latin American writing in Spanish is now reasserting its primacy over Latino writing in English, and is leading to an assertion of the Latin American connections in the new writing diverge from any posited in minority Latino texts from the 1960s and beyond. In this context, we will have to ask what will happen to English-language U.S. Latino writing in the future in its relations with the new Latin American (and sometimes "Latinoizing") writing in the U.S., and its relations also with writing in the Spanish-speaking world. However, we leave these questions for the final Post-Script of this essay. In the meantime we will deal here with what some would call Latino movement or "core Latino" writing.

II. Orientations to Latino Culture

A. Some Definitions

Questions of Chicano and Latino identity and culture have become even more complicated in recent years, first because of the social diversification and the geographic dispersion of those already here, and second, because of the massive immigration of Latin Americans for the diverse needs and motivations that caused their arrival, and finally because of the way that those who were here and the various new incoming groups have mixed and meshed together, have been transformed and have related with the other dominant and dominated groups which compose U.S. society in the context of a national and international context which has itself gone through several large-scale mutations since the 1970s.

Of course, the recent explosion of Latin American immigration to U.S. urban areas signaled more profound socio-economic, political and cultural processes in transformation and crisis at a worldwide level; and clearly, also, the new massive immigrations and related matters imply profound questions about local communities even as they try to struggle in order to survive and prosper in the midst of the global transformations.

For purposes of this essay, the word *Latino* and the related words, *latinidad* or *latinismo* will be used rather loosely, to refer to people of Ibero-American birth or family origin who have been born in or who have, willingly or otherwise, come to see the U.S. as their home. *Latinos* manifest U.S. transformations of identities formerly achieved through a syncretic process begun in Latin America (including the U.S. southwest) itself.

There is a traditionalist and generally conservative vision which defines Latinos strictly in function of their traditional language and cultural patterns; another anti-traditionalist and anti-culturalist vision, fostered by Werner Sollors and his followers (cf. Sollors 1986; also Padilla 1985), sees Latinos as products of the U.S. milieu.

The option here is for a definition rooted in distinctions emerging in the work of Raymond Williams (1981), involving dialectical transformations of past "residual" and future emergent possibilities-transformations which Juan Flores and George Yúdice (1992) conceptualize as "crossovers" in postmodern, multicultural contexts (see further on in this essay). According to this view the achieved cultural *mestizaje* of Latin Americans and especially a workingclass dimension of this identity, which corresponds to the vast majority of those who come and settle in the U.S., undergoes a series of experiences and transformations leading to a range of shared behaviors and attitudes which in turn become the pool of characteristics from which given Latino groups and individuals constitute particular selections and combinations.

This approach gives us a simple but coherent orientation that avoids excesses, especially if we remember that not every residue is reactionary (but rather that various residues can serve as progressive resources) and that not all "emergent" dimensions of culture are progressive. By underplaying what Williams would call the "residual" dimensions of culture (which are frequently, by the way, "survivals" of less alienated value systems which can provide progressive orientations, etc.), and by giving virtually all value to "emergent dimensions," we place ourselves in a position of seeing Latino identity as too much a U.S. product. To do so is to really impoverish our conception of Latinidad and the ultimate political and socio-economic implications that I believe are present in the broader definition and have hemispheric, as well as U.S.-specific consequences.

It is in the context of these perspectives that we can now reflect on our choice here of the word "Latino" as the key word to designate the object of our consideration. In recent years, we have come to employ the term *Hispanic*, and in fact it is now the word that is used most frequently in legal documents and the press. But while many "hispanos" accept the word and reject other alternatives, including the one advanced here, there are still many "hispanos" who reject that name and, in fact, prefer the term "Latino." Why? To deny that their common tie is simply Spain, perhaps even to reject a name that excludes Brazilians, Haitians, etc. But more important, they feel that the words *hispano*, *Hispanic*, *Spanish*, etc., have to do with the Anglo Saxon effort to patronize Latinos-to say, "Oh, you are really a white European... Oh you are not like the others. That is, that you are Hispanic, but not 'spic.'" In sum, Hispanic has come to prominence as a kind of left-hand compliment, by standing for "Spanishness"-that is, white, "Europeanness," even if a kind of exotic brand. The word "Hispanic" comes to suggest, then, the intent to erase (like a courtesy) the indigenous and African roots of Latin American identity. Given this hegemonic effort (in which many Latinos cooperate unconsciously and conconsciously), we have the contrary struggle for the name Latino.

Of course there is an ancient logic with the term that has to do with the Roman Empire, Romance languages, the religion and even the law of Rome. But to use the term "Latino" today is to affirm paradoxically the cultures and peoples dominated by Mediterranean civilization in its career throughout the New World. Paradoxically the term has come to connote the product of Latin-Indian and/or Latin-Black *mestizaje*. It has also come to evoke that other negativity, U.S.-based Latin American working class. I suppose in some Anglo minds, it conjures up *machismo*, black hair, gold crosses on chains, beaded curtains, tropical music, etc. But however pejorative or affirmative in connotation, the word "Latino" suggests a broad and aged otherness to Anglo American modernized norms-but an otherness constituted with the American frame. It suggests ethnic pride and cultural affirmation, not the hiding of black and brown blood that is implicit in the "Hispanic" label. Thus the term expresses paradox, complexity and defiance. It has come to stand for an affirmation of a struggle against racism and even classism. It is to affirm the workingclass base of the great majority of "Hispanics" in the U.S. It is to refuse cooperating with the racism and classism within Latinos themselves. It is to affirm Latin identity in contradistinction to an identity integrated with the dominant powers and their will to name and control. Regularly the situation of Latinos may best be understood in terms of their problems in confronting an individualist and capitalist civilization with a culture based on communal and pre-capitalist forms. Here the stress falls on cultural aspects that have to do with attitudes and customs based on the importance of kinship as central to group organization and behavior. Of course the ensemble of Latino values must be viewed not only as a synthesis of "the Hispanic," but also of the indigenous and also of the African. However, even with the specifically Hispanic dimension, the emphasis must fall on Spanish diversity, on North African roots and the role of Semitic culture (Arab and Jewish) in the formation of the attitudes that have to do with concepts of tribe, of race, of honor, of kinship, of sex roles, of land, of property, of life, death and in general identity seen as community and family-based.

A complex aspect of Latino unity has been the retention of characteristics drawn from the cultural past that have been defined as "pre-capitalist," "early capitalist," "pre-industrial," "Catholic," "agrarian," "Spanish," "dependent," etc. It has been argued that these characteristics render Latinos as relatively "dysfunctional," "underprivileged" or "underdeveloped" within the rationalized productive system governing U.S. society; but they may well prove to be a source of strength against the more corrosive effects of material and technological advance. In fact, a more humane future for all people may well depend in part on the conservation of such "residual" characteristics among the Latinos and the "Latinization" of non-Latinos. However symptomatic they may be of liberation, such matters as the rising rate of Latino divorce, ruptures of the extended family, the pressures for higher degrees of individuation, independent female participation, etc., imply cultural and psychological difficulties for large numbers.

In this sense part of the problematic Latinos face in trying to survive and live a creative life within the U.S. system has to do with the "interface" of Latin values and orientations with Anglo-Saxon/capitalist civilization. Without doubt, many Latinos suffer because they carry with them values and attitudes that in spite of their many transformations still express a communitarian, agricultural and semi-feudal logic. And we understand that there are many Latinos who are even computer experts, but we also understand that the Latino working masses have forms of life that more readily fit with pre- and not post-industrial forms. And we also know that these forms of life (including forms of courtesy and Catholicism) fit perfectly well in the capitalist world, but like forms of an "underclass" in what we call the "dual labor market." We know that the well-known Castilian motto, *Yo soy quien soy*, which is part of the Latino legacy, doesn't have to do with individualistic, Protestant or existentialist identity, but with social and communitarian forms of being. We know that honor and loyalty to one's *compadre* are forms that are out of fashion and that don't thrive in a world where the "cash nexus" and "rational self interest" rule the day. But we also know that in the carnivalesque, Baudrillardian landscape of post-industrial, postmodern values, of impersonalism, uprootedness and monadism, there is a considerable attraction to Latino values, and the hope that certain dimensions survive and thrive-not machismo, as it has been characterized and, I think, properly stigmatized, but the Latino sense of family, not *compadrazgo* to the death, but, yes, something of loyalty, something that is not pure "rational" interest, not sun-worship, "land fetishism," or blood sacrifice, but something which goes beyond a mechanical order of clocks, gears and the logic of productive efficiency. Ironically, this romantic anti-capitalism and anti-modernism comes at a time when through and structural changes involving rural-to-urban migration, as well as the migration of technologies to the countryside, etc., Latin Americans and, even more so, Latinos are undergoing intense processes of modernization, in some ways transforming, in some ways undermining any essentialist sense of Latino identity.

While there are many who have an interest in Latin culture who are not Latinos, there are also many Latinos who like Richard Rodríguez and Linda Chávez, feel that the effort to preserve Latino culture contributes to the maintenance of Latinos in situations of marginalization and poverty. And of course there are those who want the best of both worlds; they want to combine "the best of the Anglo with the best of the Latino." But there are still others who argue that the great majority of Latinos who lose their culture come to suffer from a process of uprooting that leaves them with the worst possibilities for surviving in the modern world. Above all, there are some of us who persist in their preoccupation with Latino traditions of struggle and resistance. We see a nexus between Marxist and non-Marxist tendencies (anarchist, religious and other tendencies) of opposition and various modes of populist and religious struggle of Latin Americans and U.S. Latinos. We also see a nexus between the struggles of Las Casas, of José Martí, Sandino, César Chávez. We see that the survival of Latino traditions is not necessarily a conservative matter, but one involving the survival of elements that have not suffered from complete domination and that can serve in forging a more fruitful future for Latinos and for every one.

In this sense, Latino culture, even as differentiated from Latin American-based traditionalisms, is seen to stand as an alternative to postmodernism. But others see Latino identity as acting as a positive category *within* our overall culture, providing some of the sources for the future. And so we have a paradox. At a time when many intellectuals are trying to inscribe Latin American and U.S. Latino culture as part of postmodernism and actually see the culture as anticipating or pre-dating the phenomenon (the same argument was used with regard to surrealism, so that Latin American *real maravilloso* and now magical realism are related to European modernism and the boom fiction to post-modernism) others are seeking to maintain traditions as a struggle against postmodern encroachment, and a prolongation of the struggle against assimilation; and finally there are others who see Latino subalternity (and even what remains of Latin American traditionalism) as already acting as a category within the postmodern, but as a potentially progressive, transformative current, not necessarily and inevitably submerged and dominated by it, but possibly standing as a reservoir of resistance and resistance energies, possibly providing one of the sources for future social transformations far beyond the postmodern moment-provided of course, as Stuart Hall, along with Laclau and Mouffe (2001), would insist, on how Latino dimensions become *articulated* with others in years to come.

These definitions and orientations in mind, we may turn to questions having to do with our situating theoretical concerns pertaining to Latinos in relation to their situation in the midst of past, present and anticipated changes in the U.S., Latin America and the overall global order.

B. Some Questions About the Future of Latinos

Latino culture requires differentiation from other U.S. minority or ethnic cultures, and from strictly immigrant complexes, first because of the long-standing Indian, Mexican and Puerto Rican presence within territory directly taken by the U.S.; second, because of the fact of a common border between the U.S. and Mexico; third, because of the special legal status of Puerto Ricans and Cubans; and finally, because of the long-term and continuous two-way migratory pattern between the U.S. and Mexico, the U.S. and Puerto Rico, etc. While immigration is a crucial matter, however, the main source of Latino population growth is still from the continued expansion of the existing U.S. Latino population pool.

Inevitably when we contemplate the growing Latino population, we immediately face questions of diversity and apparent disunity which prevent our overestimating the statistical growth: the U.S. Latino population does not automatically form a *bloc*; and even among many sectors with similar objective interests, it is extremely difficult to construct an effective unity. It is also hard to anticipate all the possible implications of the growth of the Latino population for the future. In spite of the new immigration policies, we can be sure that the flow will continue, because its causes will continue to be acute. The new efforts at free trade, even if successful for some, may not stem but may in fact intensify the reasons for immigration.

The obvious point to make is about problems Latinos may face in the future. First, there is the question of racism and cultural hostility, patterns of prejudice and discrimination, struggles with other minority groups-and all the rest. This is especially important when we realize that Latinos will potentially constitute a significant proportion of the workers employed or not in the country, and therefore that what happens to Latinos will be important for the future of the U.S. and for every one.

On first sight, the prospects can appear negative enough. Indeed, without some dramatic transformations and radical changes in state and corporate policies, current trends would lead to a situation in which a vast and growing population of unskilled, poorly educated workers functionally illiterate in Spanish and English, would be inserted in a society based on advanced technology and capital-intensive labor; we would have a population needing housing, social services, education and jobs in a nation whose own logic of development may well leave it ill-prepared to deal with its deepest problems. Indeed, since the median age of this population mass would be significantly lower than the U.S. majority, the nation would face an extenuation of an already existing polarization between an older, mainly white population (though with some strategic Latino intermediaries) which increasingly monopolizes wealth, resources and power, and a younger, mainly non-white population numerically dominated by Latinos, who will be waging an ever more difficult struggle to maintain and win access to institutions and resources in which the majority has lessening interest and commitment.

In this context, Latinos will have great socio-economic and political difficulties, but the cultural and psychological problem may be greater, as pressures affect family patterns and values, on sex roles, on all relations and identifications.

Such matters as gangs and drugs, the informal economy, continuing and extending anomie and the like have prevented Latino groups and other from uniting. so that, at the same time that some Latinos will rise in prestige and respect, most of the others, those thousands who can't get with the new world order will be doomed to live on the margins-if they are able to live at all.

3. U.S. Latino Literature: History and Development

A. Latino Populations and Three Phases of Migration Literature

In the study of U.S. Latino literature, we should first note the diversity and ambiguity of our object. For example, to what degree is what seems to be Spanish-language Mexican literature written in what were or are U.S. boundaries, to be considered as part of U.S. Latino literature-or literature written in Puerto Rico, or Spanish language literature by Puerto Rican university professors living in New York but ever identifying in their writing with the island and Latin America? To be sure successive generations and immigration waves of Mexicans produced a diverse range of literary forms and styles long before what we might generally recognize as even Chicano literature emerged; and it should be underlined that the various Mexican literatures are still being produced even as Chicano literature becomes more developed, sophisticated and experimental. The same may be said about Puerto Rican literature in the U.S. as it developed after 1898, and as it took off in the wake of the explosion of Puerto Rican immigration and settlement after World War II. Given cultural differences; Cuban writing was following a similar path as the Puerto Rican until the Cuban Revolution changed the class, political and ideological orientation of U.S. Cubans and made their literature difficult to relate to the Puerto Rican and Mexican counterparts. Now, most notably with the writing of Julia Alvarez from the Dominican Republic and the appearance of young sons and daughters of other Latin American migrations, we have styles, themes and forms which, taking into account historical differences, in many ways have things in common with earlier Mexican and Puerto Rican dimensions.

Although heterogeneous, the Mexican and Puerto Rican migrations were primarily workingclass, and the groups brought with them those elements of their national and Latin American culture, oral tradition and literature available to their social class and situations. For a distinct U.S. Latino culture and literature to emerge for each group in each locale, there had to be a sufficient experience of U.S. life, culture and language, to pressure Latin American cultural norms, and there had to be a sufficient degree of critical consciousness, generated through hardship, but articulated through institutional or extra-institutional/counter-cultural formations to make writing as a vehicle of cultural definition both necessary and possible. Obviously that literary expression required an adequate pooling of resources for at least minimal cultural reproduction and distribution-from self-publishing to small chapbook and literary journal production. To the degree that each emergent work of literature tended to stand in relation to broader cultural, literary and socio-psychological patterns, that work tended to follow certain general lines of "mainstream" or minority literary development dominant nationally, but also marked by certain characteristics specific to its place and group of generation. This meant that each expression by each member of a national group was at least in part filtered through a particular, sometimes regional, sometimes even a more local sense of Latino identity.

Leaving aside the Latin American literature written by professionals who have come to the U.S. as part of the brain drain, U.S. Latino literature may be divided into two major categories, (1) a literature based on and extending from long ingrained indigenous U.S. southwest homebase traditions, and (2) a literature based on the experience of those many primarily working class people who have migrated from Mexico, Puerto Rico, and other parts of Latin America to the U.S. during the course of the twentieth century.

To be sure many of the people of the first group have virtually become part of the second by a dislocation process which has uprooted them from their Southwest homes and sent them to work and sometimes to settle in other parts of the country, so that their original cultural and literary base, rooted in eighteenth and nineteenth century traditions, has been influenced, affected and at least partially merged with the newer immigrant populations, which they have in turn also influenced. And to the degree that much of the U.S. Latino population has been one in transformation, we may consider that population's literary expression as being loosely divided into three phases, through which various population strands, generations and individuals have passed through at given historical moments.

The first phase is a romantic literature attempting to replicate the homebase literary culture (whether in the Southwest or Latin America) with variations in subjects, emphases and expressive modes deriving from the particularities of the writers' origins and experience, especially as the forces of "cultural shock" and transformation begin taking their toll. This usually means a nostalgic, nationalistic poetry of loss and exile, romantic, rhetorical and declamatory in style with conventional rhythms, rhyming patterns and poetic techniques. Mexican and border-area *corridos*, Puerto Rican *plenas* and other musical forms influence this literary expression, as do folklore, sayings, proverbs, etc.

The second phase is a literature of migration or immigration, marked by hopes, but also by problems, presenting everyday life confusions, conflicts, etc., frequently exploring racism and ethnic or national identity, an affirmation of roots, appeals to justice and envisioned social solutions. This literature emerges in all genres (in song, poetry, fiction and drama), but it tends to favor poetry at first and then begin to veer toward the development of more extended dramatic or narrative forms, modeled on, but varying from the early primary ones probably because of the complex and ever shifting experiences the forms attempt to encapsulate and articulate. At first this literature is only somewhat mediated by existing literary norms. It is performative, social, didactic, hortatory; it is often bitter, militant, defiant. Still close to oral roots, it may play far better than it reads. It is meant to be read and heard, by targeted groups in specific settings. In poetry, this is a literature often without rhyme, jagged in rhythm, imitating and extending from first older and then emergent musical forms, with some influences based on forms stemming from Afro-American, Native American or other minority cultures. It is populist in orientation; but overtly or surreptitiously, in tone, gender-centering and ideology, its populism, democratic spirit and resistive counter-culturalism or otherness emerge within a patriarchal frame.

The third phase is a literature of settlement, also looking back on the homebase and immigration, but from a more settled-in framework, with an existing Latino tradition behind it, now reaching out to other minority and mainstream (U.S. mainly but also Latin American, African, etc.) to expand horizons and move either to pan-Latin American, "pan-third world" or U.S. mainstream identifications. Here the culture itself becomes self-critical and de-centered from earlier male discourse; feminist and post-nationalist issues become crucial, as do a wide range of alternative cultural models and directions. Expression is frequently more individual, subjective, inward; style replaces a generalized rhetoric. In one sense this literature may be an expression of assimilation or acculturation that may or may not represent the broader group aggregate (but rather a sector thereof); however, it may also be a literature which draws on, even as it critically distances itself from, earlier norms and suppositions.

These literatures are far from exclusive. Tendencies exist along a continuum. For example, in the Midwest, Latino literature develops late when overall U.S. Latino consciousness and literature is moving along the continuum from the second to the third phase. Even as new versions of older modes reappear in relation to recent immigration and development patterns, contemporary Midwest Latino literature tends to telescope the second and third phases to produce a literature which may still have roots in the rural land, or a *barrio* or *colonia* surrogate, but which tends to project beyond national to broader Latino and universal concerns. And the multilayered and diverse urban environments of our literary centers make it possible for a single writer to go through all three phases in a matter of a few years.

B. The Development of Chicano Literature

What we today call Chicano literature is really, first a Southwest variant of Mexican literature and then an emergent immigrant literature written by the successive waves of twentieth century immigrants and especially their second and third generation offspring. In fact, tendencies toward what we today consider Chicano, as opposed to Mexican, literature, begin to emerge in the Southwest even in the nineteenth century and on into our own time, as primarily Mexican values react to Anglo-American ones to produce Chicano identity and literature. Gradually a new Chicano literature emerges, a literature mainly focused on U.S. experiences, the clash of old and new cultural trends, the pressures on language and identification, the problems of cultural loss, prejudice, discrimination, poverty and urban blight.

Rural and even folk literary forms embodying older traditions and small town agrarian life have developed alongside with urban texts portraying barrio and prison life and efforts to defend identity through the concern with "roots" and the elaboration of a mythic source of identity-structure such as that which developed during the heydays of the Chicano movement with the concept of *Aztlan* seen as the lost promised land which must be recaptured and maintained at least in spirit if Chicanos were to survive the pressures of what many of them saw as a soulless and racist technocratic order which threatened to devour them.

From efforts to reclaim land grants to the symbolic positing of a pre-Colombian mystical realm, Chicano writers developed the concept of *Aztlan* as a pre-capitalist, land and spirit-centered basis for Chicano culture, literature and political activity. Even as Chicano literature developed throughout the 1960s and 1970s and on into the 1980s, even as new Chicano writers showed new levels of sophistication, left older modes of protest and incorporated new Latin American and U.S. models as the bases for their developing work, the *Aztlan* myth or one of its variations as a "sacred space" would still tend to characterize Chicano literature and serve as its paradigm, only to be eroded (or resurrected, in the case of Anzaldúa) by the more secular, rationalist and feminist trends that would emerge increasingly in the 1980s as a literature of settlement and acculturation began to displace the older cultural model for many writers.

No more provocative formulation of the pre- or anti-capitalist/anti-modern, land-centeredness of Chicano literature, and no better means to understand different Chicano works and trends against national norms and currents has been suggested, than the post-structuralist paradigm elaborated in relation to Chicano poetic discourse by critic Juan Bruce-Novoa in the 1970s and given most complete articulation, variation and elaboration (from paradigm to anti-paradigm) in his *RetroSpace* (1990).

For Bruce-Novoa, the surface concerns of Chicano literature point to a "deep structure" based on the loss of a world, or "*axis mundi*" and an effort to recuperate the lost world through some kind of creative recreation of space. This paradigm is played out in function of the polarities of life and death. Its deeper, anthropological roots may be found in a tribal sense of communal, sacred space. One is only alive in relation to a community which occupies and defines that space. Exiled, one enters the land of death, a world of chaos in which the "center will not hold," the spiritual disorder which is the modern experience, or the world of time as opposed to spatial values, chronometric/labor time as opposed to sun/space time: the world not of maize, but of money and machines.

As Bruce-Novoa argues, Chicano literature is the space of symbolic action between the forces of "life and death" in relation to the disappearance, survival and transformation of the Mexican *axis mundi*. Each progressive historical transformation of the *axis mundi* implies what Bruce-Novoa describes as the "erasure" (or conservation even in negation) of what is formally canceled. It is the Conquest which marks a major rupture in the violation of the *axis mundi*. The Independence and future Mexican struggles represent efforts by varying groups to "erase the erasure" and retake the Mexican space.

The threat of group obliteration intensifies in the modern world of displacement from the countryside, of migration, migrant labor and cross border immigration. Mexico is canceled by migration and displacement. A whole value world and cosmology is lost. The people try to reconstruct the sacred in their new space, the *colonia*, *barrio* or street, only to find this space and the people attacked from without and threatened by disintegration from within, with only certain possibilities for survival and reconsecration, to be found in those who, while valuing change, take on older roles of incanting the wise and magic words and enacting the proper rituals. The new turf becomes the new Chicano *axis mundi* to be held and defended, as the U.S. experience cuts the people off from Mexico and as Mexico cuts them off from the U.S. window onto the world. But the *barrio* is a fallen Mexican world, one in which there seem to be few creative avenues, in which what is left of cultural roots may hem one in and hold one down, more than provide modes of liberation. Indeed, defense of the sacred turf may lose all significant cultural reference as it synchronizes with or rather becomes reduced to generalized "underclass" or even gang orientations (cf. Horowitz 1983). The question then becomes how to find creative resolution, how to protect oneself from the identity chaos of the external world, but how on the other hand not to be trapped by what from that internalized external world's point of view is the prison of a traditional culture which no longer holds even the illusions of rewards and possibilities that it formerly offered.

The artist is seen as a kind of shaman, recreating the communal space or its surrogates and winning a war against invading forces of chaos. Of course one frequently must take on the enemy's tactics and weapons; one cannot strictly bring back the old. You cannot restore old Mexico or bring back *Aztlan*, but you can win creative space ritualistically, artistically, through creative reconstruction and projection. The space of the printed page becomes the communal writer's space of victory.

Clearly, this kind of cosmology (as projected by Sandra Cisneros and others) has ties to the evocations of structural transformations specified in the writings of Octavio Paz; as a sophisticated reformulation of the *Aztlan* construct and theme so central to Chicano cultural and literary mythology, this orientation has been subjected to intense critique as constituting an overly normative definition of Chicano literature. Interestingly, Bruce-Novoa himself has been intensely involved in the critical and deconstructive process.

Latino literary editor, Nicolás Kanellos, has attacked the ethnic immigrant narrative as an exhausted paradigm; and Bruce-Novoa has become an absolute champion of canon reform (cf. their articles in Ruoff and Ward, Jr. 1990 and Bruce Novoa 1990). But this reform has prompted continual theoretical interventions, such as the major one we find in Ramón Saldívar's *Chicano Narrative: The Dialectics of Difference* (1990), and in a variety of other, and especially feminist, critics and writers.

More overtly political than Bruce-Novoa, Saldívar uses an interdisciplinary, critical methodology involving the Derrida's deconstructionism and Jameson's "political unconsciousness" to portray Chicano literature as a part of, yet resistant to the mainstream of, U.S. literature, and to characterize it as structuring oppositional differences with respect to both hegemonic Anglo-American literary, cultural and ideological norms and the evolving socio-economic and political processes to which they are related.

By this account, deconstructionism operates to undermine the binary oppositions which seemingly structure discourse in the production of differential textual meaning. This procedure opens textual structuration to interpretations based on Jameson's conceptualization of relations between Marxist concerns in production, class and transformative action and Freudian views of such phenomena as tied to neurosis-producing repression and sublimated expression. Basing his analysis on dialectical, socially rooted difference, Saldívar sees Chicano narrative as involving deconstructions of imposed Anglo identities for the production of literary meaning. Interpretation of literary texts means understanding the relationship of their symbolic patterns to their generic conventions and the broader social and political forces which writers internalize and express through unconscious processes.

Whereas Chicano narrative may have seemed less overtly oppositional than other literary modes, Saldívar underlines its varieties of difference as they articulate themselves in relation to existent generic norms and variations which mediate between given literary works and the social world they would seem to represent. Thus, Chicano border reactions to Anglo American racism initially found expression in the border *corrido*, which solidified in the second half of the nineteenth century and then experienced successive transformations and pressures until it gave way to other expressive forms under the weight of historical change. Modern urban Chicano poetry is one mode developing out of and pressuring the *corrido* frame. But the varying novelistic forms which emerge at the time of the Chicano movement constitute the primary mode of Chicano expression in the period extending from the 1960s to present.

Most of the major Chicano narratives of the 1960s and 1970s, no matter how varying in formal experimentation, were in fact male *bildungsroman*, so that the emergence of women writers and feminist narratives in the 1980s meant a constitution of works that were multiply differential and resistant, in that they went counter not only to the hegemonic culture but also to the Chicano patriarchal patterns and even the white feminism which sought to oppose the hegemonic culture.

Starting in the 1980s, radical feminist ideologues like Norma Alarcón, Gloria Anzaldúa, Cherríe Moraga and Ana Castillo articulated a new Chicana oppositional stance by rewriting Chicano male-centered macro-mythologies in terms of feminist ones which question all fixity of gender/race/class identities and norms; meanwhile feminist fiction writers have sought to explore the micro-world of everyday life patternings to find the multiple modes of possible resistances within the seams of lived experience and creative projection.

Now, under the impact of deconstructionism, feminism, post-Marxism and other postmodernist modes of thought, much contemporary Chicano writing male and female seeks to break through beyond earlier narrow ethnic concerns to ones which require new modes of understanding and analysis to grasp how the writing maintains or transcends earlier patterns and identifications. The new writing is inevitably more urban, more closely woven with other Latino and non-Latino cultural strains, more distanced from a pre-technological, pre-capitalist world of blood bonds and sacrifices, sacramental, ritualistic and ceremonial relations with the earth and other humans; it is also distanced from the world of confrontational violence with Rangers, cops or rival gangs.

Many new writers seem intent on withdrawing from Chicano ethnic literature and from the culturalist paradigm early identified with it. Feminist Chicana writers seem to drift both from Bruce-Novoa's spatial identification or Saldívar's construction of machistic border and barrio defiance; they struggle ambivalently with the older paradigms as well as the repression and the inscribed role of women which they find as central to them and to at least certain dimensions of the Chicano movement they have been seen to represent. Still others seem fully turned toward the U.S. mainstream without struggling with the older paradigms or being particularly centered on them. More than a few have attempted to relate their work to the Latin American mainstream, or even the more minority testimonio, etc., in search of broader pan-Latin identifications.

Nevertheless, in one way or another, many contemporary Chicano writers, and especially male ones, directly or indirectly, consciously or not, project the early paradigmatic Chicano vision into contemporary settings and circumstances; and it may well be that contemporary feminist work, as well as other "new wave"-tending Chicano literature can still be shown to partake, however critically, of a land-centered structural view as a necessarily regressive, pre-capitalist oppositional mode, now refashioned to project a more progressive, late capitalist resistant pattern. If this is the case, then we would still be able to establish the core ties of Chicano writers to a vision which is very specifically rooted in a syncretic "imaginary" where Mexican and U.S. polarities find their resolution. We would still be able to speak of a specifically "ethnic" literature, rather than a general literature written by writers who just happen to be Chicano.

This orientation may continue to have importance if we believe that even the enforcement of the new immigration laws cannot resist the pressure created by circumstances in Mexico, and that, even as we have new generations of sophisticated Chicanos able to read and absorb the sophisticated writings of new writers, we will continue to have large, new Chicano social sectors who must find or create a literature expressive of and suited to their own situation and experience.

C. Puerto Rican Literature in the U.S.

Pointing to the lack of continuity and community between Nuyorican and Island writers, Efraín Barradas (1980: 11) notes that one of the most difficult tasks in explaining U.S. Puerto Rican writing is to *distinguish* between island-oriented literature (even when it is written in New York and/or is about the U.S. Diaspora), which is a branch of Caribbean or Latin American literature, and Continental U.S. Puerto Rican writing which, no matter where written, at least tends to be a U.S. ethnic literature. In attempting to make a bridge between island and Continental expression, we cannot overlook the differences, which have been felt so keenly by those on both sides of the divide.

Above all, he cites the tendency of "Nuyorican" writers toward heretical demythifications and/or mythmaking constructs with respect to Puerto Rican culture and national identity. Obviously the reasons for these constructs lie in the root causes for the immigration of Puerto Ricans to New York: the island's colonial status and the economic upheaval caused by efforts of modernization, and of course the very negative and demoralizing circumstances most Puerto Ricans have encountered in the U.S. So we have a mythifying of the island and a search for alternative role models and identifications; and we have, above all, the assertion of an injured, denied and hence defiant sense of national and cultural pride.

At times, continental Puerto Ricans have resisted dealing with themselves as a U.S. minority, because to do so would imply a negation of a focus on their island's colonial status. Even as unemployment, poor housing, drug and welfare dependency, gang and school dropout rates, etc., became increasingly endemic in the Puerto Rican community, such problems could only be seen as legitimate to the degree that they were subsumed in function of the situation of Puerto Ricans as a colonized people. And the entire immigration process, seen from the island intelligentsia's struggle to preserve a fragile, jeopardized national identity, could only be construed as loss. This sense of loss, felt in the very bones by those having their base in a U.S. enclave, and unable to recapture fully their island roots, has led to sometimes desperate alternatives-from a full-blown romanticism with respect to the island, to a rejection of the island and a search for other worlds.

Indeed, perhaps for their smaller numerical size as a population (or as a tiny writer/artist subculture), and perhaps also for the fragility and difficult-to-specify character of their sense of nationhood, U.S.-based Puerto Rican writers, more than their Chicano counterparts, have tended to decenter or go beyond national identification to Latino and third world/minority identifications even to the degree that they affirmed their nationhood. So, the first Puerto Rican writers in the U.S. learned to project their visions of island independence in terms of union with Cuba and the broader Caribbean world. And, in this century, it is no accident that in Chicago, where the Puerto Rican population exists in the context of a much larger Mexican presence, the major contribution to the developing national scene was *Revista Chicano-Riqueña*, fathered by U.S. Rican Nicolás Kanellos.

While recent Chicano critics have attacked, abandoned or transformed the *Aztlan construct*, the problem for Puerto Rican writers has been the elaboration of a series of partial, fragmented mythologies in the face of a lack of an abiding and binding Ur-myth that could give depth and unity to the epiphenomenal thematics of their work. So the occasional and topical feel and at least appearance of much U.S. Puerto Rican writing, and also the tentative and melancholy nature of the writers' heresies and mythologies; so the apparently more limited volume and elaboration of Puerto Rican literature compared to the Chicano counterpart. This is the viewpoint articulated rather arrogantly in Bruce-Novoa's *RetroSpace*. But if there is some truth in this contrast, stemming as it does from the lost past of Caribbean pre-Hispanic cultures (as opposed to the at least partial continuities involved in Mexican history), and from a lack of long-term residence or rootedness (through workforce or proprietorial relatedness achieved as permanent workers, business people or homeowners) in a land which they have felt theirs by some deep and sacred pact (the case of at least some people living in the Southwest, and part of the mythic structuration of much Chicano literature), nevertheless, this very situation helps to define the profundity behind the sometimes superficial appearances.

We have in fact just designated "the space of U.S. Puerto Rican literature" as one primarily for the exploration and forging of a new sense of identity and nation in the face of loss and disorientation, multi-ethnicity and multi-Latino identifications, in the face of the loss of myths which is increasingly the postmodern condition for Chicanos just as for others in contemporary life. The space of this literature separates even as it relates it to Puerto Rican island writing; the space is where the Puerto Rican colony or *barrio* is related to the city and its majority and minority populations, to the island, the Caribbean, Africa and the world. Gender will also emerge as a concern. In this context, the main contribution of much recent Puerto Rican writing is the insistence we have pointed to on a broad Latin and even internationalist focus even in the midst of developments emphasizing U.S. Puerto Rican nationalist, broadly minority and feminist trends. And in this context too, the question emerges (in a way it hardly ever does for Puerto Rican island writers) about what may have been *gained* by Puerto Ricans in spite of the obvious negative dimensions of the Diaspora.

To be sure, Puerto Rican literature in the continental U.S. does not begin with the Diaspora of economic refugees to New York. Flores divides Puerto Rican literature to the U.S. into three phases, preceded by a kind of "pre-phase" (Flores 1989: 39-44).[1] Extending from the last century, the "pre-phase" is generated by exiles from the independence struggle against Spain (major intellectuals like Hostos, Betances, etc., but also "a solid base of artisans and laborers"), who spent varied lengths of time in New York, forming Puerto Rican and Antillean independence support groups and writing mainly about their Caribbean struggles, but also (in the case of Hostos' diaries or the poetry of Francisco Gonzalo ["Pachín"] Marín) reflecting critically on the New York experience of arriving Puerto Rican nationals. Then there is the extraordinary case of Luisa Capetillo

(1879-1922), a labor organizer and feminist whose essays and plays extend from this pre-phase to the next period and indeed anticipate the most radical and feminist currents in more recent texts.[2]

The first phase proper, extending roughly from1917 to 1945, is mainly of auto-biographical and journalistic works expressing the efforts of first generation immigrants, many of them with the feelings and attitudes of foreign nationals and subject people (and here their difference from other immigrants), to adjust to U.S. life. This period is most fully and richly represented by *The Memoirs of Bernardo Vega* and Jesús Colón's *A Puerto Rican in New York and Other Sketches*. However, as Flores notes, this phase is also represented by fragments from a vast, still-accessible stream of oral history, and a still more accessible volume of popular music (boleros, plenas, etc.) in which Rafael Hernández and other popular song writers expressed a wide range of feelings about the experience of Puerto Ricans coming to the city.

After the initial development of agro-business, industrialization efforts under Operation Bootstrap were responsible for the massive movement of poor, country Puerto Ricans off their land and into a migratory process that brought them to U.S. cities. The period of this migration, from 1945-65, constitutes the second phase of developing U.S. Puerto Rican literature. As immigrants, the Puerto Ricans of this period arrived too late to the feast of U.S. industrial expansion. Whereas many Mexicans, lacking legal status and having to take whatever job became available, gradually integrated themselves into the U.S. workforce (albeit in marginal roles), all too many Puerto Ricans, lacking minimal skills and suffering from cultural and racial discrimination as well, failed to find permanent niches in a declining industrial base; and, as U.S. citizens, they found their modes of survival in low-paying, temporary jobs, and (the subject of Oscar Lewis' notoriously reductionist study of the "culture of poverty," *La Vida*), the famous U.S. systems of welfare and the "informal economy"-*la bolita* and *el mantengo*.[3]

The circumstances of emergent lumpenization and what many saw as a loss of Puerto Rican/Latin American values and the attendant defense of the very system which was undoing them led to the emergence of two predominant literary modes. First, there was a very powerful, negative "view from the island"-a perspective focusing on the problems of workingclass Puerto Rican immigrants shared by writers whether living in San Juan or New York and represented most famously by Pedro Juan Soto, René Marqués, Enrique Laguerre, José Luis González and Emilio Díaz Varcárcel.

Second, there was a "view from within the community" by a group of exile writers with long residence in New York (Clemente Soto Vélez and Julia de Burgos among them, and with writers such as Iris Zavala, Iván Silén and Víctor Fragoso representing more recent examples), writing mainly a literature of exile with hardly any bilingualisms and only limited reference to the immigration experience. Exceptions in this group were writers in at least a few works were Guillermo Cotto-Thorner and, above all, Jaime Carrero, who turned toward the depth exploration of the immigration experience and the linguistic and cultural "*neorkismos*," which were to become common in the next stage of U.S. Puerto Rican literature.

This third, or Nuyorican stage "arose with no direct reference to or evident knowledge of the writings of the early period... But nevertheless in prose at least [it] effectively draws together the firsthand testimonial stance of the 'pioneer' stage and the fictional, imaginative approach of the writers of the 1950s or 1960s" (Flores, p. 43). Clearly, this definition applies to such narratives of male becoming by Piri Thomas, Lefty Barreto, Nicky Cruz, Humberto Cintrón, Edwin Torres and Edward Rivera, as well as much of the work of the best known Nuyorican woman writer, Nicholasa Mohr-whose most famous narratives are, as Arnaldo Cruz-Malavé points out, "narratives of formation," or *bildungsromane* exploring the fate of outsiders caught often between one or more sets of conflictive polarities: Puerto Rico/New York, city/suburb, Latin culture/Anglo culture, semi-feudal patriarchism/capitalist feminism, etc. (Cruz-Malavé 1989: 45-48).[4]

According to Cruz-Malavé, Puerto Rican writers have been most prolific in poetry, where, more than in other genres, they have mapped out the polarities specified by Barradas between mythification and heretical demythification, which "constitute a dialectic that may be said to have its origins in the New York Puerto Rican awakening of the late 1960s" in the work of the Puerto Rican members of the Last Poets and in a group known as the Young Lords (Cruz-Malavé: 48). Early Nuyorican poetry draws on militant Afro-American and beat influences. It speaks for a community, more than an individual, and seeks to strip away false consciousness about the "American Dream" and Nuyorican colonial status in a third world ghetto; it seeks to promote action in the direction of nation-building.

Gradually Nuyorican writing becomes freer of prior models and develops its own voice, in the works of such writers as Pedro Pietri, Víctor Hernández Cruz, Miguel Piñero, Miguel Algarín, Ángel Figueroa, Tato Laviera and Martín Espada. Still tending to portray the New York ghetto world against a mythified view of an inter-racial utopia identified with a liberated Puerto Rico, these poets begin to break down the mythified strand and move in a richer, more complex frame of polarities and contradictions, which they portray not only in poetry but in plays as well. Indeed, for Miguel Algarín, by the mid-seventies, Nuyorican poetry had already developed three modes which he saw also as an overlapping continuum of phases in Nuyorican writing (cf. Algarín 1975). First there was "outlaw poetry," involving expressions of hostility, rage and violence; second, there was "evolutionary poetry," entailing a growing consciousness of the external determinations of outlaw moods and acts, as well as a movement toward transcendence; finally there was "dusmic poetry," tracing the transformation of aggression into spiritual strength, wholeness and freedom.

Even in Algarín's last phase, which parallels our view of the third stage of U.S. Latino literature in general, U.S. Puerto Rican literature does not leave specific national and ethnic considerations behind. So, in recent years, with Hernández Cruz's stylistic and thematic experiments and with the gender explorations of Sandra María Esteves, Luz María Umpierre, Judith Ortíz Cofer, Mariposa and others, we see new modes and new cultural horizons only hinted at fifteen years ago, but in no way signaling an end to Spanish, and collective orientations, in no way signifying accommodation or assimilation. Piñero is gone, but others have arrived. Ed Vega and others may parody the earlier immigrant narratives and may search for new narrative paradigms; but this, far from signaling an end, just points to the fact that, in Tato Laviera's wonderful phrase, the *carreta* has been making a u-turn. So, in concluding his essay, Flores notes that, like Chicano and other "'minority' or non-canonical literatures of the United States," Continental Puerto Rican literature since its Nuyorican phase has been, while intensely national in orientation, also "a literature of recovery and collective affirmation,... of 'mingling and sharing,' of interaction and exchange with neighboring, complementary cultures." However, while paying homage to Afro-American literature as influence and Chicano literature as cross-fertilizing parallel and presence, Flores adds that, most distinctively among these minority literatures, "Puerto Rican writing today is a literature of straddling, a literature operative within and between two national literatures and marginal in both. In this respect" he concludes, "Nuyorican writing may well come to serve as a model or paradigm for emerging literatures by other Caribbean groups in the United States, such as Dominicans, Haitians and Jamaicans" (Flores: 44).

Noting the broader perspective, and citing Pietri's work as an example of how Puerto Rican literature relates to the logic of "Late Capitalism" in the 1960s (implicitly early postmodernism, as characterized by Jameson [1984]), Cruz-Malavé (1988: 50) argues that "Because of the diversity of the Puerto Rican experience, encompassing both the Third and First Worlds, underdevelopment and advanced capitalism, oral and written traditions," Puerto Rican writing has not just been a matter of survival stories and poems "in the fringes" of U.S. society, but "the space where... the strategies for change-the many attempts to find a space of resistance and freedom outside (and inside) [First and Third World] modernization and [First World, late capitalist] consumerism-are taken to their ultimate consequences."

As we project to future phases of U.S. Puerto Rican literature, we should simply note that from the perspective of Chicago and the Midwest, the designation by Flores and Cruz Malavé (but not Barradas) of the third phase of Puerto Rican literature in the U.S. as "Nuyorican" is misleading, since it leaves out a significant area and all the other centers where the new literature developed. Future studies must include these other communities in and around New York, but the Midwest as well-wherever Puerto Ricans have gone and will be going. In further efforts, and above all in developing a more sophisticated critique of the remarkably slow and limited emergence of a Puerto Rican woman's and specifically feminist literature, however, the perspectives specified above, will continue to serve as significant guideposts even as we project to future dimensions of this literature as symptomatic and predictive of future possibilities for Puerto Ricans and the Caribbean, Latin American and still larger world of which they are a part.

D. Cuban and Other U.S. Latino Literatures

As noted earlier, the coming of Cubans, Dominicans, Central American and other Latin Americans to the U.S. has led to the emergence of new works, mainly in Spanish, expressive of their experience. To be sure, transplanted Cuban or Argentine novelists are not in any sense writing U.S. Latino literature, whether their characters twist and turn through Havana, Buenos Aires, Montevideo or New York. Only those writers representing groups with several years of U.S. residence and having had some working class as well as some *barrio* experience (including discrimination) are likely to write something which approaches community literary expression such as we find in U.S. Chicano and Puerto Rican literatures. An Argentine lawyer may write fiction in the mode of Borges or Cortázar; his or her daughter or son may outdo John Updike or Ann Tyler. But in either case, even if we find some residues, inflections, or specific "ethnic markings," the result will not necessarily be U.S. Latino literature.

Of all the groups mentioned, the Cubans certainly have had long enough residence and population density to produce a distinct ethnic literature in this country. And indeed the first steps in the development of U.S. Cuban writing tend to parallel the Puerto Rican model, in spite of initial historical and cultural differences. There is a pre-1898 phase, most famously represented by José Martí, that is virtually identical with that described by Juan Flores and summarized above. And, in spite of the differing immigration statuses allotted to inhabitants from the two islands in the wake of 1898, there was a similar development of U.S. Cuban writing throughout the first half of this century.

For the most part, Cuban immigration was never large or very permanent; and while tobacco workers migrated, many entering Cubans were from higher layers in Cuban society. Also, many politicized middle sector Cubans continued to come from the 1930s through the 1950s fleeing the regimes of Machado and Batista, some returning as new governments came to power. Still, small enclaves developed in New York and Miami, and their socio-cultural (not to say literary) history still requires study, if only because it will reveal the kinds of communities which opened the doors to the massive Cuban migration that arrived after Castro's coming to power.

Not surprisingly, what has tended to separate most Cubans and their literature in the U.S. from their Mexican and Puerto Rican cousins has been their predominantly middle class background (we refer here mainly to Cubans arriving before the Mariel exodus of 1980) and of course the political circumstances surrounding their departure from Cuba and their installation in Miami and other communities.

As Naomi Lindstrom has noted, U.S.-based Cubans have "apparently made few attempts to create a minority subculture literature such as that of Nuyoricans." Indeed, "typical of Cuban American production are the numerous works produced by anti-Castro Cubans" that are usually "right wing and conservative Catholic," and that "feature expressions of outrage..., depictions of the sufferings of upper... or middle-class families. [Here] the important elements are the continuity the authors see between Cuban culture as such and the culture they themselves represent in the act of writing... Several bibliographic summaries group these writers not with other U.S. Hispanics, but with anti-Castro writers living ... elsewhere. Spanish is their literary language, and they seldom attempt to represent the effects of continual... contact with ... English-speaking culture" (cf. Lindstrom 1982: 224-225).[5]

This tendentious Cuban exile literature has its right and also left wing parallels in other Latin American groups based in the U.S. and across the globe. In fact, a current of exile literature developed during the 1960s among some of the children of the post-Castro exile identifying themselves as the *grupo Areíto* and seeking "dialogue" with Cubans on the island. Mainly writing in Spanish, but sometimes in English, group members created their works out of pained nostalgia and a desire for reconciliation, rebelling against their parents' politics but also against their pro-U.S. elitism and their unwillingness to see themselves in relation to other Latinos except when it was convenient. In the *Areíto* group, then, were seeds of a very different orientation not only toward Cuba but toward the U.S. experience-seeds that were to grow even after Lourdes Casal's early death, e.g., in Eliana Rivero's continuing and expanding immersion in U.S. feminist writing as critic and poet. This U.S. orientation came to be shared by many other Cuban writers regardless of their stance vis-à-vis Cuban Communism. That is, increasingly albeit gradually, the sons and daughters of middle class Cuban families in the

U.S. have begun to write a literature rooted in U.S. experience. And most of them have surpassed their U.S. Cuban forerunners in this regard.

Even among the tendentious exile writers there were some who did not fully ignore the U.S. experience as such. Some stories, while haunted by the trauma of the Revolution, showed a keen eye for life in Miami and New York; some authors managed to write prose and poetry capturing major "ethnic" and "Latino" aspects of the U.S. Cuban situation: displacement, loss, confusion and re-identification; cultural shock and even Cuban worker exploitation (Kanellos 1989: xvi).

During the 1960s, talented off-Broadway playwright María Irene Fornes launched herself into the mainstream with little direct reflection of her Latin or Cuban roots-matters which only appear in her work during the 1980s.[6] Then, several years later, Oscar Hijuelos, a son of parents who immigrated to the U.S. in the 1940s, wrote a major example of Latino autobiographical fiction in his *Our House in the Last World*. But this book and many other Latino-tending Cuban works were examples of American Dream Romance too inadequate in oppositional force and perspective to constitute U.S. Latino expression as it emerged in Chicano and U.S. Puerto Rican writing. Hijuelos' more recent work, *The Mambo Kings Play Songs of Love*, is a more complexly ambivalent anti-romance, as our white Cuban musicians enter the door into U.S. acculturation only to lose their lives in machistic assertion, nostalgia and spiritual paralysis. In this work, Hijuelos bears ambivalent witness to a breakthrough toward a critical and oppositional ethnic literature accomplished only slowly in the last two decades and expressed in varying degrees also by only a few writers such as Iván Acosta, Dolores Prida, Roberto Fernández, Elías Miguel Muñoz and Cristina García.

The oldest of the group, Acosta is a gifted dramatist whose fine play (and then film) *El Super* is able to capture multiple nuances of the immigration experience, and its effect on family life, friendship, Cuban-Puerto Rican relations and sanity. Another playwright, Prida has now written a sufficient number of plays to establish herself as a talented comic writer able to grasp sex role conflicts and other critical dimensions of Cuban and more broadly U.S. Latino experience. Partaking of the wonderful Cuban talent for exaggerated extravagance, Fernández already has a considerable body of work focusing on absurdities in Miami's Cuban enclave. Significantly, his most recent novel, *Raining Backwards*, is his first written in English. Muñoz's novel *Crazy Love*, reveals his ability to portray several major aspects of immigration and settlement. His more recent writing reveals him grappling with Chicano themes and their relation to his own Cuban roots in a more generalized Latino experience he is intent on exploring. García brings a middle class feminist dimension to the mix in works that have led to her joining Fornes and Hijuelos (and perhaps the spy novel specialist Martin Cruz Smith) as perhaps the most prominent of Cuban American writers.

While these last Cuban writers and many others seem too assimilationist and conformist, they nevertheless point to an at least partial Cuban entry into U.S. Latino ethnic literature as it expands and develops. In this process, a new Dominican current is clearly emerging in the East; and a few other maturing sons and daughters of parents from varying places in Latin America-for example, Central American writers like Mario Bencastro and Héctor Tovar, representing the new crisis-years immigration wave; and South American writers like Chilean Marjorie Agosín have written works which show at least some influence of core U.S. Latino ethnic experience, perhaps interspersed with mainstream U.S. and Latin American nuances. Then too of course, there are the many Latin American elite writers like Isabel Allende, Luisa Valenzuela and Rosario Ferré who choose to live in the U.S. and write on Latin American themes but from a discourse base that seems far more Latin American and or mainstream to be easily categorized as Latino literature. And, as mentioned very early in this essay, there are new waves of Spanish-language Latin American writers in virtually every U.S. city-writers who may or may not take on Latino characteristics.

Finally, there are those non-Latinos whose life experience and capacity of creative projection have enabled them to create valuable examples of what has been dubbed *Chicanesque* literature-including the early short stories of Amado Muro, the outrage-creating book by "Danny Santiago" and the much-praised work by John Nichols and Jim Sagel.

Even as conditions improve for many U.S. Latinos, others will continue to suffer. The proximity with Mexico, U.S. relations with Puerto Rico and Cuba (even if they change), the economic and political situations which impel immigration-these and other factors guarantee, in the face of amnesty laws and new immigration crackdowns and busts, a continuing human stream into the U.S. and its joining with an even greater population of Latinos being born here already. We can be sure that this vast and varied human pool will be the source and subject of a vast and varied ethnic literary pool in the years to come.

4. Further Perspectives and Thoughts in the Age of Postmodernity and Globalization

How might we summarize the situation of Latinos as they may see and feel it, what are some final synoptic thoughts we should put forward here to frame our consideration of Latino cultural and literary matters? First, of course, we may now paraphrase what we said with respect to Latin Americans: that there are no

Latinos, that the word is a construct bringing together diverse people who while they clearly share certain bases, are often quite distinct and only identify with each other in opposition to the non-Latinos and that usually for very specific, contingent and often political, epiphenomenal and ephemeral concerns. This said, what core problems might we articulate that point toward the future-and then, what again about Latino literature as the expression of a non-existent group?

A. Some Key Perspectives

In the coming years, U.S. Latinos will be passing through a conflictive and painful process of transformation, marked by constant, contradictory efforts to hold on to their existing cultural patterns and identifications while modifying and transforming them in an effort to maintain relative balance with changes in society at large.

In this period of transition, many Latinos will seek to assimilate fully into capitalist or "Anglo" society, but vast numbers will hardly make the effort. For each person who wants to do so, there will be many others so alienated by a society pervaded by class and racial inequities, that they will not want to integrate themselves-or at least, they are going to experience a conflict between their conscious desire and their subconscious resistance. And even many Latino workers who may want to, will be unable to integrate themselves adequately into the U.S. mainstream, because their marginalized role as cheap labor source will be all too convenient for certain powerful and avid groups in this country. Thus many Latinos will continue to seek their solace from the wear and tear of social domination and discrimination in what they can salvage of their cultural relations and values.

But Latin American cultural complexes will not be able to remain the same in a changing world; and if U.S. society continues to evolve along its current road, Latino culture may prove less and less able to meet its old needs, of providing all that the governments of domination have not provided. In this circumstance, we can expect to see the possible extenuation of the worst things that are already happening to many people: increased unemployment, increased poverty, increased crime and drug abuse; increased enmity between newly arrived and less recently arrived sectors; increasing hostility among Latinos from different countries; the breakdown of families and whole communities; struggles among Catholics and new Protestant groupings; the survival and aggressive (at times chauvinistic) assertion of only the most negative, superficial and regressive dimensions of culture.

In fact, unless Latinos can develop the most positive dimensions of their cultural legacy in ways that integrate progressive political orientations that are able to win over certain communitarian divisions based sometimes on certain aspects of the culture itself (e.g., nationalism, regionalism, racism, *compadre* relations, *machismo*, *caciquismo*, etc), unless Latinos can form viable alliances and fight effectively for common values and goals, large numbers will be sunk in the backwaters of U.S. life, in a society that will move toward a greater division of rich and poor, haves and have-nots.

A progressive study of U.S. Latino culture involves examining prevalent and potential modes of Latino identification in function of their possible articulation and activation in forging group unity, alliances among diverse Latino groups, other oppressed minorities and class sectors. Identification with popular struggles in Latin America and elsewhere has been a dimension of what is at issue here. And the diversification of Latino immigration and demographic base has created this possibility. The ultimate end is to find bases for generating a viable and organizable political response to conditions of exploitation and exclusion.

While aspects of U.S. development and U.S. Latino culture and history generate growing Latino diversification and disunity (including class, political and now an increasing religious differentiation, etc.); and while certain cultural dimensions (e.g., the orientation toward space, time and death, the way of measuring and evaluating the individual and the communal, the orientation to family and the definition that is given to the family in its extended form, etc.) vitiate efforts to forge broader social unity among Latinos, as well as between them and certain non-Latino groups, there are, nevertheless, other factors, resulting principally from the effects of subjugation, that suggest greater future Latino unity and greater ability to forge at least tactical alliances.

In a progressive study of Latino or any culture, looking for practical alliances, potential openings and points of resistance, etc., distinctions must be made between a group or subgroup's ideology of culture and culture itself-also between the specific cultural products (in art, music, literature, etc.) and Redfield's "little traditions" (or de Certeau's "little tactics" of survival) -i.e., questions of language usage, popular attitudes and opinions, social interaction, etc. We must distinguish between what people say they believe and do and how they actually behave. Thus cultural analysis must relate intellectual and artistic production to more mass concerns and actualities within the groups studied. There must be some determination of the relation between what people say and do, what their leaders and writers say about the people's culture and what their culture itself is.

The matter at hand is one of social, cultural and individual possibilities in a world of limited resources. This question should be confronted at national and international levels as well as in each place where there are concentrations of

Latinos. In this regard, the relation of Latino culture and literature to Latin America and the hemisphere in postmodern contexts becomes essential.

B. Postmodern Multicultural Crossovers

In the context of these general concerns, we would do well to consider one recent development of U.S. Latino literature and popular culture, the subaltern (and often feminist) autobiographical or testimonial impulse as a current in poetry, novel and other modes, in relation to the recent debates over postmodernism and the place of minority literary forms and movements. It is not unusual to hear today that the writing of Cherrié Moraga and Gloria Anzaldúa, either exemplifies or serves as a counter-hegemonic response to dominant (capitalist) postmodernist discourse as it exists in our country and impacts the "internal colony." Here the relation of Latino themes to postmodernism is difficult to ignore.

Clearly there is a problem in applying a concept that is conceived in relation to the cultural state of the hegemonic groups of advanced capitalist consumer societies to the cultural and artistic life of subordinated, marginal and subaltern minority groups. Clearly there is also a correspondence between cultural phenomena identified as postmodernist and the present sensibility and strategies of multinational capitalism which gives some credence to the idea that postmodernism may be a new form of cultural imperialism. But it may also be that Latino culture and literature, as systems within postmodernism, may offer alternative possibilities that may affect and even transform the overall field of relations.

The implication in all this is that we must follow the lead of José David Saldívar (1991) and Emily Hicks (1992) in their effort to grasp Latino cultural and literary resistance within a hemispheric and even global political frame, in which the chances of transformative oppositional difference are greatly conditioned and configured even as they are impeded by the new emerging global order and its often intense local eruptions. Nevertheless, any appropriation of such a framework must overcome what we have characterized after García Canclini as a "Manichaean polarization" (1990). Again, as in the case of Latin American testimonio, the perspective elaborated in this book questions the status of U.S. Latino culture and literature in its relation to, or relative autonomy from, more globally-based postmodernist modes.

In sum, any given work of U.S. Latino literature is written in the midst of an already existing discourse system that has Latin American and U.S., and often broader dimensions. That system is constituted through a series of shifts and transformations that play off existing norms in ways that both sum and open up the fullest range of tendencies within the entire literary system, bringing together popular and elitist cultural trends and establishing the bases for the multivalent kinds of discourse that are now emerging in the writings of Gloria Anzaldúa, Cherrié Moraga, Sandra Cisneros and Ron Arias, Roberto Fernández, Judith Cofer Ortiz and Ed Vega. These literary transformations stand as epiphenomena for deeper structures and transactions that have to do with the effort to forge modes of resistance not outside of but directly within the frame of hegemonic forces. Inevitably, such modes of internal opposition are in danger of encapsulation, cooptation and absorption in the overall system of which they are clearly apart. Nevertheless, their option to exist within that system may also be one aimed at having some meaningful effect on cultural practice and its relation to other zones of social process.

Given the danger of Latino subordination in the U.S. and the few openings toward liberational politics in this historical conjunction, the question also becomes what broader cultural and political horizon the new literature and culture project toward in the U.S. and the relation that horizon may have with Latin America and this hemisphere as a whole. In this connection, we may again invoke Laclau and Mouffe (2001) who point to how it is impossible to totalize social process, to suture it in definitive ways-and how a grasp of the whole is only achieved through a flexible armature ever ready to grasp new Archimedean points in the shifting maze of social determinations.

This perspective, suggested by many recent Latino critics, is one that is explored at global and micro levels by Juan Flores and George Yúdice, "Living Borders/ Buscando América: Languages of Latino Self Formation," which appears in the former's *Divided Borders* (1992). Flores and Yúdice see U.S. Latino culture and literature as significant contributants to the effort to construct a new hegemony with its own cultural practices and discourses. As such, Latino culture and literature constitute more than just peripheral or "minority" modes of symbolic resistance to, but within, a hegemonic system which in effect cancels any genuine potential for agency; given the limits of current oppositional possibilities, Latino practices confront hegemonic norms by creating an alternative if not necessarily adversarial ethos.

The perspective of Flores and Yúdice is best exemplified by the Latino struggle with mainstream culture over language, and the extension of that struggle to other signifying systems. In this regard, they draw, perhaps over-romantically on the icon of Latino/a otherness lauded so by postmodern critics, Gloria Anzaldúa's border vision as expressing not just some postmodern indeterminacy, but a new ethos in the making-one which generalizes feminist critique to a series of practices in which "America" is seen as a cultural map with endless living borders. Here our critics invoke their concept of "crossover culture," as symbolic praxis, corresponding at the linguistic level to Bruce-Novoa's view (1991) of Latino discourse as a new, "interlingual" construction.

Crossover culture does not mean that Latinos seek to "make it" in the general culture; rather it is a vehicle for Latinos to create new, hybrid signifying forms that involve linkages and relations in a variety of often unexplored directions. For example, *salsa* involves a crossover combination of many musical forms, expresses multiculturalism and crossing borders, moments of alliance, convergence and clash among distinct social groups and sectors. *Salsa* means creating one's roots from heterogeneous elements rather than going back to some place of origin. The search is not for some original *axis mundi* or fixed essence, but distinct sets of identity possibilities from within the givens of an expanding multicultural universe.

Indeed, a constructivist, transformative view of cultural identity and the overall multicultural context of U.S. life is the central motif in Flores and Yúdice, for multiculturalism implies connectedness with others without any necessary submission to hegemony past or present. Multiculturalism and multi-centrism are not equivalent to some relativist fiction of cultural pluralism. It is in fact their view of identity affirmation derived from postmodernist discourse which separates Flores and Yúdice from Bruce-Novoa's early cultural paradigm and challenges his critique of Puerto Rican culture and literature, pointing to a broader, achieved U.S. Latino identity, forged out of the varying subject positions which divergent Latino groups and subgroups have experienced in the U.S. Cultural richness is not defined by past myths but the generation of new possibilities, and new, if sometimes chaotic, energies. Latino identity with all its previous characteristics and contours, crosses over in postmodern culture as posing some combination of the most retrograde and progressive possibilities for future patterns of resistance and creativity, posing some of the most dynamic points of convergence and alliance with other, non-Latino groups in a broader field of new oppositions internal to and at least possibly transformative of the entire social system of which they are a part.

C. Literature, the Midwest and Future Developments

With respect to U.S. Latino literature itself, we have to think in complex relations, in continuities and discontinuities, in approaches to and distances from concrete social processes, in the relation between the writer and the group that the writer may be assumed to represent, between a work's hypothetical public or community and the real consumers of the writer's product. Thus, in spite of the Latino population growth and the appearance of many writers and texts, and in spite of the valuable efforts of enterprises like Arte Público Press and Bilingual Review Press to produce and promote Latino literature, it is still true that there are few Latino readers of this literature, except those university students assigned to read a few key works as part of their educational experience.

Ignored or not, subsidized or not, this literature is in the course of developing and deepening; and its writers have been able to express many ideological and material tendencies at work in their communities. While clearly most Latino writers are not much distanced in class background or culture from the community about which they write, it is also partially *because* the writers are not fully typical of Latinos as a whole that they have been able to serve as their community's "organic intellectuals." Thus, more so than other members of their communities, they have been able to probe in the world of creation and imagination certain possible directions of Latino life; they have been able to express but also anticipate certain problems and solutions; they have created valuable modelic constructs which have contributed by positive and negative example to the forging of a potentially better U.S. Latino future.

Given the danger of Latino subordination in the U.S. and the importance this issue has for Latinos and the nation as a whole, the question of social and literary relations also becomes one of what broader cultural and political horizon the new literature and culture project toward in the U.S. and the relation that horizon may have with Latin America and the world as a whole. We have already pointed this issue through our look at Flores' *Divided Borders*. Before fully exploring all the great questions, however, future studies of Latino society and literature must take some time to consider regional developments as well. In this rethinking, the Latino reality must be decentered from the Southwest and New York to embrace a broader conceptualization which includes the Midwest.

Indeed Midwest Latinos and Midwest Latino literature have been greatly neglected. In the literary sphere, although Tomás Rivera wrote of Midwest migration in perhaps the greatest novel of Chicano literature, and although such key Chicano writers as Ana Castillo, Sandra Cisneros and Carlos Morton are from Chicago, and finally although there are innumerable writers who come from many other Midwest centers, the overall Midwest Latino literary corpus and its role in anticipating a Latino as opposed to a strictly Chicano or Puerto Rican emergence has been largely underplayed in the national aggregate.

In the process of rectifying the southwest/eastern seaboard centering and Midwestern exclusion in U.S. Latino literature, and also in taking into account the newer Latino migrations and cultural mixes, initial premises and paradigms become subject to reconsideration. Thus a focus on the Midwest and the new Latino immigrations affecting the overall character of the U.S. Latino population demands a questioning of the literature and mythological constructs involved in the Chicano movement and earlier expressions of U.S. Puerto Rican literature. In this context, most of the symbolic ideological systems emerging out of the struggles of the 60s, are called into question, as being virtually unknown and (here, perhaps the real point) relatively irrelevant to the new populations-even if we conclude that questions of space and time, patterns of acculturation and assimilation, etc., may well remain central to U.S. Latino life and its conceptualization. Furthermore, a Midwestern emphasis raises the question of the viability of border discourse itself as it extends metonymically to other areas and other social problematics, and as its metaphorical and more directly denotative uses become confused, blurred or displaced.

With respect to literature itself, the recent new wave of U.S. Latino literary production, spurred on by NEA grants to individuals and such entities as Arte Público Press, is so mediated by U.S. literary norms, that the relation of U.S. literary and intellectual production (and the producers) to the newer and future waves of Latino population, and to the specificities of given areas and problematics, becomes increasingly problematic.

Writers may very well express the "potential or latent consciousness" of larger social groups; they may constitute themselves as the "organic intellectuals" of subaltern sectors. However they must be ever viewed critically in this guise, and literary production must ever be viewed in relation not only to literary traditions (in the U.S. and in Latin America), but in relation to the everyday life patterns of the larger social mass. Latino writers may draw on their roots to take off, but where do they end up? Will they really be Latino writers in more than name if the older oral traditions and performative/mythic dimensions of their writing fade away?

The vast numbers of immigrants and the initial writers to emerge among them have never read or even heard of Octavio Paz, Carlos Fuentes, José Luis González, etc. (to say nothing of a Borges or a García Márquez); their culture has been somewhat impacted by these figures or at least by some of the same forces which impacted them. But to what degree? We may also note that while most of the more sophisticated contemporary Latino writers are aware of and draw upon the Latin American literary system (an early example was Ron Arias' *Road to Tamazunchale*; more recent ones are the novels of Ana Castillo), others respond more fully to dominant and minority U.S. literary constructs (Richard Wright, earlier forms of Chicano and Native American, but also Jewish, Italian and Irish American literature, etc.). Thus the question remains as to whether, in their growing immersion in a broad literary tradition and in their transcultural crossovers, they are coming to better portray U.S. Latino experience, or if they are beginning to drift from it and coming to express that process of individuation within U.S. culture which has become characteristic of many ethnic minority literatures on the road to dissolution. To choose another, related question: in what ways does the recent feminism of Latino literature anticipate the Latino future or a growing alienation between the writer intelligentsia and a broader, possibly very conservative social mass?

These are matters which only future developments can clarify. But the prediction here is that multiple forms of Latino writing will continue to exist and develop so long as Latinos continue to arrive and constitute distinct groupings; and the further prediction is that this process of U.S. Latino growth, with all its implications for U.S. and world history, will not cease for many years to come.

Here too, the final of many points I wish to stress at the risk of repetition-the fact that problems for the great Latino mass continue to be great and even worse than ever. It is not necessary to repeat all the problems, their causes and possible solutions. But we must emphasize problems and not forget them or negate their reality and see the welfare of the successful ones in relation to the situation of the many Latinos whose present and future prospects are still not pleasant to contemplate.

On the other hand, to project a less pessimistic note, we should remember that the consciousness of negative possibilities provokes many to seek a more positive future. And aspects of that future may be found in positive cultural dimensions that, often expressed, affirmed and rededicated in literature, have survived the acculturation process and may play a key role in the survival of Latinos and all of us. To say this in another way, what is at stake is the struggle to maintain what is human, human for Latinos, human for all who have paid the price of modernization and who seek their place in the famous new world order. Latinos will have much yet to contribute in the ongoing struggle for a richer human world.

5. Postscript

With the exception of one paragraph about the "pre-history" of Latino literature and a few added words on Latin and Central American writing in the U.S., the above essay is just a slightly edited version of the one I published in *U.S. Latino Literature: An Essay and Extended Bibliography* (1992). In the preface to that volume, I made the following commentary which is interesting to consider today:

> *Since the manuscript for the first edition of this text was completed, countless new works of and about U.S. Latino literature have appeared. The list of recent publications is a remarkable one, including major novels and poetry*

collections, as well as pathbreaking theoretically-driven critical texts, as integral to a spurt of cultural production that raises fundamental questions about the overall field and its conceptualization.... [Theoretical works..., as well as a number of significant feminist creative works, have appeared to point toward the weighty contribution of Latina feminism to reconstructing Latino literary theory. In addition, a whole range of polemics have come center stage-debates over U.S. and Latin American literary canons (as well as their possible inter-relatedness under the rubric of "New World Writing," etc.); over "political correctness" and "multi-culturalism" or "multicultural literacy"; over possibilities of "literary difference," "resistance" and "subaltern voice"; over the "transformative difference within difference" constituted by feminist and homosexual texts. These controversial questions, in the midst of the overall effort of mapping contemporary, postmodern culture, have brought at least certain works and indeed the entire field of U.S. Latino literature to a level of recognized significance that they had never before achieved (Zimmerman 1992: ix)

Many of the matters pointed to here and in the introduction to this volume have indeed come to pass. Latino literature has continued to develop and grow; it is now studied in many English and even some Spanish departments throughout the U.S. and in Europe-and elsewhere as well. Criticism and theory with respect to the literature has also deepened, especially in the areas of gender, feminist and queer, border, transnational and globalization studies. If I had to publish a new version of my annotated bibliography, it would be a massive volume far longer than the original (this task I leave to others!). Furthermore, the literature is now mainstreamed so that the established Latino publishers tend to publish newcomers who then sign on with agents and find larger and stronger publishing houses able to project their work for massive sales.

Above all, through the efforts of Nicolás Kanellos' Recovering the Hispanic Heritage Project, we have now far greater knowledge about Hispanic writing in what is today U.S. territory than we had even a few years ago.[7] We know of memoirs, poetry collections, novels and other texts over the past 500 years; we can trace foreshadowings and anticipations of what many of us have considered the core of Latino literature; we can even find great deviations from that core which make us question our basic definitions of the literature. Indeed, as we have learned more and more, there is perhaps an ever greater confusion as to what this literature is and what its own borders might be, especially since 9/11 and the great restrictions on immigration patterns and thus on the transnational dimension which had been growing by leaps and bounds and transforming Latino communities throughout the U.S. Nativist Latinos have been outnumbered by immigrants. New waves of Latin Americans without a historical memory of Latino conflicts have refused to conform to older definitions of what Latinos are and should be. The recent elections indicate that more and more Latinos are indeed becoming and preferring to be called Hispanics, so that the ever-so-slight leftist or workingclass bite which the Latino label evoked and I, a stubborn old leftie, continue to evoke, may be irrelevant at some future not too far off. 9/11 clearly has upset some projections and possibilities; but in the long run, it may be assumed that the Latino population will continue to grow, its literature and its critique continue to expand, and its definition continues to require revision.

One of the most striking aspects of the new situation is that while more and more Latinos born and/or raised mainly in the U.S. have been developing a literature in English, the pre-9/11 migration waves from the early 1980s on, and including a much higher percentage of middleclass and even college-educated Latin Americans than ever before, have led to a situation that Spanish language Latino-tending Latin American writing is now tending to be more prevalent than Latino writing in English. With this phenomenon and the growing interactions between Latin American and Latino writers in Spanish and English, the nature of Latino literature reaches new stages of richness and also of conceptual complication. In all of this, the relation of these most recent literary trends to trends in Latin American, U.S. and worldwide writing is ever more complex to trace, articulate and theorize. In this context, the relation of Latino literature to Latin American and to overall hemispheric developments in the age of globalization and beyond must indeed remain in a sphere of discourse beyond the range of themes that can be explored in this framing volume and even its postscripts.

Works Cited

Algarín, Miguel and Miguel Piñero, ed. 1975. *Nuyorican Poetry: An Anthology of Puerto Rican Words and Feelings.* New York. William Morrow.

Algarín, Miguel. 1975. "Introduction." In Algarín and Piñero, ed. 7-9.

Anzaldúa, Gloria. 1987. *Borderlands / La Frontera: the New Mestiz* San Francisco. Spinsters/Aunt Lute Press.

Baeza-Ventura, Gabriela. 2004. *U.S. Latino Literature Today.* New York, San Francisco. Pearson/Longman.

Barradas, Efraín and Rafael Rodríguez, ed. 1980. *Herejes y mitificadores: Muestra de poesía puertorriqueña en los Estados Unidos,* ed. Río Piedras, Puerto Rico. Ediciones Huracán.

Barradas, Efraín. 1980. "Introducción" to Barradas and Rodríguez, ed.

Bruce-Novoa, Juan. 1990. *Retro Space*. Houston. Arte Público Press.

Capetillo, Luisa. 1992. *Amor y anarquía: Los escritos de Luisa Capetillo*. Ed. Julio Ramos. Río Piedras, Puerto Rico. Ediciones Huracán.

Colón, Jesús. 1982. *A Puerto Rican in New York and Other Sketches*. New York. Mainstream Publishers.

Colón, Joaquín. 2001. *Pioneros puertorriqueños en Nueva York*. Houston. Arte Público Press.

Cruz-Malavé, Arnoldo. 1988. "Teaching Puerto Rican Authors: Identity and Modernization in Nuyorican Texts, "in ADE Bulletin no. 91, pp. 45-48.

Flores, Juan. 1988. "Puerto Rican Literature in the United Status: Stages and Perspectives," in *ADE Bulletin* no. 91 (Winter) 39-44 (and now in *Divided Borders*).

______. 1992. *Divided Borders: Essays on Puerto Rican Identity*. Houston. Arte Público Press.

Foster, David William ed. 1982. *Sourcebook of Hispanic Culture in the United States*. Chicago. American Library Association.

García Canclini, Néstor. 1990. *Las culturas híbridas. Estrategias para entrar y salir de la modernidad*. México. Grijalbo,

Hicks, Emily D. 1992. *Border Writing: The Multidimensional Text*. Minneapolis. University of Minnesota Press.

Horowitz, Ruth. 1983. *Honor and the American Dream: Culture and Identity in a Chicano Community* (New Brunswick. Rutgers U. Press.

Kanellos, Nicolás with Alejandra Balestra, Kenya Dworkin y Méndez, ed. 2001. *Herencia: The Anthology of Hispanic Literature of the United States* New York. Oxford University Press.

Kanellos, Nicolás, with Charles Tatum, Erlinda Gonzáles-Berry, José B. Fernández, and Agnes Lugo-Ortiz, ed. 2002. *En otra voz*. Houston. Arte Público Press.

Kanellos, Nicolás. 1989. "Introduction". *Biographical Dictionary of Hispanic Literature in the United States*. New York. Greenwood Press.

Laclau, Ernesto and Chantal Mouffe. 2001. *Hegemony and Socialist Strategy: Towards a Radical Democratic Politics*. London. Verso, 2nd Edition, 2001.

Lewis, Oscar. 1968. *La Vida*. New York. Mortiz.

Lindstrom, Naomi. 1982. "Cuban and Continental Puerto Rican Literature," in Foster, 224-25.

Menton, Seymour. 1975. *Prose Fiction of the Cuban Revolution*. Austin. Institute for Latin American Studies. University of Texas.

Mohr, Eugene. 1982. *The Nuyorican Experience: Literature of the Puerto Rican Minority*. Westport. Greenwood.

Padilla, Félix. 1985. *Latino Ethnic Consciousness: The Case of Mexican Americans and Puerto Ricans in Chicago*. Notre Dame, IN. Notre Dame U. Press.

Ruoff, Lavonne and Jerry W. Ward, Jr., eds. 1990. *Redefining American Literary History* (New York. Modern Language Association.

Saldívar, Ramón. 1991. *Chicano Narrative*. Madison, WI. University of Wisconsin Press.

Sollors, Werner. 1986. *Beyond Ethnicity: Consent and Descent in American Culture* (New York. Oxford U. Press.

Williams, Raymond. 1981. *The Sociology of Culture*. New York. Schocken.

Zimmerman, Marc. 1992. *U.S. Latino Literature: An Essay and Extended Bibliography* Chicago. March/Abrazo Press.

Notes

1 Flores's phases are an extension and refinement of those found in Eugene Mohr's (1982).

2 See Luisa Capetillo. 1992.

3 See also Joaquín Colón 2001.

4 This essay is the main source for what follows here on Nuyorican poetry.

5 In characterizing Cuban exile literature, Lindstrom draws on Seymour Menton 1975: 215-46; 305-8.

6 See among her recent plays *Sarita* and *Letters from Cuba* (1999).

7 See Nicolás Kanellos (Editor), Alejandra Balestra, Kenya Dworkin y Méndez, eds. 2001. *Also* see Kanellos with Charles Tatum, Erlinda Gonzáles-Berry, José B. Fernández, and Agnes Lugo-Ortiz. 2002. In these texts, Kanellos divides "Hispanic literature" in terms of their nativist, immigration or exile origins. In her collection, *U.S. Latino Literature Today* (2004), Kanellos's associate, Gabriela Baeza Ventura similarly divides the Latino literary field into native, exile and immigration, but posits an additional "transcultural" or transnational dimension indicating that actual, personal nativist, immigration or exile status does not exhaust transnational trends.

Coda:

A Final Frame, Entry Point and Postscript

To the degree that borders between disciplines, forms of knowledge and discourses continue to exist and guide the structuration of literary and extra-literary processes, the discourse patterns employed in the essays presented in this volume may be said to belong to a conceptual universe that is coming to its end. This is so even as I transcribe these words or as the words are ventriloquized from the structural position I occupy to enunciate the cultural and ideological dimensions of the literary frames under study. In the emergent post-postmodernist/ post-postcolonial moment of obscured or effaced borders and nomadic logistics, in the new world order with its new world strains, [dis]orders and (dis)harmonies, a critique of this book could well center first on the fact that globalization perspectives have already overtaken postmodernity itself as the center of theoretical debate in general, Latin American, Caribbean and Latino cultural levels (cf. García Canclini 1995 and García Canclini, ed. 1996); and second, within this context, contemporary studies by García Canclini and others do not indicate any narrowly conceived homogenization of culture. This position, alluded to by Beverley and Oviedo in the introduction to their collection with Aronna (1995), and also by Appadurai (1996) throughout his book, is well articulated by Santiago Colás (1994: 10-12) under the rubric of "dynamic heterogeneity." Drawing on economic and social theorists from Marx to the postmoderns, Colás develops an argument which he sees as running contrary to Jameson's Adorno-like vision of a postmodern cultural homogeneity against which third world narratives and actions stand as last gasp modes of resistance:

> *Capital requires differences, an exterior, to survive. If contemporary capital has consumed all difference, then it will, in effect, run out of gas. But ... capitalism engages in a constant self-refueling. As it consumes difference in one place, it regenerates it elsewhere. [10]*

In effect, heterogeneity, otherness and difference are necessary for the expanded reproduction of capital. Capitalism can only thrive on the commodification of varied use values. Most pointedly, the most varied areas of Latin America and the Caribbean will continue to count on the reproduction of otherness for tourist and export dollars as well as social ordering, just as U.S. capital has counted on racial, ethnic and cultural differentiation in its division of labor. Ironically now, otherness can only have weight and can only survive within the circuit of capital—that is, as "cultural capital." This term itself cannot be taken in uncritically as some kind of economistic reduction of cultural practice. However, it points to the accumulated repository of possibilities from which new political scenes and scenarios can develop. In this sense, such notions as transnationalization, globalization and post-colonialism, post-Marxism and postmodernism do not imply the erasure of colonialism, neo-colonialism, imperialism and Marxism, but rather mark their re-articulation in relation to new global and local interrelations.

To be sure, "hybridization," "deterritorialization," and other terms that are part of the recent arsenal of Latin American cultural studies are not innocent of existing relations and hierarchies of power and control, no matter how transformed they may be by new post-Cold War and post-dictatorial contexts. Those new contexts, however characterized, may well imply that the commodification of otherness, while fully dangerous, offers a space for oppositional articulation otherwise not available. In this sense, as globalization increases, so do the spaces for potential resistance; new social movements may emerge and lead to crises in civil society and citizenship, in governability and, yes, hegemony.

The themes articulated throughout the book engage Latin American, Caribbean and Latino specificities in terms of controversies that will repeat and echo as this still-new century continues on its way and as post-9/11 structures continue to take on a life of their own on the horizon of our fears and expectations. As such this book can provide no comfortable answers to the questions it raises; but the questions themselves will help to frame the discussions which will continue on into the future. Indeed this book goes beyond its own parameters and points to the kind of globalistic logic required by recent developments; so it joins in the music of contemporary discourse in an effort to find some new remedies for the strains and veritable pains of the postmodern condition, to find some *new* keys, some *new* strains and even (is it plausible?) some *new* dynamic harmonies that may become part of this world's future music and its non-homogeneous but thoroughly globalized cultural directions. In this sense, perhaps, our book is transitional, as it reconfirms but also renegotiates its literary emphasis as a re-articulation that is still vital to contemporary discussions.

Of course it is easy today to be "against literature" as an only illusory source of cultural resistance; it is rather easy to point to an exhaustion of differences that even obliterates the non-literary and positional illusions of Beverley, Mignolo and others. A look at contemporary world processes for the articulation of a revolutionary multitude through Luhmanesque eyes, does not readily sound the chimes of hope. But I would suggest that literature indeed persists as a possible source for imagining through and also beyond the givens of our time and place. The construction of fictive, poetic and dramatic worlds must somehow speak to possible material constructions, in spite of class, gender or ethnic biases and limits, in spite of all the negative forces at work in our historical moment.

Only future events will show, then, if Latin Americans, Caribbeans and Latinos can move from the struggles of particular sectors, groups and communities to those of peoples sufficiently united and sufficiently allied with related groups to appropriate and forge a history that can become theirs in the current era and beyond. Again, only future situations will show if, now though bereft of any oppositional position clearly outside world and national social systems, Latin American and Latino cultural and literary processes can serve any transformative role by giving expression to the realities and dreams of peoples who have persevered against existing powers and counter-powers and can now, utopian visions obliterated or transformed, in fact begin, however gradually, to remake their own world.

Works Cited

Appadurai, Arjun. 1996. *Modernity at Large: Cultural Dimensions of Globalization.* Minneapolis. U. of Minnesota Press.

Beverley, John, José Oviedo and Michael Arrona, ed. 1993. *The Postmodernism Debate in Latin America.* Durham. Duke University Press.

Colás, Santiago. 1994. *Postmodernity in Latin America: The Argentine Paradigm.* Durham. Duke University Press.

García Canclini, Néstor. 1995. *Consumidores y ciudadanos: Conflictos multiculturales de la globalización.* México. Grijalbo.

García Canclini, Néstor, ed. 1996. *Culturas en globalización. América Latina—Europa—Estados Unidos: libre comercio e integración.* Caracas. Nueva Sociedad.